Youth, D̶̶̶̶̶̶̶̶̶̶̶̶̶̶̶̶

Drugs and music have long been tied together. From marijuana and jazz, and amphetamines and punk, drugs and popular music have been inextricably joined. Today the music is electronic and ecstasy and party drugs are the drugs of choice. Raves and clubs are often treated by public health experts as merely conduits for drugs, and youth drug use is presented as an unalloyed danger. Within cultural studies, raves and dance scenes are often celebrated as liberating or transgressive, but the issue of drug use within these scenes is often ignored or brushed aside. In *Youth, Drugs, and Nightlife*, anthropologist and sociologists Hunt, Moloney, and Evans go beyond these limits and explore the attraction of the scene and the drugs to young people today. Using information from over 300 in-depth interviews with ravers, DJs, and promoters, the authors examine the interplay between dance scenes, party drugs, and these young people's identities – focusing on issues of Asian American ethnic identity, gender, and sexuality. In contrast to the often stereotypical view of young drug users as naive and poorly informed, the authors explore the sources of information used by ravers, the precautions they take before and after using, and the controls they impose on one another's use. They examine the central role that the pursuit of pleasure (generally ignored within drug literatures) plays in the practice and meanings of party drug use. We learn about these young people's frustration with legislation controlling raves and clubs, and their general skepticism about official pronouncements on the dangers of ecstasy and other drugs. The book examines youth, drugs, and nightlife in terms of local nighttime economies, but also places these happenings in the broader context of national legislation and the globalization of culture and technology.

Geoffrey Hunt is a social and cultural anthropologist with nearly thirty years' experience in planning, conducting, and managing research in the field of youth studies, and drug and alcohol research. He is a senior research scientist at the US Institute for Scientific Analysis and the principal investigator on three US National Institute of Health projects. He has published extensively on substance abuse, especially alcohol and drug use, and evaluating community prevention and intervention programs.

Molly Moloney is a senior research associate at the Institute for Scientific Analysis. Trained as a cultural sociologist, her research focuses on gender, ethnicity, and identity within street gangs and within club-drug scenes. She has published on fatherhood among gang members, on regulating the nighttime economy in San Francisco, on club-drug use among Asian American youth, on gender theory, and on global television and television critics.

Kristin Evans has a degree in sociology and psychology from the University of California at Berkeley. As a research associate at the Institute for Scientific Analysis in San Francisco she was project manager of two NIH-funded projects, on "Club Drugs and the Dance Scene" and "Asian American Youth, Drugs and the Dance Scene." Previously she worked on street gang projects. She has published a number of articles with Geoffrey Hunt on gang girls and drug use, and on drugs and the dance scene.

Youth, Drugs, and Nightlife

Geoffrey Hunt, Molly Moloney,
and Kristin Evans

Routledge
Taylor & Francis Group

LONDON AND NEW YORK

First published 2010
by Routledge
2 Park Square, Milton Park, Abingdon, Oxon. OX14 4RN

Simultaneously published in the USA and Canada
by Routledge
270 Madison Avenue, New York NY 10016

Routledge is an imprint of the Taylor & Francis Group, an informa business

© 2010 Geoffrey Hunt, Molly Moloney, and Kristin Evans

Typeset in Times New Roman by Glyph International Ltd
Printed and bound in Great Britain by CPI Antony Rowe, Chippenham,
Wiltshire.

British Library Cataloguing in Publication Data
A catalogue record for this book is available from the British Library

Library of Congress Cataloging in Publication Data
Hunt, Geoffrey, 1947–
Youth, drugs, and nightlife / Geoffrey Hunt, Molly Moloney,
and Kristin Evans.
p. cm.
Includes bibliographical references and index.
1. Youth – Drug use. I. Moloney, Molly. II. Evans, Kristin. III. Title.
HV5824.Y68.H86 2010
362.290835–dc22   2009029244

ISBN 10: 0-415-37471-5 (hbk)
ISBN 10: 0-415-37473-1 (pbk)
ISBN 10: 0-203-92941-1 (ebk)

ISBN 13: 978-0-415-37471-2 (hbk)
ISBN 13: 978-0-415-37473-6 (pbk)
ISBN 13: 978-0-203-92941-4 (ebk)

Contents

Tables

Acknowledgments

As David Matza noted in his book *Becoming Deviant*, nearly the last thing one does before a book goes to the publisher is to acknowledge one's debt to respondents, colleagues, research assistants, families, and funding agencies. This is certainly the case for us. The second point that he makes is that one has to confront the embarrassing fact that the book took so long to produce. This is again true for us. Having received the contract from Routledge early in 2005, we are only now writing this acknowledgment in early 2009.

Given this admission of poor productivity, maybe our initial thanks should go to our long-suffering and exceedingly patient editor, Gerhard Boomgaarden. Not only has he been extremely patient, putting up with my jokes about aiming to complete the book within ten years, he has also been amazingly good-tempered. One of the benefits of having taken so long to complete the manuscript is that it gave us an opportunity to get to know Gerhard well. We became close friends as a result of sharing a number of meals and drinks whenever we crossed paths at the obligatory conferences – an experience very similar to those described by David Lodge in *Small World*. Also in connection with Routledge we would also wish to thank Miranda Thirkettle for always being there when sometimes Gerhard was otherwise busy.

Our next acknowledgment is to thank the US National Institutes of Health and specifically the National Institute on Drug Abuse (NIDA), which funded both the main research in San Francisco and the supplementary work in Hong Kong and Rotterdam. As we note in the introduction, without the generous funding from NIH for qualitative research we would have been unable to interview 300 respondents. Our two main contacts at NIDA – Moira O'Brien in the epidemiology division, who was our program officer for the entire length of the project, and Steve Gust in the International division, who facilitated our crossnational research work, have always been encouraging and complimentary about our research — and we thank them for that encouragement.

Although only three names appear on the cover of the book, many more people in our team have contributed both to its overall production and also to specific chapters. Professor Karen Joe-Laidler has worked as coprincipal investigator on all our projects. She was also in charge of the Hong Kong subproject and consequently the majority of the material on Hong Kong was analyzed and written by her. But Karen's role was more than just handling the Hong Kong data; for the last eighteen years since she began working with us, she has served as an intellectual inspiration to our team and has always been able to produce imaginative ways of analyzing and presenting the data.

In terms of the book's overall production, one person – Lauren Greene – more than anyone else ensured that it was consistently formatted and that all the citations were properly included – even while the authors continually made changes to supposedly finalized chapters, forcing her to reformat, add, or delete citations once again. During this entire process she proved to be very tolerant. Lauren also collected valuable information for the book, especially for Chapter 4. Adam Fazio, one of our research associates, tirelessly analyzed the quantitative material, produced all the tables for the book, and made the final corrections to the manuscript. In addition, Adam specifically analyzed and wrote much of the qualitative material for Chapter 10.

Galit Erez's principal forte is as an interviewer. Her interviews with many of the Asian American respondents and the nighttime economy key informants were of an exceptionally high quality and she always possessed the talent to put her interviewees at ease and encourage them to tell their own stories. Her field notes and knowledge of the dance scene in San Francisco also played a major role in our discussion of San Francisco in Chapter 2 and Chapter 5. Noelani Bailey worked as a consultant interviewer for our analysis of the nighttime economy and interviewed many of the key informants as well as helping to kickstart that part of the project.

Other research assistants, who contributed either to interviewing respondents or to analyzing the data, include Eileen Wu, Katie Hendy, Neshani Jani, Meghan Boone, and Michelle Duerte. Anne Samuel worked tirelessly transcribing nearly all the interviews, the average length of which was approximately eighty pages. Finally Kathleen MacKenzie, although not directly involved in the production of the book, nevertheless played a central role in running and supervising our other research on youth gangs. In conducting simultaneous research on seemingly diverse topics – youth gangs and young drug users in the dance scene – there is always a tendency at different times to focus on one more than another. While we were more focused on the book and dance scene we always knew that Kathleen was in control of the gang projects and that the research was being conducted in an expert way and, consequently, we had little to worry about.

Our thanks also go to our other past and present colleagues at the Institute of Scientific Analysis. Special thanks go to Dr. Marsha Rosenbaum, who conducted one of the first sociological research projects on ecstasy. The results of her work, discussed in her book *Pursuit of Ecstasy*, written with Jerome Beck, was an inspiration to us and also provided the groundwork for our own research. Thanks also to Michael Jang, Director of the Institute, Maya Jang, Dr. Sheigla Murphy, and finally Lyman Louie, who was always there to handle any computer problems.

Like in all acknowledgments, we run the risk of forgetting to thank someone who made either a direct or indirect contribution to the production of the book, so we would like to thank others who contributed time to listen to our ideas and often commented on the chapters when they were in draft form. Professor Judith Barker has had to read much of our work over the last fifteen years, and whenever she does so, new ideas begin to emerge. Other people who read and gave comments on drafts of earlier chapters include Professor Elisabeth Ettorre, Dr. Jenny Mellor, and Dr. Kaye Fillmore. Dr. Fiona Measham agreed, when the manuscript had been completed, to wade through the entire book to ensure that we had not made any serious blunders. Even though she did this, we are totally responsible for any errors in the final product.

The first author would like to thank Andrea Mitchell especially for having an encyclopedic knowledge of the drug and alcohol research fields and consequently always being able to provide the very latest information on both past and recent publications. Molly Moloney would like to thank her husband, Michael Stemmle, for his support, encouragement, and humor throughout the project. Finally, all three authors would like to thank and acknowledge all those participants in this study who were willing to share intimate details about their lives with complete strangers. Obviously, without them there would not have been any book. As project manager and one of the interviewers Kristin Evans wanted to especially thank them. She felt particularly humbled by the opportunity to understand how each of them comes to experience life, even if for a moment in time. Their passion for what they believed in and their willingness to spend hours answering our lengthy questionnaire were admirable. Many did so for the opportunity to be heard and with the faith that we would honor their perspectives. We hope that we have done justice to their stories and we hope that if any of them should read the book they will feel that we portrayed their experiences accurately and fairly and that the volume has given their stories a voice.

Some of the ideas and material presented in Chapters 1, 5, 6, 7, 8, and 11 appeared originally in article form and have been elaborated on in this book: G. Hunt, K. Evans, E. Wu, and A. Reyes, "Asian American Youth, the Dance Scene and Club Drugs," *Journal of Drug Issues* 35 (4) 2005: 695–731; G. Hunt, K. Evans, and F. Kares, "Drug Use and the Meanings of Risk and Pleasure," *Journal of Youth Studies*, 10 (1) 2007: 73–96; G. Hunt and K. Evans, " 'The Great Unmentionable': Exploring the Pleasures and Benefits of Ecstasy from the Perspectives of Drug Users," *Drugs: Education, Prevention and Policy* 15 (4) 2008: 329–49; M. Moloney, G. Hunt, and K. Evans, "Asian American Identity and Drug Consumption: From Acculturation to Normalization," *Journal of Ethnicity in Substance Abuse* 7 (4) 2008: 376–403; G. Hunt, M. Moloney, and K. Evans, "Epidemiology meets Cultural Studies: Studying and Understanding Youth Cultures, Clubs, and Drugs: Addiction, Research and Theory"; G. Hunt, K. Evans, N. Bailey, and M. Moloney, "Combining Different Substances in the Dance Scene: Enhancing Pleasure, Managing Risk and Timing Effects," *Journal of Drug Issues*; M. Moloney, G. Hunt, N. Bailey, and G. Erez, "New Forms of Regulating the Nighttime Economy: The Case of San Francisco," in P. Hadfield (ed.) *Nightlife and Crime: Social Order and Governance in an International Perspective* (Oxford: Oxford University Press, 2009).

Introduction

To some readers, the arrival in 2009 of another book on raves and the culture of dance parties may seem strange when the height of the rave scene, at least in the UK, occurred more than a decade ago. Given the fact that a number of books have already been written, published, and thoroughly dissected, readers may wonder: why produce another book so long after the rave scene began? In spite of the rave/dance movement having its heyday in the early 1990s, the dance scene has since then developed globally and dance clubs are still an important element of night life in London, New York, Hong Kong, and Sydney, with a continuing flow of new and younger DJs entering the scene.[1] Consequently, a book on the dance scene is still relevant. But, besides its contemporary relevance, six other important reasons exist for why we decided to write *Youth, Drugs, and Nightlife*.

The first and most important reason for writing this book is that it is one of the first in-depth sociological accounts to be written about contemporary raves, clubs, and parties in the US.[2] In spite of the fact that the term "rave" has a California origin (J. Beck and Rosenbaum 1994) and house and garage music began in the US, the vast majority of scholarly work on raves and the electronic dance music scene has been based on research in the UK (where raves as a significant cultural form first emerged). Some of the more obvious reasons for this result from the significant initial explosion of raves in England during the second "summer of love" in 1988 and the subsequent interest in these developments by researchers such as Thornton (1996), Malbon (1999), Measham *et al.* (2001), Pini (2001), and Redhead (1990, 1997). The importance of these pioneering studies of the dance scene and their influence on our own thinking will become obvious in later chapters. While the dominance of the UK literature may be explained by the early upsurge of raves in the UK, the precise reasons for why so few detailed studies have been published in the US are more difficult to understand. Possible reasons for the absence of book-length research may include the dominance of epidemiological and psychological literature primarily found in peer-reviewed journals in the American literature on drugs, the emphasis on journal articles, impact factors, citation indexes, and the like in US academia, and the failure of contemporary sociological or cultural studies research to consider important this aspect of youthful leisure practices. This is surprising, given the interest in cultural studies in the US in other aspects of the music scene and especially that of hip-hop, which has generated a sizable literature (Dyson 2007; Maira 1998; Perry 2004; Rose 1994). However, the interest in hip-hop may stem from the relationship between music and minority youth, whereas the electronic music dance scene of raves is a scene that has traditionally been viewed as dominated by white middle-class youth (although as we'll see, 50 percent of the sample of ravers focused on in this book are people of color; see Chapters 2 and 11).

The second reason for writing this book is that, unlike many studies which have gone before it, the book is not only about young people's experiences in the dance scene but also about their experiences of using drugs. The central aim of our study, and the research on which it is based, is to explore the meaning of drugs for young people who attend raves, parties, and clubs. This focus on youthful drug use within the social and cultural context of the dance scene means that the focus of this book is very different from many other studies of this issue. With only a very few exceptions, social and cultural research on the dance scene has focused primarily on the culture of music and dancing in the scene, and only in passing have these studies discussed the importance of illicit drugs within it.[3] The absence of a detailed discussion of drug use within these studies of the dance scene is paralleled by the failure of drug researchers to explore the extensive and existing research on the dance scene within youth and cultural studies. As we will discuss in more detail in the first chapter, although these two bodies of literature are particularly relevant for the study of drugs, raves, and dance parties, they have remained largely separate from each other. While the reasons for this continuing separation are complex, clearly some of them may relate to both the dominance of different disciplines within each of the two research camps and the increasing tendency for researchers to remain firmly embedded in their own discipline. In opposition to this separation, we present here an alternative and combined approach. As researchers who straddle the fields of drug and alcohol epidemiology, sociology, anthropology, cultural studies, and cultural criminology, we have utilized material from all of these disciplines. We believe that adopting such a combined approach leads to a much more comprehensive account. Furthermore, while we value the recent developments in cultural studies research, we nevertheless believe that we should not underestimate the fact that our research participants are involved in illegal activities. However, just as we would wish to argue that cultural studies research has downplayed the illegal nature of drug use, we would also argue that our approach to examining youthful drug use differs from the problem-oriented approach normally found within much of the research in the drug field.

In examining drug use within an alternative perspective, we utilize many of the theoretical developments that have occurred in youth studies and specifically research that has explored the relationship between identity, lifestyles, and consumption. Young people are viewed "as attempting to find self-fulfillment and ways of identifying with other young people through the consumption of goods" (Furlong and Cartmel 1997: 61), especially fashion and music. Given this perspective, we locate youthful drug use both within the social context of the dance scene and as an important aspect of consumption, which, like the consumption of other commodities, is used to construct an identity. Drugs – along with fashion, musical tastes, and general lifestyles – are important symbols through which young people construct their identity. The different ways in which young people use different commodities leads to new and different hybrid forms of identity (France 1998). Unfortunately, much of the research in the drug field still represents youthful drug use as a high-risk individual activity within a social problems or public health paradigm. Consequently, existing research on young people's drug use continues to present these activities as though they occur within a social vacuum. Little of this research has made any attempt to situate youthful drug use within the contexts of young people's leisure activities. In contrast to this representation of youthful drug use, a central tenet of our book is that our respondents' drug use is essentially social and consequently any analysis must begin from this starting point. As Appadurai has noted, "all consumption is eminently social, relational, and active rather than private, atomic or passive" (1986a: 31). Within this perspective we have examined young people as neither passive recipients nor "inadequately formed adults" (Maira 2004: xxi), but have instead adopted an approach that views young people as active players negotiating their lives within certain social-structural and cultural constraints, highlighting the obstacles that young people confront today in a period of rapid social change (Miles 2000).

The third reason for writing the book is that we wish to examine the drug use and leisure activities of young people who can be broadly described as "mainstream." The development of the electronic dance music scene has come a long way since its early manifestation in the UK and its association with large outdoor or illegal warehouse parties. Today, "raves" have become "transformed into a multimillion-pound global phenomenon" (Carrington and Wilson 2004: 66). The phenomenon has become so widespread that it has been described by some researchers as "a completely normal leisure option in keeping with the times" (Tossman *et al.* 2001: 20). As a result of the widespread attraction of the dance and party scene, those who attend the dance scene are primarily "mainstream" or socially inconspicuous young adults who are integrated into the world of family, school, and work. The young men and women we interviewed come from lower middle or middle-class families, attend school – whether high school, colleges, or universities – and can be considered as relatively affluent, even if they have to rely on their parents for money. Some of our respondents are also young professionals just embarking on their careers. Because of these backgrounds, our respondents are able to pay entrance fees for clubs and raves and buy the clothes and drugs necessary for enjoying the night out. While many may decide that attending the dance scene on a regular basis is too expensive, or even financially wasteful, the majority are able to attend events without resorting to petty crime or the selling of drugs. Unlike the focus of much of the early studies on youth cultures, our respondents do not belong to subcultural groups, nor are they primarily working class, disenfranchised, poor, or underprivileged.[4] Although within the drug field our sample are similar to the young people who are regularly monitored by the US national drug survey "Monitoring the Future," they are also that sector of young people who have been neglected by much of the research in youth studies. Some of the reasons for this may relate to the fact that they are unspectacular (Hodkinson 2007), or less "spectacular" and "melodramatic" (Ettorre and Miles 2002; Miles 2000), than some of their counterparts. "Ordinary kids and normal kids were positioned as quiescent or too drab and passive to warrant investigation" (P. Kelly 2000: 308).

Our respondents are not the equivalent of the Mods and Rockers of the 1960s, the Punks of the 1970s and 1980s or even the Goths of the 1990s, and while their dress may be distinctive when they attend dance events at the weekend, for the rest of the week they are largely indistinguishable from other young people. Moreover, as Measham (2004a, c) and others (Hayward 2002) have noted, because most dance event attendees have jobs or attend full-time education, dance events occur mainly at weekends. For these young people hedonism is clearly enjoyed within a controlled manner. In focusing on these young people we do not wish to lessen the importance of documenting the lives of the less privileged sectors of young people, instead we wish to document the lives and experiences of young people who are not usually classified as problem youth. In spite of their general conformity, and the fact that these young people are not generally viewed as a problematic group, nevertheless their nighttime activities, and especially their drug use, as we will see in Chapter 4, have been described by those in authority as dangerous, high-risk, and in need of regulation and control.

Writing about the lives and drug use of "mainstream" young people is also important if we are to examine the extent to which drug "normalization" has occurred in the US. Although the debate about the normalization thesis has been given an extensive airing within the UK (see for example Blackman 2004; Hammersley 2005; Measham 2004b; H. Parker *et al.* 1998, 2002; Shiner 2009; Shiner and Newburn 1999) the thesis has been generally neglected within the research on the drug-using practices of young people in the US.[5] The reasons for this relative neglect are unclear, although one possible factor may be the tendency of drug researchers in the US to ignore contemporary research in the UK within the fields of sociology, criminology, and cultural studies. While it is important for us to identify the pertinent differences between youthful drug use in the US and the UK,[6] it is nevertheless the case that a consideration of the normalization thesis may highlight the usefulness of adopting a nonproblematic approach to drug use by young people.

The fourth reason for writing this book is to emphasize the importance of conducting qualitative research within the drug field. The field of drug research is dominated by the disciplines of epidemiology, psychology, quantitative criminology, and public health studies. Because of this, the vast majority of the research is based on quantitative survey data, and while such data are important for mapping the general picture of drug use within the country, they are much less useful when we come to consider the experiences and meanings of individual drug users. To chart the meanings young people attach to the dance scene and drug use today we have to adopt alternative research methods more suited to exploring these themes. The existing emphasis on survey research has led to qualitative research being somewhat marginalized in the drug field. While qualitative researchers are continually expected to evaluate their methodology against a positivist tradition, those who conduct primarily quantitative research are rarely expected to evaluate their work against the epistemological premises of qualitative work. "Qualitative research almost inevitably appears unconvincing within this relationship because dominant understandings of concepts of validity and reliability and representativeness are posed within a numerical rather than a process framework" (Ribbens and Edwards 1998: 3).

Although quantitative data have continued to dominate the field, qualitative studies do of course exist. Though many of these have produced important findings, their results have often been downplayed because of the use of small samples. The research results described in this book are based neither on a large representative sample nor are they taken from a small in-depth sample, instead they are based on in-depth interviews with a relatively large sample of 300 young people. Qualitative samples of this size are somewhat uncommon both because of the time necessary to conduct in-depth interviews and subsequently analyze the data as well as the overall costs of doing the work. We were able to do this research because we were fortunate enough to obtain funding from the National Institutes of Health (NIH) and specifically the National Institute on Drug Abuse. Funding from NIH allows qualitative researchers to conduct large-scale qualitative research, and explore the experiences of individual drug users. Data from these studies can then in turn be used to supplement research data generated by more quantitative focused projects.

The fifth reason for writing this book is not only to present the views of an underresearched group of young people, but also to emphasize the extent to which important differences exist within the meanings they give to their leisure activities and their drug use. In much of the early literature on raves a heavy emphasis was placed on the unity and solidarity that develop within these events. Issues of difference are crucial to understand as well. In addition to individual idiosyncrasies, significant gender and ethnic differences exist; an important feature of this book is to examine these differences. Although in the UK a number of important studies have examined the role of women within dance events (Henderson 1993a, 1999; Hutton 2006; McRobbie 1993; Pini 1997, 2001), few studies have examined the significant gender differences that exist among dance event attendees in the US. We focus on gender and sexuality in the dance scene through the eyes of both the young women and the young men in our sample, and we analyze and problematize femininities and masculinities within these scenes (see Chapters 9 and 10). We find neither that raves and dance events are unambiguously liberating nor that conventional gender expectations are reproduced intact. We instead find that among the young men and women we interviewed there is a complicated and sometimes ambivalent negotiation of gender.

In addition to considering issues of gender and drug use we also examine the role of ethnicity and the ways in which it operates in the dance scene and nightlife. Issues of ethnicity have been neglected in both epidemiological research as well as cultural studies of dance cultures. When we began our research in the San Francisco Bay Area we quickly became aware of the importance of young Asian Americans in the dance scene. While African American and Latino youth seemed less attracted to the rave scene, young Asians accounted, according to some reports, for approximately 30 percent of attendees and at some events were in the majority. As well as being enthusiastic participants, they also reported significant drug use. This finding was surprising, especially given popular (and sometimes scholarly) generalizations of Asian American youth as nondrug users. Given these findings, we soon came to focus on the involvement of Asian youth in the scene and the role of illicit drugs in their lives, examining the contributions, but also the important limitations, of how the conventional literatures on drug use, ethnicity, and immigration explain the experiences of young Asian Americans within these scenes.

The sixth and in some ways the most important reason for writing the book stems from our young respondents themselves. To encourage a young person to agree to an in-depth interview on their drug use and their involvement in the dance scene is not that easy. Understandably, young people are suspicious when researchers want to ask them questions about their drug use. Were we the police? Was the information confidential? What was going to happen to it after the interview? These were common questions that we were asked before a young respondent would agree to being interviewed. Though we assured them that we were not the police and that all information would be confidential, such assurances are only part of the reason why many ravers and clubbers ultimately agreed to talk to us. The other main reason was that they genuinely hoped that by sharing their stories, their experiences, and their views on raves and drugs they would be able to correct the erroneous picture portrayed by the media or by those in authority. Our participants described in detail how important their rave experiences were and stressed the pleasure they obtain from the music, the dancing, and the drugs. From their stories we quickly learned how important for them attending dance events was and the extent to which they viewed this activity as primarily harmless. The vast majority of the young men and women we interviewed were very reflective about their experiences in the scene, had thought extensively about their drug use, and in many cases had conducted their own research on the potential risks of using the drugs. In addition to telling us about the enjoyment and the importance of these activities, they also expressed their frustration when politicians passed legislation to control dance events. They complained that their voices as participants went unheard while the voices of the authorities and politicians, who possessed little or no real experience of either dance parties or ecstasy, were heeded. In agreeing to be interviewed they believed that they were doing something to register and document these alternative views. Because many of our respondents chose to participate in the study for these reasons, we believe that it is incumbent on us to document and publicize their views.

As feminist researchers have noted, there is a danger that the voices of particular groups may be "drowned out, systematically silenced or misunderstood as research and researchers engage with dominant academic and public concerns and discourses" (Ribbens and Edwards 1998: 2). This is never truer than in the field of youth drug use. Young people are frequently categorized as a high-risk group within the field of drug research and therefore it is very easy to commence one's analysis by accepting the notion of "problem" drug use among young people. This is not, however, our starting point. Consequently our aim is for the readers of this book to gain a better understanding of how young people view the dance scene, how they portray their role in it, and what meanings they attach to their involvement in the scene and their use of drugs. In detailing their experiences our aim is not merely to give voice to young people, albeit an important reason; it is also to contribute empirical research to the contemporary debates on youth cultures. As Pilkington and Johnson (2003) have noted, much of theoretical discussion on notions of youth cultures, subcultures, or neotribes has been conducted with "little reference ... to young people's own definitions of contemporary situations ... rather, characterizations are based on a reading of general social dynamics" (2003: 266). The bases of this book are the narratives extracted from the 300 in-depth interviews with young people, which we hope will provide a " 'thicker' subject with historical, emotional and biographical aspects than those that figure in most discursive analysis and social theory" (Pilkington and Johnson 2003: 276). Consequently, the use of these accounts will hopefully speak to the larger debates that are currently taking place in youth cultural studies (McRobbie 1997; Maira 2003).

However, in charting their views, we do not wish to imply that unanimity exists amongst the young men and women we interviewed, for, as we will show, many of our participants hold different views both about the dance scene and about drug use. Not all of them are either pro-rave or pro-drug use. Though many remained active users at the time of being interviewed, others claimed to initially use extensively but lessened use over time. The range of different experiences documented within the pages of this book emphasize the importance of realizing the extent to which young people are not a homogeneous group but, instead, a sector of the population divided by ethnicity, gender, age, as well as by lived experiences whether at school, in the family, or at work. In charting their experiences we hope to show the extent to which, even within "mainstream" youth, significant and important divisions exist. Furthermore, while government officials, prevention experts, and politicians may wish to portray all drug use and dance parties in black-and-white terms of good and bad, the voices of our participants highlight the extent to which young people today express much more nuanced and complex views about their leisure activities and drug use. In general they are aware of both the positive and the negative features of drug consumption, and their decisions to use or not use particular drugs are based neither solely on official pronouncements nor on popular portrayals but instead are founded on a wide range of information stemming from their own personal experience, that of their friends, Web sites, and even the media. Unfortunately, the dominant portrayal of young people and drug use is that they are largely ignorant, ill informed, and gullible. Such assumptions appear to be made with few or no empirical data to support them and, in fact, as we will see later, such assumptions are sharply at odds with the views of young people interviewed for this study.

Presenting the data

The book is divided into four parts: Part I, "Theory and methods for studying youth," Part II, "The global, the national, and the local," Part III, "Drug pleasures, risks and combinations," and finally Part IV, "Gender, social context, and ethnicity."

In Part I there are two chapters, "Epidemiology meets cultural studies: studying and understanding youth cultures, clubs, and drugs" and "Clubbers, candy kids, and jaded ravers: introducing the scene, the participants, and the drugs." The aim of Chapter 1 is to outline the two research perspectives that dominate the study of drugs and the dance scene. While we wish to build on the foundational epidemiological data that have documented the extent, type, and patterns of drugs associated with the scene, as well as the characteristics of the users, we also note the tendency for research to ignore three critically important features – agency, pleasure, and context. In attempting to correct these shortcomings, we then consider the available cultural studies research which has more specifically focused on these features. We divide the cultural studies literature on the dance scene into two broad emphases: that focusing on the cohesive features of dance events and that highlighting the social divisions reflected within the scene. Overall, the cultural studies literature has provided an important counterbalance to the problem-oriented emphasis of the epidemiology data. Nevertheless, while cultural studies research has produced a detailed sociocultural context of the dance scene, it has, with only a few exceptions, been somewhat silent about the use of drugs within the scene.

The subsequent chapters of our book focus on correcting this silence, beginning with a description, in Chapter 2, of the social and demographic characteristics of the 300 young people whose experiences and narratives form the basis of the book. In addition to describing our sample, we also describe their involvement in dance events, including clubs, raves, and warehouse parties. Although the boundaries between raves and clubs are sometimes unclear, it is nevertheless the case that distinctions between the two are important to our young participants. In fact, on the basis of this, we were able to construct a typology of both ravers (regular, former, reluctant, new, and returning, and non-ravers) and clubbers (former, reluctant, ambivalent, regular, and non-clubbers) based on both their involvement and progression in the scene. The final section of the chapter examines our participants' alcohol and drug use, focusing specifically on the six club drugs (ecstasy, LSD, methamphetamine, GHB, ketamine and Rohypnol) specified by the National Institute on Drug Abuse.

Three chapters make up Part II: "Clubbing, drugs, and the dance scene in a global perspective," "Youth, US drug policy, and social control of the dance scene," and "Uncovering the local: San Francisco's nighttime economy." In Chapter 3, focusing on the global context, we examine the historical development of the rave scene and electronic dance music, from its origins in New York, Chicago, and Detroit to its early flowering in the popular Spanish tourist island of Ibiza in the late 1980s and with it the development of the "Balearic beat." From Ibiza the dance scene moved to England, where many of the young devotees attempted to recreate their Ibiza island experiences. From these developments, Acid House spread to mainland Europe, Australia, and the US, and eventually to other parts of the globe. In the latter part of the chapter we examine in slightly more detail the cases of Hong Kong and Rotterdam and the ways in which specific local characteristics influence and modify the global tendencies within the dance scene.

Chapter 4 focuses on the US national context and specifically the legislative developments that occurred in the early part of the new millennium which targeted youthful drug use and the nighttime dance scene. We examine the congressional hearings and the media accounts that led up to the passing of the 2003 Illicit Drug Anti-Proliferation Act. The purpose of this chapter is to highlight the extent to which young people's involvement in the rave/dance scene quickly led not only to a series of local and federal controls being placed on these youthful leisure activities but also to the characterization of these activities as particularly risky and dangerous.

Having described the global and the national level, in the final chapter of this part we examine the local environment of San Francisco. While many of the cultural studies books that have looked at the rave/dance scene have focused on the experiences of the young attendees themselves, few of the existing studies have attempted to provide a detailed social context of the dance scene and of the nighttime economy in which the scene is embedded. To contextualize our 300 in-depth interviews, we provide a brief history of the developments that have occurred in San Francisco nightlife since the 1970s. This includes an account of the heyday of raves in the Bay Area and the expansion and retraction of nightclubs as a result of economic fluctuations. Such changes have also led to changes in the regulatory process and the establishment of the San Francisco Entertainment Commission. As well as noting these changes, we also describe within the chapter the different venues, clubs, raves, and other dance events in San Francisco nighttime economy that we mapped in the early 2000s.

In Part III we focus specifically on our participants' narrative accounts of their drug use and the meanings that they attach to their use. In Chapter 6, " 'The great unmentionable': exploring the pleasures and benefits of ecstasy," we explore a somewhat underanalyzed or rarely mentioned feature of youthful drug use, that of pleasure. One of the most striking features of our participants' accounts of why they use drugs is their emphasis on having fun and the pleasure they obtain in using drugs, especially ecstasy. In examining this feature, we highlight the way that the young people we interviewed distinguish between the immediate effects and the more enduring features of their drug use. Although much of their discussion is on the pharmacological pleasures of ecstasy, their entire discussion is couched within the context that their drug use is a social activity done with friends either at a public dance event or within a more private environment.

While we wish to document the extent to which our participants discuss elements of pleasures, we do not wish to underestimate the extent to which these young people are also aware of the potential negative or unpleasant effects of using drugs. Consequently in Chapter 7, "Drug use and the meaning of risk," we explore how risk is constructed in the narratives of our participants. We trace their sources of knowledge and information and their perceptions of risk and the extent to which they describe both the occasions when the benefits outweigh the risks and when risks overcome the pleasures. We conclude this chapter by suggesting that an intrinsic part of the pleasure of doing drugs is the risks entailed.

The final chapter in Part III, Chapter 8, "Combining different substances in the dance scene: enhancing pleasure, managing risk, and timing effects," presents an application of the issues developed in the preceding two chapters to the topic of "polydrug" use. It explores the ways in which our participants utilize a range of different substances to extend or enhance the pleasures and navigate the risks of individual drugs. As well as noting what substances work beneficially, they also describe in great detail the importance of timing in combining different substances. The substances to be combined are both other illicit drugs as well as a range of non-illicit substances. Finally, we also examine their accounts of the drug combinations to be avoided.

In the last part of the book we turn to issues of difference and identity, analyzing experiences and constructions of gender, sexuality, and ethnicity in the social contexts of the dance scenes. Chapter 9, "Drugs, gender, sexuality, and accountability in the world of raves," focuses on the relationship between ecstasy, raves, and the accomplishment of gender. Examining constructions of femininity and masculinity, we find discourses of gender malleability and challenges to conventional gender and sexual expectations among the discussions of raves from the young men and women we interviewed. But this is not a simple story of raves or ecstasy leading to some kind of clear-cut gender liberation. For we also found evidence of gender accountability and the ways in which conventional gender and sexuality norms continue to be enforced, even in this context.

In Chapter 10, "Alcohol, gender, and social context," we continue with an examination of issues of gender and sexuality, but we shift the focus to the social context of clubs and the different role that alcohol plays in that setting, compared to the more drug-oriented rave scene. Although alcohol consumption is close to universal among our young participants, the discourses they present about alcohol differ significantly from those we have seen in earlier chapters regarding ecstasy and other club drugs. Our participants associate alcohol and clubs with more onerous expectations of gender, and especially sexual, display, and alcohol intoxication is judged much more harshly than drug intoxication.

Finally, in Chapter 11, "Asian American youth: consumption, identity, and drugs in the dance scene," we focus on issues of ethnicity, particularly as they relate to the young Asian Americans in the rave and club scenes. Though the rave scene is often described as monolithically white, in San Francisco Asian Americans (from a variety of different ethnicities and nationalities) comprise a sizable portion of the scene. Fifty-six of the 300 young men and women we interviewed identified as Asian American, and this chapter focuses on their experiences, as well as the experiences of the 250 young Asian Americans we interviewed as part of a follow-up study. We examine the role and constitution of social networks in the experiences of young Asian Americans in this scene and the ways in which many of the young men and women we interviewed construct their own identities in this scene in contrast to "other" Asians against whom they define themselves. We then examine the efficacy of the traditional literatures that have been used to explain Asian American drug use – which have tended to either downplay its existence or reduce Asian American youth drug experiences to responses to immigration – either as a symptom of assimilation or as a symptom of the difficulties involved with acculturation. We find among our diverse Asian American sample a variety of discourses employed to examine and explain their own use, identifying three main narratives. While the first two narratives fit within the traditional focus on issues of assimilation and acculturation, the third, largest group of respondents instead discussed their identities as drug users, as Asian Americans, and as Asian American drug users as unremarkable and, indeed, normalized.

Part I

Theory and methods for studying youth

Chapter 1

Epidemiology meets cultural studies

Studying and understanding youth cultures, clubs, and drugs

Introduction

The use of ecstasy (MDMA) and other club drugs[1] has increased dramatically in the US since the late 1990s. This growth in use has been accompanied by an escalation in concern about ecstasy and the young people who use it. The growth in ecstasy use has many causes, chief among which is the association between ecstasy use and the popularity of raves, clubs, and dance parties during this same period. Although the peak of raves may be past (arguably, raves peaked in 1994 in the UK and a bit later, in 2002, in the US), youth nightlife and dance scenes continue, ecstasy use among youth may be on the rise (Johnston *et al.* 2007), and attempts to control and regulate youth cultures persist.

A cursory look at the public perceptions of clubs and drugs reveals the existence of two opposing and contrasting perspectives or discourses. One, an official discourse, characterizes raves, dance events, and taking drugs as situations of "excess risk" (D. Moore and Valverde 2000: 528), which need to be controlled and regulated. An indicator of the extent of the concern and the desire for regulation was the passing in 2003 of the Illicit Drug Anti-Proliferation Act, previously named the "RAVE Act," in the US. In attempting to close down raves, here the establishment revealed "a trenchant fear of youth transcendence – as authorities, suspicious of bodily pleasure, conflate dance with moral corruption" (St. John 2004: 5; see Chapter 4 of this book for more on this legislation). The other discourse, as exemplified in accounts of the participants themselves, and sometimes referred to as "subjugated knowledges" (D. Moore 2008), emphasizes the importance of dance events and club drugs for young people and the pleasures derived from attending and using. The dichotomous nature of the discourses – an official, expert, and governmental response to raves and the techno dance scene, on the one hand, and the insider perspectives of the youthful participants, on the other – is not altogether surprising; adult concerns with and attempts to control youthful practices have been witnessed many times before (Griffin 1993) and today we may be seeing an increasing "governance of youth" (Bunton *et al.* 2004b: 8).

A division between perspectives on and approaches to understanding raves and drug use, though, can be found not just in the contrast between official/government approaches and those of rave/dance club participants, but also within scholarly work. Scholarship on raves, the dance scenes, and club drugs can be divided into two immensely differing traditions: the epidemiological approach and the cultural studies approach. The epidemiological research has focused primarily on examining the prevalence of club drugs, the problems associated with their use and the characteristics of the users.[2] The cultural studies approach acts as a much-needed corrective or supplement to the epidemiological research through its introduction of a focus on pleasure, subjectivity, and social context and by more fully attending to youth perspectives. However, the cultural studies scholarship itself has important blind spots, particularly in its underemphasis on the role of drugs within the dance and rave scenes. We will argue for a third approach that utilizes the theoretical and methodological strengths of the cultural studies approach, while combining it with perspectives that allow us to comprehend the role that drugs play within these scenes and the roles of pleasure and risk within them.

Research dichotomies

Contemporary ecstasy and club-drug research

The overall aim of the available epidemiological research in charting drug use and the dance scene has been to assess the prevalence of drug use and "risk factors for addiction, psychological problems which might be treated, or a general and dangerous propensity for antisocial behaviour" (Glassner and Loughlin 1987: 3). More specifically, the extant research has emphasized the problems of using ecstasy and other club drugs, the extent of drug-using behaviors connected with the scene, and the characteristics of the users.

The problems of using ecstasy and other club drugs

First, researchers have examined the potential problems of using ecstasy (MDMA) and other club drugs. For example, in the case of ecstasy, a number of physical and psychological problems have been associated with its use. MDMA can cause psychological problems such as depression, sleep problems, anxiety, and paranoia, and the stimulant effects of MDMA may lead to a significant increase in heart rate and blood pressure, dehydration, hyperthermia, or possible seizures and heart or kidney failure (Dowling 1990; Milroy 1999; National Institute on Drug Abuse 1999). Possible long-term brain damage has also been identified (Asghar and DeSouza 1989; McCann et al. 1998; National Institute on Drug Abuse 1999; Peroutka 1990). Although MDMA is said to be physically non-addictive, users may become psychologically dependent and may subconsciously use the drug as a form of self-medication for underlying disorders (Jansen 1999). Other serious reactions include "hyperthermia, rhabdomyoysis, disseminated intravascular coagulation, renal failure, cardiac complications, intracranial hemorrhage and hepatotoxicity" (Maxwell 2005: 1212; see also Goss 2001; K. M. Smith et al. 2002).

The extent of drug-using behaviors connected with the scene

As many researchers in Australia, Canada, Germany, and the UK have documented, a strong association exists between the dance scene and specific types of drugs, especially ecstasy and methamphetamines (Adlaf and Smart 1997; Boys *et al.* 1997; Deehan and Saville 2003; Forsyth 1996; Lenton *et al.* 1997; Measham *et al.* 2001; Soellner 2005). As Measham and her colleagues note, "the key conclusion to be drawn … is that clubbers are extremely drug-experienced" (2001: 96). Not only did researchers discover that the majority of attendees use drugs at raves and clubs (Akram and Galt 1999; Boys *et al.* 1997; Ward and Fitch 1998), but also that attendees had a much higher rate of using drugs than non-attendees (Tossmann *et al.* 2001: 12. See also Adlaf and Smart 1997; Measham *et al.* 2001). Overall, these studies suggest a strong association between dance events and drug use, and most researchers have argued that increases in the use of club drugs by young adults reflect their increasing involvement in dance events.

Epidemiologists have identified ecstasy as the quintessential drug of the international rave and club scenes. Lenton and colleagues (1997) in Australia discovered that ecstasy was the only drug which was used by more respondents in association with a rave than in any other setting (for similar findings in Britain see Pearson *et al.* 1991 and Ward and Fitch 1998) and ecstasy rates among ravers and clubgoers are much higher than among youth in the general population (Tossmann *et al.* 2001: 12). It is not solely ecstasy, though, that epidemiologists have found prevalent in the dance scenes. Research suggests that marijuana may be used more extensively than ecstasy (see for example Tossmann *et al.* 2001), especially in the stages before and after the event, and high rates of amphetamine and hallucinogen use have also been documented (Van de Wijngaart *et al.* 1999; Ward and Fitch 1998).

Characteristics of the users: age, gender, ethnicity, sexuality

The age of the users is the first striking and somewhat obvious characteristic. The majority of attendees at dance events are teenagers and young adults, both male and female. From the available research this trend appears generally consistent in different countries, and ecstasy users who attend raves and clubs have some similar characteristics. For example, according to Measham and her colleagues, ravers in the north of England are predominantly young adults between the ages of 16 and 25 (Measham *et al.* 1998). A number of other studies show that the age range is generally similar, although there may be slight variations in attendees' average age; studies range from a mean age of attendees of 18.9 in Australia to 24.8 in Berlin (Boys *et al.* 1997; Calafat *et al.* 2001).

The gender ratio of the users is the second striking feature to emerge from the research literature. Although no representative surveys have been completed on the gender ratio of attendees at clubs, raves, and parties, researchers have argued that, while men are in the majority in the scene, women are a significant presence. Most studies suggest that the ratio of young men to young women is never greater than 60–40.[3] For example, the SONAR project (Calafat *et al.* 2001) showed an overall dominance of men (approximately 60 percent) but they also discovered that the precise gender ratios varied both from one city to another as well as within different scenes (see also Solowij *et al.* 1992).

The presence of women within the scene is also reflected in their drug-using behaviors. The fact that attendees at clubs and parties are "drug-experienced" is true for both young women and men. Researchers still tend to find greater male involvement in club drugs among adults (Measham *et al.* 2001: 101) but young women's use appears to be increasing, and "the once distinctive difference in the figures between boys and girls is disappearing, with young women being almost as likely to take drugs as young men" (H. Parker *et al.* 1998: 14). (For more on gender and club drugs see Chapter 9.)

In terms of ethnic characteristics, the research evidence from the national studies suggest that ecstasy users are primarily white. This predominance of white users and attendees has been noted both in the UK and in the US. For example, in the UK Measham and her colleagues (2001), in their sample of over 2,000 clubgoers in Manchester, found that only 5 percent were either Afro-Caribbean or Asian. In the US, Johnston and colleagues (2003), using data from the Monitoring the Future study, found that white high-school seniors were nearly six times as likely to report ecstasy use in the past year as their African American counterparts, and Yacoubian and Urbach, analyzing data from the US NHSDA survey between 1990 and 2001, found that "the use of ecstasy has remained primarily a white phenomenon" (2004: 75). However, there exists some local research that suggests that the ethnic composition of ecstasy users may either be altering or may be determined by geographical location. For example, Schensul and colleagues (2005b) have highlighted the extent to which ecstasy has begun to diffuse to African American and Latino youth in inner urban areas, and in some regions Asian Americans have become a significant presence within the rave and club scenes (as we will examine in Chapter 11).

Another body of research has developed in recent years focusing on sexuality and club drug use, centered particularly on analyses of drug use among men who have sex with men (MSM) in the gay club/party scenes. For example, studies have highlighted higher rates of marijuana, cocaine, and popper use (McKirnan and Peterson 1989), and higher rates of methamphetamine and ketamine among homosexual versus heterosexual drug users in the dance/club scenes (Degenhardt 2005). A particular focus of this research has centered on analysis of the connections between club-drug use (particularly methamphetamine use) and high-risk sexual practices that can lead to HIV transmission. For example, Colfax *et al.* (2005) found higher rates of unprotected anal intercourse (UAI) when MSM were using methamphetamine, poppers, or cocaine; Operario *et al.* (2006) found significant increases in risky sexual practices associated with frequent substance use, club-drug use, and polydrug use among young MSM; and Celentano *et al.* (2005) found significant associations between incidents of UAI and being under the influence of alcohol, cocaine, amphetamines, and marijuana. The research on MSM drug use, which continues to grow, remains somewhat isolated from other club-drug research, with relatively little cross-citation.

What's missing from the drug literature?

As is clear from the above discussion, there exists an extensive epidemiological literature on the potential problems with using ecstasy and other drugs, the extent to which drugs are associated with the contemporary dance scene, and the types, the characteristics of the users, and the patterns and combinations of drugs used. While this literature has been particularly important in providing information on the drug-using patterns and the sociodemographic characteristics of the users, it has nevertheless ignored three critically important features: *agency*, *pleasure*, and *context*.

Agency

First, and most important, it has omitted any investigation of young people's perspective or understanding of their own behaviors (Glassner and Loughlin 1987). "Concern with adolescent drug use … are based on assumptions about the meaning of drugs for potential users whose perspectives are very different from that of adults" (Glassner and Loughlin 1987: 1). The agency of young people is ignored or underemphasized and consequently the vast majority of research has neglected to consider the role or meaning of drugs within the lives of young people, and especially their role within young people's leisure activities, from the perspective of youth themselves. Young people are viewed within the literature as fundamentally passive, risky, or problematic consumers involved in risky consumption (W. Mitchell *et al.* 2004).

Pleasure

Second, epidemiological research in focusing on the problematic nature of drug use has ignored the importance of pleasure in drug consumption.[4] Within this research, primacy has been given to a discourse of pathology, deviance, and problems and "considerations of 'pleasure' in relation to drug use" (D. Moore 2008) have been marginalized. This neglect of pleasure and fun from much of the official drug discourse and drug research literature in general is particularly striking when we examine the use of ecstasy and other "club drugs." In spite of the fact that researchers have christened the clustering of drugs associated with nighttime dance events as "club or party drugs," the element of pleasure is still absent. It is as though pleasure has become unseeable within much of the research.

> [These discourses] tend to remain silent about pleasure as a motive for consumption and raise instead visions of a consumption characterized by compulsion, pain and pathology. Problematic substance use is said to be caused not by pleasure-seeking but by such things as … the "behavioral stimuli" of many current psychological theories of "craving" or by some bodily, social or psychological failing or deficit that pushes people to act "unreasonably."
>
> (O'Malley and Valverde 2004: 26)

The absence of any significant discourse about pleasure within drug research means that a central component of why both young people and adults use mind-altering substances is ignored. As Parker and his colleagues have remarked, "we need to place ... pleasure in the formula. Drugs are used because they give enjoyment" (H. Parker *et al.* 1998: 133; see Chapter 7 for extensive discussion of pleasure); this seemingly obvious point is missing from much epidemiological drug research. Unfortunately, because drug research focuses solely on the substances themselves and their possible dangers, researchers miss completely the point that the enjoyment of taking these substances is an intrinsic part of enjoying the event, which includes the music, the spectacle, the dancing, and, most important, having fun with friends or lovers. Furthermore, because the pleasure discourse is underdeveloped within epidemiological research, little attention has been focused on the social construction of pleasure. As O'Malley and Mugford have argued, "pleasure is not defined the same way in all societal contexts, nor are all drugs seen as desirable and pleasurable by all people in all cultures at all times" (1991: 51). Furthermore, both the sensory effects of the drugs and the very nature of the pleasures engendered by them vary based on different contexts (Duff 2007).

Context

Finally, the epidemiological literature has also ignored the social context in which young people's drug use takes place. In focusing solely on the substance itself, researchers have downplayed the importance of studying the use of these substances within a social setting. The club/rave settings are noted (as locations of ecstasy use) but these settings are rarely examined or explored. Although Zinberg (1984) produced his classic study of drug settings over twenty years ago, few studies within the drug field have located youthful drug use within a sociocultural context of consumption. Consuming ecstasy is primarily a social activity done with friends, either in a public environment such as a rave or in private at a party. However within the epidemiology literature, the young drug user is portrayed as separate and divorced from his or her social setting, and their social identities have become totally subsumed by the substance. They are defined solely as drug users, and this overarching identity becomes the individual's defining characteristic. Wagner calls this tendency to categorize individuals solely by their drug behavior a process of "decontextualization of isolated behaviors" (1997: 69). Decontextualization is sometimes so thorough that it is difficult to uncover how these individuals behave in social settings, perceive their social lives, or express their feelings and beliefs.

Therefore in order to begin to examine the social context of club-drug consumption and the social construction of the pleasures associated with it, we must now turn our attention to examining an alternative literature which has focused more specifically on examining the sociocultural setting within which these young people consume ecstasy and other drugs and experience fun. This literature explores the meanings that young people give to experiences at raves and clubs, and instead of adopting a problem perspective, it celebrates young people's active enjoyment of the dance scene. Within this literature, the neglected voices of young people are explored.

Focusing on young people, the dance scene, and pleasure: a cultural studies perspective

Given the wide-ranging nature of the available sociological and cultural studies research on youth cultures, coupled with the ubiquity of the international dance scene (Hunt and Evans 2003), it is not surprising that the literature is fragmented into different interest areas. While the available epidemiological literature has remained within fairly narrow research limits (characteristics of users, drug patterns, and problems) the topics covered by researchers who have examined the dance scene is extensive and covers such issues as gender relations, religious and trance experiences, musical taste, dance styles, changes in the urban nightlife, political protest, and global developments. Moreover, while some researchers have focused exclusively on the experiences within the clubs themselves or the dance scene in general, others have used the electronic dance music world to illustrate other, wider sociological issues (Bennett 2000; Brewster and Broughton 1999; M. J. Butler 2006; Collin 1997; Epstein 1994; Fritz 2000; Gilbert and Pearson 1999; Harrison 1998; Huq 2006; Laughey 2006; Maffesoli 1996; T. Mitchell 1996; Redhead 1997; Reynolds 1999; Silcott 1999; Skelton and Valentine 1998). Consequently, given the extent of the existing literature, it is not possible for us to cover in depth all the different strands within this chapter. Instead, rather than attempting to be fully comprehensive and review the entire literature of the field, we will focus in particular on some of the key cultural studies of the dance scene, which have been most central or influential in the field, as representative of trends observed more broadly.

The starting point for much of this alternative sociological and cultural studies literature has been the attempt to understand the rapid expansion of the electronic dance music scene in the 1990s. Even though the specific focus of individual researchers has been diverse, they have all explored the experiences of young people within this leisure activity and sought to understand the pleasurable features of the contemporary dance scene. For example, Redhead (1990), one of the earliest commentators on the scene, referred in his early work to the development of Acid House in the UK in the late 1980s as a "Dionysian" culture. Although in his later work on rave culture he argued that the "paradise regained" of the initial years may have turned into a "psychic malaise," he nevertheless believed that a central feature of rave culture was a pursuit of pleasure.

Epidemiology and cultural studies adopt significantly different research methodologies. Whereas epidemiological research on ecstasy and other club drugs has adopted, unsurprisingly, survey and quantitative methods, youth researchers today are committed to ethnographic and qualitative research. Unlike epidemiologists, who have remained separate from their research subjects in a quest for "objectivity," cultural studies researchers have been more involved with their young respondents, documenting accounts of their own experiences and uncovering the processes of being young. Influenced by developments in new thinking in anthropological research and cultural and feminist studies, especially around issues of reflexivity, these researchers have reacted against the role of researcher as the "outside expert." Instead they have emphasized the importance of doing "self as insider" research, and many of the studies we will discuss have been written by young researchers who had been involved in the scene prior to conducting research on it (Malbon 1999; Pini 2001; Thornton 1996; Wright 1999).

Studying club cultures: finding cohesion within the club and dance scene

Within cultural studies research on the dance scene, two contrasting themes can be identified. Some analysts view the clubs and dance events or the night out as *overcoming or counteracting* the wider societal divisions while others examine the dance scene *as reflecting or reproducing* the social divisions within the wider society. In the former tradition, researchers examine the elements of cohesion and, in the latter, they focus on the divisive elements within the dance scene.

With the initial development of the rave scene first in Ibiza, Spain, and then in the UK, commentators noted the extent to which young people from many different social backgrounds came together at the raves and bonded into one undifferentiated mass of humanity. "With rave, class, ethnicity, gender and other social distinctions were imagined to dissipate" (St. John 2004: 5). Young attendees described their experience of oneness, empathy, and shared communality. This sense of oneness was reflected in some of the early sociological accounts of raves and clubbing, and especially in the work of Ben Malbon. His book *Clubbing* (1999) is still the most detailed account of the internal workings of the club scene and the night out. Malbon seeks to show us the cohesive nature of clubbing, or, as Deleuze and Guattari have called it, a "Body without Organs" (Jordan 1995). The experiences of the night out are viewed as primarily a harmonious environment in which young people from all backgrounds could come and blend together. In opposition to other research, he argues that previous research neglected the "experiences of clubbing itself" (Malbon 1999: 17), by which he means the experiential interactions that take place on the dance floor. He believes that researchers such as Thornton (1996; discussed below) provide only a "background to … the practices and spacing constituting clubbing" (Malbon 1999: 18). Instead, Malbon seeks to convey the "lived, performed and emotional nature of clubbing" (1999: 18). He asks: what are the meanings that young people experience while attending dance events? And to what extent do clubbers experience a togetherness which binds disparate groups of individuals together during the night out? While he agrees with previous research that has emphasized the quality of resistance within youth cultures (a prominent theme in much of the work of the Centre for Contemporary Cultural Studies), he argues that an equally important feature, albeit a neglected one, is the desire by young people in coming together to belong. "The practices of youth cultures can be as much about *expression* as about resistance; as much about belonging as *excluding*; as much about temporarily *forgetting* who you are as about consolidating an identity … and as much about blurring boundaries between people and cultures as affirming or reinforcing those boundaries" (Malbon

1999: 19, author's emphasis). By identifying with the crowd, clubbers confirm their identity.

His interest in the internal experiences of clubbing is also important for research on clubs and drug use because he seeks to examine the relationship between sociality and experiential consumption in terms of both the experience and the drugs. However, his focus on drug use and specifically ecstasy does not emanate from an interest in drugs *per se* but more on the use of substances to achieve what he calls an "oceanic" or "ecstatic" experience – "losing and gaining control, feeling inside and outside the self, the momentary euphoria outside time and place" (Crichter 2000: 159). By using these terms, Malbon wishes to convey the intensity and specificity of the experience enjoyed by clubgoers. According to Malbon the ecstatic experience comes from a combination of dancing and using the body within a crowd, and merging with the music can be intensified or prolonged by the use of "dance" drugs and especially ecstasy. While arguing that an ecstatic experience can be obtained without the drugs, he nevertheless admits that using dance drugs, especially ecstasy, provides "an additional layer of emotional and sensational action" (Malbon 1999: 116). At the height of the oceanic experience the individual loses all sense of time and place and experiences a sense of oneness or belonging with all the other participants.

The theme of unity and the creation of a "spontaneous communitas" (Turner 1969) has been developed by other researchers who have focused on the development of "techno-communitas." The most articulated form of this research can be found in the work of Graham St. John and specifically his edited book *Rave Culture and Religion* (2004). In general, he and the contributors to the collection seek to examine the religious or spiritual content of raves. What is it that participants experience when they attend a rave or dance party? Raving is viewed as a transformational and spiritual practice in which rave attendees experience a sense of transcendent community or "indissoluble bond" brought about by their willingness to let go of their identity. Within this "dissolution of identity" (Gilbert and Pearson 1999), the participants experience a sense of intense pleasure. One of the first steps to abandoning one's identity is through the process of dressing up – a process "of deconstructing and reconstructing subjectivity" (Gautier 2004: 73). The disappearance of both one's self and "the other" experienced by rave attendees is similar to the ecstatic and trance-like qualities found in shamanistic rituals in many parts of the world (Tramacchi 2004) and is experienced by rave participants in different cultures, including the UK (Malbon 1999), France (Gautier 2004), Canada (Olaveson 2004), San Francisco (Hill 1999), and Ibiza and Goa (D'Andrea 2007). From this disappearance of self, the individual participant becomes one with the rest of the attendees.

Studying club cultures: elements of differentiation – gender, sexuality, race/ethnicity

Although a couple of important collected editions appeared prior to the publication of her book (such as Redhead 1993), Sarah Thornton's *Club Cultures* (1996) can be considered the first in-depth and probably most influential of all the later cultural studies research on the dance scene. Thornton's interest in the dance scene came out of a cultural studies perspective which sought to understand and deconstruct a significant example of popular youth culture. Her concern lay less in the internal and cohesive happenings of the clubs themselves than in the way young people use taste cultures to distinguish themselves and their own social groupings from others both within and outside the scene. To do this she modifies Bourdieu's notion of "cultural capital" and develops the concept of "subcultural capital," which like cultural capital acts to confer status on its owner. Individual clubgoers define themselves as authentic members of the rave subculture or the underground and in so doing they distinguish themselves from others who are less "cool," whom they categorize as being part of the homogeneous and indiscriminate mainstream. In other words they provide themselves an identity by which and through which they can separate themselves from others.

Issues of gender do not loom large in Thornton's work and yet, because of the popularity of the dance scene for young women, feminist researchers have examined gender issues and gender relationships (Henderson 1993a; Hutton 2006; McRobbie 1994; Pini 2001) both from the perspective of young women themselves but also, to a lesser extent, from the perspective of young men. (See Chapter 9 for our analysis of gender, ecstasy and the dance scene.) Other than a number of highly influential articles by McRobbie (1993, 1994), the most significant early study on women and the dance scene is Pini's *Club Cultures and Female Subjectivity* (2001). Maria Pini has produced an important feminist account of the dance scene. She argues that left-wing scholarship had tended to neglect dance cultures, and especially disco, on the grounds that they were fundamentally trivial and hedonistic.[5] Today, however, the world of dance cultures has "finally captured the academic left imagination" (Pini 2001: 29). Nevertheless, according to Pini, this renewed interest has remained male-centered and little research exists on women within the scene. With this in mind, Pini examines the recreational practices of young women in the dance world – a world which allows them, she argues, to live out a more liberating version of femininity.

Although Pini acknowledges the importance of Thornton's work, she argues that Thornton's study is indicative of research which has ignored issues of femininity and has focused too little attention on the "practices and experiences of women within these cultures" (2001: 7). To counter this failure she asks why women consider raving so liberating. Pini answers this by analyzing the experiential accounts of women in the dance scene and she explores how these young women seek experiences of adventure, exploration, discovery, and pleasure within the world of raves. She finds that the dance floor is a space for young women to explore the boundaries of "appropriate" behavior and that the rave scene has allowed women a new freedom in using drugs. (Though it is not a central concern, Pini focuses more on drug use in the scene than is typical in the cultural studies literature.) Pini discovered that her respondents no longer saw drug-taking as a form of personal pathology, but instead they attached a certain street credibility to getting high and looking "out of it." This freedom to consume drugs, have fun, and "go mad" within the dance scene is unusual, especially given the presence of men. In most other situations, historically, young women's ability to become intoxicated has been strictly controlled both by men and by other women.[6]

However, while noting the importance of new forms of femininities, Pini also acknowledges the extent to which this sense of feeling "safer, freer and more at home" is coupled with the extent to which notions of masculinity within the scene have also changed. As she notes, "If the rave environment is seen by these women to provide a comfortable space for the playing-out of a sense of belonging and madness this is also centrally because it is seen to involve new forms of masculinity" (2001: 114).

Issues of sexuality and sexual identity play a peripheral role in the gender analyses of dance, clubs, and ecstasy in the above examples. Sexuality is a more central focus in a key early study of club-drug use in the gay dance-club scene in Lewis and Ross's (1995) *A Select Body*. In this book, based on their ethnography of gay dance clubs in Sydney, Australia, Lewis and Ross examine the relationship between symbols in the dance scene, gay identity, political dynamics, drug use, and sexual-risk behaviors. They highlight the importance of examining these issues qualitatively, to understand the dynamic points of view of scene participants and to understand the importance of setting or social context in facilitating drug-using and sexual-risk practices. Their book is somewhat unusual among the cultural studies analyses of club scenes in that it places the issues of drugs, the experience of drug consumption, and the differential meanings of different drugs (e.g. ecstasy versus ice [methamphetamine]) for clubgoers. While this book is much cited in the literature on club-drug use among gay and bisexual men, it appears less frequently in general cultural studies club literature, which continues to focus primarily upon heterosexual clubgoers and scenes.

Ethnicity issues have tended to be overlooked in cultural studies research of the rave and electronic dance music scenes. Fortunately, today a few studies have begun to emerge which focus more specifically on ethnicity and the dance scene. The absence of studies on ethnicity and the dance scene is surprising, given the growing attention in cultural studies on rap and hip-hop and its role in black and Latino cultures. For example, writers both in the US (Kitwana 2002; Rivera 2003; Rose 1994) and in the UK (Back 1996; Bennett 1999a; Gilroy 1987, 1993) have examined the importance of ethnic identity and the culture of rap and hip-hop. Whether this gap in the cultural studies dance-scene literature is solely due to the dominance of white clubbers in the early rave scene or whether it is yet another example of cultural studies' earlier neglect of ethnic minorities (Gilroy 1987) is unclear.

The growing popularity of bhangra music both in the UK and in the US has occasioned increased interest in the relationship between ethnicity, ethnic identity, and the dance scene. This new focus on bhangra music emerges against a backdrop of historically sparse scholarly attention to South Asian or Asian American youth, especially when compared with more extensive attention paid to African American or Afro-Caribbean youth.[7] This imbalance is doubly noticeable within the field of drug and alcohol research. Since the mid-1960s Asian American youth have been stereotyped as a "model minority" and consequently of less interest to problem-oriented social science researchers. The roots of this neglect go back even further in the history of racism and legal exclusion experienced by Asian Americans since their first arrival in the US in the mid-1800s; South Asians "as a whole have in many ways remained an invisible community in the eyes of academia" (Huq 1996: 62). Research is beginning to address this neglect. Maira's book *Desis in the House* (2002) is an important example of this new interest. Maira examined Indian American youth culture and specifically bhangra remix music in New York. Her work is significant not merely because she has focused on notions of ethnic identity and the dance scene but also because she attempts to utilize and transform the work of Thornton and her theory of subcultural capital, integrating it with recent thinking on ethnicity and ethnic identity, specifically the work of Hall (1992). Hall questions essentialist notions of ethnic identity as unitary, fixed, and unchanging, and instead argues that ethnic self-identities, far from being fixed, are actively chosen, created, recreated, negotiated, and performed by individuals. Their model of ethnicity "emphasizes the socially 'constructed' aspects of ethnicity" (Nagel 1994: 101). Like Thornton's clubbers, Maira's respondents interpret different forms of ethnic identity as more or less "cool" and "hip." They use different ways of being Asian and different Asian lifestyles as key symbolic markers to position themselves in relation to others, and especially other Asians, within the scene. This process exhibits the extent to which social groups are differentiated within the dance scene. This way of conceptualizing ethnicity is in marked contrast to the way that ethnicity tends to be used in the drug and alcohol epidemiology literature, where ethnicity operates solely as an inert, individual variable to be measured just like age and sex. (We examine the experiences of young Asian Americans in the dance scene in Chapter 11.)

What's missing from the cultural studies literature?

Overall, cultural studies research on raves and the dance scene provides an important counterbalance to the problem-focused approach of much of the drug literature. Given the sharp contrast between the foci of epidemiology and cultural studies on the dance scene and their alternative foci on problems or on pleasure, it is not surprising that the implicit or even explicit conceptualizations of young people are also significantly different. These two approaches reflect dichotomous views of young people based in part on different underlying theoretical paradigms of positivism and phenomenology. While epidemiological drug research portrays youthful drug use as particularly dangerous, and young people as especially vulnerable and in need of protection, researchers trained in cultural studies begin from the position that young people are "active and creative negotiators of the relationship between structure and agency" (Ettorre and Miles 2002: 173). They are viewed as actively involved in negotiating their lives and using "modes of consumption as a means of making sense of a rapidly changing world" (Ettorre and Miles 2002: 178). These different conceptualizations of the actor are also related to the way that researchers, in both arenas, adopt significantly different research methodologies: quantitative surveys versus qualitative interviews and ethnographies.

Cultural studies researchers have provided a detailed analysis of the dance scene and the sociocultural settings within which youthful drug practices take place. Throughout much of the cultural studies analysis of the dance scene, though, there has been a curious silence about the drug use itself and any discussion of the illegal nature of drug use. Often, the importance of drugs within the scene is downplayed or brushed aside, mentioned tangentially but not as a central part of the analysis.

While it would be inaccurate to suggest that cultural studies research has ignored the importance of illicit drugs within the dance scene,[8] the role of drugs and the importance of their illegal status has been of less significance for many cultural studies researchers. For example, while Malbon discusses the use of ecstasy and the extent to which it can provide "an additional layer of emotional and sensational action" (1999: 116), and Pini (2001) makes a few references, their discussion is secondary to their exploring other more important (to them) features – in Malbon's case it is the creation of a communal oneness, in Pini's it is the gender-liberating features of raving. Thornton (1996) has no general reference to drugs and mentions ecstasy in passing only when she admits to having taken it. Bennett (2000) devotes only a small section to drugs and finally Gilbert and Pearson, while noting that drugs "are central to contemporary dance culture" (1999: 138), devote only a couple of pages to the topic. In noting their seeming lack of interest in drugs and their illicit qualities, we wish not to lessen the importance of their work but more to emphasize the need for a more thorough cultural studies analysis of youth club drug use, *per se*, especially given its importance in the lives of young people.

Furthermore, although cultural studies scholars have importantly privileged discussions of pleasure overall, the specific pleasures of drug consumption within the dance scene have not been fully explored. The pleasures of drug consumption are generally subsumed under a broader, more general notion of the pleasures of the scene overall – the pleasures of dancing and of communality. Even less examined than drug pleasures themselves within this research tradition, though, have been the pleasures associated with taking risks in using drugs, whether that be the pharmacological risks or the risks associated with an activity defined as illegal. The risky nature of doing drugs, of being involved in "voluntary illicit risk-taking" (J. Young 2007), may further enhance the pleasure. Nor have the risks of drug consumption themselves been much examined by cultural studies scholars. While epidemiologists have placed an undue emphasis on the risks and dangers associated with club drugs, the alternative need not be ignoring the question of risk entirely. Nor must an analysis of risk necessarily succumb to the problems of constructing youth as passively in danger, at risk, without agency. A cultural studies approach to the analysis of drug risks, one that takes context, agency, and subjectivity seriously seems called for. (See Chapter 5 for our take on risk, pleasure and club drugs.) Young people themselves, while wishing to have fun and pleasure from becoming intoxicated, are not without an understanding of the dangers associated with their using drugs. (See Chapter 6 for the negotiation of drug risks.) In fact, given the societal emphasis on drug problems, especially through the Drug War, it would, indeed, be surprising if young people were not aware of the potential dangers.

Conclusion

In our own approach to understanding and analyzing this youth culture of the dance scene, and its related drug use, we attempt to draw from the strengths, while avoiding some of the pitfalls, of both perspectives outlined in this chapter. In the next chapter of the book, we will begin with many of those key issues of epidemiological concern, as we introduce the specific group of young people who are the focus of our study – users of club drugs involved in the rave and club scenes in the San Francisco Bay Area. While our approach at first seems very consistent with the epidemiological approach, in the explication of the extent of drug use in the scene and the characteristics of the users, this can be only a beginning and never an end of our analysis. Therefore the remainder of the book digs deeper, to examine how club drugs, the club/rave/dance scenes, intersect with issues of pleasure, risk, identity, consumption. We examine this both on the micro level of the particular experiences of individual club-drug users in their specific social settings of raves and clubs, as well as the more macro level, situating this particular dance scene in a broader global, national, and urban context. Our work is inspired most by many scholars in the sociological and cultural studies traditions and we hope to extend many of their insights into pleasure, identity, and risk in these scenes, to include a focus directly on the experience and meaning of drug use as the central issue of concern in this book.

Chapter 2

Clubbers, candy kids, and jaded ravers

Introducing the scene, the participants, and the drugs

The thumping bass that's heard from outside the rave fuels the giddy anticipation among patrons waiting in line to get in. One could walk up and down the line and think it was a Halloween costume party; kids in fairy wings and elaborate makeup, others in pink wigs and fishnet tights, others still in oversized pants, neon shirts and mini-backpacks. The party preparations begin in line as ravers scramble to hide candy, ecstasy pills, opened packs of cigarettes, massage lotion, and other "party favors" before entering. Although security is often lax, pockets will be emptied and backpacks searched. These forbidden items are often stashed on places of the body which security can't touch. Tickets are collected but IDs are rarely checked at the door and many of the patrons are under the age of 18.

Upon entering the rave, attendees are transported into another reality, with flashing lights, fog machines, and decorations on the walls and that hang from the ceiling. The atmosphere is only enhanced by the attendees themselves, who pin small flashing lights to their clothing and carry around glowsticks and other light toys. Some immediately start dancing to the deafening music; others explore the entire premises, winding in and out of various rooms that are all pounding a different style of electronic dance music. It's a social event, and many people go to meet friends whom they maintain relationships with in the party circuit context.

The dance floor is crowded with masses of people who are worshiping the DJ, jumping and gyrating, stomping energetically to the beat. The DJ is worshiping the music, encouraged by the crowd that is cheering him on. Some dancers show off their skills in a dance circle, doing the electric boogaloo, popping-and-locking, breakdancing, liquid and wave dancing. Others perform lightshows for an entranced audience, carving out intricate geometric shapes with their neon glowsticks. Those who aren't dancing are propped up against the speakers, swaying to the music's vibrations with their eyes closed. Others are lined against the wall in "cuddle puddles," sitting with friends, talking, giving and receiving massages.

The night seems to last forever and finally comes crashing down when the music stops and the lights come up. Sweaty and exhausted, the partygoers shuffle out of the building and move on to after-parties held at other venues or in private residences.

(Compilation of field notes from raves)

Introduction

Although we draw on a variety of sources of data throughout this book – from observations at dance and club events to analysis of policy and legislation that provide the context for these events – first and foremost this is a study of the experiences and narratives of young club-drug users in the rave, dance, and club scenes in the San Francisco Bay Area. Over the course of two years (2002–04), we interviewed 300 young men and women who use club drugs and who participate in these scenes. As we will discuss below, this group of people includes those who identify very strongly with the rave or club scenes as well as those who only occasionally attend these as just a small part of their broader leisure repertoire. It includes frequent and heavy drug users, experimental users, occasional users, and former users. The young people we talked to were diverse in terms of their genders, their sexual identities, and their ethnicities. We primarily talked to young adults, aged 18–24, with some others in their late twenties or thirties and a smaller number under 18. This was a fairly well-educated group of people, or at least ones with educational goals, as many were still students. Most, though not all, of those we interviewed were from middle-class backgrounds. About half of the sample identified as white, and the other half with another racial/ethnic group (most commonly Asian American, as well as Latino, African American, and "other"). Very few of those we talked to were married or with children – not surprising, given the continued involvement in night life and club drugs of most of those we interviewed. The diversity and heterogeneity of those we interviewed means that it would be impossible to paint a picture of "the" club-drug user, "the" raver, or "the" clubber. Instead, we have noticed different patterns and constructed typologies of participants, which we will outline below. Throughout the interviews, we were very lucky to encounter the openness and willingness to share their experiences, ideas, and thoughts, of the young people we talked to, even when discussing very sensitive topics. Ultimately, we hope that the stories that we tell throughout this book are their stories.

Methods

The primary data for this book came from an ongoing study of the Bay Area electronic dance music scene and club-drug users. Between 2002 and 2004 we interviewed 300 participants in these scenes. The interviews were conducted by the project manager, Kristin Evans, and five interviewers, who were extensively trained on interviewing techniques and using the schedule.

In the first part of the interview a brief, structured quantitative questionnaire was used to collect demographic characteristics. The second part of the interview, which immediately followed the quantitative questionnaire, used a semistructured guide to collect primarily open-ended qualitative data on the participant's background and current life, alcohol and drug use, and involvement in the dance scene. Participants were given a US$45 honorarium for their participation, and the interviews generally lasted from three to five hours. While the interviewers followed a set of questions and topic areas, the respondents were given the flexibility to express issues of interest or concern as they came up during the interview process. The detailed interview guide and our respondents' desire to talk in detail about their experiences or convey their perspectives on raves, clubs, or club drugs contributed to the lengthy nature of the interviews.

Several methods were used to recruit participants, including advertisements, chain referrals from other participants, and contacts of the project staff. We advertised the study at stores throughout the Bay Area, primarily at record/music shops, but occasionally at other stores which were in the same neighborhood. We handed out flyers at dance events, we posted an announcement on a local dance scene-related Website message board, and we posted flyers at neighborhood community organizations. In addition, we sent announcements to local groups and organizations, including a harm-reduction organization that worked at dance events and some Asian American interest groups (e.g., college clubs). These methods proved successful at accessing the target population and resulted in people with a range of drug experiences and involvement in different aspects or sectors of the dance scene.

The main inclusion criterion for the study was that participants had to be involved in the electronic dance music scene in the Bay Area by attending dance events such as clubs, raves, and warehouse parties. While we interviewed a small sample of non-drug users (in total twenty-two out of the 300), the vast majority of the participants also had to have some experience using one of the six drugs defined by the National Institute on Drug Abuse (NIDA; our study's funder) as "club drugs": ecstasy (MDMA), LSD/acid, methamphetamine, GHB, ketamine, or Rohypnol.[1] As this was an exploratory study, we were interested in interviewing people with a wide range of experiences with club drugs, from those who were "new users" (having used less than five times in total) to those who were frequent users, and to those who had used in the past but were not currently using. Our initial recruitment efforts tended to produce an overwhelmingly white, middle-class sample aged 18–24, despite the greater racial and age diversity witnessed at dance events. We then made specific efforts to target for recruitment participants from diverse racial/ethnic, socioeconomic, and age backgrounds (including minors).

Our sample is more heavily weighted to those who are or had been more involved in the rave scene (as opposed to the club scene – a distinction that we will unpack later in this chapter), although that was in part due to the fact that our recruitment methods focused more on advertising in locations that were frequented by rave attendees (such as local record stores that sold tickets to rave events). We found that most of our respondents had more to say about their rave experiences, even if they had been to many more club events. Club events were often portrayed as more everyday, normal activities and hence the experiences didn't seem quite as special or memorable. We chose not to attempt to recruit directly from the club setting, because we knew that we would likely come across many people who attended club events but who had never done club drugs, which were the primary focus of the study.

Most respondents seemed to participate either because they wanted the opportunity to talk about their involvement in the dance scene, which they felt very passionate about, because of the monetary incentive, or because of a combination of both. The political climate, both locally and nationally, around rave events and drug use likely played both a beneficial and a detrimental factor in our ability to recruit people. (For more on this climate and laws targeting raves see Chapter 4.) Many participants said that the reason they agreed to be interviewed was that they wanted to talk about the "good" parts of the scene (in contrast to the attacks they felt the government and media were making) and they hoped that our research would provide a positive portrayal of the scene and dance culture. However, it was common for people calling about the study to express suspicion or concern about who we were, who was funding the study, and what our intentions were. People were often afraid that we were the government, law enforcement, or a group with anti-rave and anti-drug politics. Once we explained the approach of the study, that it was sociological research, and that we had no hidden agenda, most people were willing to participate.

One of the strengths of this qualitative approach is that we are able to explore the detail and complexity of the respondents' experiences with drugs and in the dance scene, which would not have been possible with a solely quantitative survey. Our study sought to access a hard-to-reach population that included minors, drug users, and those who attend "underground" or illegal dance events. As such, our sample cannot be said to be representative of club-drug users or dance-event attenders in the Bay Area as a whole. Readers should keep in mind that though we present statistics and details of the participants' drug use, these numbers reflect self-reported data and therefore must always be interpreted with caution. While we feel confident that we did the best we could during data collection and data cleaning to provide "accurate" data, and our interviewers were highly trained and checked for reliability, we must be humbled by the fact that there is always an unknown factor in drug data, and therefore realistically these statistics, like most drug statistics, can be taken only as estimates of drug use in this sample.

Introducing the participants: demographics

Gender

In our interviews with young club-drug users in the dance scenes, we interviewed slightly more men than women (see Table 2.1). Our goal was to interview approximately equal numbers of men and women, and we found that over the course of the study our recruitment efforts generated this ratio without us having to intentionally target either gender. Though studies often mention the over-representation of men in the club scene (see for example Measham *et al.* 1994), our study was never designed to be representative, so we cannot comment on whether our gender breakdown reflects that of the wider party scene. The relationship between gender, substance use, and participation in the dance scenes will be examined in detail in Chapters 9 and 10.

Age

Overall the men and women we interviewed were fairly young, and the majority (72 percent) were between the ages of 18 and 24. The ages ranged from

Table 2.1 Sample characteristics (*n* = 300)

	%	*n*
Gender		
Male	54	161
Female	46	139
Age (mean 21.5)		
15 and under	1	2
16–17	9	28
18–20	43	128
21–24	29	87
25–29	12	36
30 and over	6	19
Ethnicity		
White	50	150
Asian American	23	70
Latino	11	34
African American	6	18
Native Hawaiian/Pacific Islander	2	5
Native American	1	4
Middle Eastern/Arab	<1	1
Mixed	6	18
Sexual orientation		
Heterosexual	76	227
Homosexual	7	22
Bisexual	13	40
Other	4	11

15 to 47, with a median age of 20. As we will see later in this chapter, age, along with amount of time involved in the scene, plays a major role in shaping boundaries between identities and practices of different categories of ravers, clubbers, and club-drug users, with some aging out of the scene altogether, and others aging out of one scene (e.g., the rave scene) and moving to another (e.g., club scene).

Race/ethnicity

Exactly half of the respondents (150) reported Caucasian/white as their primary ethnic group, while 23 percent reported Asian American, 11 percent reported Latino, 6 percent reported African American, and 10 percent reported another ethnic group (Pacific Islander, Native American, or Iranian). There were eighteen respondents (6 percent) who identified primarily as "mixed." The dance scenes – and the rave scene especially – are often stereotyped as being largely or even exclusively white events. Based on our informal observations of dance events, as well as the descriptions provided by those we interviewed, this does not appear to be entirely true in the San Francisco Bay Area. While the rave scene was predominantly white in its earliest years, in later years the scene became increasingly diverse. Young Asian Americans (from a variety of ethnic/national backgrounds), in particular, became increasingly active in the rave scene – a transition that did not come without some tensions and antagonisms. (Chapter 11 will focus particularly on Asian American identity in the scene.) The dance club scenes have a different history of racial and ethnic affiliations – the clubs break down largely based on musical styles, which themselves are associated with different ethnic groups, though rarely in the absolute sense that they're assumed to be (e.g., hip-hop clubs attract a diverse clientele). Though the participants in this study were primarily involved in the electronic dance music (EDM) scene and clubs associated with this musical style, in Chapter 5, which focuses on the specifics of San Francisco nightlife, we will probe some of these demarcations more thoroughly.

The vast majority of the participants (87 percent) were born in the US, with 66 percent born somewhere in California. The median length of time living in the US for the foreign-born respondents was fifteen years; the majority of these respondents immigrated when they were children. The foreign-born respondents came from a variety of countries across the globe, although about half were born in Asia. While the vast majority of the respondents were born in the US, over one-third had one or both parents who were born in another country, with Asia by far the most common region of origin.

Education and employment

Overall the sample was well-educated, and 55 percent of our respondents were attending some form of educational institution at the time of the interview. Over three-quarters of those were in school full-time. In all, 60 percent of the sample had (either currently or in the past) pursued a post-high-school education, ranging from vocational training to graduate school. Less than one-quarter of participants had received a high-school diploma but had not (at the time of the interview) pursued higher education. Only 4 percent of respondents had dropped out of high school and hadn't returned.

Sixty percent of the participants were employed at the time of the interview, mostly in white-collar business or clerical jobs, education or nonprofit fields, or in retail and service. Of those who were not employed, about two-thirds of them were students. Only 6 percent of respondents worked in skilled trade or labor jobs. More than half of those employed were working part-time, but more than two-thirds of the part-time workers were also students.

The nature of their work and the types of jobs they held generally seems to fit with the overall nature of this sample. Given that the sample is comprised of primarily young adults, many of whom are students, it may not be surprising that the job types held leaned towards retail/personal service, associate professional or technicians, and the clerical or customer service sector – the types of "student jobs" or entry-level positions perhaps typical of this age and socioeconomic group. As one would expect, employment was generally correlated with age, such that older respondents were less likely to be unemployed and more likely to have business or professional positions.

Sexual orientation, marital status, and relationships

Just over three-quarters of the sample identified as heterosexual, while 7 percent of the sample identified as gay, lesbian, or queer, and 13 percent identified as bisexual. The remaining 4 percent either offered a different identification (e.g., pansexual), were questioning or curious, or felt that their experiences or desires did not match up to the standard triadic classification of hetero/homo/bisexual. Men were more likely to define themselves as straight (83 percent of men versus 68 percent of women), while women were more likely to define themselves as bisexual (20 percent of women versus 8 percent of men) or provide a different identification (7 percent of women versus 1 percent of men).

The vast majority (90 percent) of the sample were unmarried and not living with a spouse or partner, although 34 percent described having a boyfriend or girlfriend. Six respondents were married, and an additional 8 percent of the respondents were unmarried but living with a partner. Five respondents had one child each, and one respondent was pregnant.

Social class

Assessing the social class of the young men and women we interviewed is far more difficult than with the other basic demographic categories. Because so many of the respondents were students at the time of the interview, going by their own income would lead to misleadingly low numbers. Yet looking at their class of origin, for instance through their reports of their parents' incomes and class statuses, has its own problems, since these data are often quite unreliable. Still, though, we can get a general picture of their families of origin, which alongside the employment data above paints the picture of a generally, but not exclusively, middle-class group.

Around 60 percent of the participants' fathers held what could generally be classified as white-collar jobs, which ranged from bank vice-presidents and engineers to small business owners and insurance salesmen to musicians and teachers. About one-third of those held fairly senior professional positions, such as lawyers, doctors, and college professors. Twenty-one percent of fathers held "blue-collar" or labor jobs, around 4 percent each were in retail and service and the military. Almost 70 percent of respondents' mothers worked in white-collar positions, with just over 13 percent in retail and service, and 4 percent had labor jobs. A little less than 10 percent of respondents said their mothers did not work outside the home, and the remaining 3 percent were unknown, with one mother on disability. A little over 45 percent of fathers and 50 percent of mothers were college graduates, some with advanced degrees, with fewer than 10 percent of each not completing high school.

Rave and club participation

The large bodyguard, dressed in a black suit and holding a radio in one hand, stands at the entrance as he surveys the crowd. His job is to keep a long line waiting behind the red velvet ropes to give the impression that the club is particularly "hot" that night. Everyone is dressed to impress; groups of girls in high heels and miniskirts, young men wearing black dress shoes, slacks and button-up shirts. The atmosphere is heavy with glamour and sex. They chat and smoke cigarettes in line, waiting to cross through that red-rope barrier and into Clubland. Finally getting to the front of the line, patrons present their IDs to security and pay the $20 cover charge. Being let in means you are accepted, you belong. A night of decadence awaits.

The first thing to greet you inside the club is the bar. Dramatically fashioned with glass and colored lights, it displays bottle after bottle of alcohol poised for consumption. Attractive bartenders showing their midriffs have already started mixing drinks for early customers. Most patrons head for the bar first to order a drink before they walk the premises of the club or step foot on the dance floor; after all, the party gets started when the alcohol starts flowing. Groups of men hang by the bar to watch clusters of females moving to the music on the dance floor. The DJ plays house, hip-hop, Top 40, whatever gets the crowd excited. He works to build the crowd's energy as the go-go dancers by his side suggestively twist and turn for onlookers.

The club is filled to capacity by midnight and everyone is trying to cram in their fun before closing time at 2.00 a.m. The patrons who are overly intoxicated are quickly identified by Security and escorted out of the club. Everyone else finishes out their night, stumbling out of the club at 2.00 a.m.

(Compilation of field notes from nightclubs)

In order to qualify for this study, participants not only had to have used one of the six NIDA-defined club drugs in the previous six months but also had to have participated in the electronic dance music scene in the San Francisco Bay Area. We defined participation as attending dance events such as clubs, raves, and warehouse parties. This was a rather broad and open definition, which enabled us to recruit participants with a wide range of involvement in these scenes. While for some, participation in the dance scene comprised a fundamental part of their identity and a major subcultural activity, for others participation in these scenes was merely one activity within a broader repertoire of leisure and nightlife activities. People who are more heavily involved or invested in particular scenes may reflect that through their appearance, lifestyles, beliefs, and worldview. In addition, there were important lines of distinction marked by participants around involvement in clubs versus involvement in raves. While many attended both types of events, most identified with one more than the other. The type of scene in which a young person is involved is important, given that it in part determines, or at least reflects, such things as musical preference, beliefs or practices connected to leisure and consumption, and types of drug use. Consumption practices are increasingly seen as important tools that youth use to shape and perform their identities and sense of self today (Miles 2000). Because each subscene has its own norms and group behaviors, how individuals act and even what their views of the scene are will vary by what scene they are involved in. Whether people choose their scene because of their beliefs and values or their beliefs and values are influenced by the scene is not something we can completely determine, though it likely goes both ways. For example, people involved in the "older" warehouse party scene are more likely to be discreet or less open with their drug use. One must wonder if that is a function of age or rather a reflection of the norms of the scene, and the stage of progression of the participants. In general we see that distinctions made by participants – delineating their scene from others – play a major role in the construction of their own identities and particularly their identities as participants in nightlife. (See Thornton 1996 for more on the construction of identities through participation in, and investment in subcultural capital within, nightlife.)

While the divisions between raves and clubs are not absolute, some broad distinctions can be made between the two types of event, and certainly the young people we interviewed see these as quite distinct. In addition, they mark significant differences within these two major categories. Raves are centered around a DJ who plays a variety of electronic dance music, including techno, trance, house, drum 'n' bass, and hardcore. These events are strongly associated with club-drug culture and particularly the use of ecstasy (MDMA). Broadly speaking, participants attended two major types of raves, each with its own ethos and normative behaviors: underground events and massives. Underground raves are renegade dance-music parties that are often held in nonpermitted or illegal venues such as warehouses or abandoned buildings. Rave parties tend to go on all night, sometimes not ending until six or seven in the morning. Because underground raves are all-ages events, some of them attract a greater number of minors than other events. Massive raves are more commercial in nature and are held in large permitted venues such as stadiums, auditoriums, or theaters. Massives are usually restricted to those who are 18 or older and may serve alcohol to those of legal age (21+). Because massives take place in permitted venues, they are subject to city licensing policies similar to those of clubs and therefore must shut down around 2.00 a.m. in California.

We can further delineate types and styles of raves into two major categories. First, the "classic" rave scene (including massives but also smaller raves with a similar aesthetic), which attracts "candy ravers" noted for their bright clothes and candy jewelry and their loving-everyone attitudes and young ravers more generally. Second, the older warehouse party scene, which includes many who have "graduated" from the "classic" rave scene. It is in the mainstream raves[2] that one is most likely to see the stereotypical accoutrements of raves – the glowsticks and light shows, the pacifiers and childlike clothing. The rave ethos of peace, love, unity, respect (PLUR) is popularly espoused here. On the other hand, in the older, warehouse scene the ethos around dress is different (much less likely to see the "candy" style), as are the norms of drug use, which is still quite present but more discreet. Music styles also vary in as much as styles such as happy hardcore and drum 'n' bass traditionally predominated at mainstream raves, while progressive trance and house music are more associated with this older crowd.

In contrast to raves, which are generally either one-off or annual events, clubs are permitted dance-music parties that are held in established, licensed venues. To run as a legitimate establishment, nightclub venues must obtain a number of city permits, including but not limited to a cabaret license, liquor license, and in some cases an after-hours permit. Because of the industry's ties to alcohol consumption, the vast majority of clubs close at 2.00 a.m., when liquor can no longer be served legally. While most clubs exclude patrons under the age of 21, some open their doors to those who are age 18 or older. Clubs often feature a DJ who plays dance music, although nightclubs are also known to host live musical acts and MCs. Many dance clubs are seen as mainstream by our respondents because they showcase hip-hop or Top 40 radio hits while raves play less well-known underground music that is often independently produced. (Although the boundaries between "mainstream" and "underground" are themselves contested and play a part in identity construction among young people in the scene; see Hutton 2006 and Thornton 1996 for more.) While the rave scene is associated with various diverse styles of electronic dance music, this is only one slice of the club scene, which includes Top 40 music, hip-hop, rock, as well as the ubiquitous electronic dance music. San Francisco has a small number of very mainstream clubs that play Top 40-type music. These clubs are stereotyped as mostly for the purpose of people who want to have a night out, but the focus is not really on the music; music provides the backdrop for the social environment, but is not the end focus in itself. In this segment of the club scene, many people are not going to see the DJs and in many cases don't even know who they are. The focus is on the social scene, meeting romantic interests, and that is in some ways built into the advertisement for the club. Alcohol, rather than drugs, is the major substance at these clubs. Other clubs feature a particular music style such as hip-hop or Latin music or New Wave and many of our respondents attended these types of clubs. However, the club scene most associated with the young people we interviewed is large electronic dance music clubs that attract big-name DJs and draw a crowd on that basis. Some of these clubs are what the young people we interviewed called "ravy clubs" – that would get a contingent of "rave" people and have rave-like elements like glowsticks and laser lighting within the venue. While drug use is generally more discreet at these clubs than at raves, many of the patrons will be on ecstasy or other club drugs, although alcohol consumption is clearly popular as well.

Among the 300 young people we interviewed, we find more heavy participation in the rave scene than in the club scene, although most participants have attended both types of events. The majority (55 percent) primarily or exclusively attend raves, a smaller number primarily or exclusively attend clubs (32 percent), and 10 percent attend the two types of events somewhat equally.

Simply noting how often one attends club or rave events, though, does not tell us what this participation means to the young men and women. Do they identify with the scene, do they enjoy it occasionally, or do they attend with disinterest? There is a difference between merely attending raves and being a raver, and both groups were represented in the young people we interviewed.[3] We further classified the ravers' and clubbers' participation in the scenes according to a typology of five categories of rave participation and five categories of club participation, with each respondent being assigned to both a rave and club typology. We base this discussion on an analysis of a randomly generated subsample, made up of 110 of the 300 participants in the study. Here we introduce you to some of the people whom we will be hearing from throughout the book.

Rave and club involvement typologies

Among ravers: first we have the former raver, who no longer has interest in the scene and who has developed a negative impression of it. Twelve percent of the random sample fits into this category. For example, David[4] (age 25) is no longer interested in raves because he thinks the crowd is too young. Emily, 19, used to be heavily involved in raves, and has attended over 100 of the events, but no longer goes, because the ticket prices have become too high and she increasingly dislikes the people at raves. She is one to declare that the rave scene is "dead." And Kelly, 22, no longer attends raves because she no longer wants to use drugs, and her attendance at raves in the past always involved club-drug use.

An additional 12 percent can be classified as reluctant ravers. They attend raves, but only begrudgingly, to placate friends, to obtain or use drugs, or because there's nothing better to do. Serena, 16, for example, attends raves because many of her friends go, but she is not very interested in the scene on her own. Tanya, 19, used to go along with friends to raves, but is drifting away now that she's old enough to get into clubs. Participation in these scenes in terms of attendance, and in some cases frequent attendance, does not always indicate that this plays a major part in the participant's identity or even interests.

Of course, some never attend raves or have very little experience with or interest in raves: the non-raver. These make up only 5 percent of the random sample. They include Fiona, 24, who no longer uses drugs except for alcohol and hence prefers less drug-oriented nightlife venues, Chad, 22, who is more interested in alcohol and did not enjoy raves, and Monique, 22, who used to be heavily involved in the club scene but has never gotten involved with raves.

Although some participants are at the tail end of their rave career, others are just getting started, or just getting started again: the new or returning raver (16.5 percent). This fourth group has little experience with raves but has a positive impression of the events and wants and plans to attend more in the future; some were once involved with raves, but drifted away, and are now desirous of rekindling this involvement. Isabel, 19, is recently exploring raves and is particularly interested in them as a good setting for ecstasy use. Seth, 20, has some nostalgia for how the rave scene used to be and wishes he could get back into it. Kathryn, 19, is heavily involved in the Asian club scene, but is more recently involved with raves.

But the majority of the sample (55 percent) can more clearly be identified as ravers: they go to raves regularly and identify with the rave scene. These ravers vary immensely among themselves in terms of how they understand and enjoy the rave scene. Ashley, 16, loves raves and volunteers with the organization Dance-Safe, but wishes that raves weren't so focused on drugs. Donnie, 20, used to be a "Goth" but is now heavily involved with raves. He defines himself as a "candy kid" and hopes to attend raves for the rest of his life. James, 26, works as a club promoter, and goes to raves primarily for the music. Astrid, 26, is a DJ and a member of a music collective, who identifies with the community aspect of raves more than the drugs. Bahira, 17, thinks that raves are the "perfect place for ecstasy use."

Although club attendance was less prominent in our sample – with very few (2 percent) attending clubs exclusively – there are many who attend clubs frequently, and some who identify with clubs more than raves. So, just as above with the rave typologies, we also typify respondents with respect to their beliefs and practices connected to clubbing.

In characterizing club participation, the smallest category is the former clubber; 4.5 percent of the sample used to go to clubs but have since quit that scene. Monique, 22, was once a frequent clubgoer, but has since stopped attending clubs after entering a drug treatment program. Kyle, 19, is interested in DJ-ing but otherwise dislikes the atmosphere of clubs. There are fewer former clubbers in the sample than there are former ravers. This reflects, in part, the notion expressed by some of our respondents that there is a progression from raves to clubs as one gets older (although other respondents who have no interest in clubs would refute this idea).

Others are reluctant clubbers – 18 percent attend clubs, but dislike the scene, only going when friends insist, or they've only had limited exposure to clubs but were turned off by what they encountered. Antonia, 20, dislikes the pressure to dance perfectly as well as the emphasis on "pickups" and getting "hit on." Craig, 28, also dislikes the meat-market atmosphere of clubs (and this is by far the most common complaint about clubs – see Chapter 10 for more), but attends sometimes when there is a DJ he wants to see. Carlos, 18, feels at home in the rave scene, but can't connect with the atmosphere of clubs.

Twenty-one percent of the sample have never been to a club or have very, very little experience with clubs and no strong opinions about them – non-clubbers. Some of these people are involved in the rave scene and just not interested in clubs. Others are underage and find clubs difficult to attend, either because of age requirements (some clubs are 18+ but most are 21+) or because of the high cost of attendance. Cory, 16, a self-described "novice" is just beginning to explore raves and has not yet attended clubs. Mercedes, 19, identifies with the PLUR philosophy of raves (especially underground raves) and has not attended clubs due to their different ethos.

Some of the clubgoers describe a somewhat mixed response to the club scene – the ambivalent clubbers. They may have not attended much in the past, but are thinking of attending in the future. They may enjoy clubs for particular DJs but do not identify with the scene overall, or they enjoy the scene but dislike certain aspects of it. This somewhat hard to pin down category is actually the largest group, comprising 34 percent of the sample. Kelly, 22, has drifted away from raves, because she believes the attendees are too young, but has not yet fully found a home at clubs, where she finds the attendees difficult to relate to. Thomas, 21, enjoys hearing specific DJs at clubs, although he dislikes the highly sexualized environment at most clubs. Brian, 19, has started going to clubs recently, particularly gay clubs, but is not always able to get in because he is under age. He thinks that when he gets a fake ID or turns 21 he will attend more frequently.

Finally, 23 percent of the sample are clearly regular clubbers, they attend clubs regularly and identify with the scene. Donna, 26, goes to clubs regularly to hear her favorite DJs, to dance and listen to music, and to use ecstasy. Jasmine, 19, attends clubs more frequently than raves because she likes the music at clubs and because clubs are more affordable than raves. (While not all clubs have a cover charge and many charge under $10 or even under $5, with some charging $25, most raves cost $10–$40, sometimes more.) Tanya, 19, used to go to raves, but started attending clubs when she turned 18 and was able to get in. Lucy, 19, loves attending clubs and seeing her friends, and particularly attends Asian clubs.

Age and stages of scene involvement

The absence of age restrictions at rave events allows younger attendees to participate in the scene, whereas they are (officially) excluded from other "mainstream" arenas of nightlife, such as clubs and bars. While younger patrons appreciate the inclusion they are granted, older attendees often complain about the permissiveness of all-ages events, saying that they are bothered by seeing "kids" partying and using drugs at such a young age. Emilia, 19, stated that she was "uncomfortable" going to massive raves that attracted "people who look like they're 13, 14, or 15 all drugged out. Maybe getting taken advantage of, you know." Others struggle with the notion that they are too old for raves or feel out of place because they are now above the average age of attendees. However, when one respondent was asked if he would go to raves in the future, he responded that he would "probably be the oldest person there" but would most likely attend anyway, saying, "Why not? Who cares how old I am?" (Boram, 33).

We can additionally delineate participants in these scenes by marking their stage of involvement in the scene overall, or in a subscene in particular. Although youth drug use and participation in nightlife are often presented as something static, it became clear in our interviews that young people's involvement in the dance scene develops through different stages. These different sequences, while not necessarily linear, are associated with different levels of involvement – initial intensive involvement developing into regular but less active attendance to developing into more sporadic involvement or ultimately drifting away.

One distinction along this continuum that held a great deal of salience for many was the difference between candy ravers and the jaded ravers. Though people in both groups may have similar levels of involvement in the scene, the way they talk about their involvement and their views about the scene will be different. One self-described "candy kid" explains, "There's the candy kids who are dressed in the brightest colors possible, and they've got the fuzzy backpacks and the fuzzy pants, and they're just like, you know, the cute ones. They're just so, like, happy" (Alicia, 17). Gloria, 19, explains why she's drawn to the candy kid ethos:

> Like when I give my candy [plastic beaded jewelry that candy kids hand out at raves] to somebody – you know, bracelet, to somebody – I'm giving them like a little piece of me, to remember me by. It's just a way of, like, introducing yourself to somebody. It's fun, it's a type of party kid that's, like, pretty much how I associate myself with. Kinda fits my personality, really like a goofy, happy.

Whereas the candy raver is characterized as someone who is young, wears bright colors and candy jewelry, uses ecstasy, and listens to trance or happy hardcore music, the jaded raver has been in the scene longer, is portrayed as less idealistic, is more likely to wear muted colors, is more critical of the scene (especially critical of the candy ravers) and is less likely to use drugs and/or openly display intoxication during dance events. They're less likely to espouse the PLUR ethos of raves, or at least are somewhat more cynical about it.

The jaded ravers rarely identify themselves with quite these terms, but tend to define themselves and their roles in the rave scene in opposition to the candy ravers, about whom they often express bemusement, frustration, or occasionally outright aggression. Some have become reluctant ravers at best, while others remain active in the rave scene, despite their misgivings about where the scene is headed. The candy kids tend to be the "others" against whom their own rave identities are constructed. Julia, 20, shows disdain for the candy kids: "Um … as for the candy kids, I mean … the girls with the fuzzy things in the front and the fuzzy fucking boots. What the fuck is that? I … I seriously don't understand it at all. It doesn't make any sense to me." Justin, 24, concurs. He tries to describe candy kids' attributes: they listen to "CHEESY trance [music], wearing really colorful clothes, sucking on pacifiers and lollipops, talking about DJs, not knowing really about the DJs, just saying how much they love them, but not knowing anything about them. Really media induced … colorful again. Irritating." (Laughs.) Justin says that he's been there, done that, and that over time he drifted from the candy scene to the "junglist" scene, associated with "drum 'n' bass" music. He explains that:

> [At] jungle parties, people are a little more thuggish … you can't really … open up to somebody else and say, "Hey, can I give you a massage?" or whatever, you know. Like, "Get away from me." 'Cause, you know … 'Cause it all goes along with being jaded too. I mean, like … if you're a junglist you cannot be, like, a … candy kid, you know. You can't be … happy core kids.

Junglists themselves are often associated with a particular clothing style, especially emphasizing an urban look, or camouflage clothing, but this seems less central to their identity, which is based around the music style of drum 'n' bass (a harder, faster, and sometimes darker music style), and certainly not all junglists conform to these clothing standards. As with Justin, many, but not all, jaded ravers started off as candy kids and feel they have matured or progressed beyond this.

These divisions and hostility among rave subgroups belie the notion common in some analysis of raves, particularly in the earlier years, that raves and the dance scene uniquely promote a unity among participants, that the ecstatic dancing allows people to overcome barriers and distinctions (Avery 2005; Malbon 1999). Instead, we see many of the types of distinctions of subcultural capital, in which clothing, music style and knowledge, and depth of knowledge of the scene confer status and provide the basis for identification and prestige within the scene (Thornton 1996). It is important to note that the length of time in the scene may be much more important than the physical age of the ravers. Overall, the jaded ravers tend to be older, but an individual candy raver may be older than a jaded raver in years. Thus we emphasize the importance of a developmental perspective featuring progression of stages.[5] This development of stages within the scene may influence dress, musical tastes, and drug use. While these different groups can be associated with different types of events – the candy kids more typically at massive raves, junglists and other jaded ravers at smaller house parties, warehouse parties, or underground scenes – they can also all be found under the same roof at the same rave, particularly in the larger raves with multiple rooms of different musical – and affective – styles.

We do not find so clear a distinction within a clubber progression, and certainly not with the recognizable terms (jaded, candy) we find among ravers, although we can identify individuals' progressions in types and levels of engagement, involvement in the club scene, propensity for binge drinking, etc. These progressions may be within a scene (as with the rave scene) but can also appear as progressions through scenes (progressing from mainstream raves to older warehouse raves, or from raves to clubs). There is certainly a sense among some of those we interviewed that clubs are the natural progression after the rave scene, especially as one ages. These different levels of involvement in the scenes are also mirrored in their consumption of drugs. Their drug use often follows a similar progression of initiation, followed by extensive use, eventually leading to more moderate and occasional use, and finally a gradual "maturing out."

Subculture? Scene? Tribe?

Given the wide variety of levels and types of involvement in raves, clubs, and club drugs, how should we characterize the broader group affiliation of these young people? Do raves represent a distinct subculture? While the concept of "subculture" has been foundational in studies of youth culture, particularly those centered in a cultural studies tradition, in recent years many scholars studying youth nightlife, raves, or clubs have become increasingly critical of using the subculture label here. Subcultural youth studies originating from the Birmingham cultural studies tradition that grew out of the Centre for Contemporary Cultural Studies (CCCS), such as foundational works *Subculture: the meaning of style* (Hebdige 1979) and *Resistance through Rituals* (Hall and Jefferson 1976) continue to be influential in their focus on agency and resistance, style and culture, youth and social class. Critics charge, however, that many of today's youth-cultural formations lack the cohesiveness, homogeneity, or durability that "subculture" may imply (Huq 2006; D. Moore 2004; Muggleton 2000), or that subcultural studies overemphasize resistance at the expense of acknowledging youth embeddedness in corporate culture and nightlife (Chatterton and Hollands 2003; Miles 2000; Perrone 2009). In subculture's place, a number of alternative frameworks or concepts have been offered. One of the earlier challenges was Redhead's (1993, 1997) focus on club cultures rather than subcultures. Others theorize youth cultural formations as tribes or neotribes, seeing tribes as more fluid and temporary than subcultures and more open to multiple identities (Huq 2006; Maffesoli 1996; Malbon 1999; Muggleton 2000). Miles (2000) argues for shifting from subculture to analyses of youth lifestyles that emphasize the centrality of consumption and consumerism in the construction of identities in late modern society (Miles 2000). Others focus on scenes, which is seen as allowing for more heterogeneous formations than subculture's focus on normative values and beliefs typically allows for (Bennett 1999b; D. Moore 2004; Straw 1997). We find these debates somewhat frustrating, as the concept of "subculture" is often set up as a straw figure, and treated as inherently more static, homogeneous, deterministic, or all-encompassing than is necessarily the case for the concept. Wouldn't it be possible to offer a more nuanced understanding of subcultures than to throw the concept out entirely? Yet, at the same time, even a more elastic and dynamic understanding of subcultures would not seem to apply across the board to the types of involvements and affiliation that our respondents described and displayed. While some were heavily involved with raves, which comprise a fundamental aspect of their identity, style, consumption, and life in general, others were only tangentially involved, attending raves, clubs, and dance events as an occasional leisure activity, one of many, and not involved in a distinct subcultural formation in any major sense. Hence one of the more provisional, flexible concepts seems more appropriate in these contexts. While the boundaries between these various frameworks are not set in stone, and we draw inspiration from the work of many of these theoretical traditions, which hold much in common in their emphases on culture, meaning, and agency, we tend to fall back on the concept of the "scene" most often in this book. One advantage that this concept has is that it is the one that seems to have most resonance with the young people involved, who frequently invoke the term "scene," and their own understandings of it themselves.

The dance scene

There are many appealing elements to the dance scene: social, romantic, and sexual encounters; opportunities to use drugs and alcohol; a fantastic reality in which to escape. In addition to these elements, the dance scene is foremost a *dance* scene – a place to hear dance music and move to the groove.

Because of electronic music's focus on rhythm and repetition, the music is "specifically geared to dancing rather than to listening" (Walsh 1993: 113), thus making it a perfect fit for dance clubs and dance parties like raves. Many of the young men and women we interviewed discuss dancing at rave events and make connections between the dancing and the drugs. More of these discussions connect dancing with ecstasy than with any other drug. They often talk about ecstasy giving them the feeling of being physically "free" to move their bodies, of being better able to appreciate music, and understand rhythm. Mishti, 22, explains why she loves dancing on ecstasy at raves: "[I'm] in my space, and no one can … bother me there … I'm free and I'm happy and I'm dancing … one of the greatest things was dancing on E." Many young men and women describe feeling uninhibited in their dancing as a result of the ecstasy and the setting of the rave. Participants also describe more practical reasons for the ecstasy/dancing connection: using the drug to have the energy and stamina to dance all night at rave parties. Shelley, 18, notes that taking ecstasy makes her feel "like you could just dance forever."

Although many of the young men and women identify the pleasure and sometimes the practicality of taking ecstasy at a rave while dancing, some participants do voice a desire to enjoy music and dancing while sober. Some of these respondents talk about this as a stage one progresses to within the rave scene:

> My involvement with the [rave] scene has changed over the years. When I first started, it was like, "Oh, do ecstasy, and go see how many people I can meet. And just have a great time that way." Now I'm much more into the music and dancing and stuff, and ecstasy doesn't make me do that. It puts me on my butt. It doesn't make me get up and wanna dance.
>
> (Craig, 28)

Some young men and women argue that dancing can provide a "natural high." Garret, 25, argues that dancing at raves "is what I get high off these days, instead of the drugs ... that and the music."

Many ravers discuss the spiritual aspects of dancing within the rave scene and the sense of community they get from their participation at rave and dance events. Leann, 18, acknowledges the connection she feels with other dancers, saying that "dancing with other people feels better ... if you're dancing with someone, you feel like you're connecting with them." Craig eloquently describes dancing as community, even applying it to notions of global unity:

> There's just something about being in a mass of people that are all throbbing to the same beat ... there's a unity, a realization that whatever differences we may have outside of this just really don't matter ... There's a desire for that to ... expand beyond just that setting to, like globally. I think the human race could learn something from that.

Ben Malbon writes extensively about the phenomenon of community and connectedness at dance events. He writes that "sharing of emotion" and common purpose facilitate feelings of belonging and "consolidates attachments and identifications" (1999: 72). All this combines to create "a notion of the crowd as in some way superseding the individual" (1999: 71). Additionally, Measham and colleagues explore how "communal dancing" can be a religious experience for participants and often "evoke feelings of tribalism" (2001: 26; see also Diebold 1988). Although the idea of community and the collective are significant, it should be noted that participants also value their individual selves and are concerned with finding a balance between belonging to the crowd and establishing individuality within it (Fikentscher 2000). Ling, 18, emphasizes this element: "That's the cool thing about raves ... it's like everyone has their own style ... Like they dance their own way, and they express themselves."

Drug use

Dancing is undeniably a central, defining element of the scene. Rivaling this element for centrality, though, may be the presence of illicit drugs. Thus far in our discussion of this scene (or these scenes, as there is certainly no single unitary scene here), one important aspect has remained somewhat tangential: the issue of drug consumption within these scenes. Yet the importance of drug consumption within these scenes should not be underestimated. Consumption is seen as increasingly important in the creation and performance of identities and lifestyles for youth – this includes the clothes, music, and styles discussed above, but also can include the consumption of drugs and alcohol. While not everyone involved in raves, clubs, and other dance events consumes drugs, and not everyone who uses drugs there sees these as a central activity in these scenes, certainly drug use is a notable practice at these events and is cited by some as the key activity within them. In this next section we sketch a broad picture of the level and scope of drug use among those in our sample. And in later chapters we move beyond these statistics to examine the meaning, practices, and interpretation of drug consumption by young people in these scenes.

As mentioned above, the goal of the project was to interview club-drug users who attend clubs, raves, and other dance events. We also interviewed a small subsample (twenty-two out of the 300) of dance-event attendees who had never used club drugs. Because of our sampling strategy, which targeted drug users, our subsample of non-club-drug users cannot be said to represent their proportion in the overall dance scene. Rather we made the decision to interview them when they inquired at our office about the study. In our advertisements we did note that drug use was a focus of the study, and consequently the vast majority of people who contacted us about the study had used club drugs at some point in their lives.

Given the focus of the study, it is therefore not surprising that almost the entire sample had tried marijuana (97 percent) and ecstasy (92 percent). The lifetime prevalence of these drugs (the number of respondents who reported trying them at least once) equals, or nearly equals, that of alcohol. Mushrooms was the only other drug that more than three-fourths of the sample (77 percent) had tried, although more than half of the sample had tried cocaine (60 percent), LSD (59 percent), methamphetamine (55 percent), prescription opiates (55 percent), and nitrous oxide (62 percent). Other prominent drugs that respondents reported trying include ketamine (37 percent), GHB (25 percent), opium (30 percent), prescription amphetamines (30 percent), and prescription tranquilizers (28 percent).[6]

Other researchers who are studying dance-scene populations have described their sample as "drug experienced," because of the generally high percentage (in comparison with the general population) who have tried different types of drugs, including marijuana, ecstasy, and other stimulants and club drugs (Measham *et al.* 2001). While we do not feel that we can label the overall San Francisco dance scene population in this way, primarily because of our selection criteria (this is primarily a sample of drug users so naturally they are drug experienced), we can say that a portion of our sample are clearly experimenting with multiple drugs, certainly at a higher rate than the general population. Two-thirds of the respondents say they have tried seven or more drugs[7] in their lives, and 43 percent say they have tried ten or more.

We can see from our data that, while most of the men and women in our sample are likely to experiment with and try different drugs, for some, the extent to which they use these drugs is limited. As is true in the general population, marijuana was the most extensively used drug, and 28 percent of the respondents claim to have used it on at least twenty days in the last month. Approximately 71 percent of respondents had used marijuana in the last thirty days, compared with 37 percent for ecstasy, 14 percent for methamphetamine and 15 and 17 percent for cocaine and mushrooms respectively. However, all of those current ecstasy, cocaine, and mushrooms users, and five out of seven of the current methamphetamine users, had used it on five or fewer occasions in the last month. While these respondents are clearly using at rates higher than the general population, these data, although limited in terms of sample size, suggest a picture of primarily recreational or "weekend," rather than daily or very frequent, use.

Gender and drug-use rates

Although traditionally drug users have been stereotyped as male, within studies of club and rave scenes many have wondered or conjectured whether women's drug use has caught up to or is at least nearing that of men. In our sample, though the women are clearly experimenting with drugs, the men generally tend to have tried more drugs. Whereas 49 percent of men say they have tried ten or more drugs, only 36 percent of women say the same. Age could be a confounding factor here, as the age of men in the sample is slightly higher than that of women. Among the young people we interviewed, women's use of many drugs is approaching that of their male counterparts, though the men did have the highest prevalence rates for most drugs. Women and men were fairly similar in their lifetime prevalence (the number of days they estimate having used a drug in their lifetime) of alcohol, marijuana, ecstasy, cocaine, crack, heroin, PCP, prescription amphetamines, and a few of the other psychedelic drugs mentioned such as salvia.[8] The men had slightly higher prevalence rates for methamphetamine, mushrooms, ketamine, 2CB, pill opiates, opium, and a few of the other drugs, though these differences were not statistically different. The men had statistically higher prevalence rates for LSD, GHB, nitrous oxide, MDA, and poppers. For more on the relationship between gender and drug use (especially ecstasy use) see Chapter 9.

Drugs used

Alcohol

Alcohol was a universal substance among all of the young men and women we interviewed, with the exception of two 17 year olds who said that they had never tried any form of alcohol. Almost all respondents had tried beer (98 percent), wine (95 percent), and liquor (98 percent). Most users were drinking on a weekly basis,

Table 2.2 Drug-use rates in the sample (n = 300)

Drug	Lifetime use		Past year use		Past month use	
	%	n	%	n	%	n
Tobacco, alcohol, marijuana						
Cigarettes	93	280	73	219	59	176
Beer	99	296	89	268	74	223
Wine	95	286	83	248	47	140
Liquor	98	293	89	268	77	231
Marijuana	97	291	88	263	71	212
Club drugs						
Ecstasy	92	276	80	239	34	101
LSD	59	177	17	52	4	11
Mushrooms	78	233	54	163	17	51
Methamphetamine	55	165	33	100	14	41
Ketamine	37	111	22	67	2	7
GHB	25	75	12	36	3	8
Rohypnol	1	3	<1	1	0	0
Other illicit drugs						
Cocaine	60	181	41	123	15	46
Nitrous oxide	62	186	34	103	10	31
Poppers	12	35	5	15	2	5
Inhalants	10	30	1	3	1	2
Crack	11	34	3	8	1	2
PCP	8	23	2	5	1	2
Heroin	8	23	2	6	<1	1
MDA	14	41	7	21	<1	1
Opium	31	92	12	36	3	8
Quaaludes	4	11	0	0	0	0
2CB	13	38	8	23	0	0
2-CT-7	3	8	1	2	0	0
Other psychedelics	28	84	10	30	2	6
DXM	11	33	4	12	<1	1
Prescription drugs						
Pill opiates	56	167	40	121	14	41
Amphetamines	31	92	13	38	5	15
Sedatives	2	6	1	2	0	0
Tranquilizers	29	86	14	41	4	11

with almost three-fourths using some type of alcohol in the last week, with 18 percent drinking at a rate of three to four days per week. The issue of alcohol and social setting will be explored in detail in Chapter 10.

Marijuana

Like alcohol, marijuana was fairly ubiquitous in the sample, with 97 percent of respondents having tried it and approximately 70 percent reporting use in the previous month. Of the nine who had never tried it, eight of them had never used drugs, and the other respondent had only ever tried ecstasy. Some of the young men and women we interviewed did not view marijuana as a "drug," and like alcohol it was used both in party settings as well as in more "everyday" situations. Slightly less than 40 percent of the current marijuana users were daily or almost daily users (using about five days per week or more), with the same number having used on five or fewer days in the last month. The bulk of the recent marijuana users were split between infrequent and daily/almost daily use, though an additional 27 percent of those who had ever used marijuana had not used in the previous month at all.

Ecstasy

As noted above, ecstasy was second only to marijuana as the most prevalent drug in the sample, with 92 percent of respondents having tried it. There were only two respondents in the sample who had not tried ecstasy but had used other "club drugs." About 80 percent of the sample had used ecstasy in the prior year, and approximately one-third of the sample had used in the last month. Though the prevalence of ecstasy use in the sample was high, the lifetime frequency of use was much lower than for marijuana or alcohol (though still higher than for other drugs), primarily because ecstasy was used at the weekends in the context of parties or other leisure activities, whereas alcohol and marijuana are considered to be more "everyday" substances. While some respondents used ecstasy on a weekly basis or had periods of heavier use, most tended to use less frequently.

LSD and mushrooms

Just under 60 percent of the sample had tried LSD; however, most had not used recently: about 17 percent of the sample had used in the year prior, and only 4 percent of the sample had used in the last month. Even among those who had used in the past year, most only used a handful of times or less. Mushrooms was somewhat more prevalent in the sample, with more than three-quarters (78 percent) reporting lifetime use, 54 percent using in the last year, and 17 percent using in the last month. Around 43 percent of users had used mushrooms on five or fewer days in their lives, with only 6 percent saying they had used it fifty or more times. Mushrooms was generally viewed as a more natural and less risky drug, which may explain its higher prevalence rate in the sample, as some respondents were willing to try mushrooms but not acid. Though interestingly the frequency with which respondents used mushrooms is lower than for other psychedelics, suggesting it is a drug which the majority of respondents wanted to try but not a drug that is used heavily. Although mushrooms is not included by the National Institute on Drug Abuse as one of the "club drugs," we found it to be more commonly and consistently used in these rave and club scenes than many of the "official" club drugs.

Methamphetamine

Though methamphetamine is listed by NIDA as a "club drug," many of the users in our sample did not use it in conjunction with the party scene in the way that they used drugs like ecstasy. This is not to say that methamphetamine is not used at parties and events, but rather that it does not have the same association with the party scene that psychedelic drugs do. Methamphetamine also has a more negative connotation among respondents, even among those who have used the drug. This may be partly due to personal experience, but may also be due to the general perception and viewpoint that is put forward by the media and prevention campaigns, which essentially equates methamphetamine with drugs such as crack cocaine. Because of methamphetamine's perceived greater addictive potential, it is seen by our respondents as a "harder" drug with greater risks than ecstasy or acid. Fifty-five percent reported using methamphetamine in their lives, with one-third of the sample reporting use in the last year, and 14 percent using in the previous month. Methamphetamine has a distinct pattern, in contrast to many of the other drugs our respondents consume. Although it does not have the highest prevalence rate, it seems that, of those who use methamphetamine, they use it more frequently than other drugs with similar prevalence rates. This is likely due to the fact that methamphetamine is used in the course of everyday situations as well as during leisure activities, whereas hallucinogens like mushrooms and LSD tend to be almost exclusively used in dedicated leisure activities and therefore their use is a little more self-limiting.

Ketamine, GHB, Rohypnol

The remaining club drugs, ketamine, GHB, and especially Rohypnol, were used by far more limited numbers of our study participants. Thirty-seven percent of respondents had tried ketamine, with 22 percent using in the previous year and 2 percent using in the past month. In the sample there were only a couple of respondents who were semi-regular users, the majority had only used it one to five times. (In Chapter 3 we examine the very different rates of ketamine use in other international cities.) One-quarter of the sample had tried GHB, with 12 percent using in the prior year, and only 3 percent reporting use in the last month. More than three-quarters of the GHB users had used it on five or fewer occasions in their lives. Even those who had used it recently were limited in their use. It should be noted that more gay and bisexual men had tried GHB (64 percent) than heterosexual men (24 percent) or lesbian/bisexual and heterosexual women (22 percent and 16 percent, respectively). Similar trends emerge for ketamine. These significant differences may be interpreted as a reflection of the historically high rates of drug use within the context of gay dance clubs and circuit parties (Halkitis and Parsons 2002; Lewis and Ross 1995; Mattison *et al.* 2001). However, our quantitative data do not include information about the precise location of our respondents' drug use, therefore it is difficult to know whether this drug use is in fact taking place at gay dance clubs and circuit parties. Rohypnol is classified by NIDA as a "club drug," so we specifically asked the respondents if they had tried it. The vast majority of them did not even know what it was, so we feel fairly confident in saying that Rohypnol is not part of the scene in the Bay Area, nor is it a drug of interest for these respondents. Only three respondents said that they had tried it, and two of them said they had only used it once or twice.

Cocaine

Although not officially classified as a club drug, and certainly not limited to that social setting, cocaine is increasingly reported as popular within the club scene. The lifetime prevalence for cocaine in our sample was just over 60 percent, with 41 percent of respondents using in the last year, and 15 percent using in the past month. There were only a couple of respondents who had used heavily in the last year. Like methamphetamine, cocaine tended to be used in a variety of situations, and some respondents tended to use much more often than others. Though there was a range of lifetime frequencies of use for cocaine, most of the recent users were limited in their use, such that just over three-quarters of those who had used in the last year only used it between one and eleven times. While some respondents did talk about periods of heavy use, most respondents tended to use cocaine in the course of leisure activities, whether at clubs or just hanging out with friends. It was much more commonly used by respondents at clubs or bars than raves. Though some respondents were opposed to using cocaine, whether because they did not want to snort a drug or they were not partial to stimulants, cocaine did not carry as much of a negative connotation as methamphetamine.

Nitrous oxide, poppers, inhalants

Nitrous oxide was by far the most frequently used inhalant, with 62 percent of respondents having tried the drug at some point in their lifetimes. Far fewer respondents had tried poppers (11 percent) or any other inhalants (10 percent). While nitrous was among the more commonly used drugs in our sample and was frequently cited as being used in the course of an evening out at a rave or a club, it was rarely used by itself, and was generally described as being of relatively little significance.

Drug use within the scenes

We also found significant variations in current drug use patterns on the basis of our respondents' involvement with clubs or raves. There were few significant differences in young people's lifetime prevalence of illicit drug use on the basis of the type of event they attend most frequently (raves versus clubs). Ravers and clubbers were generally likely to have tried the same numbers and types of drugs. However, we found a strong correlation between club or rave attendance and their current drug use patterns. For example, the young people we interviewed who attend primarily clubs were more likely than those who attend raves to have used beer, wine, or hard liquor in the past month. They were also far more likely to use some form of alcohol at least once per week, on average. Take, for example, beer, which was used once per week or more by 56 percent of young people who attend primarily clubs, versus only 22.5 percent of young people who attend primarily raves. These data support what many of the young people we interviewed say about alcohol use: it is uncommon and, often unacceptable, to use alcohol in the rave scene, whereas in the club scene it is seemingly ever-present. (For a further discussion of alcohol use as it relates to social context see Chapter 10.) In contrast, the young people we spoke with who attend primarily raves were more likely than respondents who attend primarily clubs to have used a number of illicit drugs in the past month or year, including ecstasy, mushrooms, LSD, and nitrous oxide. When looking at the frequency of drug use, we found the most significant differences in our sample's use of ecstasy: 34 percent of rave attendees who had tried ecstasy used the drug, on average, at least once per month, versus only 13 percent of club attendees. It is not entirely surprising that we see higher rates of use of these drugs among young rave attendees, given that these drugs are frequently described as being among the most popular in the context of the rave scene.

Thus, to understand their drug use, it is important to understand the contexts in which it occurs. In later chapters we examine the specific contexts of clubs and raves, examining how pleasure and risk are negotiated within them, and how identities based on gender, ethnicity, and sexuality shape and are shaped by experiences with these drugs and these settings. In the very next part of the book we take a step back and turn to the much bigger context in which these scenes and these individuals are embedded. We examine the broader global context of the international dance scene and offer comparisons between three international cities in Chapter 3. We turn to the US national context and look at legislative, policy, and media responses to the dance scene and club-drug use in Chapter 4. And in Chapter 5 we hone in on the specific urban context of the San Francisco scene, examining the shapes and contours of nightlife in the city, differentiations between types of clubs and raves, and the economic and regulatory context that helps shape these.

Part II

The global, the national, and the local

Chapter 3

Clubbing, drugs, and the dance scene in a global perspective

Introduction

The study of cultural globalization has been a major area of research and debate within contemporary sociology and anthropology, leading some to refer to an "explosion in writing" in this field since the 1990s (Pilkington and Bliudina 2002). While cultural globalization cannot be said to be a new development, it certainly appears to be "currently at an accelerated stage" (Pilkington and Bliudina 2002: 1), especially as the rapid spread of new technologies in the media, communications, and information has intensified the spread of global cultural flows.

The global development of the electronic dance music scene is an important and relatively recent example of global cultural flows. The dance scene and its associated drug use have emerged center-stage as a global phenomenon, and with its distinctive and fluid lifestyle in dress, music, setting, and drug use it is flourishing across the world, from Europe to the Americas, to Australia, and most recently to Asia. However, while it is the case that sociologists, anthropologists, and cultural studies researchers have examined in much detail the development of globalization, it is much less the case that researchers have focused on the dance scene as an example of the key role that youth play within any study of globalization. Indeed, youth culture has not been a prominent focus in studies of cultural globalization. Yet "Youth ... are at the center of globalization" (Maira and Soep 2005: xix), a point made strongly by Pilkington and Bliudina, who note that the "wider cultural practice of youth appears to confirm a 'global identity' " (2002: 14). Further remarking that whereas the "older generations" may have difficulty coping with the "information overload," "young people appear to move effortlessly between texts, in and out of real and virtual spaces, borrowing images, catchphrases and symbols as they go and reinventing them in the process of identity formation" (ibid.). While the development of the dance scene may have been uneven, it is nevertheless the case that contemporary youth dance scenes in different parts of the globe highlight the extent to which young people borrow, develop, and modify cultural practices, including dance, music, dress, and drugs. "The evolution of 'club cultures' around the world can be attributed ... to the ongoing global processes of cultural borrowing" (Carrington and Wilson 2002: 74). Given the increasing fluidity of contemporary society (Bauman 1998), young people identify less with "real" communities based in specific locales than with "taste communities or lifestyle enclaves" (Pilkington and Bliudina 2002). As a result of the globalized dimensions of communication, young people in San Francisco can not only learn immediately about the latest developments in London, Manchester, Rotterdam, New York, Sydney, Bangkok, or Hong Kong and exchange views about events, music, and dance-drug experiences, but also adopt, adapt, and utilize these practices for their own use (Malbon 1999; Thornton 1996).

Sociologists and cultural studies theorists examining the processes of club and dance cultures, like their counterparts in the general globalization debates, have attempted to assess the extent to which these processes can be viewed as either yet another example of Westernization leading to increasing homogenization or as an example of hybridization in which the local modifies and reshapes global culture (Howes 1996), a process that some cultural theorists refer to as "glocalization" (Crane 2002). For example, Carrington and Wilson examined the "hazy relationship between a 'global' club culture and various 'local' club cultures" (2002: 75) and noted that "while core members of the world's various dance music communities might have a shared understanding of the origins of their 'global scene' ... the various national and regional club communities still maintain a 'local' knowledge/flavour" (ibid.). Even in cultures where the dance/drug scene has been a more recent development, the settings are varied and reflect the influence of the local on modifying the global. For example, in Bangalore, India, youth dance culture has been situated in pubs rather than clubs. These venues provide entertainment during the afternoon instead of in the evening to accommodate the lifestyle and restraints on young middle-class women (Saldanha 2002) and in the UK some bhangra events are held in the day-time to accommodate the restrictions on many young Asian women's leisure. Such local specificities suggest that, while global homogenization is a growing trend, we should not underestimate the extent to which imported global universals become transformed and translated by the local context and culture. Such local adaptations are important features that emerge in cross-national research, where "the articulation between global and local" (Howes 1996: 6) becomes played out in different ways in different social settings and cultures. This process has been referred to by Lull as that of "cultural reterritorialization," which he defines as "a process of active cultural selection and synthesis drawing from the familiar and the new" (1995: 160). Consequently, in examining and comparing/contrasting local dance scenes in different parts of the world, we need to examine how it is that local audiences rework these global processes "in such a way that their meanings become inextricable from the everyday settings in which they are experienced" (Lull 1995, cited in Bennett 2000). The San Francisco dance scene, as with other dance scenes around the world, must be viewed not in isolation, then, but in this broader global context. Each dance scene can be viewed individually as a different constellation of the youth dance/drug scene, operating within a context of global influences, each with its own starting point, its own subgenres of music, its own styles of dancing, its own physical and sociogeographical makeup of venues and clubs, and its own drug-using preferences and practices.

Unfortunately, while researchers within the field of globalization and youth cultures have seen the importance of examining the dance scene within a comparative and global perspective, researchers in the drug field, with only a few exceptions, have restricted their enquiries on drugs and the dance scene to single cultures and locales. By focusing solely on drug use within individual cultures, researchers may miss an important opportunity to examine the extent to which either similar processes have developed in a number of different dance-scene locales or are specific to particular dance scenes. In other words, to what extent do the specifics of the scene and the accompanying drug-using practices reflect either the characteristics of the local music scene, including musical tastes, types of dance venue, characteristics of attendees and their expectations and intentions, as well as the prevailing local drug markets, or the extent to which these characteristics are influenced by more global cultural flows (Bennett 2000; Weil 1972; Zinberg 1984)? One such exception is the work of Agar and Reisinger (2003), who, in their study of ecstasy, attempt both to understand the global interconnections of ecstasy production and distribution as well as examine ways in which the global phenomena are privileged over the local practice. Researchers' reluctance to position their work within a more global perspective is somewhat surprising, given both the topic itself and the existence of cross-national research in other areas of the drug field. For example, many cross-national studies on drug trafficking, drug policy, drug problems, and dependence and cross-national studies of drug treatment exist (Klingemann and Hunt 1998; Klingemann and Sobell 2007; Levine 2003; Reinarman 2003; Room and Paglia 1999; P. H. Smith 1992). There are also a number of comparative cultural studies on drugs, including Furst's (1976) and Dobkin de Rios's (1990) research on hallucinogens and Eliade's (1964) work on shamanism.

Consequently, and in spite of the increasing globalization of the dance scene, our knowledge of the globalization of drug use and the dance scene is somewhat limited. Like studies in other locales, our research primarily focuses on one specific site – San Francisco. As our study progressed, we recognized from our other work in Hong Kong and Rotterdam that there were, at least on the surface, a number of commonalities between these sites which required further investigation. Based on a comparative study, it became increasingly clear that, on the one hand, there were overall features constant to the scene, including the shift from an occasional or transitory dance-drug scene to a permanent, flourishing, and highly lucrative entertainment industry with a dynamic drug market. On the other hand, the expression or articulation of the scene has very much been locally and culturally defined. Instead of examining drug consumption and drug-using practices within only one culture, we need to compare contrasting social and cultural contexts in order to highlight the regularities and the differences that are occurring in this period of rapid social change in the lives of young people (Miles 2000). By adopting a cross-national approach and comparing the dance and drug scene within similar but different social and cultural contexts, we can begin to examine both the elements that remain constant regardless of context and those elements that are more socially and culturally influenced. In the following chapter, we sketch out the emergence of the global dance scene and its connection to youthful drug consumption and its manifestation in two locales. In doing so, our aim is to develop a transcultural approach to the study of the dance-drug scene (Bucholtz 2002).

Raves and clubs: the start of a global movement

In 1999, when Martin called the rave/dance movement "the biggest, most universal, British youth culture since the 1960s" and "the largest, most dynamic, and longest-lasting youth subculture or counterculture of the postwar era" (D. Martin 1999: 77), he probably did not imagine just how global the dance scene was to become. The growth of electronic dance music and dance parties is generally attributed to developments in Britain from the late 1980s and early 1990s and in some cases it is certainly correct that both the scene in the UK and specific DJs have had an important effect on the development of the global rave and club scene. However, although the UK scene played a significant role, the origins of electronic dance music and the incorporation of ecstasy to enhance the impact of dance music began not in the UK or even on a Spanish holiday island but in the US.[1]

According to Wilson (2006), the rave scene can be traced back to four related movements.[2] The first element that can be identified is the New York dance scene of the 1970s and specifically that centered around gay African Americans and such clubs as Salvation in the Hell's Kitchen district. The importance of the gay and black scenes for the origins of the rave scene are not that surprising, according to Collin, given the fact that "Black and gay clubs have consistently served as breeding grounds for new developments in popular culture, laboratories where music, drugs and sex are interbred to create stylistic innovations that slowly filter through to straight white society" (1997: 12).

The second element – the Chicago house-music scene – was initially developed by DJ Frankie Knuckles, from South Bronx, who in 1977 migrated to Chicago and introduced electronic soul music at the Warehouse club.[3] Although according to Collin (1997) and Kempster (1996), Knuckles was not the only significant DJ at the time creating house music, he certainly became well known and was an early exponent of taking records apart and reediting them, a technique that had not been used in Chicago prior to his arrival.

Interestingly enough, even in those early days of house music, divisions in style and taste were already developing. This division in musical tastes and clientele was also reflected in the different drugs used by the respective audiences. The older group who followed Knuckles tended to use acid and MDA, while those who followed other DJs used cheaper drugs, such as PCP, and especially drugs which induced maximum energy (Wilson 2006). The identification of different drugs with different musical styles was to become a significant feature of the contemporary fragmentation of the rave and club scene.

The Detroit "techno" sound was the third element that contributed to the development of the rave scene. While house music was being developed in Chicago, in Detroit DJs were producing "an electronic and futuristic sound" (Wilson 2006: 46) or as Collin notes "attempting to translate the electric dreams of European pop into visionary sci-fi" (1997: 23). DJs like Juan Atkins were particularly influenced by

Kraftwerk – a minimalist quartet from Dusseldorf – and other New Wave electronic music. "The new sound relied on synthesised drums and base, stripping music of tangible lyrics in favour of a new African American futurism" (Connell and Gibson 2003: 99).

The fourth and final element was the Ibiza–UK connection. Although many writers trace the development of DJs and clubs to DJ Alfredo in 1985 in Ibiza (also known as the White Island), others, such as S. Armstrong, have argued that the music and club scene on the island actually began in the 1950s with an ex-GI, Bad Jack Hand, who ran the Jamboree Jazz Club in Barcelona. From Barcelona he moved to Ibiza, where he "threw open-air jams and parties on the beach near Figueretes" (2004: 302).

One of the first clubs started in the 1960s in Ibiza was Amnesia, which was an old *finca* and became used as a bohemian and hippie venue (Garratt 1998). By the mid-1970s, as disco took hold, other clubs developed, including Pacha and Club Raphael. The latter was soon renamed Ku and by the late 1970s it had become a glamorous nightclub appealing to the international celebrity set, including Boy George, Grace Jones, Tina Turner, Joni Mitchell, Led Zeppelin, and many others. However, the success of the 1970s soon came to an end and by the mid-1980s these clubs were struggling financially. They were saved, according to S. Armstrong, by the arrival of MDMA (ecstasy), stockpiles of which, with the closing of Bagwan Rajneesh cult's workshops on the island, "were released into Ibiza's flourishing dope, speed and acid market" (2004: 307). Initially, however, the effects of ecstasy did not mix well with the dominant music played on the island ("white-boy funk," S. Armstrong 2004: 307), and it was not until the mixing abilities of an Argentinean ex-journalist and would-be DJ, Alfredo, that the music and drugs came together to produce an irresistible combination. Alfredo played tunes based on a wide and eclectic range of music, including underground disco from New York, house music from Chicago, British synth bands, indie rock, Euro-disco, and reggae. From this mixture of sounds a different type of scene developed. "These eclectic sets, mixed with MDMA and the dawn sunshine on Amnesia's open-air dance floor, started to attract clubbers from all over Europe" (S. Armstrong 2004: 309). So began what became called the "Balearic beat."

In the summer of 1987 four young friends from England – Paul Oakenfold, Danny Rampling, Johnny Walker, and Nicky Holloway – arranged to meet in Ibiza to celebrate Oakenfold's twenty-sixth birthday. All of them had heard about the new drug, ecstasy, and Oakenfold and Rampling were keen to try it. One evening they set out clubbing and someone suggested they go to Amnesia. As Walker recalls, going to Amnesia "was a completely new experience. Just feeling absolutely wonderful. ... it was all new ... it just blew me away ... And the whole thing was enhanced ... by being on a really good E" (Garratt 1998: 100). From the experience of this one evening, their lives were to change. The next day the four of them discussed their experience of the previous night and planned how to translate the experience back to London.[4]

Chicago house music had been available in the UK since 1985, but, as Rietveld makes clear, until late 1987 "there was no sign of a house ... craze amongst British youth" (1998: 47). However, by the end of 1987 its popularity was increasing, but what was needed for house music to become successful was an environment in which "a sound system is good enough to drive its frequencies into the body and loud enough to stifle any lengthy conversation, in addition to light effects which disorientate the visual and rational cognitive field, [where] music can become a dominant factor ... [and where] ... A recreational drug such as MDMA ... could open the mind" (Rietveld 1998: 51). This is what Oakenfold and Rampling supplied. As Melechi has noted:

> The British phenomenon of Acid House ... [was the attempt] ... to relive the *jouissance* of the Mediterranean holiday in the pleasures of dance, music and drugs ... Acid House would be born of this nostalgia and by the end of the summer of '87 holiday-sick clubbers arrived back home in London intent on resurrecting the spirit of Ibiza Town.
>
> (Melechi 1993: 30)

Soon the Balearic sound was becoming increasingly well known. By the autumn of 1988 the music spread across Britain and beyond. Its popularity was encouraged by the media, which, while initially positive about this new "Acid House" music scene and its association with MDMA, suddenly within a few weeks ran headlines warning about the "evil of ecstasy." However, if the aim of media attention had been to alert young people about the dangers of the scene and the drugs, thereby keeping them away, it had exactly the opposite effect. "The scaremongering tabloid and television coverage did not have the intended effect of discouraging the youth of Britain. If anything, 'it just helped it grow even bigger'. The result was an influx of younger kids and suburbanites on to the scene" (Reynolds 1999: 67).

In addition to the increasing popularity of the scene, and the activities of the four young men who had imported the "Balearic beat," other would-be promoters became involved in arranging parties and subsequently began the start of special dance events designed not just to attract a couple of hundred partygoers but instead thousands. "The agenda had changed: this was no longer about club nights, one-off parties. It was about *events*, about spectacle" (Garratt 1998: 145). These events, which could be attended by as many as 20,000 people, became synonymous with raves. They took place in large spaces such as aircraft hangers, derelict churches, film studios, disused warehouses, equestrian centers, and open fields. As Connell and Gibson (2003) have noted, the use of space is important and gives a new music scene credibility. In the case of raves, this occurred by taking over unused urban industrial premises, thereby altering the original role of the space from industrial production to the playing of music. "It was the temporary and transgressive nature of the warehouses that made them special, feelings amplified by the illegal use of the premises and often by the consumption of drugs ... This sense was heightened by the fact that the partygoers did not know at the beginning of the night where the party would take place" (Ingham *et al.* 1999: 293). Promoters transformed not only disused industrial space but also the interior of clubs into "imaginative landscapes" (Gibson 1999, quoted in Connell and Gibson 2003). This included "the physical space – its size, position of DJs, chillout rooms for relaxation, quality of lighting rigs – and attempts through decoration and interior design to construct imaginary playscapes" (Connell and Gibson 2003: 204).

Acid House goes global

From these early beginnings in London and then other parts of the UK, Acid House began to spread, first to Europe and then Australia and the US, and finally to other parts of the globe. However, unlike previous developments in rock and pop music, where the impact of developments in one country suffered a time lag prior to influencing young people in other countries, the followers of electronic dance music and culture no longer relied solely on the record corporations or music publications for their information. In fact, partly as a reaction to the domination of the music scene by large corporations, clubbers and ravers kept themselves informed about global developments through a proliferation of grass-roots Internet websites, chat rooms, and listservs, that supplied information on the latest music, new and past raves, new and up-and-coming DJs, dress fashions, and different dance scenes. Adolescents and young adults in Hong Kong learned immediately about the latest developments in Berlin, London, Manchester, New York, Leipzig, Ibiza, or San Francisco and not only learned about them but also exchanged views (Malbon 1999; Thornton 1996). These trends and developments in the scene were further fueled by corporations through advertising and marketing, which simultaneously absorbed and utilized "the overt and subliminal language of new youth trends" (European Monitoring Centre for Drugs and Drug Addiction 1997). Even the music, which initially had appeared so shocking, gradually became absorbed within the mainstream culture so much so that "electronic dance music came to be consumed in ways similar to other previous eras ... from the use of dance music in aerobics classes to techno segued to car advertisements or sports shows" (Connell and Gibson 2003: 207). This process of incorporation of oppositional cultural commodities has been discussed by Hebdige, who argues that subcultural styles become quickly converted into mass-produced objects: "Youth cultural styles may begin by issuing symbolic challenges, but they must inevitably end by establishing new sets of conventions; by creating new commodities, new industries or rejuvenating old ones" (1979: 96).

In fact, it appears that a somewhat common development had occurred in many of these sites. Initially, dance events were one-off events organized around particular themes or particular genres of music. Some of these events were legal/licensed and some not. Gradually, as the authorities began to exercise increased control of the events and restrict their operation, the rave parties gradually became incorporated with the existing nightlife infrastructure. (We discuss San Francisco's nightlife and rave history in Chapter 5.) More established clubs, whether independently owned or part of a multinational entertainment corporation, began to offer these events on a regular basis, thereby capitalizing on this new musical event. One indicator of the extent to which the rave scene became an important feature of corporate profits can be seen in a 1993 report on recreational activities by the Henley Centre for Forecasting, which noted that the "value of the rave market was calculated to be £1.8 billion ($2.7 billion)" (Thornton 1996: 15). Such developments encouraged the increasing globalization of the dance scene.

In addition to the latest developments in communication technology, a worldwide expansion in relatively inexpensive tourism and the declining cost of international package tours also encouraged the global spread of dance-club culture. Magazines catering to dance-club attendees, such as *Mixmag* in England, began to detail the best vacation places to visit, the clubs to go to, the DJs that would be playing, and recommended the cheap hotels to stay in. Young clubgoers could now not merely read about developments in the dance scene in Ibiza or Goa but could experience them for themselves (Sellars 1998). However, for those clubgoers who wished not to venture abroad the mainstream media provided spectacular information on the foreign scene for home consumption. For example, British television and satellite companies presented programs such as *Ibiza uncovered* and *Around the World in Eighty Raves* to allow viewers to experience clubbing abroad (Carrington and Wilson 2002). As Lipsitz has remarked, "the interdependence of people throughout the world has never been more evident ... New technologies and trade patterns connect places as well as people" (1994: 6).

However, it was not only news about the music and the DJs that spread worldwide, the development of a global drug-using culture was also developing. In charting this development, as noted above, few cross-national studies exist; nevertheless, we are able to construct a global picture of drug use and the dance scene from a number of individual studies.

Drug use within a global context

The first and most obvious characteristic in discussing drugs and the scene is the extent to which the two are inextricably tied. Researchers in many different countries, including Australia, Canada, England, Scotland, the US, Germany, Italy, the Czech Republic, the Netherlands, Sweden, Finland, and Estonia, have noted a strong association between the dance scene and specific types of drugs, especially ecstasy, amphetamines, and cocaine (Barrett *et al.* 2005; Degenhardt *et al.* 2004; Duff 2005; Gross *et al.* 2002; Measham *et al.* 2001; Salasuo and Seppälä 2005; Sjü 2005; Tossmann *et al.* 2001; Winstock *et al.* 2001). Although research has suggested that marijuana may be used more extensively than ecstasy, especially in both the buildup to an event and the period after, it is ecstasy, more than any other substance, that has been identified as the quintessential drug of the international club and rave scene. It provided, as Carrington and Wilson noted, "the most visible exemplar of an emergent global culture" (2002: 74). Ecstasy is "the prototypical drug of the rave scene, the mental state it produces being intimately related to the sounds, designs and concepts of house music culture" (Newcombe 1992: 14), a point reinforced by Beck and Rosenbaum when they remarked that ecstasy was the ideal drug for "prolonged trance-dancing" (J. Beck and Rosenbaum 1994: 54). But it was not merely its suitability for extended dancing that made it so attractive; it also possessed other appealing characteristics. First, its street name conjured up pleasurable and nonproblematic experiences, unlike other "hard" drugs such as heroin or cocaine. Second, ecstasy was extremely easy to administer – just pop a pill. Third, it had no association with "sleazy and unhygienic lifestyle associated with heroin" (Redhead 1993: 97). Given these positive features, ecstasy has consequently been strongly associated with the dance scene and those who attend. For example, Riley and colleagues (2001) found that 82 percent of the rave attendees in Edinburgh had used ecstasy in the previous year, a point confirmed by many other studies in many different countries. However, as Tossmann and colleagues (2001) note, the dominance of ecstasy was not necessarily found in all European capitals, thereby suggesting the effect of local drug markets. Whereas "the use of ecstasy is especially widespread in Amsterdam ... this substance is comparatively less likely to be used in the eastern metropolitan cities of Prague, Berlin and Vienna" (Tossmann *et al.* 2001: 22).

Recent research has also suggested that other substances may be gaining in popularity. For example, reports from Europe suggest that ketamine may be gaining in popularity, with seven countries reporting for 2006 lifetime use. These range from 6.7 percent in the Czech Republic to 10.8 percent in Italy and 16.4 percent in France to 20.9 percent in Hungary (European Monitoring Centre for Drugs and Drug Addiction 2002, 2007; Joe-Laidler and Hunt 2008). Also in the UK there has been an increase in experimentation and the development of "an established user base" (Nutt and Williams 2004: 4) in certain locales and among subgroups within the dance scene, which led to ketamine's classification as a Class C drug in January 2006 (European Monitoring Centre for Drugs and Drug Addiction 2002; McCambridge *et al.* 2007; Release 1997; Riley and Hayward 2004). Nevertheless, there still exists a strong association between using ecstasy and involvement in the dance scene. A number of writers went as far as to suggest that it was precisely this combination of ecstasy, dancing, and the environment of the event that made Acid House so popular and attractive to young people: "The atmosphere is one of unity, of dissolving difference in the peace and harmony haze of the drug ecstasy" (McRobbie 1994: 168; see also Collin 1997; Reynolds 1998b). The symbiotic relationship between illicit drugs, music, and dancing is not a new phenomenon and has had a "long and diverse history" (Shapiro 1999: 18), and although researchers have debated the relative importance of drugs (Shapiro 1999) versus the music (Reynolds 1998a) versus the experience (Malbon 1999), what is clear is that the elements of dance, music, drugs, and setting are intimately tied together in the global culture of dance clubs and dance parties.

Finally, the available research suggested that attendees at dance parties experimented with new and varied combinations of substances. For example, Hammersley and colleagues (2002) showed that few users, if any, use ecstasy on its own. However, in tracing the precise characteristics of this polydrug use, researchers have uncovered different drug-using patterns depending on the location of the study. For example, in their multi-city European study of the techno-party scene, Tossmann and colleagues (2001) found that the most common combination was ecstasy and cannabis followed by ecstasy and alcohol, whereas Barrett and his team (2005), studying raves in Montreal, found that cannabis and amphetamines were the most popular of club drugs used in combination with ecstasy. However, regardless of possible local variations, the types of drugs adopted tend to favor certain particular varieties and combinations. As Hammersley and colleagues note, "Overall there is a clearly a preference for co-use of hallucinogens and stimulants" (Hammersley *et al.* 2002: 637; see also Allott and Redman 2006).

From this brief overview of the association between the dance scene and drug use it is clear that, while certain global features exist such as extensive use and experimenting with different combinations, specific local practices are also important. Researchers who have examined the development of youth cultures have emphasized the importance of local social and cultural influences in determining the characteristics of individual scenes. As Weber has noted, "a unique local scene ... [is] derived from both the local, national and international influences" (1999: 333), and as Bennett has remarked, the local reflects the way in which "clubbers articulate their commitment to a particular dance music style, club or event in a language designed to construct a sense of place within a particular set of 'local' circumstances; a particular version of everyday life" (2000: 84). In the same way that local characteristics may influence the global features of the dance styles and music, so also do local features influence the preferred drugs used.

Local developments in drugs and the dance scene: the cases of Hong Kong and Rotterdam

In order to examine in more detail the extent to which the local features operate to modify the more global characteristics of the dance scene and produce within the local scene their own particular characteristics, whether that be in terms of a distinctive musical style or in the type of drugs preferred, we now examine two case studies further. We draw on the research of ourselves and our colleagues, who conducted 100 interviews in Hong Kong and seventy-five interviews in Rotterdam, Netherlands, using comparable interview schedules to our San Francisco project, allowing us to compare some key patterns among club-drug users in these three cities. While both of these cases – Hong Kong and Rotterdam – reflect global developments within the electronic dance music scene, they also illustrate, in different ways, the importance of considering local characteristics, whether that be in specific drug-using practices or in preferred types of music.

Hong Kong

Despite the globalization of the dance-drug scene, our understanding of the phenomenon has principally been informed by the experiences and developments in the UK, Europe, Australia, and North America. While this is not surprising, given the origins of the rave scene, it does highlight the extent to which the experiences of Asian countries have been largely ignored in these international discussions.

Hong Kong's nightlife has traditionally centered around Victoria harbor. The north shore of Hong Kong Island has three districts, Central (LanKwaiFong), WanChai, and Causeway Bay, which are the center of Hong Kong's business sector, leading tourist destinations, and home to most of the restaurants, pubs, bars, and clubs on the island. Across Victoria harbor is the Kowloon peninsula, the southernmost tip of the mainland, which is home to two districts, Mongkok and TsimShaTsui (TST), which are also known for an active and lively nightlife.

Hong Kong's elite business district, Central, is a landscape of high-rises, world-class hotels, elite shopping streets, swanky bistros, and hip bars and clubs. Bordering Hong Kong harbor, from which it sprawls steeply uphill, Central is the literal and symbolic center of Hong Kong's capitalist power and urban professional sophistication. It has an extremely dense concentration of some of Hong Kong's trendiest bars and clubs. The streets are closed on the weekend, and the streets are filled with weekend revelers. Most of the bars open on to the street, allowing the overflow into this regular weekend multi-bar party. Many of the venues along this street are popular with a mix of urban professionals, both expatriate and local, some local college students, and foreign tourists. Eschewing both the local Hong Kong bar style and the chic and sleek Hong Kong elite lounge style, the area is noisy, friendly, and a mix of mostly middle and upper middle-class revelers of varying ethnicities.

The WanChai district, also located on Hong Kong's main island, was in the past a favorite haunt for American sailors and boasted a dense concentration of "girlie" bars, massage parlors, and street prostitution. Currently it is home to a large number of foreigner-friendly bars and discos with large numbers of local Hong Kong Chinese customers who appreciate the laid-back and lively environment of these bars. The nightlife in the area begins quite early, being a popular first stop for urban professionals, both locals and expatriates, for after-work drinks. Later in the evening, live music venues become extremely busy, especially from Thursday to Saturday. Across the harbor is the Kowloon peninsula, with TST at the southern tip and Mongkok just slightly north. TST is located along the mainland's southernmost point, across Victoria harbor from Hong Kong island. The district is associated with foreign tourists, having a number of moderately priced tourist hotels, open markets, Western-style pubs, Internet cafés, and moderately priced restaurants. It is an extremely vibrant, lively, diverse part of the city, with a mix of tourists (primarily Caucasian), immigrants, and local Hong Kong-Chinese of varying classes. The TST nightlife scene is equally diverse. Several Western-style pubs are in the area, catering heavily to foreign businessmen as well as local expatriates, but are also frequented by business-class Hong Kong Chinese locals.

More prominent are the "local-style" bars, primarily clustered in groups along smaller streets dotted also with small shops and restaurants, some of which feature karaoke. Connected with the more prominent "local bars" are several "local-style discos" that have dominated the area's disco scene more recently. These clubs are generally small, dark, and sophisticated in their decoration. They tend to serve a somewhat young and upscale professional clientele that is almost entirely local Hong Kong Chinese. The TST district is an extremely "mixed" nightlife district, retaining in general its somewhat distasteful associations with "local-style" establishments, but also developing upmarket venues.

Similar to the experience in other countries, the rise of the dance-drug scene did not originate in these long-standing entertainment districts. That was a gradual process. Instead, organized dance parties and raves first surfaced in Hong Kong in 1993. These occasional events were imported from the UK and North America primarily by the expatriate community. The frequency of these organized events grew until approximately 1997 but since then they have declined.

The limited success of organized rave parties was related to the density of living and lack of space in Hong Kong, but it was also due to the increased policing of these events and the government's enactment of legislation mandating organizers and promoters to meet stringent health and safety requirements (Joe-Laidler 2004). The popularity of these organized events began to diminish by 1998 as many Hong Kong entrepreneurs recognized the potential profits of converting existing karaoke bars and restaurants into permanent venues for dancing and clubbing.

From 1998 onward the dance party scene began to take hold, and established itself in different venues, which attracted a wider audience and became integrated into the entertainment scenes in Central, Wanchai, and TST (Joe-Laidler *et al.* 2000). The differences between organized rave parties and the developing club scene during the latter part of the 1990s can be understood in terms of the music and the people who attend these two types of scenes. While the music at raves was typically from abroad, and without lyrics, more permanent local venues tended to include local Cantonese pop music. Raves were also recognized as sites with a high degree of anonymity, thereby allowing participants to be bolder and freer than in discos and clubs where space is more constrained and the risk of knowing or being under the scrutiny of others is greater.

The proliferation of more permanent discos and clubs has resulted in a range of dance venues catering to different types of participants and experiences. At one end are large clubs which can accommodate at least 400 attendees. Such clubs tend to charge relatively high entrance fees ranging from about US$35 to US$65, and drinks are expensive when compared to smaller discos. These large dance venues have strict security controls, trying to ensure that minors do not gain entry. Participants are fully cognizant of the differences between large clubs. For example, Club Space[5] has been characterized as being a very trendy, upscale, clean, and spacious venue with Western-style music and expensive décor. VIP rooms are available to rent and typically groups of friends pool their money to share the expense of about US$150. The patrons of this club are described as young but mature and professional. Club 6 is also a very popular venue, but tends to attract more "gangster-like" patrons. Aside from these large clubs, there has been a growth in the number of discos, clubs, and lounges catering to working-class youth as well as the affluent. Unlike the larger clubs, smaller clubs were more likely to be short-lived, often closing and reopening months later with a different name and a modified style.

This was certainly the case with the district of Mongkok, which came to be defined as a center for clubbing and discos for working-class youth. Mongkok is noted as being one of the most densely populated areas internationally, and its streets are packed with crowds around the clock. Mongkok is home to primarily lower middle-class local Hong Kong Chinese, a vast array of inexpensive shopping opportunities, a thriving sex-work industry, and a large number of "local-style" bars, clubs, and discos. While English is commonly heard on the streets of Central, Wanchai, Causeway, and TST, one is more likely to hear colloquial Cantonese and Chinglish spoken in Mongkok.

Various aspects of the Mongkok club and disco scene have typically been associated with particular Triad groups, such as management, security, and drug distribution

(Joe-Laidler 2005). Triad members frequent the clubs and discos there, and reportedly fights within and outside of these venues are a nightly occurrence. The door charges for these venues are relatively inexpensive; however, once inside, drinks (including water) are expensive. In addition, drug sales often take place within these establishments, and drug use within the clubs is evident. The potential for violence and the apparent drug consumption have led to increased policing and surveillance. Given these characteristics, many describe the Mongkok club scene as "dangerous," "dark," and "low." In fact the district of Mongkok serves as a distinctive cultural marker of working-class locals, against more affluent locals and nonlocals characteristic of cosmopolitanism, internationalism, and refinement. But not only has the district become synonymous with the locale, it has also become associated with a particular working-class youth style – the "MK" style – against which more affluent youth often judge themselves. Consequently, Mongkok has an extremely prominent place in Hong Kong's cultural landscape of social class, style, and nightlife consumption. It also has an important place as the center of open club-drug consumption. Perhaps because of its prominent visibility, this district became one of the main targets of police raids and licensing checks, so much so that the main venues in this area for dance and drug use have closed.

Despite, or perhaps, in spite of, the ongoing displacement and replacement of these venues, many young persons, particularly those from working-class backgrounds, have taken advantage of the choices for dance, leisure, and drug consumption across the Chinese border in Shenzhen. In this "sister city" to Hong Kong there are many attractions for Hong Kongers, including the relatively cheaper prices for entrance and drinks, the quality and less expensive cost of drugs, perceived freedom from police surveillance, and new alternative venues (Joe-Laidler 2005).

In comparing Hong Kong to Rotterdam and San Francisco we find significant differences in drug-using patterns among young people in the dance/club scenes. In Hong Kong the most striking difference is the popularity of ketamine. With the exception of marijuana and ecstasy, which were nearly universally used by respondents in all three cities' samples, ketamine is by far the most popular drug in Hong Kong, used by 85 percent of the young club-drug users interviewed. This sets Hong Kong apart from other cities, where ketamine is used by a smaller number of respondents (37 percent in San Francisco; 9.5 percent in Rotterdam) (see Table 3.1). While we see fairly comparable rates of ecstasy use in Hong Kong compared to the other two cities (88–92 percent in each of the cities in the sample), other drugs appear to be used much less. For example, Hong Kong respondents were less likely than San Francisco or Rotterdam respondents to report lifetime cocaine use (32 percent versus 60 percent and 73 percent), methamphetamine use (31 percent versus 55 percent and 67 percent), mushroom use (9 percent versus 78 percent and 64 percent), and GHB use (3 percent versus 25 percent and 25 percent). None of the people in the Hong Kong sample reported lifetime use of crack, nitrous oxide, MDA, 2CB, and poppers. In fact, Hong Kong respondents reported the lowest rates of drug experimentation of any subgroup; more than half of Hong Kong respondents had used three or fewer drugs in their lifetimes versus less than a quarter of

Table 3.1 Lifetime drug-use rates, by location

Drug	San Francisco	Hong Kong	Rotterdam
Marijuana	97	89	93
Ecstasy	92	88	92
LSD	59	8	17
Mushrooms	78	9	63
Methamphetamine	55	31	67
Ketamine	37	85	10
GHB	25	3	25
Cocaine	60	32	73
Nitrous	62	0	35
Poppers	12	0	50
Crack	11	0	8
MDA	14	0	4
2CB	13	0	1

San Francisco and Rotterdam respondents. While there were relatively few differences in the ages at which club drug users tended to start using drugs, Hong Kong
respondents tended to start using cocaine, LSD, and mushrooms later than respondents from San Francisco or Rotterdam, but started using ketamine at a significantly
earlier age.

Rotterdam: the development of gabber

Rotterdam, located on the Maas river, has a population of 600,000, which makes it
one of the largest cities in the Netherlands. It also has one of the world's largest con-
tainer ports, and consequently plays a vital part in the Dutch economy. Rotterdam's
nightlife, unlike some other cities, is concentrated not in one single location but
instead is spread around a number of different areas, including the city center,
the Westelijk Handelsterrein, the historic Delfshaven, the Old Harbour, Witte de
Withstraat, the Nieuwe Binnenweg, and the Stadhuisplein. Over the last twenty years,
more new nightlife areas have been developed and an explosion of cafés, restaurants,
clubs, and discothèques has occurred. Today, there are between 100 and 125 venues
in Rotterdam, and most of these have a dance floor as well as "ambient" rooms for
smoking or relaxing.

Areas of the city with a thriving nightlife include West-Kruiskade, Nieuwe
Binnenweg, and Witte de Withstraat streets in the center, which have a range of
different bars, cafés, small clubs, and venues. The more well-known venues include
Nighttown, Calypso, and "Bootleg." The latter, for example, is a small late-nightclub
with electronic music, popular among the after-party people. Farther down the river is
Westelijk Handelsterrein, another relatively new area, where new and trendy restaurants, galleries, and clubs can be found in renovated warehouses. Land van Waas
for example is known to the 30-plus crowd and hosts a few clubs and DJs that play
"broken beatz" and "future jazz."

Stadhuisplein, situated in the center of the regular shopping area, has a number of small discothèques and bars. In addition, there are approximately forty music bars and venues, such as the Skihut and the Coconut Bar. Nearby is the popular venue Off-corso, in a building that was once a theater, which now offers many different styles of music, from hip-hop to salsa lounge, dance, and urban. Close to Rotterdam Central Station is the Hollywood Club, which caters specifically for the very young (under 21) and attracts a lot of people from outside Rotterdam. Club Revolution, which is also in the neighborhood, is especially popular among the after-party people and is open until eleven o'clock in the morning. Finally in this central area is the Park, which is a magnificent public urban garden bordering the river. Within its confines there is a splendid building that now accommodates Parkzicht Restaurant. Parkzicht is seen as the place where gabberhouse music was born.

In the north, at Zomerhofstraat, big party locations can also be found, such as Atlantic Palace, which has the Dancehall and Bubbling parties, and in the south/center of the city at Kop van Zuid (viewed as the "new" center of Rotterdam) other big venues include Las Palmas, Cruise Terminal, and Club Rotterdam. Finally further south, Now and Wow, a large venue located in an old grain silo, which hosts dozens of clubs, can be found.

Special dance events are also held in big venues such as Ahoy, Binnenmaas (Decibel Outdoor by Back2School), the former Holland-America Line cruise terminal, and Tropicana (Keifland, Lunapark) as well as the world-famous Heineken Fast Forward Dance Parade, similar to the Berlin Love Parade, which occurs every year and is sponsored by all the main clubs and record companies.

The arrival of English Acid House and the development of gabberhouse

English Acid House music became popular in the Netherlands soon after its development in the UK, and in the summer of 1988 English rave organizations, such as Sunrise, began to arrange parties in Amsterdam. According to Rietveld (1998), this early influence was the result of Amsterdam's attractiveness to people in the UK for its more liberal attitude to drug use, licensing laws, and sexual practices. In fact, London-style acid parties had come to Amsterdam in 1987, but their appeal was relatively exclusive and parties were attended only by a relatively small Amsterdam avant-garde "in" crowd. Other than these events, the new music had, overall, made few inroads in other parts of the Netherlands until the end of 1988. Rietveld, for example, cites a Dutch magazine at the time that described the initial impact of Acid House in Rotterdam: "A while back they organized an Acid House party in a club in Rotterdam. Its usual disco clientele came in, looked around and left in shock" (Dibbets 1988, quoted in Rietveld 1998). Nevertheless regardless of these setbacks, the popularity of house parties, especially in Amsterdam, began to increase steadily and the influence of the London scene was obvious, with, for example, large parties being named "London comes to Amsterdam" and English DJs, such as Danny Rampling, being major attractions. However, attendance at these events was still relatively exclusive, and to gain entry clubbers needed to possess an invitation or flyer. These invitations were distributed only at prior events.

The exclusivity of the scene in the early period soon began to evaporate as the popularity of Acid House increased, and more people wished to attend. However, its growing popularity began to create divisions within the fans between those who saw themselves as the original party elite and who felt that only they really understood the spirit of the movement and those who were perceived as the new "second-generation" partygoers. The "old-timers" increasingly complained that the newcomers were encouraging violence within the scene and had little or no idea of the original rave philosophy and its sense of community and togetherness. In constructing the scapegoat, commentators in the media characterized these new antisocial clubbers as "uneducated, inarticulate, violent, racist, homophobic and sexist" (Marshall 1993: 85, quoted in Verhagen *et al.* 2000: 147), and "blind to creativity" because of their "taste for a heavier type of music" (Verhagen *et al.* 2000: 149). Furthermore, they were scorned because they were not exclusive ecstasy users, but instead preferred cheaper amphetamines, and also consumed large amounts of alcohol and became drunk; the consumption of alcohol was viewed as further evidence of their ignorance of the philosophy of raves. Their characterization became confirmed in the Dutch media when they were described as "shameless morons, layabouts and aggressive bastards" (*Algemeen Dagblad* 1992: ml 15, quoted in Verhagen *et al.* 2000: 151).

Soon they became christened "gabbers," which has its roots in the Dutch word for "mate." The origin of the term as a way of characterizing these new ravers, according to one apocryphal story, cited by many commentators, is that on one occasion a young male raver had wanted to get into the Roxy, a fashionable club in Amsterdam, and was turned away by the bouncer, who said, "No, gabber, you can't come in here" (experiencefestival.com). To enhance their group identity, they developed their own distinctive dress style, which according to Ter Bogt *et al.* (2002) involved "Male gabbers walked around in track suits, brand Australian, and on Nike Air shoes, their heads shaved and one earring in each ear. Gabber girls just wore tracksuit pants combined with a little top, their hair shaved up the neck and above and behind the ears, the long hair on top of the head tightly fixed in a pony tail" (Ter Bogt *et al.* 2002: 164).

Their characteristic dress style was also reflected in a specific musical style. Using Reynolds's (1999) initial classification of types of dance music, Ter Bogt and Engels (2005) argue that divisions within clubbers and ravers became reflected in different tastes in music between those who preferred club music, also called club mellow in the Netherlands, and those who preferred hardcore. The former was generally played in more exclusive venues for an older artistic crowd, while hardcore was played at parties with "an adolescent crowd with predominantly a lower education" (Ter Bogt and Engels 2005: 1480). These young clubbers began to demand a faster and louder variant than the style associated with the more mellow form of house music. This musical style became christened "gabberhouse" – a term attributed to the DJ Hardy Ardy Beesemer, who described it in the following way: "Gabberhouse could be compared to hardcore punk: easy to make at home, purely technological, rough and very energetic because of its high tempo" (Rietveld 1998: 86). The music was characterized by hard driving beats at between 150 to 210 b.p.m. (beats per minute).

Gabberhouse became increasingly associated not with Amsterdam but instead with the industrial city of Rotterdam and specifically with club Parkzicht, where Rotterdam football fans tended to congregate. However, the development of gabberhouse in Rotterdam was not accidental and many commentators have argued that the hardcore flavor of the music was influenced by the characteristics of the people of Rotterdam. As Rietveld (1998) notes, "With its working-class tradition of being no-nonsense and 'straightforward', the hardcore attitude, as opposed to soulful gentleness, suited its population better" (Rietveld 1998: 91). The style of dancing associated with gabberhouse adopted characteristics from movements displayed by fans of Feyenoord (Rotterdam's football team). "Gabbers from Rotterdam danced like they were riding a horse, a movement which was reported to be used on football terraces the year before" (Rietveld 1998: 82). This type of dancing was called "hakkuh," chopping (Verhagen *et al.* 2000). Not only did the music reflect the characteristics of the people of Rotterdam, it also, according to Rietveld, reflected the industrial nature of Rotterdam itself. The sounds of Rotterdam city with its "noises of pile drivers and circle saws ... and the sounds produced by tugs, boats and cranes on the busy river Maas" (Rietveld 1998: 91) was evident in the "super-fast brutal beats [and] speed metal riffs" of the music. But while the origins of gabberhouse began in Rotterdam and its culture, its influence soon spread, and by 1997 gabber music dominated the Dutch music scene and it ruled the Top 40 charts in the Netherlands.

It is not only the music that differs in the Rotterdam scene, but the drugs favored by young people within these scenes as well, when we compare Rotterdam club-drug users with those in Hong Kong and San Francisco. While all three sample populations were similar in their high rates of use of marijuana and ecstasy, the Rotterdam sample reported by far the highest rates of cocaine, methamphetamine, and poppers use (73 percent, 67 percent, and 50 percent respectively). The most striking of those differences is with poppers, which was used by half (50 percent) of all Rotterdam respondents versus only 12 percent of San Francisco respondents; no Hong Kong respondents reported any lifetime poppers use. Like respondents in San Francisco, Rotterdam respondents reported relatively high rates of mushrooms use; however, very few (17 percent) reported having ever tried LSD, which was used by more than half (59 percent) of the San Francisco sample. No Rotterdam respondents had ever used PCP, which was used by a small number of respondents in both San Francisco and Hong Kong (8 percent and 2 percent respectively), and, as was the case with Hong Kong respondents, relatively few reported having tried MDA, 2CB, DXM, and amphetamines. While respondents in Rotterdam reported having tried on average more substances other than alcohol than respondents in Hong Kong (five substances versus three substances), they still reported lower rates of drug experimentation than respondents in San Francisco, who had tried, on average, seven drugs.

The internal developments within the dance scene in the Netherlands and specifically Rotterdam transformed the original UK-inspired dance-music scene, but its influence did not remain within the confines of the country but instead began to spread outside its borders and into other parts of Europe. Soon it became particularly popular in Italy, Belgium, Switzerland, Germany, and the Czech Republic. The Rotterdam dance scene is clearly involved in global cultural exchange and influence, both shaping and being shaped by the contours and specific practices of other international scenes. Yet, at the same time, the Rotterdam scene remains distinct, embodying an ethos, musical style, and dance-club practices unique to its particular history, social background, and cultural styles. Just as the drug-using practices featuring ketamine in Hong Kong differ in important ways from that of other international club-drug scenes, the music and dance of Rotterdam retain their unique elements, despite the flow of global cultural capital across national borders. The San Francisco scene, to which we devote most of this book, is found within this same global cultural nexus – and, like these other scenes, is also shaped by the particular social contexts in which it is embedded – shaped for example by the national US media and public policy context analyzed in the next chapter and the particular policy and cultural elements of San Francisco's nighttime economy, examined in the chapter after that.

Conclusion

The development of the electronic dance music scene geared primarily to young people is now established in all parts of the globe. From its tentative beginnings at club Shoom in south London and the one-off illegal events to the development of megaclubs like the Ministry of Sound in London and Manumission in Ibiza, the scene has become a multimillion-dollar enterprise in which large-scale corporations earn huge profits. From DJ Alfredo's development of the Balearic sound, which appeared initially so shocking, to the cultural absorption of electronic dance music into everyday life, it is clear that the once oppositional cultural commodities have gone from being part of a subculture to an accepted part of the mainstream.

Part of the scene's initial impact and its continuing success as a global phenomenon have been its association with a range of illicit substances. In fact, marketing the scene also meant marketing illegal drugs, especially ecstasy, and the belief that a "chemical generation" had developed. However, while sociologists, anthropologists, and cultural studies researchers have examined in much detail the development of globalization and the extent to which a global youth culture has emerged, researchers in the drug field have spent much less time examining the global nature of drugs and the dance scene. While they have certainly identified regional variations, they have neglected to examine the extent to which the meaning of drug use within these youthful events contains both similarities and dissimilarities.

In tracing the way in which the global and universal features of the dance scene have been adapted and modified by local characteristics, whether in terms of the nighttime economy, musical preferences, specific dance styles, or preferred forms of intoxication, we have utilized data from our comparative qualitative research in two very different social settings, namely Rotterdam and Hong Kong, and next we turn to the American context generally, and to the San Francisco context specifically. While there are many important historical and cultural specificities to the San Francisco setting, these particularities must be viewed against the broader global backdrop established within this chapter.

Chapter 4

Youth, US drug policy, and social control of the dance scene

Starting with a highly indeterminate space/time unit (the rave or even vaguer the party) and with an amorphous set of substances (date rape drugs, club drugs) and placing them in a circular relationship to one another [we] end up with a conglomerate of risks of truly frightening proportions.

(D. Moore and Valverde 2000: 520)

Introduction

On April 30, 2003, President George W. Bush signed into the law the Illicit Drug Anti-Proliferation Act of 2003,[1] previously named the RAVE (Reducing Americans' Vulnerability to Ecstasy) Act (S. 2633, 107th). This was the third piece of legislation enacted since the start of the new millennium designed to target drug use and the nighttime dance scene. This law was the culmination of concerns which arose in the mid to late 1990s as a result of an increase in young people's involvement in using ecstasy and attending rave parties. Given the upsurge in the media publicity surrounding raves and club drugs, numerous claims makers (politicians, law enforcement, anti-drug associations, concerned parents, government agencies and local authority representatives) argued that the country faced a growing drug epidemic centered around raves. Issues of risk, threat, and danger dominated official discourses about raves and club drugs. In fact the two main Senate hearings on the problems of ecstasy in 2000 and 2001 were respectively titled "Ecstasy: Underestimating the Threat" and "America at Risk: The Ecstasy Threat." According to politicians and law enforcement officials, steps needed to be taken quickly in order to curb the drug epidemic among young people and to protect a future "generation of leaders."

In passing the Illicit Drug Anti-Proliferation Act, President Bush and Congress followed the earlier steps taken by the British Parliament in 1994 when the Criminal Justice and Public Order Act became law, which made raves illegal in the UK. Like the UK authorities, US politicians accepted the argument that raves were, as then Senator Joseph Biden noted, "havens for illicit drug use" (Biden 2002); in these accounts raves are reduced to nothing more than venues for the dispersal and consumption of drugs, especially ecstasy. The relationship between illicit drugs, music, and dancing is not new and consequently it was not too surprising that lawmakers should have emphasized the connection. In earlier periods, drugs, music, and dance had been intertwined, for example the use of cocaine and marijuana in the jazz era of the 1920s and 1930s (Berridge 1988; Holiday 1956), and the use of LSD and psychedelic music in the 1960s (Joyson 1984; Stevens 1987; Winick 1960).

However, what was more significant – in the wording of the Acts, in the Senate hearings and testimony about the Acts, and in the media coverage surrounding both the RAVE Act and the Illicit Drug Anti-Proliferation Act – was the extent to which the official and dominant discourse characterized dance events as inherently spaces of "excess risk" (D. Moore and Valverde 2000: 528) which needed to be controlled and regulated (Hier 2002). In this chapter we analyze the official constructions of risk in the arenas of the media and the political/legal sphere. Later, in Chapter 7, we return to the issue of risk, examining how it operates in the particular experiences of the young men and women themselves involved in the dance scene so under scrutiny.

Official discourses of risk

Within the official constructions of risk, as D. Moore and Valverde (2000) have noted in another context, officials and concerned individuals constructed a homogeneous notion of a dance event which lumped together under the heading of raves a wide range of different types of nighttime dance events. This includes upscale and fashionable nightclubs, one-off unofficial and unlicensed raves held in disused buildings or abandoned spaces, and a wide range of private parties held in hotels or apartments. Collapsing all of these events into a single category obviates the important differences in culture and ethos that characterize each of these settings. Just as different types of dance events were collapsed under the single heading of raves, so also was a wide range of different illicit substances – ecstasy, GHB, Rohypnol, ketamine, methamphetamine, and LSD, each with its own distinct set of pharmacological effects – all enclosed under the quasi-scientific umbrella term of "club drugs"[2] (or, in other instances, all drug use in the rave scenes gets reduced to ecstasy use). "Club drugs" becomes a "category of governance even though its content cannot be either legally or pharmacologically identified" (D. Moore and Valverde 2000: 523). As D. Moore and Valverde (2000) remarked, the fact that in many of these nighttime venues both alcohol and marijuana are also consumed in large quantities is never acknowledged. This socially constructed risk discourse is "focusing on the social space of the rave coalesced with one centered on illegal drug ab/use" (Hier 2002: 36). However, while the events and substances may be diverse and wide-ranging, the official discourse contains only two common elements. First, the focus is on events attended primarily by adolescents and young adults and, second, these events take place at night. The combining of youth and nightlife has meant that these "space-times [were] thought to be fraught with sexual and pharmacological risks" (D. Moore and Valverde 2000: 516). Moreover, this focusing on dance events and drugs has the effect of identifying "raves as the core site of youth drug activity and confirms this youthful arena as the legitimate site of public and policy concern" (Giulianotti 1997: 427).

This perspective, developed by government agencies, "politico-moral entrepreneurs" (Reinarman 1997) and other interest groups, warning of the hazards and dangers connected with dance events and drugs, has become, as we will see in the legislation, coupled with law enforcement strategies to curtail such activities. In fact, one of the key moral entrepreneurs was the Drug Enforcement Administration (DEA), which possessed a "high media profile" (Crichter 2003). As Jenkins has noted, "News reporting of drug issues over the last quarter century has largely consisted of reprinting or paraphrasing DEA press releases" (Jenkins 1999: 21). A dominant theme to emerge, having joined together raves and drugs, is for these interest groups to emphasize that "the legal powers enjoyed by agents of social control are potentially insufficient for dealing with the scale of drug activity" (Giulianotti 1997: 427). New powers need to be provided to law enforcement to handle the new threat. The reduction of raves to drug use, and of ecstasy to use in raves, and the association of all of these with risk and danger, have become so common and deep-seated in these discourses as to comprise an almost unquestionable common sense, an assumption that is taken for granted and asserted but rarely completely backed up by evidence, in the discourses leading up to the passage of these laws. Alternative perspectives and voices are glaringly absent in these accounts. Decoupling raves from club drugs (treating these as related yet independent) and problematizing the presumed uniformity and homogeneity of these categories is important to consider if we are to truly understand the processes by which claims makers ensure that their views of youthful activities, and only theirs, are dominant and enforced.

Consequently, an examination of the hearings, the legislation, and the media accounts is an important contemporary illustration of the ways in which youthful activities become demonized and then criminalized. While the avowed aim of the legislation, according to its proponents, was to protect young people from a host of possible criminal activities, including, according to DEA administrator Donnie Marshall, "rape, property damage, gang violence, drug sales, robberies, assaults and murder" (US Congress Senate Caucus on International Narcotics Control 2001a: 32), the actual effects of the legislation, at least at one level, was to increase controls on young people's ability to enjoy youthful leisure activities. Indeed, the legislation targets not only illicit drug use but also rave parties more generally and the items and accoutrements associated with this youth subculture or scene. Under the guise of protecting young people, policy makers targeted and curtailed social and leisure activities and the cultural expression of many young people. Furthermore, an examination of those who presented evidence at the official Senate hearings highlights the extent to which organizations or individuals representing either young people or those involved in organizing rave events were absent. The voices of the consumers (the young dancers and attendees of raves) or the producers (DJs, party promoters) were silent in the official proceedings (though their voices can be heard in the protests to the Acts that followed their introduction). The absence of an insider perspective is not altogether surprising; adult concerns with and attempts to control youthful practices have been witnessed many times before, and rarely have the authorities listened to the voices of young people (Griffin 1993). The discussions that led up to the passing of the Illicit Drug Anti-Proliferation Act are also important in order to understand the way in which the latest "drug scare" (Reinarman 1997) developed. The manner in which the hearings took place and the choice of those invited to present evidence is an important case study to examine in more detail, if only to understand how the authorities, in attempting to close down what the *New York Times* called "the most significant and innovative American youth dance culture today" (Samuels 2000), revealed "a trenchant fear of youth transcendence" (St. John 2004: 5).

Given the focus of the Illicit Drug Anti-Proliferation Act and the aim of politicians and law enforcement officials to close down raves, just as they had in the UK, we were surprised to find that these pieces of legislation have not received more coverage within the extant sociological and cultural studies literature. Other than a few articles in law journals (Dore 2002; Haas 2005; Kardan 2003; Levy 2004; Sachdev 2004) and a couple of references in the social science literature, little discussion has taken place. While the law-journal articles have importantly focused on whether the Illicit Drug Anti-Proliferation Act is unconstitutional, due to its overreach and its possibilities for stifling free expression, many important sociological issues connected to this legislation remain unexplored. The coalescing of fears about drugs and fears about youth would seem an important contemporary development. The absence of any significant sociological literature on this legislation and its potential impact on young people is in sharp contrast with the available literature in the UK, where a more extensive sociological and cultural criminology discussion has taken place (Manning 2007; Presdee 2000).

While researchers in the UK have had longer to consider the implications of the Criminal Justice and Public Order Act of 1994, the absence of an available literature in the US may therefore tell us something about the contemporary state of youth studies and drug research in America today. With this in mind, the aim of this chapter is to contribute to an area of contemporary youth and drug policy as yet largely unexplored and to examine the ways in which a significant form of drug policy legislation came to be enacted. In doing so, we can begin to situate the individual experiences of the young men and women we interviewed. Furthermore, we will explore the broader context of national policies of control and the media depictions of the scenes in which they are involved.

Ecstasy and the development of raves in the US

By the beginning of 2000 the use of ecstasy (MDMA) and other drugs associated with nighttime dance events had increased in the US since 1998 and with this had grown an escalation in concern over and interest in their use. According to the Federal Drug Identification Network (FDIN) database, over 12 million tablets of MDMA were seized, a tenfold increase over the 1.2 million seized the previous year (US Congress Senate Caucus on International Narcotics Control 2001a: 47). The DEA also estimated that the US was now the largest consumer of MDMA, followed by Britain (ibid.). In the same year the DEA seized 2,155 methamphetamine labs, an increase from 1,627 in 1998 (Drug Enforcement Administration 2000). Reports of increases in other club drugs had also been noted. For example, the Community Epidemiology Work Group (CEWG) reported that Rohypnol was becoming one of the fastest-growing drug problems in the US (Community Epidemiology Work Group 1995). However, "since legislation of recent years," reports of its use were declining in CEWG areas by 2001 (Community Epidemiology Work Group 2001). Overall these increases reflected, according to law enforcement and public health officials, the recent growth in the popularity of these drugs for adolescents and young adults.

According to the Monitoring the Future study, lifetime ecstasy use increased for college students from 2 percent in 1991 to 13 percent in 2001. For young adults the percentages for the same time period rose from 3 percent to 11.6 percent. However, since 2001 ecstasy use among eighth, tenth, and twelfth-grade students had begun to decline.[3]

In concert with the increasing use of club drugs, incidences of associated problems had also escalated. According to the Drug Abuse Warning Network (DAWN), estimates of hospital emergency room mentions for MDMA rose from 319 in 1996, and 637 in 1997, to 1,143 in 1998 (Drug Abuse Warning Network 2004). From 1994 to 2002 hospital emergency room mentions for MDMA rose from 253 to 4,026. In addition, emergency room mentions of GHB increased from fifty-six in 1994 to 3,330 in 2002. Emergency room mentions of Rohypnol also increased from 1994 to 1998, although specific numbers are unavailable. Emergency room mentions of LSD dropped from 5,158 in 1994 to 891 in 2002, although mentions increased from 4,982 in 1998 to 5,126 in 1999 (ibid.).

While the upsurge in the use of these drugs may be attributed to a number of factors, researchers have argued that a strong association exists between their current use and the popularity of dance events, particularly raves. In many of these accounts it is clear that illicit drugs are a central component of raves, and writers have emphasized the extent to which the development of raves has coincided with an increase in ecstasy and other drug use. In fact a number of researchers and popular writers have gone as far as to suggest that it was this combination of drugs, especially ecstasy, dancing, and the environment of the event that made the scene so popular and attractive to young people. Clearly, the rise of raves and the rise of club drugs (and perhaps declines in both) are deeply interconnected. We would not wish to suggest otherwise – and indeed, in the first chapter of this book we have criticized cultural studies scholars for not sufficiently attending to the importance of drugs when studying these youth subcultures. Yet, at the same time, we will suggest that it is also misleading to completely reduce ecstasy to raves or raves to ecstasy use. But, in order to understand the background to the legislation, we need also to examine, not solely the use of ecstasy and other drugs, but also the development of raves in the US.

In the previous chapter we focused on the global dance scene and its history and in Chapter 5 we will hone in on San Francisco's particular history of nightlife, raves, and dance clubs. This chapter, however, focuses generally on the US context more broadly – specifically on the level of policy and legislation. Providing an overview of raves in the US is difficult, for two reasons. First, in the same way that sociological discussions of the legislation are rare, so also are discussions of the development of American raves. While the UK rave scene has been extensively documented and dissected for many years now, considerably less scholarly attention has been paid to the rave scene in the US. Instead of gleaning information from a body of sociological literature, information about raves in the US has to be taken from a few significant accounts by music writers and dance-event commentators. Second, because of the geographical and sociocultural heterogeneity of the US, it is difficult to generalize about raves for the entire country and instead what becomes clear is that the development of raves in, for example, New York, was significantly different from developments in San Francisco, or Florida, or the Midwest. Consequently, within this chapter we provide only a brief and incomplete snapshot of raves in different parts of the US.

The growth of electronic dance music and dance parties in the US is generally attributed to developments in Britain from the late 1980s and early 1990s. In certain cases it is certainly correct that both the scene in the UK and specific DJs had an important effect on the early manifestations of the rave scene in the US. However, although the UK scene played a significant role, the origins of electronic dance music and the incorporation of MDMA to enhance the impact of dance music began not in the UK but, as we showed in the last chapter, in the US. As we saw, much of the music identified today as rave music can be traced back to Chicago's urban dance music "house," "techno" music from Detroit, and "garage" music from New York (Foderaro 1988). And as we will discuss in the next chapter, it can be argued that the beginning of raves themselves can be traced to developments in the mid-1960s in San Francisco (J. Beck and Rosenbaum 1994).

By 1991 the British "rave scene" started to move back to the US. In New York early raves called STORMraves (Reynolds 1999) took place in woods or other abandoned areas in the neighborhood of Queens. These early manifestations of raves had by 1992 moved from the outer boroughs of New York to Manhattan and were held in well-known nightclubs such as the Palladium, the Limelight Club, and the Tunnel. The latter two were closed in 1996 after a DEA investigation "alleged the existence of a 'drug supermarket' where massive amounts of ecstasy, as well as cocaine, the animal tranquilizer ketamine and the depressant Rohypnol were used as promotional tools to lure patrons to the club" (Jenkins 1999: 166; see also Owen 2003).

On the west coast the development of the rave scene can be attributed in part to "British expatriates" in San Francisco and Los Angeles (Reynolds 1999; Silcott 1999). San Francisco's early raves tended to have a spiritual flavor (sometimes of a Mother Earth bent, other times distinctly cyber-influenced) (Silcott 1999), whereas Los Angeles's were more fashion-conscious and explicitly hedonistic in tone (Reynolds 1999). San Francisco's early importance in the dance-club scene has been attributed to a number of elements, including its role in the 1960s psychedelic movement, the prominence of San Francisco's gay community and clubs, and finally a good supply of drugs from west-coast labs. In addition to these two areas, raves also developed in other parts of the US: the most significant, according to Reynolds (1999) and Silcott (1999), were that of Milwaukee, other parts of the Midwest, and Florida. According to these commentators, raves known as the "Further" series, took place in the wilds of Wisconsin, starting in 1994 and continued until 1998. Also raves in Orlando, Florida, began in 1991 and Florida soon competed with California as the No. 1 rave state in the US.

Writers such as Reynolds have argued that raves in the US never really became established in the way they had in the UK, noting that raves had a hard time "establishing roots in America ... [and consequently] never became a mass working-class movement" (Reynolds 1999: 314); raves, in the US, certainly never achieved the status of the predominant site of youth culture, as they arguably did in the UK. Yet raves did become a significant site of social expression, consumption, and leisure for many American youth. And, certainly, reaction by local authorities (police or government officials) increased dramatically during the late 1990s – even while the number of raves – at least in their prototypical form of unofficial, underground parties – had already begun to decline (in part as a result of increased local controls). For example, according to the Department of Justice *Informational Bulletin*, "cities such as Chicago, Denver, Gainsville, Hartford, Milwaukee, and New York ... reduced rave activity through enforcement of juvenile curfews, fire codes, health and safety ordinances, liquor laws and licensing requirements for large public gatherings" (National Drug Intelligence Center 2001: 5). In Chicago, promoters, club owners and even performers could face a fine of $10,000 for participating in an unlicensed rave, and in Seattle the authorities passed a teen dance ordinance which required that children under 18 be accompanied to raves by a parent (Eliscu 2001). This is precisely the time when the federal government began to curb ecstasy and raves.

Congressional legislation

As Philip Jenkins shows in his book *Synthetic Panics* (1999), the media coverage around ecstasy and other "club drugs" had been gaining momentum since 1993. In 2000 alone "the media had produced no less than 1,000 print and electronic stories ... the vast majority alarmist" on ecstasy (Rosenbaum 2002: 139). While ecstasy was clearly identified as the " 'quintessential' rave drug," much of the initial focus that inspired drug legislation at the turn of the twenty-first century was on two other substances: GHB (gamma-hydroxy-butyrate) and Rohypnol (flunitrazepam). Although Rohypnol was also mentioned in the subsequent Act which outlawed GHB, it had already come under federal control in 1996 under the Drug Induced Rape Prevention and Punishment Act of 1996 (H.R. 4137, 104th). Consequently most of the discussion at the hearings prior to the passing of the Hillory J. Farias and Samantha Reid Date-rape Drug Prohibition Act of 2000 (H.R. 2130, 106th)[4] centered on GHB.

GHB, a naturally occurring neurotransmitter, had been legally available (especially via Internet sales) and widely used as a nutritional supplement found in health food stores. It had also been found to stimulate the release of a growth hormone, which likely accounts for its popularity among body builders (Jenkins 1999). Partly as a result of this popularity with the body-building fraternity, GHB began to be used in the gay club circuit and then in the general club scene. In addition to its ability, at lower doses, to relieve anxiety and produce relaxation, users of GHB especially enjoyed the "empathogen" aspects of the substance: features similar to those attributed to ecstasy, and hence its popular name "liquid ecstasy." Furthermore, GHB has "fewer consequences in terms of serotonin depletion, dehydration, and subsequent depression, and jaw-clenching" (Barker *et al.* unpublished). While some consumers report feeling energized by GHB, more comment on "enjoying the loss of social inhibitions, enhancement of tactile sensation, sexual stimulation, and the mild hallucinations that sometimes accompany GHB ingestion" (Barker *et al.* n.d.). In spite of its popularity for providing these pleasure-giving, ecstasy-like properties, GHB soon became identified in media accounts with possessing a totally different feature. Although GHB had been attracting some bad publicity, partly as a result of being identified, wrongly as it later transpired, as the cause of death of the actor River Phoenix in 1993, it was not until 1996 that media attention transformed its primary purpose. GHB became identified as a "rape weapon" (Jenkins 1999) because of its ability to render "women unconscious for sexual purposes." "It's the perfect crime in a pill" (Oprah Winfrey 1996, quoted in Jenkins 1999: 167 and in D. Moore and Valverde 2000). This change in the drug's perceived purpose – from that of a pleasure-giving substance to a dangerous weapon used on unsuspecting women by predatory men – appears to have stemmed from the publicity surrounding the death of one teenager in Texas. In 1996 Hillory J. Farias died, according to the newspaper reports, from GHB contained in a bottle of soda which she had consumed while spending an evening at a dance club. According to the initial coroner's report she had died as a result of someone putting GHB in her drink, with the implication of someone sexually assaulting her. Although subsequent investigations revealed that little or no GHB was in her body, and certainly not enough to cause her death,[5] nor was anyone ever charged with deliberately lacing her drink, she nevertheless became a *cause célèbre* and an important case for the media's subsequent labeling of GHB as a date-rape drug.

The second incident that provoked significant media coverage involved another teenage girl, Samantha Reid, from Michigan, who also supposedly died from a GHB overdose in 1999. In this case, an autopsy did reveal the presence of GHB, but the medical examiner also found significant levels of alcohol and THC. However, unlike in the case of Ms. Farias, rape was never suggested, as the three young men who were indicted were charged not with sexual assault but with manslaughter. They were initially found guilty, but the conviction was subsequently overturned by an Appeals Court judge. The media handling of these two cases illustrates the way in which in the media engage in what Reinarman has called the "routinization of caricature," by which he means the media process of "recrafting worst cases into typical cases and the episodic into the epidemic" (1997: 101). Moreover, the media's interest in stimulating anxiety in the public concerning drugs and young women can be traced back, at least in the UK, to the early 1900s (Kohn 1992). As Blackman points out, "The media representations ... are meant to be disturbing ... The charm and beauty in these girls' faces calls out for us to condemn drugs as the suggested cause of their death" (2004: 171). However, the focus is not only on the innocents at risk; "There is usually a role for the 'evil' individual seeking to lead 'innocents' astray" (Manning 2007: 160). In the case of GHB, the evildoer is the unspecified male, whether friend or stranger.

As a result of these incidences and the media attention, the deaths of these two young women became symbolic of the sexual and pharmacological dangers of taking "club drugs." They became the US equivalent of Leah Betts[6] and received the dubious honor of having their names on the subsequent Date-rape Drug Prohibition Act, signed into law by President Clinton in 2000. As a result of the media and political campaigns, the Act outlawed GHB by reclassifying it as a

Schedule 1 drug. As one commentator remarked, GHB became illegal "not because of its actual effects but because of its alleged or even potential role in date rape" (Reilly 2001).

The passing of the Date-rape Prohibition Act was followed closely by the Children's Health Act of 2000 (H.R. 4365, 106th), within which were contained two anti-drug Acts: the Ecstasy Anti-Proliferation Act of 2000 and the Methamphetamine Anti-Proliferation Act of 2000. For the purposes of this chapter, we will focus only on the former. Prior to its enactment, a hearing ("Ecstasy: Underestimating the Threat") took place earlier in the year. It was held by the Senate Caucus on International Narcotics Control, an entity then respectively chaired and cochaired by Senators Charles Grassley and Joseph Biden. While both Grassley and Biden organized the event, Senators Grassley and Caucus member Bob Graham made the opening statements.[7] At the hearing, evidence was given by interested people, the majority of whom were representatives of different branches of federal enforcement offices. These included the Office of National Drug Control Policy, based in the White House; the International Narcotics and Law Enforcement Affairs, part of the Department of State; the Drug Enforcement Administration (DEA); and the US Customs Service. Two other individuals were chosen to give evidence: one was the Assistant Director of the Center for Drug and Alcohol studies at the University of Delaware and the other, the sister of an "ecstasy victim."

In the opening comments Senators Grassley and Graham set the tone of the hearings. Grassley stated that the drug ecstasy was extremely dangerous and that they must "fight" ecstasy "before it explodes any further ... Ecstasy is out there. It's time we stop it" (US Congress Senate Caucus on International Narcotics Control 2001a: 3). Senator Graham quickly confirmed this statement, noting that in his state (Florida), "in the first four months of this year, there have already been six deaths directly attributed to ecstasy" (ibid.: 8). Following these opening statements, each of the witnesses began, in very similar ways, to describe the extent of the ecstasy epidemic and the importance of quickly controlling it. For example, the DEA representative, George Cazenavette, said that "the increasing use of synthetic or club drugs ... by our youth is quickly becoming one of the most significant law enforcement and social issues facing our nation today" (ibid.: 42). He went on to establish the connection between ecstasy and the club scene by informing the Caucus that ecstasy's ability to suppress the need to eat, drink, and sleep meant that it enabled "club scene users to endure all-night and sometimes two to three-day parties" (ibid.: 43). Because "club drugs" had become an integral part of the rave scene, there was little "attempt to conceal their use" (ibid.: 45).

Dr. Vereen, the representative from the Office of National Drug Control Policy at the White House, further emphasized the increasing use and dangers of ecstasy and its connection to raves. He described how raves had chillout rooms – "large lounge areas where attendees can lay and hold each other" – some specifically designated for sex (US Congress Senate Caucus on International Narcotics Control 2001a: 21). His evidence emphasized the sexual component of ecstasy by noting its use in risky behavior. "With one's mood altered and reasoning faculties impaired, such experimentation often results in unprotected sex, sex with multiple partners, unwanted pregnancy, and sexually transmitted disease including hepatitis and HIV" (ibid.). Here we see the way in which sexual and pharmacological risks are brought together, thereby confirming raves as "spaces of excess risk" (D. Moore and Valverde 2000: 528).

In concluding his evidence, he warned the Caucus members that although the use of ecstasy was "often associated with the underground 'Rave youth subculture,'" the real problem was not just one type of event but young people in general wherever they might congregate (US Congress Senate Caucus on International Narcotics Control 2001a: 19). In this, he explicitly stated the subtext of most of the testimonies: youth are vulnerable, involved in risk-taking, in need of protection, and, most important, requiring external control. Young people were portrayed as both gullible and highly vulnerable to drug sellers, who could easily seduce them into buying and consuming drugs. Drug dealers were able to target young people, according to the Office of National Drug Control Policy, and snare them into buying drugs by attracting them "with a seemingly positive message." The message was based on the latest hip philosophies, including "New Age, Zen, self-awareness, Harmony with Nature and other philosophies" (ibid.). In this hearing connected to the Ecstasy Anti-Proliferation Act of 2000 we see a specific type of discourse dominating the debate, a discourse that will also be found throughout the vast majority of testimony supporting both the RAVE Act and the Illicit Drug Anti-Proliferation Act. In these discourses, youth are inherently vulnerable, portrayed as passive victims in need of control and protection, raves are inherently risky spaces that are out of control and worthy of dismantlement, and everything at raves is either the result of or for the purpose of facilitating drug use.

Having set the right tone for prohibition and control, and with the hearing completed, the Ecstasy Anti-Proliferation Act became law. As a result, the US Sentencing Commission, at Congress's behest, changed the sentencing guidelines for the manufacture, importation, or trafficking of MDMA, raising the minimum sentences from "just over one year to five years for possession of 200 grams of MDMA and from three years to ten years for 2,000 grams" (Rosenbaum 2002: 140). It also authorized increased funding for school-based programs and community-based prevention programs to target MDMA, related drugs, and other drugs referred to as "club drugs." Although the original Bill had been touted as one that would add significant money to research, the bulk of the $245 million allocated went to law enforcement, with only $1.5 million going to research (Rosenbaum 2002). Finally, because of the increasing worry about unofficial Web sites, especially those that discussed the effects of ecstasy and production of ecstasy as well as the "locations of ecstasy use" (in other words, raves), the law instructed all federal departments to develop "appropriate" Web sites where anti-drug messages could be placed.

The Illicit Drug Anti-Proliferation Act, the final piece of legislation, was passed close on the heels of the other two. It began life as the 2002 RAVE (Reducing Americans' Vulnerability to Ecstasy) Act. Unlike the previously discussed legislation, which targeted specific drugs (GHB, ecstasy), the focus of the proposed RAVE Act (as its initial name implies) was not directly drugs; rather, the Act targeted raves and rave organizers/operators as dangerous in and of themselves, due to raves' presumed purpose of spreading club drugs to young people. As with the Ecstasy

Anti-Proliferation Act, a hearing was convened by the Senate Caucus on International Narcotics Control. Called "America at Risk: The Ecstasy Threat," it took place in 2001 and was again organized by then Caucus chairman Senator Grassley and cochairman Senator Biden.[8] As in the previous hearing, the witnesses were chosen primarily from federal and local law enforcement agencies. These included the Office of National Drug Control Policy; the Drug Enforcement Administration (DEA); the US Customs Service; the Florida Office of Drug Control; the Delaware Police Department, and the US Sentencing Commission. In addition, the Director of the Gateway Community Services – a residential and outpatient treatment and rehabilitation center for addiction based in Florida – was chosen, along with two "recovering" teenagers who had used ecstasy.

Significantly enough, given the above discussion on the manipulation of public anxiety around young women with drugs, Senator Grassley opened the proceedings by discussing the case of Brittney Chambers, a 16-year-old girl from Boulder, Colorado. She died from hyponatremia six days after taking ecstasy and consuming, according to Senator Grassley, "three gallons of water in forty-five minutes" (US Congress Senate Caucus on International Narcotics Control 2001b: 3). Senator Biden later emphasized the connection between ecstasy, club drugs, and "all-night dance parties." He criticized two magazine articles, one in *Time* and the other in the *New York Times Magazine*, the latter of which suggested that ecstasy could lead to "greater self-awareness." He disparaged these pieces by noting, "If you believe what you read in *Time* and the *New York Times Magazine*, you would think that ecstasy is the key to enlightenment" (ibid.: 23). Interestingly enough, Biden singled out two articles which were unusual in that unlike many, many others they had not adopted an alarmist stance against using ecstasy. In so doing, Senator Biden established from the outset at these hearings that such perspectives were absurd or out of bounds.

The Office of National Drug Control Policy's representative was the opening witness and he began, somewhat surprisingly, given other witnesses' attempts to tie the use of the drug to late-night events, by arguing that ecstasy use was no longer confined to the rave scene but had expanded "from nightclubs and raves to high schools, the streets, neighborhoods, and open venues" (ibid.: 11). While suggesting that ecstasy may not be so inextricably tied to raves, a connection made by all the other main witnesses and in the proposed legislation, there was still no real space or discussion for acknowledging or understanding (much less combating) so-called club-drug use in non-club (or rave) settings. By so tightly coupling raves and ecstasy there appeared to be a blindness to those other possible contexts in which they are decoupled.

Following this testimony, "two teenagers who have used ecstasy" gave evidence. Both teenagers were clients of a treatment center, whose headquarters were in New York. Vinnie, the first teenager, admitted that he had "experimented with ecstasy three times" and as a result it had made him "just want to go to a party and get into some trouble" (US Congress Senate Caucus on International Narcotics Control 2001b: 16). He, like other witnesses, associated ecstasy with clubs and noted security at these venues should be increased. He also supported the idea of penalties being increased, noting that "If people saw that the penalty was worse and more busts were being made, I feel that the ecstasy's quantity would lessen drastically. I feel ecstasy is overlooked and needs to be dealt with, with more force" (ibid.).

Michelle, the second teenager to give evidence, admitted that she had tried many drugs but the one she "liked the most was ecstasy" (ibid.). Supporting the notion that young people and especially young girls are highly vulnerable, she explained how she had been introduced to ecstasy by her boyfriend, who had told her "that it was amazing and that I would really feel better" (ibid.). This proved to be true, at least for her, as she admitted that "Everything was wonderful and I had no inhibitions." Unfortunately, what her boyfriend had not told her was that she would want to take ecstasy all the time. "After a while, I felt as though I would not be able to live without it. I began to steal things from my parents and cut classes so that I could get high" (ibid.). Today, however, although she is now sober, she still misses ecstasy: "I miss the peaceful feelings and the illusion that everything is okay." These two young people were the sole representatives of a "youth perspective" in the hearings and it is interesting to note that, although both teenagers were attending drug treatment services, they were nevertheless chosen as representative witnesses.

The DEA representative then gave his evidence and began by confirming the importance of the title of the hearings and emphasized that "America is *indeed* at risk, and ecstasy has shown itself to be a formidable threat" (author's emphasis) (US Congress Senate Caucus on International Narcotics Control 2001b: 32). Raves, he argued, were a lucrative business and frequently the sites for crimes such as "pharmaceutical diversion, rape, property damage, gang violence, drug sales, robberies, assaults, and murder" (ibid.). He did not, however, present evidence of these sensational links. Raves were particularly pernicious because many of them were "advertised as 'alcohol-free,'" giving partygoers and parents a false sense of security" (ibid.: 33). (Thus ignoring, or showing little awareness of, the ways that such events are often much less violence-prone or sexually charged [and sexual harassment-filled] than many typically alcohol-fueled nighttime events – a point made again and again in young people's comparative discussions of raves and clubs, as we will show in Chapter 10 – a point missing from any of these official discourses.) The connection between ecstasy and raves was established further by the representative of the US Customs Service, who argued that the primary and "obvious" motive of club owners is to "help traffickers push ecstasy." According to this official, because organizers "are in it for the money … it is not surprising that we have seen them come under the spell of organized crime" (ibid.: 43). Discourses such as this confirm the point that drug use at raves is neither incidental nor even merely tolerated, but actively promoted, and indeed even aggressively pushed, by party organizers and all those involved. The witness concluded by noting that drug traffickers were assisted not only by club owners but also, according to him, by an "unlikely source": social scientists and "others in the so-called 'harm reduction' movement who claim that the real damage is caused not by ecstasy and its pushers, but by the laws designed to curtail them" (ibid.: 41). He noted that social scientists had fueled the myth that "American law enforcement is out to criminalize the 'harmless' experimental behavior of a whole generation of young Americans" (ibid.). This antipathy toward harm-reduction efforts can be seen elsewhere in the fact that practices such as providing water for sale and having paramedics on standby, in case of emergency, has been used as evidence of drug facilitation and collusion on the part of rave organizers in the prosecutions brought against them (Kardan 2003). This Customs representative stressed the fact that law enforcement was not there to "jail teenagers who make the mistake of experimenting with ecstasy" but instead their aim was to jail the traffickers and their partners in crime (US Congress Senate Caucus on International Narcotics Control 2001b: 41). However, while the question of who, exactly, are traffickers' "partners in crime" remains unclear, at least for those who gave evidence at the hearing, the answer is clear: it is the rave organizers and promoters. The result of the testimony and the subsequent Act was to automatically tarnish all organizers of rave events (and even those who own the property that raves are held on) with that label.

Finally, in the testimony given by a police officer from the Delaware Police Department, we witness the first admittance that raves are part of a distinctive youth subculture whose meanings and practices may not be readily understandable by adults. The police officer complained, somewhat plaintively, that investigating the "subcultures" of raves was particularly difficult because many of his officers "investigating drug crime are well into their twenties, and are unable to associate in this society of young adults" (ibid.: 95). Because it was a subculture of young people, he and his officers had to learn about all the "specific colors, brands of clothing, jewelry, and clothing styles" which signified whether a person was looking to get high or looking to sell drugs. Furthermore, because much of this information was "communicated by an underground society on the internet," it meant that it was "increasingly difficult to investigate and penetrate these organizations" (ibid.). Though this testimony focused on the operational difficulties, from a law enforcement perspective, of "penetrating" youth subcultures, it is significant, here, because in most of these official discourses the world of raves and drug use are generally treated as obvious (as in: obviously just about drug-pushing and nothing else) and hence not really in need of careful examination. They obviously constitute a problem, and they obviously need to be stopped.

As the 2002 RAVE Act became more publicized and its precise details better known, reaction from other interested but officially unrepresented parties grew. Stakeholders who were not heard within the legislative hearings made their voices heard in contexts outside of it. Organizations such as the Electronic Music Defense Fund, the American Civil Liberties Union, the Drug Policy Alliance Network, and DanceSafe, as well as many interested individuals, all began to campaign against the passing of the Act. The proposal to utilize the 1986 "Federal Crack House Statute" (Controlled Substances Act, 21 U.S.C. 856) was the most controversial aspect of the RAVE Act. It aimed to modify the original Crack House legislation to ensure that the law would apply not just "to ongoing drug distribution operations, but to single-event activities, such as a party where the promoter sponsors the event with the purpose of distributing ecstasy or other illegal drugs" (Haas 2005: 536). It noted that each year "tens of thousands of young people are initiated into the drug culture at rave parties or events," and highlighted the use of drugs as "deeply embedded in the rave culture." Raves, according to the National Drug Intelligence Center, had "become little more than a way to exploit American youth" emphasizing yet again the idea that raves are there primarily to distribute drugs. Specifically itemized in the RAVE Act were the use of neon glowsticks, massage oils, menthol nasal inhalers, and pacifiers, all of which were described as drug paraphernalia or items used to enhance the pleasures drug use.

Opponents to the proposed RAVE Act argued that by using the 1986 Crack House legislation the federal government was accusing rave organizers of running twenty-first-century crack houses. Moreover, the ACLU began to mount a campaign against the inclusion of infant pacifiers, objects that glow, vapor rub products and inhalers, dust masks of any description, masseurs or massage tables, and chill rooms as evidence of drug use, arguing that banning these legal items and attempting to ban raves outright was an abridgement of the First Amendment right of free expression.[9]

As a result of the increasing campaign against the RAVE Act, two cosponsoring Senators – Leahy of Vermont and Durbin of Illinois – withdrew their support for the RAVE Act and it died in committee. However, the main sponsor, Senator Biden, undeterred by this setback, renamed the RAVE Act the Illicit Drug Anti-Proliferation Act and made a few minor changes, including the removal of the list of items whose presence could be used as proof that the promoters or owners had " 'knowingly' let their customers and guests use drugs" (Brown 2003). According to the Drug Policy Alliance Network (2003), supporters of the Illicit Drug Anti-Proliferation Act included the Act under a miscellaneous category of the 2003 PROTECT Act, also known as the Amber Alert Act. This Act increased penalties against child sexual abuse, kidnapping, and domestic or international child sex tourism. It also implemented a nationwide coordination of notification and communication networks regarding child abductions (the Amber Alert system). The final version of the PROTECT Act was sent to Congress for an absolute yes or no vote: "Even those that opposed the [Illicit Drug Anti-Proliferation Act] had to vote for the final 'Amber' bill because they wanted to enact the provisions preventing child abductions" (Drug Policy Alliance Network 2003). If the construction of youth at raves as deeply vulnerable, in need of protection from predators and predatory environments, wasn't clear enough in the initial debates about the RAVE Act, subsuming the Illicit Drug Anti-Proliferation Act within the Amber Alert legislation appears to cement the connection.

Conclusion: continuing the regulation of youth

The passing of the Illicit Drug Anti-Proliferation Act as the culmination of an official narrative about the dangers of raves and drug use is the latest in a series of legislation that has sought initially to demonize and subsequently criminalize a contemporary and highly popular youthful activity. It is also yet another example on a long historical trajectory of adult concerns with youthful behavior, especially behavior that occurs outside of education, waged work, or the gaze of adult supervision. As researchers have noted, the precise forms of adult and societal concerns with youthful activities have fluctuated in different locations, in different historical periods, and with different sectors of youth. Sometimes concerns have focused on working-class white youth, as in the case of Mods, Rockers, Punks, and Goths. At other times the focus has been on ethnic minority groups, as in the case of youth gangs (Brake 1985; Griffin 1993; Hebdige 1979; Hodkinson 2002; Muggleton 2000; Thrasher 1927; Willis 1977, 1978). Today that concern, as we have tried to show, has been directed not at the underprivileged or ethnic minority youth but instead at the relatively affluent white middle-class youth and specifically young white girls. As noted in the text of the Ecstasy Anti-Proliferation Act of 2000, the target population is "college students, young professionals, and other people from middle to high-income families." This is the group identified as primarily involved both in the rave scene and in using ecstasy, and the group that has been designated as gullible and vulnerable to the ecstasy epidemic and its dangers. Under the guise of protecting youth, the legislation ultimately enacted further controls on the activities of young people. Although the reasons why young people today are specifically targeted are complex, two contextual factors appear to be particularly relevant.

First, contemporary notions of health and self-care have focused increasingly on the body and those unhealthy substances that are consumed, for example unhealthy food, cigarettes, alcohol, and illicit drugs.[10] Locating the site in which risk occurs, namely the body, is an essential feature of what D. Armstrong (1995) categorizes as "surveillance medicine," of which public health efforts comprise a crucial component. Discussions about "healthy" bodies emphasize the extent to which "the body has become a project to be 'worked on'" (Petersen and Lupton 1996: 23) and "an entity which is in the process of becoming" (Shiling 1993: 12; see also Bunton and Burrows 1995). "Investing in the body provides individuals with a sense of self-expression" (ibid.). The body as a project implies that it is plastic and changeable in line with the designs of its owner. The focus is no longer on understanding body signs and symptoms or on cataloging or curing discrete diseases in the present, but on "transforming the future by changing the health attitudes and health behaviors" (D. Armstrong 1995: 402). Therefore the healthy body is no longer solely about warding off disease, but also involves how "we present our bodies to ourselves and others" (ibid.). Increasingly identity is tied to practices, activities, and lifestyles. Within this framework, the youthful body is portrayed as a "body in ascent" (Ettorre and Miles 2002) or as the "unfinished body" (Lupton and Tulloch 1998). It is also viewed as "unruly, uncontained, uncontrolled and therefore in need of careful monitoring, regulation and instruction" (Lupton and Tulloch 1998: 22). Consequently, youthful illicit drug use "demonstrates a lack of successful socialization in appropriate techniques of self-surveillance and self-control" (Ettorre and Miles 2002: 181), and the concerns, specifically around ecstasy, illustrate the extent to which the "meanings associated with it transgress norms of risk avoidance and bodily discipline" (Manning 2006: 53).

Second, as a result of the weakening of traditional sources of social differentiation based on social class and communities, as noted by Furlong and Cartmel (1997) and Miles (2000), young people today are viewed as attempting to construct their identities through the process of consumption, whether that be consuming fashion, music, or drugs. However, while young people may seek to construct their identities through the process of consumption, they become increasingly identified as "risky consumers" involved in risky consumption (W. Mitchell et al. 2004;

see also Ettorre and Miles 2002). They are portrayed as having a disordered relationship to consumption, especially drug use (Griffin 1997). Given the societal urge for new and exciting experiences or as C. Campbell calls it "the ceaseless consumption of novelty" (1989: 205), coupled with the desire to seek new identities through the consumption of new commodities (Miles 2000) plus the desire to discover new thrills to overcome the mundane and inspire "pleasure, excitement, exhilaration, and desire" (Lupton 1999a: 167), it is obvious that ecstasy and other mind-altering substances would have such a widespread appeal for young people, especially within the exciting, transgressive, and pleasurable context of the dance scene and its electronic music (see Chapter 6). Because of these new and, according to the authorities, dangerous tendencies, young people must be protected from becoming "victims of their own irresponsibility" (Ettorre and Miles 2002: 178). Consequently, those arenas, such as raves, or activities in which drug use is perceived as commonplace and endemic, are viewed by adults as unruly, problematic, and "undermining the social cohesion of the local community" (France 1998: 104). Therefore they must be controlled and regulated. As Aitchison has noted, given the "increased anxiety … in activities deemed to be 'risky' … where leisure participants may be seen to be 'at risk' … leisure sites and activities have become the focus of a society preoccupied with minimising risk" (2004: 97).

As researchers have noted, and we hope that this case study has illustrated, a key area of control and regulation has been young people's leisure activities associated with ingested substances such as illicit drugs. "Adolescent drug use scares adults. The spectres of addiction, psychosis, alienation and rebellion provoke dramatic responses; legislators enact laws and create control agencies; therapists invent treatment and prevention programmes; parents worry and try to protect their children … all of these efforts are documented, evaluated and modified" (Glassner and Loughlin 1987: 1). Furthermore "the discourses of anxiety about 'substance misuse' frequently identify certain social groups with which to symbolically associate drug consumption and risk" (Manning 2006: 50). This is the situation today in the authorities' concern with raves and drugs. Youthful drug use is portrayed as particularly dangerous because young people are perceived as "a highly vulnerable sector of the population" (Ettorre and Miles 2002: 176).

The strategies examined above are yet another example of the move towards increasingly regulating, controlling, and imposing curfews on young people today (N. D. Campbell 2000). In fact the recent anti-ecstasy and anti-rave legislation supports the case made by Males (1999), who argues that the current historical period can be described as "the most anti-youth period in American history" (Males 1999, quoted in Giroux 2000). The attempts to curtail raves and ban the use of ecstasy must therefore be seen within this overall context as one of the latest chapters in the saga of attempts to manage and govern youth more generally. And the experiences of the young people we interviewed for this book must be seen against this broader backdrop.

Chapter 5

Uncovering the local
San Francisco's nighttime economy

Introduction

Since the 1980s, social researchers have developed a growing interest in city centers "as symbolic of the urban way of life" (O'Connor 1994). From the 1970s many cities in both the US and the UK have experienced extensive deindustrialization, with significant declines in city centers. Today, with the development of the post-modern or post-industrial city, a marked "revalorization" of the city centers has occurred. This redevelopment took place not as a result of traditional production but as a result of the development of a consumption-based economy, which began to play a major role in the reinvigoration of the inner-city areas. Specifically, this economy was based on the consumption of entertainment, leisure, and culture (O'Connor 1994). The city has become "an Entertainment Machine leveraging culture to enhance its economic well-being" (Lloyd and Clark 2000: 1). Because much consumption of entertainment takes place at night, scholars have increasingly viewed the nighttime economy as an important area of research. Until very recently, research on the nighttime economy had been marginalized: "the night-life of a city was not a legitimate object for attention ... other than as something to be regulated and contained" (Lovatt 1996: 143).

To understand the context of nightlife scenes, it is important not to just put this in a global context, or even a national context, as the previous two chapters have. In addition, it is important to examine the particular local, urban, or suburban context of these scenes. The contours of nightlife are shaped by local cultures and musical styles, but also by things like city policies toward urban development, the growth or decline of local economies, or regulations and zoning delimiting what sort of entertainment is permitted where. Examining the specific local, urban context of one nightlife scene, in this case that of San Francisco, California, does not mean, however, that this has lessons only for those interested in this particular city. For the questions raised here about urban economies, development, and regulation are the sort that can and should be raised about the context of other scenes and subcultures across the nation and around the world. And the happenings of this particular city do not happen in isolation, but are part of broader trends of changing economic bases for cities and changing approaches to regulating (and resisting regulation of) nightlife and entertainment.

Few cities would seem to better encapsulate the model of shifting to an idea- and service-based economy, away from traditional industrial models, than San Francisco (and the Bay Area). Close to Silicon Valley and the home of many technology-oriented companies, in addition to its strong role in finance (sometimes called the "Wall Street of the West"), San Francisco's economy is increasingly dependent on conventions, entertainment, tourism, the arts, and multimedia (Godfrey 1997). In one measure of nightlife, San Francisco boasts a ratio of restaurants/bars/entertainment venues to population (thirty-nine to 10,000) just under that of New York City (forty) and twice that of Los Angeles (seventeen) (San Francisco Mayor's Office 2007).

San Francisco has long been associated with nighttime entertainment. For example, the Avalon Ballroom and the Fillmore Auditorium were famous in the 1960s for dance events, hallucinogenic experiences, electronic sound, and flashing lights. In fact according to J. Beck and Rosenbaum (1994) the first rave took place in San Francisco in 1965 at the Longshoremen's Hall. San Francisco's importance in the nighttime club and rave scenes has been attributed to a number of elements, including its role in the 1960s acid rock and psychedelic movement, the strength of its gay community and their involvement in the club scene, and more recently its close proximity to Silicon Valley and the development of "cyber-tech" culture (Silcott 1999).

The 1970s ushered in a new wave of club culture as disco music infiltrated the nightlife scene. This was an era of hedonism; all-night "mega-parties" fueled by the use of cocaine and other drugs took root in San Francisco, setting the stage for a thriving after-hours scene. Clubs like Trocadero, the Endup, the City Disco, and Dreamland were renowned "high-energy dance palaces" for events that would go all night and into the next morning (Diebold 1988). Initially, many of these events were geared toward the gay male population, spurred on by gay musical icons of the time like Frank Loverde and Sylvester (who both later passed away from AIDS-related illness). On writing about the San Francisco dance scene in the 1970s, David Diebold speaks of the "absolute devotion to the dance experience, the fervor with which the disciples seek it, and the lasting world view which the experience engenders in its participants" (1988). He compares the dance club to a church, a gathering place of people seeking a "true religious experience" where the preacher at the pulpit is replaced by a DJ at his turntables. This era (1978–83), coined "San Francisco's Golden Age of Dance Music," was the beginning of DJ stardom and brought about the Bay Area Disco DJ Association (BADDA).

With the mid-1980s came the mega-clubs, marked by the opening of spacious venues such as Club DV8 in 1985 and Ten15 Folsom (which is still operating today) in 1986. Mega-clubs are high-production nightlife events that take place in large venues, often two or three stories high. They are known for their large capacity; some mega-clubs in Europe can host over 5,000 guests (S. Armstrong 2004: 44), although the largest in San Francisco have tended to be in the 1,200 patron range. Despite their massive numbers, mega-clubs are often quite exclusive and expensive. One appeal of mega-clubs, aside from their size, is their ability to attract big-name DJs of international reputation. They are also known for their high production aesthetics, including state-of-the-art lighting and sound systems, themed décor and stage performers. These venues and others like them hosted extremely successful, long-running house music events all over San Francisco (Chonin 2002). During this period key venues of gay nightlife in the city took a hit due to scares over the AIDS crisis. Bathhouses were forced by city ordinance to shut down (Associated Press 1984), nightclub attendance declined and nightlife culture stagnated for much of the 1980s.

The early to mid-1990s brought the heyday of raves in San Francisco (Silcott 1999). The legendary "full moon" raves put on by the British music collective Wicked, with their neo-pagan naturalism and spirituality, attracted thousands of young people to the annual beach events (Reynolds 1999). Slightly after this, the technology-oriented Toon Town raves (also organized by British expats) ushered in the soon to become stereotypical garb of raves, with the children's clothing, psychedelic colors, wraparound glasses, etc. San Francisco's rave scene was distinct from some other rave scenes in the US, though, in its emphasis on spirituality or enlightenment, a product of the British rave influences mixing with the local history of psychedelic exploration, New Age philosophies, and cyber-tech DIY (do-it-yourself) culture (Reynolds 1999). Ravers could soon be seen throughout the city, although the Haight area, most famous for its hippie past, was the daytime hub, with stores selling rave paraphernalia popping up throughout the neighborhood (Silcott 1999).The electronic dance music (in a variety of styles and subgenres) that raves popularized seeped into other nightlife outlets and mainstream clubs as well. This founding period of San Francisco raves ends in the mid-1990s, amid internal strife, the ebb and flow of musical tastes and styles (and a backlash against the British sound), but also as a result of increasing police crackdowns on unlicensed events. Whereas in the early years the police turned a blind eye on the raves for the most part, these events were increasingly targeted, leading some events to flee to the suburbs and others to cease to exist entirely (Silcott 1999). However, the rave scene did not disappear, particularly in its more commercial forms; massive for-profit raves with thousands of guests flourished up through the early 2000s.

With the dot-com boom and economic expansion of the late 1990s there was a resurgence of nightlife in San Francisco, and many operators of the nighttime economy achieved great success in this period. The city seemed to be filled with young people with unheard-of amounts of money, ready to spend it lavishly on entertainment. Clubs were booming, with long lines of patrons seeking admission. This was also the height of the mass popularity of raves in the area. Though the underground rave scene was smaller, had moved on, or transmogrified, the massive licensed commercial raves took off in prominence, attracting growing numbers of young people from the city and the suburbs. During this period of economic prosperity, nightclub operators and promoters began to organize and attempt to effect change in the regulatory process shaping San Francisco nightlife. Previously both the issuance and the enforcement of permits were largely under the purview of the San Francisco Police Department, an arrangement which some charged as leading to conflicts of interest, with the police playing "judge and executioner" in nightlife issues (J. Sanders 2002). After a series of high-profile conflicts between the police and nightclub owners and party promoters, over police actions deemed by critics to be capricious or heavy-handed, the San Francisco Board of Supervisors established a new Entertainment

Commission, comprising members of a number of constituencies (neighbor groups, police, nightclub owners, public health), removing the license-issuing powers of the police. (For more on this see Moloney *et al.* 2009) Initially this seemed to promise a major shift in the balance of power in struggles over nightlife regulation. Although the commission was the first of its kind in the US (Harnden 2006), the broader trend of a shift from police regulation over nightlife to increasing influence from the private sector is one that is seen in nighttime economies elsewhere, and which has been particularly studied in the British context (see Chatterton and Hollands 2003; Hadfield 2006; Talbot 2007).

This period of economic prosperity dwindled after the dot-com bust of 2001 and San Francisco's nighttime economy took a significant hit. With less money to spend on expensive entrance covers and $10 drinks, "nightlife slowed to a crawl," making it impossible for larger clubs to fill their once packed venues (Zinko 2005). Nonetheless, the San Francisco dance scene "survived the blows" (Chonin 2002) and things started to turn around in 2005. At this time, people seemed to be opting for smaller, "mellower" venues over the giant mega-clubs of the late 1990s (Zinko 2005), something that might be attributed to the aging of generation X as well as the economic recession. The preference for small, intimate clubs remains the trend today in San Francisco, where the "high-tech atmosphere" of clubs of yore is quickly losing its foothold in the city (Zinko 2005). And, during this same period, the clout of the nightlife operators once again diminished, and the Entertainment Commission was increasingly viewed as ineffective, or at the very least as work in progress (Lagos 2008; San Francisco civil grand jury 2007). And in this decade the prominence and frequency of raves, which were ascendant at the turn of the century, began to wane – with some claiming that rave culture was dead or dying while others argue that it has transmogrified and spread into other nightlife and leisure domains. And the raves that did prosper in the early twenty-first century were less and less often the grass-roots underground parties of the earlier period. In their place we saw the emergence and increased popularity of the commercialized massive raves, which differed greatly in that they were highly publicized, required expensive tickets, involved big production values, and were held at permitted venues that allowed alcohol consumption (whereas alcohol consumption was distinctly against the norm at many earlier raves).

Tracking San Francisco raves and clubs

From 2001 to 2003 we began mapping the public world of dance events in the San Francisco Bay Area and continued to collect some data through 2008.[1] Through the mapping process we have identified and documented venues, clubs, raves, and other dance events. It is important to emphasize the extent to which the scene is fragmented and changing. Although "the scene" is often referred to as a unified entity, it is divided by musical genre, age, ethnicity, sexual orientation, drug use, and numerous other variables. Although there is a global nature to the dance scene, it is also necessary to highlight the extent to which these global developments are continually modified and reinterpreted by local cultural forces. These local forces circumscribe the way global tendencies are experienced by local audiences. The dialectical interplay between global and local highlights the extent to which local participants are active players in creating the local scene, with its own musical and dance styles and its own distinctive drug-using practices. Youth may understand dance and drug use similarly (that which is global), yet they may also have different experiences, depending on their particular cultural space and location (that which is local).

One way that we began tracking dance events, clubs, and raves was through analyzing the flyers that have traditionally been used to promote these events. Although event flyers are considered the "traditional form of club advertising" (Osborne 1999), the Internet Age has introduced a new means of promoting dance events. With entire Web sites dedicated to club culture, one can view event calendars, learn about DJs on the line-up and chat with other club enthusiasts on online forums. We began gathering information on San Francisco nightclubs primarily through Internet sources such as nightlife and entertainment Web sites. The Internet plays an important role in the electronic dance music scene, as Web sites and e-mail lists are used by attendees, promoters, DJs, venue owners, and others as a way of advertising and discussing various aspects of the scene. We have documented approximately 250 Web sites that are focused on the Bay Area dance and music scene. In addition, we have collected and documented magazines, flyers, and other related print media, as flyer dissemination has remained a popular and effective way to advertise raves and club nights.

Flyers are designed to give the reader an idea of what's to come, from the date, time, and location of the event to the DJs and styles of music that will be played. Event flyers are also scanned for more covert information; readers may draw conclusions about the type of crowd the event will attract based on the flyer design and through the types of images, wording, and font used. For example, a club flyer with a picture of a scantily clad woman on the front gives the impression of a sexy, heterosexual atmosphere and a crowd that is "dressed to impress." Additionally, readers look for what types of behavior are permitted/not permitted at the event. One rave flyer states that drugs, alcohol, and "bad vibes" are not acceptable but "cameras, smiles, and dancing shoes" are encouraged. These guidelines indicate the promoter's intention to host a friendly, fun, and safe event. The placement of flyers can further determine the targeted population. By placing flyers in record stores, piercing/tattoo shops, and smoke shops, the promotion company intends a certain type of person to view it and possibly attend the event. Similarly, disseminating flyers at other rave/club events and at street fairs is sure to reach an already seasoned dance enthusiast. These help establish and maintain boundaries of who is in and out of the scene, who is desirable or not desirable to attend.

It is important to distinguish between club flyers and rave flyers. Although they both serve the same general function of providing the reader with information, rave flyers can be less direct or detailed in the information they present because of their sometimes "renegade" nature. For example, a rave flyer may state whether or not the venue is confirmed and/or permitted. If the event is not permitted, its location will not be printed on the flyer and instead a hotline number will be provided to attendees so that they can obtain the event's location on the date it is scheduled. This hot line may direct them toward a "map point" – a place they must go to on the night of the event to obtain directions to the rave's actual location. Such measures provide an extra layer of security (from police shutdown) for the event organizers. This sort of exclusive promotion, along with advertising raves only on "members only" Web sites, also creates a feeling of being "in the know" among attendees, who consider themselves "outside and in opposition to the 'mainstream' " (Thornton 1996). Indeed, these types of underground events are less likely to attract a mainstream crowd that prefers the more easily accessible dance clubs.

Raves and underground events

Although the accurate mapping of clubs raised methodological challenges, the problems proved to be even more substantial when we commenced our monitoring of dance events, including raves and dance parties. These are much more difficult to plot accurately than either venues or clubs, because while some are large events which are highly publicized, many are described as "underground" (Reynolds 1999; Wright 1999) and are known only to certain networks of people who find out about the location of the event on the day that it is scheduled to take place. A single rave will be promoted only for a short period of time, since it's a one-time event, whereas even a small club will be constantly promoted because it takes place on a regular basis. Raves were a strong force in the San Francisco nightlife in the early 2000s, evidenced by their prominence in the early part of our research. In our initial years of tracking raves and dance parties we documented almost 500 separate events. These events occurred every week in the San Francisco Bay Area and almost always on Friday and Saturday nights. The venues in which these events take place can vary widely, and include large exhibition halls and auditoriums, as well as warehouses, commercial buildings, private residences, and outdoor private and public land.

Some raves, such as "massive" raves, are licensed events held in legal venues and accountable to city and state laws regarding age of admittance (usually 18+) and closing hours. The "Cyberfest" rave we attended in 2003 was held just outside the city at the Cow Palace expo grounds and featured about 1,500 guests – late teens and twenty-somethings, primarily, and the "Popsikle 4" rave in 2002, for example, had over 3,000 patrons and was held at the city's Bill Graham Civic Auditorium. Other raves have traditionally been unlicensed affairs, held in makeshift venues, sometimes referred to as "underground" events. Not all underground parties are raves (which typically feature electronic dance music) – certainly a variety of scenes and subcultures can be found at different underground parties. Their prominence in San Francisco nightlife has waxed and waned throughout the past few decades, and they continue to be of significance today.

The Bay Area is home to a number of artist collectives that are loosely organized. To a certain degree, the sense that they are their own community is born from the idea that they are different from the mainstream. One collective that a few of the people we interviewed were involved in is generally based on the principles of DIY, political radicalism, and non-mainstream art/performance. Some in this community also use the self-described term "mutant." Here, a mutant (or a freak/phreak) is a positive thing: an assertion that one is happy to not be a part of the mainstream, whether this is because of lifestyle, appearance, or beliefs. For some of these, living in low-income communities, shared warehouse space, or even squatting, is sometimes common.

While this group doesn't fit neatly into being a nightlife subscene or a distinct part of the rave scene, *per se*, there is a large electronic music and dance-scene element to this group. Participants throw renegade and warehouse parties with electronic music, but that music is rarely what you would find in a club, with an emphasis on experimental music. These underground parties will not usually be elaborate or fancy as commercial raves, as they are being thrown with little money.

Underground or unlicensed dance events/parties have a curious place in the regulatory framework of the nighttime economy. While there have been raids on the parties in the past (most notably in the 1990s) and police closings do still occur (particularly since the Internet makes the parties easier to find not just for patrons but also for police and regulators), for the most part the parties seem generally tolerated/allowed to continue, except when receiving sufficient neighborly complaints. Undergrounds were once associated primarily with being truly alternative or oppositional, featuring avant-garde musical styles or radical political and social norms. However, many of the present-day events appear to differ from mainstream clubs primarily through the fact that they are unlicensed (and hence more profitable for organizers), but without a noticeably different ethos than that of a mainstream nightclub. These events, which are billed as underground, may be advertised online and through handbills/flyers, have cash bars, and play a variety of musical styles. The events may also be less security-focused than licensed clubs (both in the positive sense of having less onerous surveillance and in the negative sense of having more dubious safety/fire plans), although having bouncers and checking IDs is not unheard of. Among our interviews with nightclub operators, owners, and promoters there seemed to be a split in attitudes about undergrounds. Some resented those who threw underground parties for not having to go through the regulatory hoops that they went through, and for bringing a bad name to all clubs when problems arise. One promoter who we interviewed complained:

> It's a problem for legitimate business owners like myself who are trying to depend on this to feed their families by doing things the right way when you've got these kids who are throwing a party and who are allowed to operate after hours, serving liquor until six o'clock in the morning. They're chargin' covers; they have no permits, they have no fire exit or responsibilities. No nothing. It's in a warehouse … It's one thing to have a party once in a while but it's another thing to advertise as a weekly event and the police are sitting outside and they're not doing anything. That is bad. They're the ones who are affecting the livelihoods of legitimate club owners.

Yet other club owners and promoters we interviewed support the presence of underground events as contributing to the general vibrancy of nightlife in the city:

> I – I think – I'm okay with it, actually. I think that it's sad that these guys can't be legitimate, you know? And they can't be legit. because the rules and regulations and permits and hours of operation and all that stuff, you know, are prohibitive. … It doesn't detract; as a matter of fact it – um, any opportunity that

gives people – anything that gives people the opportunity and the encouragement to go out more often, um, is okay with me. I want people to go to restaurants, I want people to walk around the neighborhoods at night, you know, I want there to be sidewalk cafés; because all that stuff for me – yes, it's potentially competition – but it encourages a – a way of being in the world where people go out, you know?

The importance of raves/massives has clearly diminished over the decade; some argue that the rave scene is altogether dead. In her interview with people in the San Francisco dance music industry, Sheerly Avni writes that "the good days are over" and the general consensus among many scene insiders is that "rave culture has given way to club culture, to the mainstream, to the media focus on ecstasy as the drug that fuels the culture" (2001: 89). However, many party and club promoters see it differently, extolling the benefits of introducing the subculture to the mainstream.

Another example of subculture meeting the mainstream can be found in the increasing number of Burner-type parties taking place throughout the city. Burning Man, which started as a small gathering on Baker Beach in 1986, is now a massive event that attracts more than 35,000 people to Black Rock Desert each year (Chonin 2002). Burners, characterized by their "postapocalyptic fashions ... which convey both tribalism and a sense of whimsy," stand in contrast to the mainstream club style meant to exude glamour, money and sex (Jones 2005). Nonetheless, Burning Man culture, attitude, and attire have infiltrated the city's nightlife and its influence has created a scene that is unique to the San Francisco Bay Area. In the months leading up to the event, Burning Man organizers, DJs, and participants throw their own playa-inspired parties at club venues likes Ten15 Folsom, Club Mighty, and DNA Lounge to fundraise money for their camps; as a result, there is a "year-round Burning Man scene in San Francisco" that is accessible to more mainstream clubgoers (Jones 2005). While there are overlaps between Burning Man culture and rave culture, including overlaps of organizers or participants, many involved with Burning Man actively police their scene from devolving into "mere" rave culture, however, and would not want to present the two as too closely aligned.

Clubs

Using Thornton's definition of a venue as "license-holding architectural space" (1996: 22), we identified 126 different venues which hosted events with dance music during our initial 2001–03 mapping.[2] Venues are the physical structures within which clubs and events operate, and within any one venue a number of different clubs or types of events may take place. The venues in San Francisco range from more traditional nightclubs to "DJ bars" and restaurants. In recent years the DJ bar has grown in popularity in San Francisco. Many times these venues do not have a marked dance floor and instead focus on the skills of the DJ to set the mood while patrons socialize and drink cocktails. The majority of DJ bars in San Francisco are located in the Mission district, where former "dive bars" have been converted (or sometimes simply turntables and a mixer have been placed in the corner) to form a small, club-like atmosphere. One of the more popular DJ bars is Amnesia on Valencia Street in the Mission district, a venue where they feature some of the city's most talented house and funk DJs. While Amnesia can get very crowded, without much room for movement to and from the bar, let alone room to dance, there is an "in the know" feeling there. Some veteran clubgoers in San Francisco claim that some of the best music can be heard at these DJ bars. Ultimately, the precise dividing lines between small clubs and DJ bars, and DJ bars and regular bars are unclear, and consequently it is difficult to know whether we have identified all the possible venues and clubs in San Francisco.

Clubs refer to the individual events which take place in venues, and they are organized primarily either by the venue or by an independent promoter. Our research documented approximately 475 dance-music clubs in San Francisco. Given the fact that clubs come and go relatively frequently, and often without any notice, a precise number of clubs within any one geographical area is difficult to calculate. Clubs cater to different clientele, varying by age group (18+ or 21+), sexual orientation, ethnic group, as well as musical style. While the term "club" gets deployed by different individuals and groups in various ways, for the purposes of our overview a club is an organized, licensed party, within a venue, that occurs on a regular basis (at least once a month) and has a DJ playing records (and possibly some live music as well). Clubs can be any size and attract any type of crowd, although the vast majority of club events we tracked required that patrons be at least 18 years of age, and more often 21 years of age. Club nights may move from venue to venue, from one neighborhood to a completely different one. For instance, the popular gay club event "Fag Fridays" had its weekly Friday-night party at the Endup in the SoMa district, but has since moved to a different venue in a different district. Many times, if a club changes venue, there is an attempt made for it to be located in at least the same neighborhood. One example of this happening is with Da Joint, a hip-hop and dancehall club that attracts a diverse crowd, which used to be located at Rawhide II in SoMa (which has since closed down) but is now taking place at Border Cantina, about a block away.

It is worth noting that many club events occur outside the immediate control of venue owners and managers. Although promoters are hired directly by the venue, they rarely work with owners or managers on creating an event. Instead, they set up a club night independently and depend on the venue to house only that particular event. This is often a point of conflict; independent promoters – who are contracted by nightclub owners to drum up business for the club, and who typically receive the money from the door entry costs (whereas the owners receive the money from the bar) – are frequently cited by other stakeholders as a source of problems. Police and nightclub owners in our interviews describe problems with promoters bringing in too large crowds of the "wrong sort" of people. One of the hallmarks of a bad manager/owner, according to our interviews with nightlife operators, is handing over too much power to promoters one knows too little about. They argue that the problem with promoters stems from the short-term interests of promoters (versus the long-term interests of club owners), and while owners have to go through a great deal of vetting through the licensing and permitting process, typically promoters are accountable to no one. In early 2008 the city convened a "Nightlife Safety Summit" after a string of violent incidents associated with nightclub events occurred, bringing together police, club owners and managers, promoters, and security workers. (The constituency notably missing from this event: the consumers of nightlife entertainment themselves.) One of the recommendations to come out of the summit, and which is in the process of being adopted into the legal code, is to require promoters of more than two events per year to be licensed and bonded.

The one constant in the San Francisco nightclub scene appears to be variation. Though the overall scene is long-standing, individual clubs, even individual scenes, are largely ephemeral. Music scenes and taste culture are constantly evolving. After tracking the many clubs in San Francisco for several months via the Internet and local magazines, we can present only a momentary snapshot of this city's nightlife. During the course of our research, nightclub venues closed, new venues opened, club nights changed venues, and some club nights disappeared altogether. Additionally, there is a wide assortment of different club types, from large, multi-level dance meccas to casual, intimate DJ bars.

Nightlife districts

Nightclub venues are spread throughout the districts of San Francisco. However, more than 60 percent of them are concentrated in four areas: SoMa, the Mission, the Tenderloin, and the Castro. Other areas, such as North Beach, long known for its restaurants and bars, have begun to have more clubs licensed in recent years (and in the case of North Beach the district has become notorious for a string of violent bar- or club-related incidents, Lagos 2008). The first district, which contains the largest concentration of venues, is called South of Market (SoMa) because of its location to the south of Market Street, which is one of the main thoroughfares in the downtown area. SoMa contains mostly commercial buildings, although there has been an increase in residential units in recent years. Once a largely industrial part of the city, over the past decade neighborhoods, "live–work" units, and high-end condominium projects have popped up all over the district, in addition to being a hub of dot-com and other new technology-focused companies and "multimedia clusters" (Graham and Guy 2002). And even in this time of real estate contraction in much of the country (and much of the SF Bay Area), new condo developments are being built and continue to sell in 2008.[3] One newspaper account reports that, of the new buyers in the area, "About 50 percent hold at least a graduate degree … Almost all earn at least $100,000 and many make between $250,000 and $500,000. Buyers most commonly work in high-tech or high finance" (Temple 2008). According to one estimate, 83 percent of the SoMa residents have moved in since 1990 (South of Market Health Center 2007). With (middle-class) families with children increasingly priced out of San Francisco (and/or avoiding the SF public schools), two other groups primarily comprise this market: young well-to-do professionals and "empty-nesters" whose own children have grown up. Access to San Francisco nightlife seems to be a driving factor for the first group, but a source of conflicts for the latter. The SoMa area has long been a scene of nightlife in San Francisco, preceding the entry of these residential developments, with its many warehouses being a prime spot for underground parties and artist studios, and with a number of nightclubs peppered throughout the region (Godfrey 1997).[4] There are at least fifty venues in the district offering dancing and entertainment, and over 100 sites with liquor licenses. "The SFPD [police department] estimate that around 8,000–10,000 people come to SoMA on a typical weekend night, and believes that most clubgoers are not SF residents but visitors from surrounding East Bay, South Bay, and Marin counties. Some club owners believe the opposite, estimating that the majority of their patrons are local residents" (San Francisco Civil Grand Jury 2000). But, whereas these nightclubs were once in areas that did not have sleeping residents near by, condos are being built next to or on top of these venues – and not all of the new condo owners appreciate their nightlife neighbors. Thus there have been an increasing number of disputes and complaints filed by neighbors and resident groups about the noise and other nuisances of nightlife. This in turn led to restrictions imposed by the Entertainment Commission and other regulatory bodies and ongoing tension between nightlife operators and patrons and the new residents.

While those in favor of nightlife expansion may clash with the police, even bigger disputes arise between nightlife operators and resident/neighbor groups. One Entertainment Commissioner opined, "neighbors and police are always going to align, always, always, always" (interview). Writing in the media, one proponent of San Francisco nightlife argues that this is the biggest thorn in the nighttime economy's side: "One of the biggest obstacles to a healthy nightlife in San Francisco is other San Franciscans. Neighborhood groups hold far more power than local businesses, artists, and musicians. One resident citing noise issues can put a club that serves hundreds of people out of business – because city regulations place a higher value on residents than on nightlife businesses" (English 2004). This is a very different impression from what has been noted in the UK: "In spite of small victories which residents might gain, their perception is that licensing procedures are heavily weighted in favor of the trade, its legal advisers, statutory agencies, and the court, who all use the system regularly" (Chatterton and Hollands 2003: 65). One difference here may be in the power of "repeat players" versus "one-shotters" (Galanter 1974). As discussed in the sociology of law, "repeat players" who are often able to work the system in a way that benefits them in the long term have advantages over the less resourced "one-shotters" whose priorities are more short-term and thus disadvantaged. While the repeat players are generally thought of as large corporate interests (as in the case of the corporate brew pubs in the UK), within this San Francisco context it may actually be the neighbor groups and the police who are the repeat players and thus in the advantage. One reason for this (and for the general inability of nightclub interests to fully "capture" their regulators, as many feared) may be the lack of conglomeration and corporate ownership of nightlife venues in San Francisco. Unlike the situation in the UK, which is described by many as increasingly dominated by a few chains of branded bars, pubs, and clubs (Chatterton and Hollands 2002; Talbot 2007)[5] (and certainly such chains exist in other parts of the US as well), they have not established a foothold in San Francisco. Indeed, San Francisco has specific growth-control ordinances aimed at stopping chain bars (or restaurants or clothing stores) becoming too dominant within the city's landscape.[6] Instead, the vast majority of bars and clubs in the city remain local, independent establishments.[7] These local independent

establishments (or groups of establishments – a few of the more prominent propri-
etors own multiple clubs in the city) may lack the large scale and resources to truly
capture regulators. And, particularly in these down-economic times, the various owners may be too much in competition with one another to unite sufficiently to push
their interests more effectively than other stakeholders, like the police or neighbors.

While this points to structural issues in the design of governance that lead to one
type of conflict management, we must also look to structural issues in the city's planning that lead to these conflicts in the first place. San Francisco is a geographically
small (forty-eight square miles) dense city (among major US cities it's second only
to New York in population density) (Godfrey 1997), which increasingly has "mixed-
use" development. This means that residences and businesses (including late-night
business) are often in very close proximity. The 1990s brought increasing numbers
of expensive condominiums, "live/work" spaces, and loft developments into areas
formerly dominated by warehouses, which over the previous few decades have developed a vibrant nightlife. And the new, often very wealthy, neighbors often come into
conflict with nighttime entertainment owners. The Entertainment Commission (EC)
and SF nightlife more broadly, then, must operate in the context that "entertainment
venues and residences may be uncomfortably close and that goodwill must be fos-
tered by all sides to keep the City both a wonderful place to live and a wonderful
place to play," as the grand jury report put it (San Francisco Civil Grand Jury 2007:
22). A newspaper article covering the EC's proposed creation describes it thus: "Two
years in the making, Leno's plan is the latest stab at answering the 'How can we get
along?' question, in a city where apartment buildings and lofts are creeping on to
blocks where music clubs and performance spaces once stood unbothered" (Garofoli
2002). This presents a twist on some classic scenarios of gentrification and nightlife
expansion. It's not that the clubs, restaurants, and parties are invading previously
residential areas, but the reverse.

This is not the only story of nightlife transformation in the city, however. For
example, in the nearby Mission district, which traditionally has been the home
of working-class immigrant groups, particularly Latinos, these families have been
increasingly pushed out due to rising housing costs and increasing evictions, as
wealthy, primarily white, new residents move in, with more traditional gentrification patterns. Expanded nightlife has played a role in this gentrification. Although
working-class families and recent immigrants from Latin America still call the Mission home, an influx of young upwardly mobile professionals is transforming the
neighborhood's character. High-end restaurants, night spots, and "live–work" spaces
have displaced low-income households and local-serving businesses (Alejandrino
2000: 9).[8] The Mission is now home to an array of restaurants, bars, and shops
in addition to a number of smaller clubs and DJ bars. Like SoMa, the Mission is
generally a popular night spot and is home to approximately fifteen major nightlife
venues.

The Tenderloin, in contrast to the first two areas, is not an official district, and is
known as a place where drug dealing and prostitution are commonplace. Depending
on where the boundaries are drawn, the Tenderloin both borders on and/or includes
the area from Union Square to the Civic Center. It is one of the busiest areas in

San Francisco, both during the day and at night, and contains tourist sites, theaters, bars, and commercial and residential buildings in addition to thirteen club venues. Despite being sometimes described as "seedy" or the "underbelly" of the city, it is home to a number of hip bars, clubs, art galleries, and restaurants. Although it has nightlife appeal, the Tenderloin continues to be perceived by many outside it as a dangerous district, putting off those who feel it is unsafe, especially late at night when the clubs let out. For those commuting into San Francisco from other cities, there is a particular concern about leaving one's car parked in the area because of its reputation for car break-ins and theft.

The hub of San Francisco gay nightlife is in the Castro district where some of the more popular bars and clubs are located, including the Bar, Café, and Jet. To be exact, there are eighteen gay nightlife venues in the Castro district as well as a number of gay venues located outside of the Castro, such as the Stud and Lone Star Saloon in SoMa. Additionally, San Francisco is packed with nightlife venues that host weekly, monthly, or even annual gay club events. Ruby Skye, the mega-club located downtown, boasts a monthly gay event called "Fresh" and DNA Lounge hosts "Escandalo," a gay Latino club night on Fridays. While some gay nightlife venues are known for being mellow or low-key, others are known for big events that boast a circuit party-type atmosphere permissive of drug use. As with clubs in general in the city, there is no single model of a gay club that is representative of gay nightlife as a whole, as different venues cater to different clientele of San Francisco's diverse gay communities.

There have been significant changes within San Francisco's gay scene since the mid-1990s. The Castro district was known to be ethnically homogeneous, catering mostly to older white men. Many gay and bisexual men of color felt unwelcome or excluded from Castro nightlife, which was predominately Caucasian. Some venues were even considered to have discriminatory admission policies; Badlands in the Castro was caught up in a controversy regarding their favoritism for white patrons (McMillan 2005). Now a more diverse population frequents venues in the Castro, including young lesbians, heterosexuals, and people of color. These changes are encouraged by a younger generation that is interested in having a diverse nightlife experience. It is also indicative of a younger generation of Asian Americans that is integrated into San Francisco gay culture.

While each of these nightlife districts offers a variety of venues, clubs, and scenes, and none can be reduced to a single, homogeneous style or clientele, each also has its own flavor and types of venues that predominate. Although the Castro is a nightlife destination, it doesn't offer the same type of mega-clubs that SoMa offers. Instead many of its most popular spots are neighborhood bars. Similarly, the Mission offers a more intimate, DJ bar-type scene. On the other hand, people who are interested in big mega-clubs will typically go straight to the SoMa region.

Club trends and variations

Wherever they are located, clubs and nightlife venues can be compared by looking at a number of structural features which shape who wants to attend, who is admitted, and the experience inside and outside their doors. These features include venue size, age requirements, dress code, hours of operation, and cost of attendance, as well as issues of the ethnic, sexual, or musical orientation of the clubs. All are themselves shaped by local regulations and the economic scene and all play important roles in shaping the contours of nighttime entertainment in the city.

Venue size

One primary way to distinguish types of clubs is based on the venue's size. Sizes of venues can fit into three broad types: large, multi-room club; mid-size, single dance-floor club; and smaller DJ bar. The largest clubs most often draw patrons not only from San Francisco but from all over the Bay Area and beyond. For example, Ten15 is an internationally known club with several rooms and three levels located in a warehouse-style venue in SoMa; this type of venue is very popular with both local San Franciscans and "bridge and tunnel" clubgoers. A medium-sized club venue such as Club Six might be attractive to those who want to dance in a less overwhelming environment. This venue has two floors, with the top level consisting of a more lounge-like atmosphere with several plush couches and chairs and the bottom level being basement-like with open space to dance, but it is not very large. Some of the smaller-scale, more intimate clubs appeal to those who want a somewhat relaxed night out. One venue may be more appropriate for going out with a group of friends while another may be a better setting for a date.

Many of the smaller entertainment venues in the city do not immediately catch one's attention if one is not in the know. These buildings are often converted warehouse or garage spaces whose rough exterior gives way to a more aesthetic interior. One fieldworker describes such a venue in the Castro district:

> From the outside, Jet, which is located less than a block from the intersection of Castro and Market Streets, is rather inconspicuous-looking, and is in fact easy to miss due to its small sign and the absence of a large crowd standing outside, which is typical of many bars and clubs in the neighborhood. From the street, the only evidence of the venue is a single entry door with a bouncer standing outside, and a gray metal garage-style door with the pink and black Jet logo projected on to it from above. Patrons enter the club through a single door at the start of a long mirror-lined hallway. After turning the corner in the hallway to enter the main portion of the venue, patrons are immediately enveloped in a pink/red light emanating from hundreds of small dressing-room-style lights located on the opposite wall and the ceiling. Jet relies heavily on colored lights and other lighting effects to create a luxurious lounge-type feel.
>
> (Field notes)

This stands in contrast to the city's mega-clubs, which advertise themselves as nightlife destinations from the get-go with giant marquees and spotlights. Unlike the less obvious, single-door entry of Jet, Ruby Skye, the 800 person-capacity venue located in downtown San Francisco, attracts customers with the "see and be seen" mentality often exuded by larger and more "glamorous" clubs.

> Ruby Skye has a large sign protruding out over the sidewalk from the building of the club. The inside of the sign is white, but there is a bronze-colored, scalloped border running around the edge. Inside the sign, in red cursive letters, Ruby Skye is written. Below the name, in small black print, "Explore your rhythm," is written. This design is the logo for the venue, also printed on the cocktail napkins in the club and on the Web site. The building itself is three to four stories high. Two sets of glass doors leading into the club are set three or four feet off the sidewalk, under an overhang. Ruby Skye has restricted entrance to this area and claimed part of the side walk space in front of the venue by roping it off. Movable poles about three feet high are placed so that they form a rectangle with the front of the venue. Black ropes are clipped to the tops of these poles. The ropes can be unclipped to allow entry and exit from different areas. There is a third door, which we entered the club through, set apart from the other doors, on the right-hand side of the building.
>
> (Field notes)

Clearly, the experience within these two types of venue will differ greatly, despite both being under the general rubric of dance clubs.

Age

The 21-and-over clubs differ in some respects from the 18-and-over clubs in San Francisco. Most obvious is the fact that there are fewer venues in the city that cater to those 18 and over; clubgoers who are 21 and over have a much more varied selection of dance events from which to choose. The 18+ clubs serve as an introductory for most young people to club nightlife, and accordingly, those who promote such clubs spend time on creating an elaborate, exciting atmosphere, with DJs who spin popular tunes. For example, 715 Harrison is one of the premier 18+ venues that host City Nights, one of San Francisco's longest-running clubs. City Nights contains a multilevel dance floor with go-go cages high up on the walls for individuals to display their dancing skills under flashing lights while locally famous radio DJs spin on the turntables. Clubs for individuals 21+ are free to serve alcoholic beverages to their guests, and there are myriad styles of clubs for this age group.

Enforcing an age restriction is one way in which club operators exclude less desirable patrons. When we asked one venue owner why he encourages only customers age 25 and up to frequent his club, he replied that:

> People under 25 typically is where a lot of your violence – a lot of your problems, um, occur. Probably because they're not as experienced in going out, in socialization – haven't quite matured, and even at 25 ... you're just probably entering the work force with a real job, or getting out of

school and looking for a real job, so you're – you're just starting to really become a real independent adult – or – or moving in that direction pretty substantially.

This venue owner deemed patrons under 25 less mature and thus less likely to conduct themselves in an appropriate manner at entertainment venues.

For many of the young people we interviewed, clubs are associated with public alcohol drinking, which is itself seen as symbolic of nascent adulthood – and the age requirements and enforcement in clubs can be seen as establishing and demonstrating one's adult status. (See Chapter 10 for more on this.) One of the appeals of raves, on the other hand, is precisely the more open, sometimes all-ages, format of the events. While massive, licensed raves generally enforce age restrictions (albeit of the 18-and-up rather than 21-and-up variety), other more underground raves sport no such age restrictions and many more teenagers can be found at these events than at clubs. The absence of age restrictions at rave events allows younger attendees to participate in the scene, whereas they are excluded from other "mainstream" arenas of nightlife, such as clubs and bars.

Youth itself is celebrated in the traditional rave garb, emphasizing bright colors, childlike clothes, even pacifiers. As discussed in Chapter 2, though, raves are not without their tensions between older and younger ravers, as well as different styles of ravers who embrace or reject the "candy kid" image of raves.

Cost

The entrance fee, or cover, for clubs also varies widely. The cover charge becomes a fundamental aspect of club events because the cost to enter a club can influence a person's decision or ability to attend one. Some clubs in San Francisco charge up to $25 to enter, while others do not charge anything. The cover is generally higher for clubs that take place in larger venues or for clubs that are on Friday and Saturday nights. The clubs that are free are either smaller clubs or DJ bars. Many clubs also have varying entrance fees on the same night, depending on the time of entry or the gender of the patron. Some clubs will charge less for those who arrive early, generally within the first hour that the club is open. A small minority of clubs will have different covers for men and women, always charging the women less. This is generally a practice used by clubs where the majority of patrons are male. Some clubs will combine the two strategies, for example allowing women to get in free before a certain time.

The matter of entrance fees become even more complicated with VIP and guest lists for certain clubs. A prime example of such varying cover charges is at "Escape," an Asian-promoted party at Club NV (which has since shut down) where people who signed up for the guest list on the promoter Web site got in for free before 11.00 p.m., the discount guest-list members paid $10 before 11.00 p.m., the VIP members got in for free before 11.30 p.m., and general admission was $15. In addition to the cost of admission at these clubs, there is also the high cost of drinks, which range from $4 to $10, generally, with the typical price of cocktails being approximately $7.

When renowned DJs or performers come to a particular venue, prices may increase substantially. For example, Ruby Skye often hosts special performance events with internationally famous DJs and musicians that can cost $30 or more for admittance. The cost of entry paired with the cost of drinks (and sometimes drugs) can create quite an expensive night out. An establishment that hosts such costly events excludes patrons who may not be able to afford it, thus attracting a mostly middle-upper to upper-class crowd. Costs also alter according to the current economy. This element of clubs is thus the most changeable of the categories. Yet there are still the club events that are known to be expensive and those that are thought of as affordable, regardless of minor variations in cover charge.

Entrance fees at raves are typically more expensive than club cover charges. The size and cost of raves varies more widely than clubs. There are sometimes free raves, although that is rare, and most cost between $10 and $40. Most rave promoters sell tickets prior to the event at local record stores, and sometimes tickets will be sold "at the door" of the event. Some of the larger events cost as much as $70 at the door. Like the entrance cover at clubs, the price of rave tickets may exclude those who cannot afford the cost, especially taking into account the extra money that might be spent on drugs, costumes, party favors, or other accessories. Some respondents associated the increased cost of rave events with their increased commercialization or mainstream appeal.

Hours

Many of the larger clubs start between 9.00 p.m. and 10.00 p.m. and stay open until 3.00 a.m. to 7.00 a.m. There are only four venues that have clubs on Friday and Saturday that stay open until 6.00 a.m. to 7.00 a.m. After-hours clubs in San Francisco have had their share of trouble, from battles with local police to complaints from neighbors. In the late 1990s some popular late-night clubs shut their doors forever (e.g., DV8), and other venues felt pressure to close down as well. The San Francisco Late Night Coalition (SFLNC) was formed in 1999 by DJs, promoters, club owners, record producers, and dance enthusiasts to address these issues and to keep after-hours clubs open. Venues such as Ten15 and the Endup have been able to remain open late with the help of SFLNC. Many of the smaller clubs and DJ bars stay open until 2.00 a.m., although because some of those are bars and restaurants they are open before 9.00 p.m. In those cases the music generally does not start until 9.00 or 10.00 p.m. Clubs operate on a regular basis, usually weekly, bimonthly, or monthly. A weekly club will be at the same venue, at the same time, on the same day of the week, and will be organized by the same promoter. What generally changes is the DJ line-up, although many clubs have resident DJs who tend to play either every time or frequently. A club will generally play the same types of music each week, although there will be variations, depending on the DJ.

The hours for a rave depend on the type of rave that it is. Underground, unlicensed, unpermitted events do not conform to state codes regarding hours of operation and can go into all hours of the night. However, the massive raves held at large public venues operate under permits and thus are under the same restrictions regarding closing hours and hours of alcohol sales as nightclubs are, generally closing at 2.00 a.m., and some of these open in the very early evening.

The hours of club operation have been a matter of great controversy since the millennium. For the most part, operating hours are determined by California state law, which requires that establishments stop serving alcohol at 2.00 a.m. However, cities are able to issue "after hours" permits to stay open (but not serve alcohol). Proponents of these permits argue that it allows there to be a "cooling off" period before (drunken) patrons are ushered out on to the streets and that it also enables a series of staggered closing times, so that the streets aren't overwhelmed by all club and bar patrons being turned out at 2.00 a.m. A perceived moratorium on these permits was one of the galvanizing factors in the creation of the Entertainment Commission, to remove the permitting role of police, and the number of permits granted for this have grown a great deal since the EC's inception. (Of the 108 current permits, twenty-five have been issued since 2004: A. Sanders 2005.) At the Nightlife Safety Summit in 2008, however, some club owners complained that it's still impossible to get extended-hours permits due to the zoning in their districts.

Others focus on transforming the state laws to extend the hours of permitted alcohol sales. In 2004 State Assembly Member Mark Leno (the former San Francisco Supervisor who sponsored the Entertainment Commission legislation in the first place), proposed Assembly Bill 2433, which extends alcohol "last call" in some cities to 3.30 a.m. or 4.00 a.m. This was supported not only by owners of bars and clubs in San Francisco. (One nightclub owner argued for it on these grounds: "He said the initiative would calm crowd noise by creating a 'trickle out' effect. Also, he said, because most nightclub patrons don't go out until 11.00 p.m. or so, and last call is generally at 1.30 a.m., the short drinking time creates 'an atmosphere of frenzy and binge,'" A. Martin 2007.) The legislation also had considerable political support in the city. "The SFLNC, the Entertainment Commission, nine out of eleven [city] supervisors, and Mayor Gavin Newsom approved it, and a bus load of SF clubbers went to Sacramento to support it" (English 2004). Despite this support in San Francisco, they found no traction in the State Assembly. "Police Officers from Oakland, a MADD mother, and members of the Youth Leadership Institute spoke in opposition … the proposal didn't make it out of committee" (English 2004). The fact that it had such overwhelming support in San Francisco, but still was not able to pass in at the state level, indicates that while much of nightlife policy is controlled on the local/city level, it is still within the general confines of state legislation to which the cities must accede.

Dress code and entry requirements

Some clubs have "dress codes," rules about what patrons can and cannot wear. Dress codes most often mean that patrons cannot wear one or more of the following: hats, jeans, sneakers, tank tops, or other casual athletic wear. Sometimes the dress code is stricter for men than for women, and even if a club says it has a dress code, it is up to the Door Security and staff to enforce it. Many of the venue owners we interviewed spoke about using dress restrictions as a "tool," saying that individuals who dressed disrespectfully would be more likely to act disrespectfully toward the venue and other patrons. One owner in particular talked about the "respect quotient" increasing in his venue after he implemented a dress code. Another owner equated the dress code to a "filtering process," saying that he discourages styles of dress (such as overly baggy pants) that he considers a sign of lack of self-respect.

One female clubber echoed the owners' sentiments, stating that clubs who enforced dress codes were more pleasant for the patrons in attendance:

> ... I like there to be a dress code, I think. You know? At least for the boys. Like, you know, no ... no sports attire, like jerseys or anything like that. 'Cause ... when I ... I've noticed when I go into places, like clubs like that ... there tends to be, like, a lotta fights and stuff, and I don't wanna be around that.
>
> (Brenda, 25)

The norms of clothing at clubs are also deeply connected to the culture of sexuality and the perception of dance clubs as "meat markets" – an issue which we probe in greater detail in Chapter 10. Women are generally perceived by the young men and women we interviewed as having an easier time gaining admittance to dance clubs. They are seen as more likely to be admitted and less likely to be subject to pat-down searches upon entry. Not all women experience this equally, though – this may particularly be the case for women dressed in stylish, sexy, or provocative clothing. When our respondents contrast the rave experience with that of dance clubs, the two major (and not unrelated) areas of difference noted are the centrality of alcohol at clubs (versus ecstasy and other club drugs as raves) and the dominant focus on overt sexuality and hookups at clubs (versus the less sexually explicit ethos of raves). One key part of this latter distinction is focused on differing norms regarding clothing. The young men and women discuss the pressure to "dress to impress" at clubs – with an emphasis on skimpy, sometimes uncomfortable clothes for women, in contrast to the norms allowing "anything" to be worn at raves, right down to fuzzy pajamas, and where dressing too stylishly or too provocatively is itself a violation of rave norms. While the norms of dress may not always be enforced by formal dress codes, the informal expectations among clubgoers can themselves be quite powerful.

Dress code requirements are often posted outside of the club's entrance and/or on the club's Web site so that patrons can prepare their attire accordingly. One popular venue, in anticipation for their upcoming hip-hop show, posted its club policies on the Web site: it explicitly states that a dress code is "strictly enforced" and that "athletic wear, sweats, jerseys, baseball hats, overly baggy pants, and work boots" are prohibited. The promoters of the event also clarify that "entrance is at the complete discretion of the security team," meaning that the doorman will be responsible for determining whether or not someone is dressed appropriately and according to the dress code, but which also means that dress codes may be enforced selectively, targeting certain groups more than others. One nightclub promoter (from a different club) that we interviewed described using a dress code as part of a strategy of "fading people" (selectively denying access to patrons deemed undesirable):

> You don't let them come in and you implement a dress code and there are times where we fade people. So when a line accumulates, there may be people … they could be totally dressed nice, but they may not have the right attitude and so having properly trained security and staff that can recognize that is really the key. So a lot of times what we've done in the past is, we – in the lines – is keep people waiting. You know, have our line-host walk the line and pull people out and take them to the front. That might be discriminatory towards certain people, but at the same time these other people see the "right" people are getting into the club and the next time if they want to come into the club that's kind of what we want them to understand. This what you have to [do].

Dress codes establish an event's particular style and atmosphere; typically, parties with strict dress codes aspire to be upscale affairs where patrons are encouraged to be, in the words of the promoters, "high-fashion," "classy," "strictly upscale," and "dressed to impress." These guidelines also serve to establish the event's reputation. For special events the attendees may be asked to wear clothing to match the theme, such as island wear for a tropical party or white attire for an all-white theme. While this is rarely required for admission, one can obtain benefits by wearing the encouraged attire, such as getting in for free.

An enforced dress code may encourage some individuals to attend, appealing to those patrons who enjoy dressing up and being surrounded by fellow clubgoers adorned in polished, chic clothing. Brenda commented that the main appeal of going out to clubs was "dressing up like a slut" and observing what other women were wearing. Arun, 18, said that he would choose to frequent a club with a dress code because getting dressed up made him feel more mature:

> Oh, yeah, 'cause Underworld [Asian party promoter] is the type where it's … conservative … You have to dress a certain way to get into the parties … You have to have a button-up shirt and … or, like, a collared shirt … I mean … like, who doesn't like … who doesn't like feeling … like, who doesn't like dressing up, you know, a little bit older, you know, feeling a little bit more mature?

Getting into a club can be a source of excitement as well as a source of dread, particularly for those who get rejected by the gatekeepers (i.e., bouncers). (For more on the ambivalences of waiting in line and getting into clubs, see Malbon 1999.)

Some patrons prefer to dress in a more casual manner and would not choose to attend a club that enforced a strict dress code. Many of those we interviewed who identified more with the rave scene than the club scene cited clubs' onerous entry restrictions as a major source of their dislike of clubs. These entry requirements include the dress code, but also include the contraband searches they must endure before admittance to many clubs (as well as to licensed massive raves). They cite not only the greater freedom to bring in substances that they wish to ingest, but also avoidance of the humiliation and abuse that they describe being vulnerable to when getting admitted through Security. While few seemed to have difficulty smuggling illicit substances into the clubs (and women in particular cited increased chances, due to hiding things in their bra), it was the general treatment at the doors they found dispiriting.

In addition, some of the young African American men we spoke to felt that dress codes at clubs served to exclude them, especially those that forbade "ghetto" or "urban" attire. (See May and Chaplin 2008 for more on this topic.) These types of restrictions hint at racially discriminatory overtones; as one young man explained, individuals dressed in a hip-hop fashion are often perceived negatively and subsequently treated unfairly (Marcus, 23). And, indeed, there is sometimes a paternalistic tone to the defenses of dress codes offered by nightclub owners and managers that we interviewed, and one that specifically invoked them as an exclusionary process. As one nightclub owner comments:

> Well, the dress code thing is – it's a filtering process. You know – what's – what's in style and what's chic right now is showin' the world your underwear ... hanging your pants around your knees – and um – I personally wouldn't go to a place like that. I wouldn't feel safe ... and I don't think it's reflective of a high degree of self-respect. ... If going out to you means you wear the same thing you wear to the corner liquor store, this probably ain't the place for you – you know what I mean? There's other places you can go where you can look that way.
>
> (Interview with club owner)

Another club owner we interviewed said that he didn't want to have to impose a dress code, but that he felt he had to, to exclude "undesirable" patrons:

> We are starting to see the quality of our crowd degenerate, um, a little bit. And I resisted ... and I was, like, "No, I shouldn't have to do this." Like, people should be able to dress however they want, and it's so stupid not to allow people to wear a baseball cap, you know – um, but – in the end – I hate to admit it, but in the end, after doing it, the respect quotient in the bar is a lot higher.

While some of the clothes prohibited are generically casual (e.g., baseball caps), among the prohibited clothes is also the hyphy (local hip-hop variant) "uniform" of baggy pants and huge white t-shirts. Clothes associated with "thuggery" or "street life" are what this club owner wants to avoid:

> Um, so dress code is number one. No baggies. You got jeans comin' down to your crotch or lower, you're not comin' in. Um – you're – if you got a white tee that's like a, you know – 8 XL, um, you're not comin' in. Uh, if you have an airbrushed tee – because most of the time in Oakland the airbrushed tees have to do with like, street life, thuggery – you're not comin' in. Um, ball caps are – any

athletic wear, actually, is excluded. Um, including ball caps. Ball caps in general are excluded. Sneakers are okay, jeans are okay, um – it's like athletics – the big things are the baggies, the athletics and the graffiti.

(Interview with club owner)

"Thuggery" here seems to operate as code for young African American men wearing urban styles of clothing, perhaps associated with hip-hop or hyphy.

Music

But the most important organizing principle distinguishing one club from another is probably musical style. Music has played a primary role in the entertainment world of San Francisco for decades. From Beatnik-era jazz to classic rock shows at the now defunct Winterland to the rise of house music DJs, San Francisco has served as a home to musical creativity which has inspired international trends. Thus, music may be the most important factor when it comes to individuals choosing which San Francisco club to attend. Further evidence of its importance can be found on nightlife Web sites such as Nitevibe.com where one can search for a club by music genre. Club-night flyers also highlight the musical styles to be featured at their particular event.

While raves typically offer three or four different styles of music, permitted by the larger, multi-room venues in which they are held, all but the largest clubs usually feature just one specific genre of music, or sometimes a few types that are similar. There is sometimes an exception with larger clubs that have a number of separate rooms, like raves, and offer a different musical selection in each room. For example, a mega-club like Ten15 or Ruby Skye may put a headlining trance artist in the main room while the two or three smaller side rooms are occupied by resident DJs offering other musical styles such as house, hip-hop, Top 40, 1980s pop/rock or mash-ups. A fieldworker describes one club that offers its patrons two types of music to choose from:

The club was separated into two distinct dance and bar areas, each with its own DJ and musical style. Downstairs, the music was primarily dance remixes of Top 40 music similar to that which is played at many of the other gay clubs in San Francisco. Upstairs, the musical style was hip-hop.

(Field notes)

Generally speaking, house music has dominated the local scene for much of the time of this study, and the majority of venues featured at least one night per week of house music. There are approximately 181 club nights that mention "house" (and its varieties such as progressive and deep house) as the primary music style played, which does not include the other events which may play house music along with the other main styles for those clubs. Additional common musical styles found at San Francisco clubs are hip-hop, drum-and-bass, downtempo, funk, R&B/soul, reggae/dancehall, Latin/salsa, 1980s, and other electronica such as breakbeats and trance. There are some club nights that are known for their amalgam of various music genres but most focus on one or two styles. Some club nights are even more specified by subgenre, such as progressive house or underground hip-hop. When talking about the dance scene, there is often a focus on electronic music or "dance music," leading to the assumption that this is the only type of music played at clubs. In fact the San Francisco club scene offers a number of other prominent music genres, including hip-hop and popular rock. While house music may be the most dominant form of music found at events in the city, other music which does not fit into the electronica category is represented notably at many nightclubs. Hip-hop music is featured as the primary music genre at approximately sixty-six club nights in San Francisco at the time of this writing, which is the second most common style played next to house.

As noted earlier, much of the music identified today as rave music can be traced back to Chicago's urban dance music "house," "techno" music from Detroit, and "garage" music from New York (Foderaro 1988). San Francisco has placed its own stamp on this musical scene, from its importation and transformation of British beats in the early 1990s to the rejection of the British influence later in the decade which engendered a period of local music emphasis (Reynolds 1999; Silcott 1999), to today's uniquely San Francisco mash-ups. While the origins of the current dance scene can be traced back to musical inventions in Chicago or Detroit or New York, the more recent developments have their origins in the popular Mediterranean tourist island of Ibiza, Spain, in the late 1980s along with the start of a style of music that became known as the "Balearic beat." Over the years, new styles of electronic dance music (EDM) have emerged, while existing genres have given way to subgenres and crossbreeds. House music can now be progressive, soulful, or hard; drum 'n' bass has given way to jungle, hardcore has given way to gabber, and techno has become an outdated term in its generality. Although there are sometimes raves that feature a specific type of EDM, most events have several different genres that are played within separate rooms in the venue. Smaller raves may have only one or two rooms of music, while larger raves can have five or more.

Ethnicity

Ethnicity as a demarcating characteristic has tended to be overlooked in much of the literature on club, rave, and dance scenes, both drug-specific and sociological, and in fact much of the research in the UK has emphasized the all-encompassing social and ethnic attractiveness of the dance scene. (For important exceptions see Huq 2003, 2006; Maira 2002.) Yet a more detailed social contextual analysis of the scene may reveal the extent to which ethnic differences play a significant role in distinguishing which ethnic groups are attracted to which sectors of the scene. Are particular types of music representative of specific ethnic identities? This is often the perception; many of our respondents associate hip-hop and reggae with African Americans and Latinos, while electronic dance music and pop are more frequently connected with whites and Asians. What became apparent in our own research was how these perceptions, and the scene itself, were changing. For example, in San Francisco and its surrounding cities African Americans are not necessarily the primary ethnic group to attend hip-hop events; a large diversity of ethnic groups consider themselves active participants in the hip-hop scene. On the other hand, ecstasy has certainly spread from the rave and electronic dance music scenes and is increasingly present within hip-hop (especially local hyphy scenes). At the same time, raves have become more ethnically diverse. One young man talks about these changes:

> … I remember when the rave scene changed. I saw it change when it was goin' from all whites and Asians and stuff, then you'd gradually see gang bangers kinda comin' there too, a lot of Latino guys comin' in. Then you'd very gradually see more blacks comin' in. The next thing you know, you realize, you don't have to go to a rave to pop a pill [take ecstasy], you can go to the club and pop a pill. Or you don't even gotta go to the club, you can go to a sideshow [illegal car race], pop a pill, and that – and get all crazy.
>
> (Steven, 22)

After reviewing Internet and e-mail sources, it became apparent that Asian-focused club nights were the most prominent of ethnic-specific events in the San Francisco scene. We have identified fourteen different venues that host Asian club events and our research has documented an additional sixty-one clubs in the San Francisco Bay Area that appeal specifically to Asian American communities, forty-four of which are mainly Asian American. Some evidence of the predominance of Asians in San Francisco nightlife resides in the fact that there are a large number of renowned Asian DJs and promoters. For example, Shortkut, a world-renowned DJ who is a member of the now defunct Invisibl Skratch Piklz and of the current Triple Threat DJs, is a Filipino American who often performs at Asian parties as well as at mixed-ethnicity events. Hip-hop and Top 40 are most popular at Asian-specific club events. Depending on how many rooms are in the club, there may also be a room playing trance music or "old school" hits. At some of the rave events we attended for fieldwork in 2002–03, Asian Americans made up the single largest racial group at the event, sometimes topping 50 percent of the patrons.

Given our increasing awareness of the involvement of Asian Americans in the dance scene, we conducted preliminary observational work at two clubs catering primarily to Asian Americans. Our fieldworkers reported that over 95 percent of the attendees were Asian American, the majority of them in their early twenties. All the DJs were also Asian American. As a result of our fieldworkers' ability to integrate into some of the clubbers' networks, we were also fortunate to be able to attend a private Asian American dance party.

Asian party promoters, such as Saga Promotions and Synergy Promotions, send out massive e-mail lists and flyers targeting Asian Americans. There are also Asian-specific club guides online, such as ClubZen.com, that send out a weekly newsletter detailing all of the predominantly Asian club events taking place in the Los Angeles and San Francisco Bay Areas. One popular Asian club night was "Pulse" at Space

550, which occurred twice a month and was heavily promoted by Asian-focused promoters Abzolut and Climax. There are even events that target young Asian professionals who are 23 or over, such as the one-off parties (one-time events) promoted by Saga Signature, a division of Saga Promotions. Interestingly, Saga Promotions (now defunct) often displayed the phrase "Asian-friendly" next to a few of the events on their Web site. It's a vague term that seems redundant to use in an Asian nightlife guide – does it mean that it is not a predominantly Asian event but that Asians would be comfortable there? Does "Asian-friendly" imply that an Asian individual would not get turned away from the event? The meaning behind this term is unclear. One party description also included the phrase "mixed crowd" next to "Asian-friendly"; this might indicate that while the majority of attendees may not be Asian, a person of Asian descent might still enjoy him or herself there. The party promoter's effort to describe the ethnic composition of the crowd demonstrates how ethnicity – in addition to cost, venue, music, and venue size – is a deciding factor for many individuals in whether or not they will attend a particular event. "Asian-friendly" events may attract those who feel more comfortable in a club setting with similar people; others who prefer a more ethnically diverse nightlife experience might choose an event deemed "mixed." In Chapter 11 we will return to the issue of Asian American involvement in clubs, raves, and club drugs, focusing on issues of identity, consumption, and normalization.

Nightlife and violence

While the major source of complaints and actions against clubs are connected to noise issues, from the point of view of those who we interviewed in our study of regulation – police, club owners and promoters, staffers involved with the city's Entertainment Commission – the second most pressing social problem connected to nightlife is "undesirable patrons" and the violence they bring. This side of nightlife is often neglected in studies of rave scenes and club cultures. As drug researchers we were struck by how far removed issues related to drug use were in the problems-narratives in our interviews with those associated with the nightlife industries, be they police, nightclub owners, or city officials. As one promoter put it:

> I'd trade the guns for the drugs any day. I'd trade the drugs for the knives …
> I mean, a knife or a gun is most likely going to be a serious if not fatal decision.
> Most of the cases with drug use [in the 1990s], we did not see death.[9]
>
> (Interview with promoter)

The city and the police clearly see violence as a major problem facing (and stemming from) nighttime entertainment venues. In January 2008, after two shootings outside nightclubs in just a few days, the mayor's office convened a "Nightlife Safety Summit" bringing together police, security companies, nightclub owners, and promoters. Nightclub owners, and by extension the Entertainment Commission, were chastised for not taking better control of nightlife, for being irresponsible. "It won't be allowed to continue … We're here to help you, but we are going to make some changes," a city official argued (Bulwa 2008). They announced that police officials plan to inspect every nightclub in the city at least once in the next year to make sure they are living up to their responsibilities as holders of liquor and entertainment permits – perhaps indicating a swing back toward police control.[10]

Among stakeholders in San Francisco nightlife there is an ongoing debate about the relationship between nightclubs and violence. To what degree is violence engendered by nighttime entertainment? Are nightclub operators to blame for violence that happens outside their premises? Those who defend the nightclubs frequently point to the fact that there are violence and shootings in many parts of San Francisco life, not just in the nighttime economy. For example, both at the Nightlife Safety Summit and in our interviews, nightclub owners brought up the example of a 2007 shooting at the Metreon mall, in which a teenager shot someone, allegedly for moving too slowly on an elevator. In citing this incident, they argue that violence is possible anywhere, even somewhere as innocuous as a mall, so it doesn't seem fair that nighttime venues should be seen as particularly problematic. A nightclub owner similarly claims that responsibility is a societal one, not something specific to the clubs. Closing down clubs is not the solution, he argues:

> The nightclubs don't create the problems; they're created by society and are played out at the nightclub, just like the problems of poverty are played out by shoplifters or other emotional problems, but they're not caused by the stores. The existence of the store does not make someone a thief, just like the existence of a nightlife doesn't make them a homicidal maniac.
>
> (Interview with club owner)

Yet, at the same time, nightclub owners and those working in security do concede that violence is a problem in their industry in a way that it never was ten or twenty years ago. Throughout the Nightlife Safety Summit people referred to a "sea change" that has happened, with problems with patrons reaching levels never previously experienced. One owner remarked, "This isn't 1985 any more." A former nightclub owner argued that in the 1980s or even 1990s "you never saw a shooting or stabbing," that they maybe happened "three times a decade" whereas now, he argues (somewhat hyperbolically), "it's every goddamn weekend" (interview). When discussing the greatest challenges in the nighttime economy today, most of the nightclub owners and promoters we spoke with identified the need to defuse potentially violent situations in and around their club, as well as effectively "weeding out" potentially problematic patrons before they are even admitted to the club. In these discussions we see arguments about what makes a good/effective/responsible nightlife operator and what makes a problem operator, and the ability to properly attract and dissuade the right people comes up again and again as a major defining characteristic. (See Talbot 2006 for parallels in a British context.)

Running throughout the discussions of good versus bad managers is the ability to attract or dissuade desirable versus undesirable patrons to one's venue. When nightclub owners talk about "desirable" versus "undesirable" patrons, generally, it's often connected to who will or will not cause confrontations, fights, or other problems for the club: "Good behavior is people that go out, enjoy themselves, leave and don't cause a ruckus on the way out," with bad behavior "People who take out their inability to problem solve and their aggressions in physical ways – That's bad behavior" (interview).[11] One former nightclub owner describes what he sees as a continuum between problematic and nonproblematic nightlife. At the nonproblematic end he (intriguingly) places gay leather bars, while at the problematic end are clubs with "gangsta rap." The key difference along the way is (his estimation of) the propensity for violence.

> Now if you have, for example, a bunch of leather boys who are 40 to 60 [years old] … the amount of violence and the amount of problems is probably gonna be one per 100,000 customers … so that's the least problematic. And then the next one is probably the twinky gay boys with, you know, look like Abercrombie & Fitch ads, so they don't cause much problem, except they tend to, you know, pass out on ecstasy and GHB, and the ambulance … has to come and cart 'em off to the hospital. So then you go down … Top 40 no problem, this and this and this, and then when you get all the way down the scale to gangsta rap, then you're havin' a problem every day and night you're open, unless you have extremely tight security and even then … These kids …
>
> (Interview with club owner)

Often, this issue of desirable (or acceptable) patrons gets mixed up with issues of musical genre – with some musical content (most notably, hip-hop) presented as being more problem-prone than others. (And, lurking beneath these discussions of the problems of hip-hop, are implications about the problems of patrons who listen to hip-hop, particularly young African American or "urban" men – rarely stated outright, but this seems to comprise some of the subtext of conversations.) In the days before the Entertainment Commission the police were often explicit in the connections they made between undesirable patrons and undesirable music. Until court cases found that regulating musical content was a First Amendment violation, police-issued permitting requirements for nightclubs "sometimes forbade clubs to play rap music or loud rock music" (Harnden 2006). (And, indeed, this was one of the many issues leading up to the creation of the Entertainment Commission, with the police being seen as having gone too far in their restrictions.)

One media account of the time asked, "Why rap music? Why not opera? Or country music? The question of discrimination and racial profiling inevitably comes up when local club owners talk about police censorship" (Miller 2002). This reporter quotes one neighborhood group representative as arguing that "Rap music attracts a certain 'element' that may or may not be desirable." Similarly, a police captain argued that "hip-hop music often draws gang members," thus justifying censoring the music that could be played in venues in the Mission district. "We often prohibit hip-hop music. Historically there have been problems – fights and violence – at hip-hop events," he says. However, he doesn't have any evidence of this in the Mission. "There are no specific instances of this because we haven't had any hip-hop shows," he says. "But just look in the news at Oakland and Richmond" (Miller 2002).[12]

A city staffer concedes that it was once common with the police, but is adamant that such "music profiling" no longer occurs: "that's racist and it's unconstitutional, and so we don't regulate content." Yet, it's not clear that such profiling is entirely obsolete, and some argue that it is still occurring, albeit more subtly. Such sentiments are echoed by a promoter involved in the EC who sees hip-hop as a major source of problems, arguing that he would never play it (or certain variants, at least) within his clubs: "If you play gangsta rap and thug hip-hop, you're gonna have somebody killed outside your venue eventually ... doesn't matter where it is, it's not the place, it's the programming which attracts the patronage" (interview).[13] And to the degree that promoters and owners have themselves internalized the music-profiling message, strongly avoiding programming that attracts the "wrong" crowd, it may not even be necessary for the regulators to enforce these exclusions. But the end result is the same.

One club manager explains that his club does not get hassled or surveilled by the police, because it's not the sort in which fights break out. He contrasts this with problem clubs:

> I'm not saying African American, but ... if somebody's using ghetto thug music, like people smoking marijuana outside the club, or people hiding Hennessey in the bottle outside, drinking and stuff, I'm sure police would keep an eye on it ... you don't do that kind of party. You have to be smart enough not to deal with that. It's too risky.
>
> (Interview with club manager)

Here, as in some of our other interviews, "ghetto thug music," drugs, inappropriate behavior, and the mentioned-but-not-mentioned African Americans are interwoven. And all are seen as sources of "too risky" behavior, not worth it for a smart businessperson. This Bay Area DJ is quite explicit about the problems with programming hip-hop. It attracts undesirable people, by which he means those of the "lower" class who are "ghetto":

> But, you know, from a hip-hop aspect, you know, I've done hip-hop events where it unfortunately attracted crowds from [working-class African American suburb] Oakland, and it's just not a positive thing ... The people that are listening, you know, tend to act out what they're hearing, so and then they bring that to the clubs. And that's something we just can't deal with, or we can't tolerate, in my opinion. ... because I think the masses are, you know, lower-income, very ethnic culture.
>
> (Interview with DJ)

In contrast, the demographic he is trying to attract is "young professionals, ethnically diverse, that, you know, dress well and behave themselves, they are mature, that go to a nice upscale lounge and, you know, listen to hip-hop. That's more who I would like to target." He warns, though, that there's a persistent danger of attracting a "ghetto" crowd instead.

But others (and, not surprisingly, people involved in working with hip-hop events) argue that it's not the music/programming that leads to violence. One promoter at the Summit, for example, argues that while there have been some mêlées associated with some hip-hop events, this has more to do with the fact that the events were promoted endlessly on the radio and didn't have a cover charge, which led to a crowd much too large to control, and the fact that the events were insufficiently staffed, and not to some inherent tendency in either hip-hop music or hip-hop music fans. He argued that "It's not the program but the execution of the program."

Even among those who support hip-hop, or who oppose profiling based on musical content, may themselves engage in profiling acceptable and unacceptable forms of hip-hop. One EC staffer who opposed the idea that the music is the problem, and the practice of music profiling in licensing/enforcement, does find one form of music troublesome – "hyphy." "In its language and lyrics of behavior to hyphy, hyphy promotes 'go crazy, go wild,' crazy-ass shit, and although fun in theory, in practice, if you want to go crazy and do the hyphy thing you're going to cause problems" (interview); in this interview, as in others, even in the midst of arguing that no particular type of music (or music fans) are the problem, such opinions manage to sneak in. And in the Nightlife Safety Summit some major hip-hop promoters argued that they wouldn't program hyphy because of the problems it entails: kids that "act up" violent, uncontrolled energy, kids who can't get into clubs because of money or age restrictions loiter outside the event and cause problems.

These narratives about the prominence of weeding out those who are not wanted as part of this nightlife indicate that while various stakeholders talk about diversity, inclusion, and expanding the nighttime entertainment economy, exclusion is fundamentally central as well. As Chatterton and Hollands have argued, "Spaces of consumption, then, are an important component of social exclusion" (2003: 184). Despite the ethos of unity and inclusiveness that dominates much discussion of club and rave cultures, long-lasting and continuing exclusions must be acknowledged and understood as well.

Conclusion

Throughout this part of the book we have focused on the big picture, the broader context of rave, club, and dance scenes – at the global, national, and local level. This context is crucial for understanding these social settings and cultures. Yet, at this broad level, it is easy to lose sight of the specific experiences of the individuals within these scenes. In the next part, we turn to the more fine-grained experiences of those involved in the scene. In particular, we examine issues surrounding club-drug use within these scenes, focusing particularly on the constructions of and negotiations of issues of pleasure and risk as they shape and are shaped by the experiences of the young people we interviewed.

Drug pleasures, risks, and combinations

Part III

Drug pleasures, risks, and combinations

Chapter 6

The "great unmentionable"

Exploring the pleasures and benefits of ecstasy

Basically that's how I could describe it, a pleasure overload.

(Lily, 19)

All my friends say, like, you know, I get very, very friendly. They say, like, they look at me and they think that I've got like sunshine flying out of my butt. Like, I'm so happy … It's like … I can't be any more happy.

(Jamie, 16)

Introduction

Legal and illegal ingested substances have long given pleasure to those who have consumed them, from the Yanomamo using tobacco in Brazil (Chagnon 1977), Hippies smoking marijuana in Haight Ashbury (Cavan 1972), Africans drinking beer in a Bulawayo beer garden (Wolcott 1974) to English youth popping ecstasy pills in Manchester (H. Parker *et al.* 1998). Given the extent to which these substances have provided individual pleasure, as well as social and communal enjoyment, one is forced to ask the question: why then is it that so much of the research on ingested substances has ignored this central feature? Why, to quote D. Moore and Valverde, is pleasure the "great unmentionable?" (2000: 528). While it may be understandable that drug and public health researchers should focus more on the social and personal problems and risks, it is nevertheless surprising that the element of pleasure should have been so overlooked in the thousands of articles written on the use of illicit drugs.

This neglect of pleasure and fun from much of the drug research literature is particularly striking when we examine the contemporary research on ecstasy and other "club drugs." While researchers have labeled the group of drugs typically associated with electronic dance music events as "club" or "party" drugs, the discussion of pleasure is still absent. It is as though pleasure has become unseeable within much of the research. Even when notions of pleasure or fun are allowed to enter the picture, they are mentioned merely to be denied or negated. For example, the title of an informational article on a government prevention Web site speaks for itself: "Club drugs aren't 'fun drugs' " (Leshner 2000). "Governmental discourses about drugs and alcohol … tend to remain silent about pleasure as a motive for consumption and raise instead visions of a consumption characterized by compulsion, pain and pathology" (O'Malley and Valverde 2004: 26). The absence of any significant discourse about pleasure within drug research means that a central component of why people use mind-altering substances is ignored. As Parker and his colleagues have remarked, "we need to place ... pleasure in the formula. Drugs are used because they give enjoyment" (H. Parker *et al.* 1998: 133).

While many different social, historical, and political reasons could be suggested as to why the pleasure element has been largely ignored in so much of the research literature, one possible contributory factor would seem particularly relevant.[1] Bearing in mind its underlying public-health philosophy and associated problem-focused perspective, research in the drug field has focused understandably on illicit drugs as dangerous substances, which, unless strongly controlled by enlightened social policy, create problems and entail social and physical costs for the individual and for society as a whole. This approach views youthful drug use as especially dangerous because young people are perceived as "a highly vulnerable sector of the population" (Ettorre and Miles 2002: 176), involved in risky consumption and likely to be "victims of their own irresponsibility" (2002: 178). Young people are viewed as essentially passive and in need of protection, and consequently "the agency of young people is largely neglected" (2002: 174). Given such a perspective on the dangers of drugs, it is not surprising that the active pursuit of pleasure on the part of young people would be downplayed or ignored. Furthermore, focusing on the risks and problems of drug use is not surprising given the extent to which notions of risk permeate much of contemporary thought, not solely within the drug and medical professions but also within society at large. This preoccupation is also true within other social science research literature, which has emphasized the role of risk in everyday life (U. Beck 1992; Douglas 1985; Giddens 1990). Unfortunately, by examining risk solely from a problem perspective, drug researchers have tended to ignore the possibility that for many young people taking risks may be an important source of pleasure and excitement (Hayward 2002; Reith 2005), issues we explore in more detail in the next chapter.

Overall, while this literature has been particularly important in providing information on the problems associated with ecstasy, contemporary drug-using patterns, and the characteristics of the users, it has generally ignored both the role of pleasure and fun in consuming the drugs and the social context in which this consumption takes place. The young drug user is portrayed as separate and divorced from his or her social setting, and their social identities have become subsumed by the substance. They are defined solely as drug users, and this overarching identity becomes the individual's defining characteristic. Wagner calls this tendency to categorize individuals solely by their drug behavior a process of "decontextualization of isolated behaviors" (1997: 69). Decontextualization is sometimes so thorough that it is difficult to uncover how these individuals behave in social settings, perceive their social lives, or express their feelings and beliefs. Furthermore, because the pleasure discourse is underdeveloped within epidemiological research, little attention has been focused on the social construction of pleasure.

In order to begin to readjust this imbalance, and in an attempt to relocate enjoyment at the center of the drug-using equation, the aim of this chapter is to explore the elements of pleasure in the drug-use narratives of our study participants. Unlike much of the research on youthful drug use, which views young people as both passive recipients and "inadequately formed adults" (Maira 2004), we adopt an approach that views young people as active players negotiating their lives within certain social-structural and cultural constraints. Utilizing recent theoretical developments in both cultural studies and cultural criminology, we examine our in-depth qualitative interview data to explore the ways in which these young people experience the pleasures – and fun – in taking ecstasy and attending dance events. In so doing we hope to shed light on why taking these substances is so appealing to so many young people.

As O'Malley and Mugford have argued, "pleasure is not defined the same way in all societal contexts, nor are all drugs seen as desirable and pleasurable by all people in all cultures at all times" (1991: 51). Given the tendency of traditional drug literatures both to downplay the importance of pleasure and decontextualize the user, we will now examine an alternative literature which has focused more specifically on examining the social setting within which these young people consume ecstasy and experience fun. This literature explores the meanings that young people give to these experiences, and instead of adopting a problem perspective, it celebrates young people's enjoyment of the dance scene.

Focusing on pleasure: an alternative perspective

The starting point for much of this alternative sociological and cultural studies literature has been the attempt to understand the rapid expansion of the electronic dance music scene, discussed in Chapter 1. Even though the specific focus of individual researchers has been diverse, they have all explored the experiences of young people within this leisure activity and sought to understand the pleasurable features of the contemporary dance scene.[2] Redhead's (1990) early commentary on the rave scene, for example, highlighted the pursuit of pleasure as a central feature of rave culture.

This focus on pleasure was further developed by writers such as Malbon (1999), who provided the first detailed account of the internal workings of the club scene and the night out. Malbon sought to show us the "lived, performed and emotional nature of clubbing" (1999: 17). His interest was to explore how this pleasurable state, what he calls an "oceanic" or "ecstatic" experience, was achieved. Other studies, while focusing on different issues, have also emphasized elements of pleasure. For example, writers such as Bennett (2000) and Gilbert and Pearson (1999) have focused on the pleasure of the musical aspects of the scene, while others have concentrated on exploring the pleasurable elements of dancing (Thomas 1997). Finally, because of the popularity of the dance scene for young women, feminist researchers have examined the relationship between gender and pleasure (Henderson 1993b; McRobbie 1994; Pini 2001) both from the perspective of young women and also, but to a lesser extent, from the perspective of young men. (See Chapter 9 for more on sexuality, gender, and ecstasy.)

As discussed in the first chapter, cultural studies research on raves and the dance scene provides an important counterbalance to the problem-focused approach of much of the drug literature. Given the sharp contrast between the foci of epidemiology and cultural studies, it is not surprising that the implicit or even explicit conceptualizations of young people are also significantly different. These two approaches reflect a dichotomous view of young people based in part on different underlying theoretical paradigms of positivism and phenomenology. The epidemiological drug research typically portrays youth as vulnerable and in need of protection, and their drug use as especially dangerous. Cultural studies researchers, in contrast, emphasize the ways that young people actively and creatively negotiate the world around them (Ettorre and Miles 2002: 173). They are viewed as actively involved in negotiating their lives and using "modes of consumption as a means of making sense of a rapidly changing world" (Ettorre and Miles 2002: 178).

As noted earlier, cultural studies have highlighted the pleasurable features of attending dance events, whether that be obtaining an ecstatic experience (Malbon 1999), enjoying the music (Bennett 2000), or exploring new boundaries of femininity (Pini 2001). However, in spite of this emphasis on elements of pleasure and fun, these studies have considered the use of mind-altering substances largely as an adjunct to other issues.[3] While, for example, Malbon discusses the use of ecstasy and the extent to which it can provide "an additional layer of emotional and sensational action" (1999: 116), his discussion of drugs is secondary to exploring other salient features, primarily the creation of a communal oneness.

In focusing on these features of raves and dance events, researchers have downplayed the extent to which using drugs may also be an important and even normalized part of young people's leisure activities and an essential contribution to their overall enjoyment of the night out. As H. Parker and colleagues (2002) have argued, drug use among young people who attend dance events has become increasingly culturally acceptable or normalized and integrated into their leisure and lifestyle. The use of drugs that can bring about marked mood alterations and are themselves illicit pleasures may further "enhance the excitement" (O'Malley and Mugford 1993: 204) of the event. One of the key attractions of attending dance events and doing drugs is the possibility of being involved in an exciting and nonmundane activity.

Having fun and finding pleasure

A variety of drugs are used by the young men and women in the San Francisco Bay Area dance scene (see Chapter 2 for details). After marijuana, ecstasy is by far the most popular drug, used by 92 percent of our study's participants. And it is in discussing ecstasy that our participants provide the most detailed and nuanced discussions of the pleasures connected to the drug.

An important and not surprising feature to emerge from the participants' accounts of ecstasy is the extent to which having *fun* is a central component. Time and again, participants, when asked what they enjoy about using ecstasy, utilize the word "fun" to describe their experiences: "To me E is like the funnest drug. It's the funnest. It's so much fun. And, like, the high was great" (Miranda, 22). The importance of having fun is not surprising, given both the significance of attending dance events for many young people as a valued leisure activity as well as the extent of ecstasy use at dance parties. They frequently described how ecstasy, especially when used within the dance-event setting, allows them not just to have a good time but to experience a superlative level of fun. The element of fun is therefore a central feature of these discussions of pleasure, and within their narratives having fun is an integral part of the other more specific effects and benefits outlined below. In addition to the general feature of fun, the descriptions on pleasure and ecstasy can be divided into two general types: those that focus on the immediate effects while under the influence and those that emphasize more long-term pleasurable benefits.

Immediate effects: transforming the everyday

Although participants did describe negative experiences and effects from ecstasy (explored in the next chapter), the majority characterize their experiences as largely pleasurable and positive. For some, the pleasures center solely around enjoying an exciting night out, while for others the pleasures experienced are life-changing. Ecstasy users described how they perceive themselves, experience the environments in which they use, and relate to others, highlighting the *extraordinary* or transcendental nature of the experience (Lyng 1990). As O'Malley and Mugford have noted, "in such a cultural milieu ... illicit and even dangerous drug taking as a leisure activity appears as an intelligible form of the normatively sanctioned search for the extraordinary" (1991: 57). Ecstasy changes the ordinary and the familiar into something that is "out of the ordinary." It operates not only to disrupt or "break the routine" of life (Stanley Cohen and Taylor 1976: 45), but also to transform mundane activities and interactions into ones that are deeply pleasurable, satisfying and exciting.[4] Going beyond the everyday – "alterity," as Malbon (1999) calls it – removes the ecstasy user "from the 'normal' times, spaces and social relations of their everyday lives" (Malbon 1999: 83). Transforming the everyday, "transgressing boundaries," and inspiring "pleasure, excitement, exhilaration and desire" (Lupton 1999a: 167) are central and fundamental features of ecstasy's appeal:

> So the first time ... and every time, you're a kid in the candy store. But the first time, you're just going crazy. You just want ... you have so much energy and just like ... it's like a new ... it's just brand-new. It's a whole other way of looking at the world and seeing people and stuff.
>
> (Malia, 20)

For this woman, ecstasy use is energizing, novel, and radically transformative of her outlook on the world. In citing ecstasy's transformative capacity, the pleasures of ecstasy go beyond mere "fun" to something else. The descriptions of the immediate pleasurable aspects of participants' ecstasy experiences can, for the purposes of this chapter, be divided into three distinct but interrelated and often overlapping components – the physical experience, the emotional experience, and the experience of sociability and interacting with others.

The physical experience

An increase in energy and a heightening of the senses are the primary physical effects of the ecstasy "high" as described by the participants. The pleasures of these physical effects are often tied to the social context within which they use the drug. For example, because many participants use ecstasy at dance events, they note a connection between the drug and their enjoyment of music and dancing. Many ecstasy users are able to enjoy music and dancing even more than they normally do, because the music sounds "better" or they can "feel" the music, and they can dance for longer periods:

> When you're listening to the music, it's not like you're just listening to it, like you can feel the pulsations of the bass or the drum, and it's not just something that you're there listening to, it's like you're feeling it. It sounds weird but ... And the people around you are feeling it too, and it's just such a vibe of positivity.
>
> (Magdalena, 24)

Here ecstasy transforms the physical experience of the music, and the fact that this effect is shared by others further intensifies the pleasure of the experience. Similarly, Justin explains how ecstasy leads to pleasurable body effects and disinhibition which themselves make dancing better:

> And then I started to feel good in my body internally and just ... it overcame my ... my body basically ... made my dancing a lot ... easier. Yeah, in ... and uninhibited ... Yeah, that was always one of the ... one of the greatest things was dancing on E, yeah.
>
> (Justin, 25)

Participants also described the pleasures of visual effects and their sense of touch while on ecstasy. This heightened sense of touch makes physical contact with others more pleasurable, as Conrad, 21, says: "I was just sitting against the wall with my girlfriend lying against me ... It felt so good. It feels good to have human contact. Like ... you feel a warmth. Not just from physical but also, like ... you feel ... emotionally warm." Again, the physical pleasures of the drug are intimately connected with its social aspects. Overall, these physical effects allow young people to experience their environment in new and exciting ways. Experiencing these physical and sensory pleasures offers, according to Jackson (2004), "an alternative collective social order where people are granted access to explore sensual indulgences" (O'Brien 2004: 596) and shake off their "constricted, urbanized body" (Jackson 2004: 167).

The emotional experience

Many of the pleasurable effects of the ecstasy high have to do with its impact on the users' emotional state and their sense of well-being. Participants enjoy their ecstasy experiences because they feel "good," "happy," and "relaxed." As Conrad remarked, "It makes you feel very, very, very, very, very good." Another said that ecstasy feels "like happiness that's about to like explode out of you" (Anna, 23). Some even described their state of mind as "blissful" (Dylan, 21). This sense of increased well-being allows ecstasy users some respite from everyday worries and allows them to focus on enjoying themselves and being present in the moment:

> When I was on E, it was just great, everything was great. "Life's great, da, da, da," you know. It's just like ... you had no cares in the world. Time was time at the moment you're in. Don't worry about tomorrow. That's the way it was for me, when I was on it at the parties.
>
> (Victor, 23)

In addition to this sense of well-being, participants also described feeling a sense of freedom that allows them to behave in a less self-conscious or self-critical way. They feel free to act openly and authentically, to dance without worrying about whether they are "good," and to generally express themselves without fearing what others might think:

> You, like ... you open up to people. Like ... I mean ... I don't know. Like, you don't feel like threatened by anybody, there's no, like ... worrying about trying to be something you're not. Like, you can just open up and talk about whatever you want and ... dance and ... do anything you want. It's like ... I don't know, it's just ... a really great feeling.
>
> (Paul, 21)

In this interview, and in others, participants emphasize the way that ecstasy facilitates not so much a transformation into someone or something new, but rather ecstasy enables them to finally be and act as they really are, unfettered from the artifice of everyday life. Ecstasy's impact on people's physical and emotional state, its enhanced sociability, combined with a meaningful social context, fosters interactions with others that leads users to feel the benefits of ecstasy are beyond simple physical and mental effects.

Interacting with others

Ecstasy transforms the users' connections with others by altering the norms and expectations of everyday social behavior. The social constraints and barriers that exist in everyday social interactions, for example being too emotional or too open, are suddenly lifted by the effects of ecstasy, which make people feel much more sociable and empathetic:

> [It] gave me a perception of, like ... there's people all, like ... you know, there's certain definite things that everybody responds to from being human and, like ... you know, ecstasy basically allows you to like overcome a lot of ... weird stupid

social barriers that like ... might exist in a person. And it helped me to, like, overcome ... those barriers when dealing with other people.

(Deep, 23)

This young man experiences ecstasy as enabling not just superficial effects on sociability but a deeper dismantling of social barriers. Ecstasy can produce, as Jackson has noted, "a temporary and partial dip in the feeling of fear and anxiety, which suffuses much of our social experiences" (2004: 64). As Chelsea, 17, claimed, "it removes the fear factor ... You know, you still know your boundaries ... you still know when there's some things that you just shouldn't say, but you're not afraid to say some things." Because norms of appropriate social and personal behavior and notions of privacy are transformed, people often become much more eager to interact with others and are willing to share their personal thoughts and feelings. Such thoughts and feelings would, in more "normal" circumstances, often be kept secret:

There's inevitably that talking point where you're sitting down and, like, talking to people. And you just, like, talk about all kinds of stuff and maybe, like, you say things that you wouldn't normally say, I guess. But then at the time it doesn't seem like that, or even afterwards it doesn't seem, like, really abnormal. Like, I was never, like, "Oh, I wish I hadn't said that," or something ... You just like tell people that you appreciate them or remember fun things that you did, that maybe you just like forget about that like normally. But then you don't when you're on E, so then you say it ... I thought that was fun.

(Kristin, 18)

Here the openness engendered by ecstasy is described not only as novel or interesting, but explicitly as fun; this openness becomes a source of the pleasure of ecstasy. This openness in turn not only leads ecstasy users to bond more closely with friends and partners but produces in them an eagerness to meet new people. Participants who described themselves as normally shy told of how they become more outgoing and their uneasiness about talking to strangers diminishes:

Because it kind of, like, lets the guard down ... it makes people feel so happy and so like love, that people come together and, like, hug and talk, and, like, want to listen and, like, know you, how you feel. And ... that would never happen in a normal circumstance. There's definitely a lot of, like, meeting new people and talking to new people ... And, like, new people you meet, you're, like, "You're my best new friend." And, like, you feel like they are, you know. You don't feel, like ... you don't feel, like, hesitant or sketchy towards people. Like, you're just really, like, open to, like, meeting new people.

(Dana, 22)

The use of the word "love" in this and in so many of the interviews should not be underestimated or dismissed. It reflects for many of the participants the deepness of the feelings that they experience while on ecstasy with others. Ecstasy users talked about trusting others who are on ecstasy and feeling closer to "strangers." They described experiencing feelings of love or a sense of "being loving" towards both friends or partners and others in general. Feeling closer with friends and being able to easily meet and connect with strangers, and thus transforming the "normal" boundaries of social relationships, is something that many feel is one of the most important benefits of ecstasy. Overall, many participants indicate feeling free of the constraints and pressures of everyday interactions and hence they value these opportunities, even if, as many noted, it is drug-induced.

This change in notions of social boundaries also results in a diminution in the perception of social distance between people, which normally operates in day-to-day life. Spencer describes this process as "the abolition of difference and the creation of a sense of 'communion' " (1985: 154, cited in Malbon 1999). Participants described how they become more accepting of others and less judgmental while on ecstasy. They become more open to sharing and finding connections with others who seem, at least on the surface, to be very different:

> Everybody ... you just feel, like, so much love toward people. You kinda, like ... all your barriers and ... discriminations, prejudices, everything just goes away, like, everybody's equal, and it feels really good, it feels ... I don't even know. Like, words can't even really explain it, it just feels amazing.
>
> (Ynez, 22)

While some argued that these connections with strangers are fleeting and superficial, and limited to the context in which they occur, others noted that the experiences are enjoyable and beneficial regardless of their ephemeral nature. Ynez elaborates: "I'd rather, like, live knowing, like, how great people can be in certain situations, even though it's, like, drug-related, you know. I think it's amazing, like, knowing how people can be."

In the context of a dance event or party where others also use ecstasy, respondents feel a freedom of social interaction often missing in their normal lives. Of course the setting of the dance event as the context within which this interaction takes place, coupled with the use of ecstasy, is significant in creating these experiences. As Jackson notes, in many ways "ecstasy is the direct antidote to the sense of underlying anxiety that infects modern, urban life. It allows you to experience the crowds ... in a very different way. Certainly part of this encounter arises from the social rules that surround much of clubbing, but ecstasy allows you to experience those rules fully" (Jackson 2004: 66).

Using ecstasy in an environment where others also use, coupled with the agreed-upon social norms of the event, they set out to participate in a new and exciting shared experience – a sense of "being together" (Malbon 1999: 73). An essential part of the pleasure experienced by participants within this setting is knowing that others are "on the same level," and therefore would reciprocate this behavior:

Interviewer.   What was great about it at a rave? That's like the place you like to do it.

Dana.   Because, like, it was just everybody was in your same boat. It wasn't like you were the only one on the drug ... So it was like everybody feels what you're feeling. So everybody's so happy and it's just, like, all around. You know, like, it's just like everybody's there on your same level. They're all, like, on a drug and like all feeling the same way and all feeling like this energy.

(Dana, 22)

Participants find satisfaction, comfort and a sense of belonging in knowing that others share in and are committed to the same pleasurable experience. Thus, in addition to their individual pleasures, they also find pleasure from feeling and knowing that they are part of a collective. This sense of collectivity has been noted by other researchers who have emphasized the pleasurable nature of merging with others. For example, Lupton, in discussing risk and pleasure, uses the Durkheimian concept of "collective effervescence" to describe such group experiences, in which "participants may lose a sense of their autonomous selves, becoming, at least for a brief time, part of a mass of bodies/selves with a common shared purpose" (1999a: 153).[5]

> I remember there was a time when ... I don't even know what songs were playing, but it was, like, really good. And ... along with the lights and I just ... felt, like, really peaceful and calm and everything, and then ... the feeling of being connected to everybody around me, 'cause everybody else was feeling it too, like, I looked around ... The DJ put on like a really good track, and then everybody ... like, right, when they hear the first beats they all cheered ... we were all ... like, I felt really connected to everybody. And then just that with the whole atmosphere and ... the music and light shows and like ... it felt, like, really moving, like, I ... I almost started crying, because it felt so good, you know, and ... nothing else could ... could evoke that feeling like ecstasy.
>
> (Joe, 21)

This young man described a profound shared pleasure and an intense human connection unattainable without the aid of ecstasy. This pleasure of shared collectivity, unity and commonality in which "the everyday is disrupted, the mundane is forgotten and the ecstatic becomes possible" (Malbon 1999: 164) is, according to many participants, another important reason for using ecstasy at dance events.

Enduring effects: transcending the experience

In reflecting on their experiences of using ecstasy, all participants discussed the transitory and immediate effects; however, some also described more enduring and even permanent benefits.[6] Longer-term positive effects produce changes both in their sense of themselves and in their subsequent social behavior and interactions with others.

As noted above, participants described how ecstasy facilitates the transformation of everyday experiences and accepted norms of behavior in ways that they feel are self-revealing and enlightening. While some ecstasy users believe that these effects are ephemeral and confined to the intoxicating influence of the drug, others seek to capitalize on the experience of ecstasy and integrate these newfound sentiments and ways of relating to others into their everyday lives. The pleasures of ecstasy thus contribute to a longer-lasting positive experience. Having experienced feelings of empathy and self-contentment, and becoming aware of previously unexplored means of relating to others and the world in general, participants believe that they can recreate some of these positive and pleasurable ways of being into daily life.

> I think the way to come down [off of ecstasy] is to just to take pause. Like, to go outside and like take pause, "Yes, I'm coming back to the real world, but that doesn't mean it's over." Like, try to … it's kind of … it's spiritual in the fact that like everyone's, like, take God with you in your everyday life. Like, you can do the same thing with E, like take back the feeling you had, the compassion, the empathy, all that stuff, take it back to the world … So the best way to come down is to be able to remember what you learned, write it down, do whatever you can to remember what happened and be able to remember it and take it back to like your real life.
>
> (Malia, 20)

Malia is not alone in attributing to the pleasures of ecstasy a spirituality. And she highlights a view shared by others, that elements of the ecstasy experience can be captured and transferred into their everyday selves. While we are not suggesting that ecstasy users suddenly transform and become happy and empathetic all the time, they nevertheless believe that the insights and benefits gained from taking ecstasy can be incorporated into their day-to-day lives. The "drug self" can merge with and bring pleasure to the "everyday self."

For those who hold this belief, ecstasy serves as a catalyst for creating new possibilities in how they perceive and relate to themselves and the world around them. The experience on ecstasy and the opportunity to experience life and interactions with others outside of everyday norms and expectations uncover a way of being that they had previously not experienced or had not been aware of, but which they find pleasing and preferable. They described how ecstasy has "opened" them up to an altered consciousness and they now find themselves having a "new perspective" on life. As one woman described, "it gave me a way of being able to feel, like, whether it's, like, calm or open, or loving. It's like, to me, that's an opening up of a certain kind of consciousness" (Courtney, 22). For some, this new perspective is at the level of how they relate to others or their outlook on life, while for others this takes on a meta-physical/spiritual undertone in which ecstasy is seen to open them to understanding a greater purpose or meaning in life:[7]

> There had never been anything esoteric in my life … it [ecstasy] allowed me to have esoteric experiences which allowed me to reflect different on … how my life … is. And then also kind of … there's that idea that you get a glimpse of … not like divination, more like … you're given opportunities to see different ways

of seeing things. And I think … having those opportunities has been … what has been life-changing … When you take something like ecstasy you're just like, holy shit … You know, there's like the spectrum of the rainbow … You've been doing your couple of routes that work for you, and all of a sudden there's this, there's a rainbow … of interaction and experience and … like … You know, what do you do with something like that? It's life changing. And it was for me and I know for a lot of people, a lot of friends, it has been.

(Eve, 30)

The new "consciousness" that some described, and ecstasy's ability to be life-changing, is often tied to a process of self-discovery. Transcending the mundane and escaping the routine of everyday life provides people with a sense of personal autonomy, self-discovery, and self-actualization (Lyng 2005a; O'Malley and Mugford 1993). While most had not started using ecstasy with the deliberate intention of promoting self-change, nevertheless many did describe how ecstasy ultimately induces a shift in how they perceive themselves. As Reith has noted, drug users may leave their "everyday personas behind" (2005: 237). This, according to Lyng, "leaves them with a purified and magnified sense of self" (Lyng 1990: 860). They believe that the positive and valued attributes of the self while intoxicated can be used to improve the everyday self:[8] "Like … I really do think that it's a learning experience, no matter what people say. Like you really can learn something about yourself … you can … understand yourself, in ways that like I couldn't before. Which I thought was really neat" (Iliana, 18).

Having experienced a level of self-acceptance and openness with others while under the influence of ecstasy, and realizing the pleasurable and beneficial nature of this, participants try to simulate and reenact these feelings in their everyday lives:

Todd.   My use of MDMA was … really, like … pivotal in me becoming who I am now, which is like … a lot more adjusted … I really feel like I've been able to open up and, like … be more okay with who I am.

Interviewer. And do you feel like when you're not on ecstasy you maintain that ability?

Todd.   Absolutely.

(Todd, 24)

Participants described that an increase in self-confidence and self-esteem are some of the most important effects that ecstasy has on their personal development. Many claimed that while under the influence of ecstasy they worry less about what others think of them and generally feel more accepting of and confident in themselves. For example, one young man described how he had been more introverted in the past: "I was more … introverted, not quite as social. Now in everyday life I'm much more outgoing and … confident and … yes, very confident" (Conrad, 21). They described how they had come to realize that their insecurities were related to their self-perceptions, and having once experienced a readjustment of these perceptions while on ecstasy, they began to work towards regaining that sense of self-confidence in their everyday personas. Becoming more outgoing and sociable are said to be some of the benefits of this new perception, especially for those who feel they once struggled with shyness:

> E broke the ice … probably to this day, if I never did E at a party, I would probably still be antisocial and probably wouldn't even go to parties. But now that I've experienced the drug side … I like the sober side now.
>
> (Nita, 17)

Participants realize, on the basis of their ecstasy experiences, that new and more positive ways of interacting with others are both possible and desirable. Having experienced the pleasures of being more sociable and open with both friends and strangers while on ecstasy, some seek to translate these experiences into their everyday interactions and consequently they described how they now found it easier to meet and talk to people.

> You feel, like, this deep connection to like everyone around you. And it changes the way you look at, like, interactions with other people. You become, like … I always tell them, like, "Yeah, I think ecstasy has made me a much more extroverted person than before." I think … I don't know, like I tell 'em, I think it changed my life. I think I'm a new person because of it … I used to be, like, pretty shy and, like, you know, not really, like … feel like, uncomfortable, like, in social situations. But, like … I don't know, ever since I started taking ecstasy I've become, like … like I said, I've become much more extroverted. Like, it's really not hard for me to, like, talk to people. Like, to just go up and talk to anybody, and just communicate with people.
>
> (Melody, 20)

Overall these young men and women believe that their experiences with ecstasy bring about beneficial changes in their normal lives. In these cases, ecstasy is portrayed as a tool that facilitates changes which potentially have long-term benefits; as one woman noted, "It made me have a more positive outlook on life" (Mia, 18). Such changes are especially welcomed by some participants, for whom the ecstasy experience represents aspects of themselves or their lives they already hope to manifest. Fortuitously, ecstasy use, at least in part, provides them with the impetus and opportunity to initiate such changes.

Conclusion

For the purposes of this chapter, we have concentrated on the participants' discussions of the pleasures of using ecstasy. Though we made reference to the dance scene as an important element in experiencing the pleasures and benefits, much of our discussion did concentrate on the use of ecstasy largely in isolation of the multiple social contexts in which it was used. Consuming ecstasy is primarily a social activity done with friends, and as we have noted throughout the book, the enjoyment of the experience is connected to the music, the dancing, the light shows, and being with other users. The pleasures of using ecstasy are embedded within this wider context and cannot be easily or accurately divorced from the enjoyment of these other elements of the experience. Therefore, while we hope this chapter serves its purpose in highlighting the users' perspectives on the pleasures of ecstasy use, we do not wish to ignore the extent to which ecstasy and the dance scene are integrally interwoven. We must underscore the point that to fully understand the meaning of drug use in the lives of the users, it must be contextualized.

In exploring the meanings of ecstasy use we have attempted to correct a research imbalance which has concentrated on the dangers and ignored the pleasures. We believe it is important to examine the pleasures associated with drug use and dance events in order to understand why young people use illicit drugs and why they seek out the excitement of the rave and club scene as liminal zones "where the impermissible" (O'Malley and Mugford 1993: 210) is valued and pursued. However, it is not our intention to give the impression that youthful drug use occurs without any problems or that the users are not aware of the potential risks involved in consuming illicit drugs. While our data certainly highlight the enjoyable and positive nature of ecstasy use, it is also the case that some participants described negative or unpleasant effects. In fact, as we detail in the next chapter, these young men and women are not only well aware of the potential dangers associated with using ecstasy, they also take proactive steps to minimize the risks of using.

Despite these risks, most participants believe that using ecstasy is ultimately a positive decision. While for some the importance lay solely in the ability to have fun, others value ecstasy because it allows them a glimpse of an alternative way of being and interacting with others. The possibility of viewing the world differently and interacting with others in a more meaningful way may reflect, as some commentators would have us believe, the alienated state of modern youth.[9] However, other researchers have suggested that the desire to transcend the mundane is not specific to young people but instead reflects a more general tendency within postindustrial societies where individuals in general seek out "emotionally exciting activities, including leisure activities ... to offset the suffocation of an overcontrolled, alienated existence within the mundane reality of modern life" (O'Malley and Mugford 1993: 206). The accuracy of either contention is difficult to assess and certainly outside the scope of this chapter. We can only suggest that, at least for some, the experience of using ecstasy is so significant that they wish to recreate the experience in their everyday lives.

Discussions of youthful drug use have been largely determined by adults, who have emphasized the potential dangers of using drugs, while the meanings that young people themselves give to their drug use have been explored less frequently. While contemporary drug research on ecstasy has emphasized the dangers, young people also emphasize the pleasures, the benefits, and the fun. Although the absence of a pleasure perspective within the drug field is not surprising, its omission may have serious consequences, especially in prevention and harm reduction efforts. Contemporary prevention messages, which solely emphasize the dangers of ecstasy, and erroneously claim that "club drugs aren't fun drugs," have little chance of resonating with the lived experiences of young drug users. If our sample of users is any indication, it is only too obvious that public health messages which fail to acknowledge the enjoyable and beneficial aspects of ecstasy use will be viewed with doubt and suspicion by many young users. Consequently, if prevention or harm-reduction efforts are to be effective, they need to include some recognition of the potential pleasures of consuming ecstasy, and respect for the opinions of users who feel that it is a "life-changing" experience.

Yet issues of risk do not disappear entirely and remain important – and navigation of the pleasures of drug consumption is intertwined with navigation of the risks involved. These should not be viewed as wholly separate issues, but, rather as part of a general constellation of issues that the young club drug users we interviewed negotiate. The next chapter, then, brings us back to issues of risk, but in a way that keeps at the forefront the users' agency and interests in pleasure.

Chapter 7

Drug use and the meaning of risk

Introduction

As the previous chapter showed, scholarship on substance use has tended to overemphasize the risks and underemphasize the pleasures of drug consumption. That does not mean, however, that issues connected to risk should be ignored or underestimated in turn. An examination of the position of risk in drug discourses reveals a disconnect between notions of risk as portrayed by the "experts" and the "lay knowledge" about risks to the users themselves. The differences point to the "disjunction that often exists between the ways in which risk is characterized within prevention science debates and the ways it is negotiated within youth cultures" (Duff 2003: 290). This dichotomy is not surprising and sociologists and cultural studies researchers have recently spent a good deal of time examining competing notions of risk and why certain notions become so prominent in public health arenas. In fact, in the late twentieth century, the concept of "risk" had become a defining feature of biomedically and epidemiologically-oriented work. However, while the debates on the role of risk in contemporary society are extensive and an increasing literature has developed on uncovering "lay knowledge," especially in areas of health and leisure,[1] within the field of drug research few studies are available. Even fewer exist in examining the sociocultural meanings that young people give to risk-taking in the arena of youthful drug use.[2] Given the extent to which health-promotion experts and the authorities have targeted young people and especially their drug activities as being "high-risk" behavior, the relative absence of studies on the meanings that young people give to their own drug use is somewhat surprising. One possible reason for this neglect may relate to the fact that young people have been portrayed as generally passive, whether when viewed as casualties of unemployment, teenage pregnancy, or drug use. Rarely is it the case that "official" discourses on youthful drug use, and especially prevention literature, address the possibility that young people who use drugs may be interested in learning ways both to heighten these pleasurable effects, while at the same time minimizing the harmful consequences (Shewan et al. 2000). Much of the available prevention literature either assumes that young people are ill-informed and fail to fully understand the harmful consequences of drug use (Bukoski 1991), or argues that young people's desire to take risks is based on a failure of proper socialization and the result of "receiving bad messages at vulnerable times" (Heaven 1996, cited in France 2000: 321). These assumptions are made with few or no empirical data to support them. As Paglia and Room have noted, "the prevention literature fails to recognize how the phenomena of drug use appear to youth themselves" (1999: 37). Such perspectives portray youthful drug use as problematic and risk-taking as inherently negative, and fail to consider the possibility that using drugs may be viewed by young people as normal, positive, and pleasurable (Stanley Cohen and Taylor 1976; H. Parker *et al.* 1998).

With this in mind, the purpose of this chapter is to explore the way in which young people conceptualize and talk about their use of drugs and notions of risk, and how they situate those risks in terms of potential pleasures. We wish to explore their knowledge about drugs, risk-taking, and pleasure, and hope to show the extent to which drug use and risk-taking is not necessarily viewed as either inherently negative or positive. We will explore the ways that young people, while not completely rejecting the official hierarchies of risk, produce their own (Abbott-Chapman and Denholm 2001). We will see the way that these respondents engage in a process of negotiation – balancing the perceived risks against the expected pleasures. Furthermore, using contemporary sociocultural theories of risk discussed below, we will begin to uncover the way that young adults socially "construct" notions of risk and pleasure around their drug use. Within the young club-drug user narratives, we will uncover a "subtle and complex framing of risk taking" (Bunton *et al.* 2004b: 9) and pleasure which tie notions of risk and pleasure not only to the substance, but also to the social context.

A sociocultural theory of risk

While some researchers have argued that sociological studies of risk have existed since Durkheim published his classic work on suicide in the late 1890s, it was not until the 1980s that theories about risk and risk-taking took center stage in sociological debate. Most commentators point to three major theorists – Douglas (1966, 1985, 1992), U. Beck (1992, 1994, 1995, 1996), and Giddens (1990, 1991, 1994, 1998). Given our interest in examining the sociocultural context of drug-using practices, we will focus primarily on the work of the anthropologist Mary Douglas and her sociocultural theory of risk. Her starting point is to question the "realist" perspective found principally in technical and scientific approaches (see for example Bradbury 1989). Within this "realist" model, risks are believed to pre-exist in nature and are considered objective phenomena which can be scientifically measured. This scientific or "expert" assessment is compared to the "subjective" approach held by the lay public. This latter subjective appraisal is viewed unfavorably and characterized as unscientific, inferior, and unsophisticated. Douglas (1985, 1992) criticizes this portrayal because it adopts an individualistic account and ignores "the social and cultural contexts in which risk is understood and negotiated" (Lupton 1999a: 24; see also Lupton 1999b). In putting forward a cultural relativist position,[3] her aim is to uncover how our understanding of these dangers is constructed through social, cultural, and political processes. Through these processes certain dangers and hazards become defined as "risks" while others do not. In order to understand this selection process we have to adopt a cultural analysis and consider the sociocultural context of which risks are a part. In essence, Douglas argues that risks cannot be viewed as uncontested facts isolated from their sociocultural, political, and historical contexts.

The importance of Douglas's theory for our research on drug use is not only because she focuses on the cultural context of risk, but also because she provides important insights into the ways that societies operate to sectionalize and control those sectors of the population who involve themselves in risky activities. Once certain groups have been singled out "as likely victims of hazards [and] 'being at risk' " (Lupton 1999a: 49), their state of being "at risk" justifies bringing them under control (Douglas 1985: 57). To be designated as "high-risk" in comparison with others in society means to be singled out for expert advice, surveillance, and control. One such group that has increasingly been subjected to these forms of control and regulation is youth. Although Douglas does not specifically examine youth as a targeted sector for control, she nevertheless does provide us with a sociocultural framework in which to consider young people's risk-taking behaviors.

Targeting youth as at risk

The behavior of young people has long been of major concern to adults, especially behavior that occurs outside education, waged work, or adult supervision. As Griffin (1993) has remarked, the history of research on youth is both a history of "young people themselves. ... [and also] a history of adults' preoccupations and panics" (1993: 23). The precise issues of concern have fluctuated in different locations and in different historical periods. One key area of control and regulation has been young people's leisure activities and especially activities associated with ingested substances such as illicit drugs. Youthful drug use is portrayed as particularly dangerous because young people are perceived as "a highly vulnerable sector of the population" (Ettorre and Miles 2002: 176). As a result of the weakening of traditional sources of social differentiation based on social class and communities, as noted by Furlong and Cartmel (1997) and Miles (2000), young people today are viewed "as attempting to find self-fulfillment and ways of identifying with other young people through the consumption of goods" (Furlong and Cartmel 1997: 61), especially fashion and music. However, while young people may seek to construct their identities through the process of consumption, whether that be fashion, music, or drugs, they become increasingly identified as "risky consumers" involved in risky consumption (W. Mitchell *et al.* 2004). They are portrayed as having a disordered relationship to consumption, especially drug use (Griffin 1997). Consequently those arenas, such as raves, in which drug use is perceived as commonplace, and which are viewed by young people as places of excitement, adventure and risk, are perceived by adults as problematic. They must therefore be increasingly controlled and regulated (N. D. Campbell 2000). As Aitchison has noted, "leisure sites and activities have become the focus of a society preoccupied with minimizing risk" (2004: 97).

Given the increasing efforts to control young people and to characterize their behaviors as disruptive or deviant, especially around their drug use, it is our intention in this chapter to explore the experiences of young people who use drugs and who are involved in the dance scene. In examining their accounts, we hope to highlight how these young users, far from being passive, ignorant, or ill-informed of the dangers of using drugs, operate and actively engage in an elaborate system of techniques designed to minimize a sense of uncertainty associated with their drug use.

Young drug users' constructions of risk

Drug knowledge and sources of information

Not surprisingly, the participants vary in terms of the amount of knowledge they have about the drugs they use, and even how much effort they put into learning about these substances. However, contrary to the notion that young people choose to use drugs because they are ignorant of the "real" consequences, researching drugs in order to better understand their effects and consequences is common in our sample. For example, Jason, 20, notes how he researches both drugs that he has used as well as some of the adulterants that are present in ecstasy (MDMA) pills so that he can be prepared in case he unknowingly ingests them:

> I have found myself going on the Internet … looking at not just ecstasy and what's in ecstasy and what's been sold as ecstasy, but researching on pretty much all the drugs I've done and drugs that I haven't done, and seeing what the effects are and stuff like that. … And then I look at the pills that have been cut with other stuff that I've never heard of and wonder – whoa – in case if I do take one of these at some point in time I wanna know what this drug's like. What the effects are.

While there are certainly some who try drugs with little knowledge of the effects or risks, many of the respondents spend time, whether before or after first using, learning about drugs through online sources, books, classes, or experienced friends. Chace, 26, discusses the different sources he uses to gather information on drugs:

> From the Internet, from Dancesafe. There's a book that was published last August, I think, that's really useful. It's *Ecstasy: The Complete Guide*. … that book is really good. … I like the book 'cause it's really neutral and nonjudgmental. A lot of the books I've read about ecstasy, they're from the pro-ecstasy, let's everyone go get high, turn on, tune in, drop out, E-is-gonna-save-the-world point of view. Which is just flat out annoying. … But then again, a lot of the other literature is from, like … the government, doom and gloom, it's gonna put holes in your brain. Which is actually disproven by … the British National Institute of Health and Science in Britain. … Another good place I go is … there's this Web site called PubMed.

While not all users can be said to be as thorough or motivated as this young man when researching drugs, many do use a combination of sources, although the importance placed on individual sources varies for each person. In addition to using the Internet and published material, many participants trust information that they gain from friends and more experienced users. As a result of their research, they gain a better under-standing of the effects and consequences of using drugs. A striking feature in many of the narratives is the sophisticated level of knowledge they have about drugs. Deana, 18, described the effects of ecstasy on the brain:

> What happens in your brain, when you start developing holes in your brain, is that the receptors that were picking up serotonin run out of serotonin, and because dopamine is closely linked to serotonin it looks similar to them, they start picking up dopamine. And it starts to break them, the receptors. So that's what's actually happening. It's like everything negative, all the, like, comedown stuff, is you're still trying to roll. Like, your body is still trying to pick up serotonin and there's no more serotonin left.

Many users have at least some knowledge of the connection between ecstasy and serotonin, even if they are not necessarily able to articulate with as much detail as Deana. By learning about the effects and consequences of drugs, participants often feel that they could employ harm-reduction strategies to allay some of the risks (Akram and Galt 1999). When asked if it is possible to use drugs safely, Keith, 32, replied:

> You can ingest whatever you want to … if you're educated, within reason, and if you use it in moderation, whether it be 2CB, acid, ecstasy, whatever these drugs may be, you can have a rocking good time and still find yourself safe.

What became clear in the participants' discussions is that most of them are aware of prevention messages and information, but they are skeptical or unsure about these messages, including the threat of severe brain damage and other serious conse-quences, primarily because they feel that either the messages are government propa-ganda or because they know people who did not suffer from serious consequences. For example, Curt, 20, discusses this view and his belief that educating himself about the effects allows him to reduce the risks:

> Before that I did like 'shrooms and acid, and I never had troubles. … I'd heard some bad things. … you know, anti-drug propaganda, it was … all political and not really, you know, education or … like, reason-based at all, it was just scare tactics. And that was pretty much confirmed by my use. … I mean, you can tell when you're on it, I think, that, like, it's not natural. … but whether or not that is so detrimental, as some people say, I think is questionable. Especially later, once I started becoming more educated, I would take more precautions.

Participants are neither ill informed nor unaware of the effects of drugs. However, scientific information, especially that gained from more "official" sources, is not necessarily viewed as the only valid source, and respondents frequently combine this information with knowledge gained from their own or their friends' experiences with drugs. As Mayock has noted, "young drug users constructed an alternative discourse of risk founded on their everyday experiences" (2005: 361). It is not that these young men and women ignore prevention or government-sponsored messages, but rather that those messages only serve as part of their overall drug knowledge. However, whether the information comes from official sources, books, friends, the Internet, or their own experience, the knowledge they acquire has an impact on what they perceive the risks of drugs to be.

Perceptions of risk

The participants' perceptions and assessments of the risks associated with drug use, and with specific drugs, are based on numerous factors, including the nature of the drug itself, how seriously the drug alters their behavior, the context in which they use, and the precautions they take. From their perspectives, the risks are not confined solely to physiological effects, they also consider risks related to the actual experience (e.g., a bad trip) and to the social context within which they use. We will provide below an overview of the participants' views about drug-related risks, briefly highlighting those risks that are most salient to them, some of which are also part of the official discourse.

Many informational and prevention messages on ecstasy emphasize the potential for brain damage as one of the most serious risks.[4] In the period before and during our research, this point was publicized in the media, and the majority of those in our sample were aware of it. So much so that the phrase "holes in the brain" is a catch-all phrase used by many young men and women we interviewed to represent concerns about the long-term effects of ecstasy. However, although many of the participants are aware of the "holes in the brain" theory, there are differences in how they perceive this risk. Some cite it as a serious concern, some believe it constitutes scare tactics, while others have mixed feelings about the issue. Many participants are aware of the potential for long-term consequences, but some believe the risks are more dire than other respondents, and not all are in agreement with how those risks are portrayed in the media and in prevention messages.

The participants' assessments of the short-term side effects and other consequences of drug use, such as dehydration, nausea, and depression, show the same diversity of opinions as that of their assessment of the potential for brain damage – some are more concerned than others. However, it is interesting to note that these negative side effects are sometimes spoken about in a matter-of-fact manner, as though there is a certain level of inevitability to them. While unpleasant, they are an accepted or normal part of taking drugs. In some cases, participants may not even perceive certain effects as inherently negative. For instance, vomiting is seen by some as integral to fully experiencing ecstasy, because it alleviates stomach pain and enhances the ecstasy high. During the course of their use, some young men and women simply refer to these effects and risks as something to manage or deal with, rather than be seriously concerned about. As Pilar, 22, notes, "I figure that the short-term effects that I've experienced so far, they're dealable.

There are things that you can do that will get better or minimize them as much as possible."

In describing the risks of a particular substance, respondents often compare and contrast one drug with another, noting that not all drugs carry the same amount of risk. This approach would appear to undermine the belief that young drug users adopt a generic perspective of drug use (Duff 2003). For example, marijuana and mushrooms are often favorably compared because they are characterized as natural, and therefore less risky, than other substances. Ecstasy is perceived by many as a fairly pleasurable and low-risk drug, although some do raise concerns about adulterants, side effects, and the possible long-term impact. Miranda, 22, shares others' sentiments about ecstasy:

> I think that it's one of the lesser harmful drugs out of like the drug spectrum. As long as you make sure you don't get dehydrated, or get bad stuff, you're gonna be all right. ... You're not gonna overdose off of it, as long as you don't take a whole bunch of it. And ... you know, it's usually a pretty good experience.

Overall, drugs like methamphetamine are seen by the men and women we interviewed as much more risky, because of the perceived risk of addiction and side effects of heavy use. The perceived addiction potential of different drugs is important in the construction of a drug hierarchy, which is partly why ecstasy (which is not generally viewed as addictive), even with some of its other acknowledged dangers, is generally seen as more acceptable than drugs like methamphetamine, heroin, and cocaine.

What is important to note here is that risk is often not viewed in absolute terms, but is relative. Not all drugs are seen to pose the same risks, or even the same degree of risk. But just as the risk of using different drugs is relative, some respondents also argue that the potential harm of any one substance has to be evaluated against other everyday dangers. These other day-to-day dangers are sometimes perceived as more harmful, and so the risk of using drugs does not necessarily pose any greater concern. As a result, the pleasure gained from drugs, despite their risks, is seen as ultimately worthwhile. "As young people point out, not all risks are harmful or 'bad' and every life choice involves risk" (Abbott-Chapman and Denholm 2001: 282). Keith, 32, captures a point made by other respondents: "I have concerns about ... the long-term effects. I have concerns about ... the long-term effects of me breathing smog here, though, as well. So I don't ... concern myself with ... the use of a drug more than any other thing in my environment." Finally, when describing the potential risks of ecstasy, many respondents feel that the dangers come not from the inherent properties of MDMA, but rather from the adulterants that a pill might be cut with. In this way, the respondents do not view the risk as situated solely within the drug, but rather within its illegal status.

While the prevention discourse is mainly concerned with risks related to the pharmacology of drugs, many of the respondents note risks that are more connected to contextual or external factors than physiological effects. Even side effects of the drugs, such as dehydration and overheating, or even anxiety and paranoia, are viewed as risks that are also tied into the environment in which a person uses. If they use the drugs in a well-ventilated, not overcrowded, safe space, the risks of the drugs are diminished. Not only is risk connected to the physical environment, but respondents also talk about how the specific effects of a drug interact with other social factors to influence the potential risk of using. The risk of a "bad trip" figures prominently in their narratives, and is connected to many factors, including their frame of mind before using, who they are with, and the context in which they use. As we will see later, respondents view a bad trip as a function of the social context as well as the drug, and a risk that could be mitigated.

When benefits outweigh risks

Most young men and women do not approach drug use from the perspective that it is all fun, with no risks or consequences. While they may disagree about the nature or severity of the risks, or how to deal with those risks, the majority of the respondents engage in a process of negotiation – balancing risk with pleasure. The balance between risk and pleasure is important in the decision of whether or not to use drugs. While many respondents acknowledge the potentially harmful effects of some substances, they feel that the benefits gained from using are "worth" the risks. As Rhodes (1995) has argued, "the long-term threat of risk tends to be weighed up by individual drug users against a range of more immediate benefits that are influenced more by cultural and social factors than by the possibility of physical harm" (cited in Shewan *et al.* 2000: 450). For example, Priscilla, 17, notes that before even trying acid she believed that the benefits outweighed the risks:

> My friend mentioned it to me. And so I went on line, and I looked it up … just read up on it. And I knew that even that one time could make me retarded. Like I was prepared to understand that. But I also knew that it could be a very enlightening experience. I don't regret me doing acid, because … I would not be this person at all if I'd never done acid.

While reflecting on their experiences with drugs, participants not only speak of pleasure and fun, but many also feel that they gain something valuable. As shown in the previous chapter, benefits therefore include not just transitory experiences such as release from everyday pressures, but also involve enduring effects such as bonding with friends, and even on occasion profound changes in their mental well-being and subsequent social behavior. Laura, 19, talks about how ecstasy positively impacted her friendships and self-worth:

Laura.   I've gained like two best friends out of it. … I think it's more like … the friends that I've gained, the bonds that I've made, and … every time I've done it, I've come out of it like … learning so much more about myself, and, like, my confidence just … goes up …

Interviewer.   So what are the disadvantages to it?

Laura.   I think, the physical disadvantages. Or, like, the next day you're just
           kinda, like ... worn out. ... like, when you're going down off of it, you
           feel really shitty ... the only thing, like, I hated about it is, the next
           day, like, my jaw would be, like, so fucked up, like the inside of my
           mouth, and I couldn't eat for like a couple days. But then, like ... in
           the end it was totally worth it. So I don't see, like ... the disadvantages
           outweighing the advantages at all.

Having made the decision to use, many respondents actively engage in a process
of risk management, so that they may achieve the most benefits while reducing the
potential harm. Of particular significance is the fact that the respondents' perceptions
of risk and how to minimize them are tied to the social context and social nature of
their drug use.

Maximizing pleasure and minimizing risk: risk within a social setting

Participants employ numerous strategies to maximize pleasure while minimizing risk,
often configuring a set of practices and preferences that would create the optimal
combination of drug, set, and setting (Zinberg 1984). This is not to suggest that they
always use drugs within this optimal framework, or that each drug-using occasion is
carefully planned out, but by examining their preferences we can uncover the ways
in which they conceptualize and negotiate risk and pleasure. Although many of the
participants are aware of and acknowledge the effects and potential consequences
of their use, their perceptions of the risks and the ways of managing those risks are
more complex than is often portrayed.

Though the social context within which these young people consume drugs is
important in how they manage risk and pleasure, they also take individual steps to
mitigate some of the negative physiological effects, including using harm-reduction
strategies, such as drinking water or taking breaks from dancing to prevent dehydration, and taking vitamins and supplements to assist the body and protect against
some of the negative effects. Moderation in either dosage or use frequency is seen
as a way to allay some of possible short and long-term effects, as it would limit the
potential for harmful consequences. There is a sense that, by controlling these factors
that are within their ability, they can ensure that the risks are at least diminished.
Many participants believe that, given the right choices and circumstances, drugs can
be used in a safe and controlled manner.

Though participants employ some of the strategies listed above, a striking
characteristic of their drug descriptions, and how they negotiate pleasure and
risk, is the way their narratives illustrate the social nature of their drug use. By
choosing to use with particular people, and in specific settings, the young men
and women we interviewed believe they can reduce the risks of drugs while at
the same time maximizing the pleasure. Many users talked about how particular effects of a drug interact with social and contextual factors to impact the
potential risk of a drug-using experience, including what is characterized as a

bad trip. For example, Karl, 20, highlights the importance of friends and the social environment:

> The same thing with having, you know, bad trips. People using it in ignorance, in the wrong places, in the wrong settings, around the wrong people. ... I think it has a very bad potential, if you're not using it right. ... We're talking about something that's exploring the frontiers of the human mind, you know. Exploring your inner consciousness and psyche. You can't take that lightly, you know. And so anyone who does take that lightly doesn't know what they're messing with. You know, you play with fire, you're going to get burned.

While much of the drug literature has tended to focus on the pharmacological qualities and effects of individual substances (see Hunt and Barker 2001), the majority of the drug users in our sample view their drug-taking and the associated risks not solely in pharmacological terms, but also consider the uses and effects of these substances within a finely articulated social setting. This social quality illustrates the extent to which, as Appadurai has noted, "consumption is eminently social, relational, and active rather than private, atomic or passive" (1986b: 31). These young people discuss their drug consumption within a social context of structured relationships, and their discussions highlight the extent to which they "are conscious of their social context and their own role as actors within it" (Taylor-Gooby and Zinn 2005: 6). The meanings they give drugs and the potential risks are all socially embedded and socially determined. They rarely view individual drugs as inherently risky or pleasurable devoid of a social context, but instead discuss the risky and pleasurable nature of a particular substance within the parameters of a social event. They delineate the benefits and problems of individual substances from a number of different perspectives, which includes the people and social groups to be involved, and the social settings where they intend to use. In so doing they conceptualize and experience risk and pleasure not solely as an atomized and individual response but as a socially embedded decision. They develop a series of social practices, which determine these preferred social settings and the overall nature of their use. As Duff has remarked, "[T]hus it is not the drug itself which is risky, rather it is the way in which the drug is used ... [and] the context in which it is used" (2003: 293).

The importance of the social environment

As K. Moore and Miles have noted, "the apparently mundane contexts in which young people consume drugs are particularly useful in understanding what drug consumption actually means" (2004: 508). Moreover, only by examining the context in which drug use takes place can we begin to understand the ways in which assessments about risks and pleasures "emerge and take meaning" (Duff 2003: 296). Almost all of the young club drug users we interviewed have beliefs about what constitutes the best places or contexts in which to use certain drugs, and that varies by respondent as well as by drug. While using drugs at raves and clubs is preferable for many, this context also carries extra risks because the users have no control over the environment.

Some of the risks associated with drugs are not just about the drug itself, but about the drug within a particular environment. Curt, 20, explains:

> I've been at parties where later I found out, like, someone died. … It's from, like … you know, heat stroke or something, which … you could say, "Well, that's from the party being too hot." Which is definitely true, you know, but if they hadn't taken ecstasy they probably wouldn't have died. But I don't think … really anyone has died from actual ecstasy overdose, like, by taking too much ecstasy.

Given the belief that some drug-related risks are tied to the environment, respondents maintain that by choosing to use within particular settings they can palliate the risks and make the experience more enjoyable. Sometimes respondents have completely opposite views about the best place to use a particular drug, but they cite similar reasons for their choices. Many feel that the social context helps play a role in whether they would have a bad trip, have access to people or items that provide comfort, or generally have more fun. The following two participants are good examples of these opposing views, the first believing that ecstasy is better suited to raves and the second preferring to use it within a home environment:

> I don't like to do it outside of the rave scene. I seem to get a little bit more emotional when somewhere else. And when I'm at a rave, I can … I think I can control myself better around a lotta people and just can be happy.
>
> (Gabriel, 20)

> But actually I really didn't like doing E at a rave, I like to do it when I'm at home, like, on my couch and just chillin' and safe. You know, I don't have to worry about like people … just hurting or whatever.
>
> (Tali, 20)

Although a strong association exists between the dance scene and using drugs, and many experiment with new substances at dance events, there nevertheless are differences of opinion as to whether trying certain drugs for the first time at a rave is a good idea. For example, Audrey, 16, notes, "I wouldn't wanna try any new drug at a rave, because I don't know how I'm gonna react to it. Like, acid or something. I would never do that at a rave." For others, using a drug for the first time at a rave depends on the size and nature of the event, as that affects whether the respondent feel "safe." Notions of safety when using drugs is an important element within these narratives, and is determined by both the setting and the individual's social group.

Certain settings are portrayed by the young men and women we interviewed as more fitting for the use of specific substances, while others are considered less ideal. This matching of specific drugs to specific settings illustrates further the extent to which these club-drug users possess a detailed knowledge not only of the drugs themselves but also of the best environments within which to use. In other words, our respondents adopt a series of strategies that maximize the pleasure by matching the drug to the setting. For example, ketamine use on its own is considered by some respondents to be inappropriate for a rave or party because "it makes you basically numb and, like, kinda tired" (Veronica, 20), whereas ecstasy is often seen to be ideal. While it is the case that many respondents believe that raves and taking ecstasy go well together, they also develop a body of knowledge about using particular drugs that allows them to better prepare for the experience, and therefore better manage the risks and pleasures.

The importance of friends

Throughout their narratives, these young men and women consistently emphasize the importance of using drugs with friends they trust. Like choosing the right setting, using with friends not only plays a role in the pleasurable aspects of the experience, but it also helps to foster a safer experience, since friends would be there to help with a bad trip and look out for one another. The relationship between trust and risk has been noted by a number of other researchers. For example, Lupton and Tulloch have noted a "symbiotic relationship between trust and risk, for trust serves to minimize the dangers to which particular types of activities are subjected" (1998: 28). Young people often handle risks "by sticking together" (Bunton *et al.* 2004a: 170). Using drugs in the company of friends is particularly important if they are taking a drug for the first time, a feature well-illustrated in the following description of a first experience with ecstasy. Alicia, 17, explains:

> It was really like … fun, because they knew, you know, how I was going to be the first time, so they knew, like, to take care of me and always, you know, like, give me water. And, like, I was sitting in the balcony the whole time, 'cause they knew I'd feel safer, like, with just them, like, in the front row, like, looking over at all the dancers, and stuff like that. … They were just, like, you know, always reassuring. Like … 'cause at one point I got kinda scared. … And they were just talking to me about like, you know, normal things, and like keeping me level-headed so that I didn't bad-trip and, like, go all crazy.

Although respondents choose to use drugs because they feel that the benefits outweigh the risks, they are nevertheless still conscious of the possibility of having a bad trip, experiencing negative side effects, or even the potential for greater harm. Having friends present, especially those who are trustworthy and knowledgeable, offers respondents some reassurance that they could rely on someone to deal with any problems. A number of respondents note that the protection friends offer can be especially important for women, who may be vulnerable to unwanted advances, being taken advantage of, or personal harm.[5] Being surrounded by one's friends both improves the enjoyment of the experience and minimizes the risks. Friends are able to enhance the pleasurable aspects of drug use in part because it is a shared experience among people who understand each other. This social bonding is an important feature of doing drugs with friends.

Risks overcoming pleasures

While we have presented data to show how club-drug users perceive risk and pleasure when making the choice to use drugs, it is also important to note that there are many instances when their assessment of drug-related risk results in the choice to either stop or reduce their use. For some participants, the risks and side effects experienced after their initial use of specific drugs are not "worth" the benefits, and so they choose not to use again. For others, this is a process that develops over time. Whereas initially the benefits and pleasures of using may have far outweighed the risks, at some point the side effects and concerns over the risks started to become more salient. This change emerges in different ways for different participants, but is often a result of feeling that they have already gained enough from using, the positive effects are diminishing and/or the negative effects are increasing, or they are maturing out of drug use because of lifestyle changes. Ultimately, some users reach a point where they feel that the risks and consequences of using outweigh the benefits.

Throughout their narratives, participants negotiate the potential negative effects of a substance against its potential pleasures. Some said they decreased or discontinued using because the negative effects were too unpleasant or their concerns over the health consequences became more significant. In these cases the negative effects outweigh the benefit: "like the night of bliss wasn't worth, like … two weeks after of just, blah" (Violet, 19). While Violet still emphasizes the positive side of her experience, in the immediate short term at least, ultimately she concluded that the pleasure was undermined by the drug's negative effects. Adopting a slightly different approach, some respondents decide to reduce or stop using *prior* to experiencing any detrimental effects. Their decision is premised on the notion that because they had already experimented with the substance they should stop before any serious problems or negative consequences occur.

Just as social factors play a role in how respondents manage the risks and pleasures of using, these factors also influence decisions to reduce or stop using. Some respondents assert that their drug use and their general party lifestyle began to negatively impact other areas of their lives, including social relationships and their ability to perform in professional or scholastic arenas. For some, the responsibility or desire to succeed at work or school is a major factor in their decision to stop. Others speak of wanting to stop using a specific drug in order to *prevent* conflict within their personal relationships. Audrey, 16, described having to choose between using methamphetamine and her boyfriend, who did not approve of it:

> You have to think about what's more important. … There's no way that I'm gonna keep smoking and stay with him. It's not gonna work out. … if I slowly just stop doing it, then I can stop doing it and have nothing to risk any more.

In understanding the processes by which participants assess the risks and benefits of using drugs, it is also important to remember that many of these young men and women are at that stage in life when they are transitioning from school to college or from college to work. Consequently, the significance of the negative effects of using may become heightened because of increased responsibilities and lifestyle changes.

Theorizing the pleasures of risk

How do we situate these seemingly mundane negotiations of drug risks within a broader context of youthful leisure and consumption practices? Today the desire to discover new and exciting forms of consumption can be seen in contemporary leisure practices which are increasingly associated with elements of the novel, the extraordinary, and the transcendental. These features are seen in either the more benign forms of tourism or in more dangerous and risky forms of leisure such as rock-climbing and hang-gliding. These increasingly risky ways of achieving excitement and pleasure have been examined by Lyng (1990), who, building on Katz's (1988) seminal work on the seductions of crime, develops the concept of "edgework."[6] Basing his theory on contemporary sociological theories of risk and societal notions of insecurity, he explores the existential and pleasurable nature of "voluntary risk-taking," or edgework. Lyng examines the attraction of dangerous sports and argues that people deliberately involve themselves in such risk-taking behaviors as a way of seizing control and reacting against "the unidentifiable forces that rob one of true individual choice" (Lyng 1990: 870). The need to transcend the normal or the mundane has been noted by other writers, such as Stanley Cohen and Taylor (1976), who examine the increasing need for leisure activities to be out-of-the-ordinary, and to have the potential for disrupting or breaking the routine of life. Emotionally exciting activities "offset the suffocation of an over-controlled alienated existence within the mundane reality of modern life" (O'Malley and Mugford 1993: 206). "Transcending the mundane" (O'Malley and Mugford 1993) and escaping the routine of everyday life provide people with a sense of personal autonomy, self-discovery, and self-actualization (Lyng 2005a).

The search for new and exciting experiences, or, as C. Campbell calls it, "the cease-less consumption of novelty" (1989: 205) and "the endless emergence of new wants" (O'Malley and Mugford 1991: 57), create a vital demand for the consumption of new commodities, including drugs. Today, modern consumerism can be characterized as "a longing to experience in reality those pleasures created and enjoyed in imagina-tion" (C Campell 1989: 205), a longing which results in "our social relationships and self-identities, our forms of cultural expression ... increasingly constructed and negotiated around the consumption of a wide range of mass-produced commodities and activities" (Reith 2005: 228).

Given the desire to seek new identities through the consumption of new commodi-ties (Miles 2000) plus the desire to discover new thrills to overcome the mundane and inspire "pleasure, excitement, exhilaration, and desire" (Lupton 1999a: 167), it is obvious why ecstasy and other mind-altering substances have such a widespread appeal for young people, especially within the exciting, transgressive, and pleasurable context of the dance scene and its electronic music.[7] The epidemiological litera-ture, discussed in Chapter 1, documents just how widespread this appeal is; what epidemiology has not been able to do, though, is to theorize fully the reasons and context for it. Though it is important not to reduce motivations for drug consumption solely to these issues, one of the key attractions of attending dance events and doing drugs may be the possibility of being involved in an exciting and non-mundane activity. Young people are in search of "heightened experiences and extravagant pleasures" (Collison 1996: 430). As Malbon (1999) has noted (though he downplayed the drug-specific elements of this), the experience of clubbing allows the individual participant to overcome their "mundane" and everyday life. "The everyday is disrupted, the mundane is forgotten and the ecstatic becomes possible" (Malbon 1999: 164). Or, as O'Malley and Mugford argue, "in such a cultural milieu ... illicit and even dangerous drug taking as a leisure activity appears as an intelligible form of the normatively sanctioned search for the extraordinary" (1991: 57). Moreover, the excitement of attending a dance event and using illicit drugs allows young people to "get their kicks in spaces they know well," spaces that Hayward (2002) has called "performance zones." These zones become the "site of excitement and social contestation, of experimentation and dissonance" (Hayward 2002: 88) and, of course, pleasure. The dance club also operates as a place within which transgressions (Douglas 1966; Turner 1969) can take place. Transgressions are defined as "a process which allows the individual to carry out activities that are otherwise forbidden" (Lalander 1997: 35). Intoxication within these settings allows a transition into what Turner (1969) calls *liminality*. This liminal period "is characterized by an absence of the social structures that normally order the subject's world ... or the replacement of one paramount reality by another reality which does not have much in common with the paramount reality" (Lalander 1997: 35). In this state activities not normally acceptable can be performed.

In other words, within the context of the rave or club, and with the use of mind-altering substances, young people can transform the routine and subvert the elements of control that take place in their everyday lives. As they stand in line outside the event, the anticipation of what is to come increases the excitement, especially given that not all attendees are necessarily allowed in (Malbon 1999). However, once gaining entry, their everyday lives become reversed. A night out at an event becomes "a celebration of irrational ecstatic behaviour. Night becomes day and specialist clothes are worn not to work but to play. Consumption rather than production is all-important" (Presdee 2000: 119). The purpose of the night out is to consume and enjoy the immediate, whether that be in the form of drugs, or music, or the spectacle. It is, as Presdee has called it, "the perfect form of consumption, without context or content" (2000: 122), "it is a carnival of 'otherness', of 'difference' and defiance" (ibid.: 120). Given the extent to which young people today are regulated, curtailed, and controlled, once inside they can do the one thing left to them, consume. As the "technologies of surveillance and control have expanded and become more efficient" (Lyng 2005b: 43) avenues of resistance or reaction are still sought. Young people seek new ways of being and interacting with others. While the dance scene is not reducible to club-drug use, nor do all participants consume drugs, drug consumption is not incidental or tangential to this excitement, defiance, or celebration. Indeed, many young participants of the dance scenes described club-drug use as fundamentally shaping their experiences within it.

However, it is not only the mind-altering and transcending qualities of the drugs or the exciting sensory stimuli of the rave that makes drug use within this setting so appealing. It may also be the idea that young people are pursuing an activity that is defined, at least within the official discourse, as a risky activity.[8] Not only do the drugs' mood-altering qualities "enhance the excitement" of dance events, but also the illicit and risky nature of using drugs may further this excitement. Young people like taking risks (Collison 1996; M. Plant and M. L. Plant 1992), and doing something illicit or risky contributes to the pleasure and the excitement of the activity (Hayward 2002; Reith 2005). "Young people show a willingness to experiment with and enjoy a range of risk-taking, exhilarating, and aspirational activities and sensations which includes the experience of intoxication" (Measham 2004b: 211). By not analyzing the risks (and perceptions of risk) involved with drug consumption, the extant cultural studies scholarship on the dance scene may also be missing the appeal of risk connected to drug use in the scene. In fact, some researchers, such as Reith (2005), have argued that using drugs is the quintessential form of risk-taking because it enables the user to transcend or transgress boundaries – the boundaries of the mundane and the extraordinary, consciousness and unconsciousness. While the specific form of the "high" varies, depending on the particular drug ingested, all illegal drugs share one common feature: that of "transgression" from "straight to wasted" (Reith 2005: 236).

And yet the young club-drug users we interviewed most certainly do not embrace risk with complete abandon. Indeed, as we have shown throughout this chapter, they attempt to engage with risk by managing it through a variety of strategies and tactics – ranging from controlling the setting and context in which they consume drugs to changing the substances they choose to consume, to educating themselves through a variety of information channels. These young men and women, far from being passive victims of drug problems, actively assert themselves to find the right balance between pleasure and risk and the right balance between the thrill of risk and taking these thrills too far.

Conclusion

As many writers today have noted, youth and youthful activities have become increasingly the site for surveillance and intervention (Cieslik and Pollock 2002; France 2000). Within this environment of "tackling the youth problem," the architects of public policy have increasingly turned to the social sciences to understand and solve the problem. The involvement of the social sciences in monitoring and controlling youthful behavior is particularly apparent in the field of drug research, where epidemiologists track the patterns and behaviors of youthful drug use, and prevention and intervention researchers suggest a wide array of programs and messages designed to encourage young people to refrain from using drugs. Today this concern has focused on young people's use of club drugs and their involvement in the electronic dance-music scene. Using drugs and attending raves or parties are portrayed as exceedingly risky activities that should be avoided. The portrayal of youthful activities as inherently dangerous and risky is unsurprising, given the prevalence of risk as an essential component of prevention and intervention discourse.

Unfortunately, while the prevention science literature continues to burgeon, few studies exist on young people's knowledge about the meaning of drugs and associated risks and the role of these drugs in their lives. Given this discrepancy, one cannot help but question whether there is somewhat of a disjuncture between the users and their own sense of drug use, and the prevention methods and discourse that are meant to encourage young people not to use.

Overall, we have attempted to show the extent to which young clubbers and ravers are neither completely unaware nor ill-informed about the drugs they use and their associated effects. Viewing young drug users as simply misinformed or incapable of making rational decisions oversimplifies and disregards the multiple reasons why youth choose to participate in these activities and how they view their own involvement. Their drug-using narratives highlight the ways in which the respondents conceptualize both their drug use and the potential risks and pleasures. While these conceptualizations are often more complex than the views portrayed by government officials or the media, it is important to note that our sample is composed primarily of educated, middle-class young people, who, because of their social position, have easy access to drug information sources such as the Internet and published books or articles. They can be viewed as generally thoughtful about their drug-using activities, and many are influenced by a sense of social norms and expectations of appropriate behavior which lead them to use within a structured framework. Consequently, from one viewpoint, this sample could be viewed as atypical. However, the characteristics of this sample may not be atypical of young people who are involved in drugs and the electronic dance scene. The majority of our sample engage in drug use as an integral and normal part of their recreational and leisure activities (H. Parker *et al.* 1998), which, by and large, take place at the weekends or occur at semicontrolled intervals, and rarely on a daily basis.

Of particular significance in their narratives is the extent to which notions of risk are tempered by notions of pleasure. In weighing the possibilities of risk against the possibility of pleasure, many of the participants, although being aware of the risks, ultimately believe that using particular drugs is "worth it." In examining their notions of risk and pleasure we do not wish to imply that their decision-making processes are always calculated and rational. On occasions they engage in drug use with little or no forethought and decide to use on the spur of the moment, perhaps influenced by their friends or the social circumstances (Mayock 2005). (We will focus more directly on such spontaneity in the next chapter's analysis of polydrug use.) Although they may not make calculated decisions or weigh benefits and risks each time they use, over the course of time or at particular periods in their drug-using careers they engage in information-gathering and thoughtful consideration about their drug use. And yet such portrayals of these young people being driven by risk–benefit calculations in shaping their drug use run the danger of missing the emotional or affective elements of risk, which we believe are equally important to understand.

Just as young clubgoers do not passively succumb to risks (*contra* the presentation in much of the epidemiological literature) neither do they passively ignore the real risks that do accompany drug consumption. Ravers and clubbers do not simply use drugs in spite of (or because of) the risks, they also actively manage the risks they face. Nevertheless, their assessment of these pharmacological properties, and hence their assessment of the potential pleasures and risks, take place within particular social contexts. This confirms both O'Malley and Mugford's (1991) call for an examination of the way that pleasure is socially constructed, as well as Douglas's (1992) point that risks cannot be viewed as uncontested facts isolated from the sociocultural context in which they operate. The meanings that young people give to the drugs they use and the potential pleasures and risks associated with them are all socially embedded and socially determined. The premise that risks and the perceptions of risk are inherently social flies in the face of much of the drug literature, which has tended to focus solely on the inherent pharmacological qualities and effects of individual substances (Hunt and Barker 2001). On the other hand, the cultural studies project to understand youth cultures associated with raves, clubs, and the dance scene will not be complete until it begins to fully grapple with issues of drug use head-on, including the particular pleasures of drug use and the meaning, construction, and contexts of its risks.

Chapter 8

Combining different substances in the dance scene

Enhancing pleasure, managing risk, and timing effects

Introduction

Though much of our discussion of drug risks and pleasures has focused on the drug ecstasy (MDMA), this drug is far from the only one consumed within the rave and club scenes, and those who use ecstasy rarely use it in isolation from other drugs. Instead, within these scenes we see patterns of multiple or polydrug use. An examination of the ways in which our study participants combine drugs and how they understand these combinations provides a helpful on-the-ground example of their negotiations between pleasure and risk.

The practice of combining multiple mind-altering substances, whether legal or illegal, has provoked calls of concern among drug researchers for over thirty years. Alarm about these practices is fueled by worries about the negative synergistic interactions these combinations can result in. Today the recreational practices of young people, particularly those who attend electronic dance music parties, are described as especially worrying (Byqvist 1999; Hammersley *et al.* 1999; Merchant and MacDonald 1994; Riley *et al.* 2001). In fact, it is generally accepted by drug researchers that a key characteristic of using dance drugs or club drugs is young people's experimentation with new and varied combinations of substances (Measham *et al.* 1994; H. Parker *et al.* 1998).

Yet, while scholarship on this topic is not new, the reasons why different substances are combined have been relatively unexplored. Given the worry that young people are increasingly combining different mind-altering substances, the aim of this chapter is to analyze the different combinations used by the young people in our study. In examining these combinations, our purpose is not merely to describe the different combinations used, but instead, to explore the reasons why some combinations are chosen and others avoided. We examine both the thinking behind their drug-using practices and the range of procedures adopted by young people to enhance the pleasures achieved and to control the potential problems and minimize risks. In our analysis we categorize the different motivations that polydrug users cite for their differing drug-combining practices and we highlight the key role that temporal organization has in structuring their polydrug practices.

Clarifying the meanings of polydrug use

Which drugs to include?

Research on polydrug use among young adults is not new, but ambiguities remain in the field over how to operationalize drug-combining and what kind of substance use should qualify as polydrug use. Early research into the drug consumption patterns of young adults found that "multiple drug use" (Sidney Cohen 1981; Simpson and Sells 1974; Single *et al.* 1974) was prevalent.[1] Studies were initially designed to evaluate heroin addiction but, as marijuana became increasingly identified as central to the drug problem, research on polydrug use gradually evolved to include nonopiate drugs (Douglass and Khavari 1978; Sample 1977). The significance of marijuana, alcohol, and tobacco in this research has been inconsistent. In the early polydrug research of the 1970s there was concern about these substances both for their own mood-altering effects as well as because they were seen as contributory to heroin addiction (Johnston 1975).[2] Yet, even when they were found to be used extensively, many researchers excluded these legal or "soft" drugs from their polydrug analyses, following the then policy of the National Institute of Drug Abuse (NIDA) (see, for example, Sample 1977). Although today "soft" drugs are more often included than in the past, the focus is still primarily on investigating illicit drugs as opposed to the combining of legal and illegal substances.[3] However, as we will demonstrate, to fully understand polydrug use of those within the dance/rave/club scenes it is crucial to include not only "club drugs" within the analysis, but also marijuana, alcohol, and other ingested substances such as nutritional supplements that users consume to transform and manage their drug-using experiences.

Questions of timing

In addition to contested definitional issues of which drugs to include, a lack of agreement on issues of timing also exists. As early as 1975 researchers sought to clarify and standardize a single definition. Writing in an early NIDA research monograph, Johnston (1975) sought to define the term "polydrug use" by delineating the different concepts then available and noting the conceptual and measurement problems that existed. Researchers since then have attempted, with little success, to reach consensus on the precise operational characteristics of the term. Schensul and colleagues highlighted some of the contested issues, noting that "the terms reflecting the combinations of drugs within different periods of time are confusing and inconsistent, involving problems in the definition of time period, number of drugs, and the interactive effects of the drugs" (Schensul *et al.* 2005a: 572).[4] More specifically, they identify timing as a key issue. In what time frame do two or more substances have to be consumed in order to constitute polydrug use?

To answer this question, many researchers distinguish between consuming two or more drugs *concurrently* and consuming two or more drugs *simultaneously*. Whereas concurrent polydrug use is a "style of ingestion where different drugs are consumed on separate occasions" (Earleywine and Newcomb 1997: 353; see also P. Collins 1998), simultaneous polydrug use refers to "the use of two or more substances on the same occasion" (Ives and Ghelani 2006: 226); other researchers draw a similar distinction between "separate" polydrug use and "synergistic" polydrug use (Boeri *et al.* 2008). Simultaneous or synergistic forms of polydrug use have been viewed as particularly dangerous from a health perspective because of the potential negative consequences associated with the synergistic interaction of multiple drugs (R. L. Collins *et al.* 1999). Simultaneous polydrug use is especially prevalent within the club-drug scene and will be the particular focus of our analysis. As we will demonstrate, however, the concurrent versus simultaneous distinction in definitions does not clear up all potential ambiguities about questions of timing. Different patterns of timing *within* simultaneous polydrug use are also in need of delineation.

Issues of timing are key to understanding prevalent polydrug-using practices at dance-music events. Researchers have identified the existence of different stages or phases that occur during a night out (Malbon 1999). For example, phase one is the experience in social settings prior to arrival at the dance club or dance party, phase two is the dance event or party itself, and phase three is the "after-dance" period where users "come down" or "chill out" (Boys *et al.* 1997). These phases have significant substance-use implications because different drugs and different combinations are used in each phase. For example, Boys and colleagues (1997) discovered that whereas cannabis and amphetamines were the most common drugs used prior to a rave, ecstasy was the most common during the rave, and cannabis the most popular after the rave. Although many other researchers have similarly noted cannabis as a drug consumed during the "chilling out" or "coming-down phase" (Ward and Fitch 1998), others have discovered variations. For example, Forsyth (1996) discovered that the majority of his respondents, instead of taking cannabis, used depressants, especially in the form of temazepam, at "chill out" parties. But what do these different phases, and the different drug combinations consumed within them, mean to the drug users themselves? What degree of control or autonomy do drug users exert over the timing of their drug combinations within these scenes?

Agency and meaning

While much of the debate within the drug field has focused on definitional issues and attempts to reach a consensus, little research has focused on the users themselves and the reasons they provide for combining two or more substances.[5] Notions of agency have been largely ignored within the drug field and young users, in particular, have been portrayed as passive actors. Yet, as some researchers have noted, using drugs is about "doing," and what we need to know is how young people "go about doing drugs" (Mayock 2005: 363). Unfortunately, only rarely in the literature are drug users depicted as "active and creative negotiators" (Ettorre and Miles 2002: 173), consciously involved in negotiating their lives and using "modes of consumption as a means of making sense of a rapidly changing world" (Ettorre and Miles 2002: 178). Because of this tendency to represent the user as passive, analyses of the reasons associated with combining two or more substances have also been neglected. In recent years, however, some corrective to this tendency has been started.

Qualitative researchers have begun to highlight the range of reasons provided by drug users as to why they use certain drug combinations and what it is that they hope to achieve in using particular drugs (H. Parker *et al.* 1998). Such discussions illustrate the extent to which drug users assess the risks and benefits of using drugs. As Williams and H. Parker have noted, "Young adult recreational drug users ... have made reasoned choices about the role of psychoactive substances. They believe their self-regulated drug use to be functional and consistent with otherwise conforming, productive lifestyles" (2001: 411). While not wishing to overemphasize the rational decision-making choices of young people (Mayock 2005), such studies highlight the reflections and intentions of young people in using various drug combinations. It is in the spirit of furthering this nascent work that this current chapter is framed.

In attempting to correct some of these shortcomings and examine young drug users as active agents, we will examine our participants' discussions of their drug-using practices and the reasons they provide for consuming a range of substances. Going into this project we asked, Do polydrug users extensively plan the timing of their drug consumption and drug combining, or is their polydrug use largely impulsive or spontaneous? What we discover, though, is that our respondents are not so neatly dichotomously categorized. We find both explicit planning with the intention of maximizing benefits and minimizing risks *and* spontaneous, unplanned drug-combining, including sometimes within the same users. These two drug-using narratives are not necessarily contradictory but instead when combined suggest a more accurate and realistic account of how young people use drugs. The temporal organization of these two styles of polydrug use, though, do differ in subtle but important ways as we will show.

Polydrug use in our sample

Given the focus of the research, interviewing users of club drugs who attend clubs, raves, or dance events, it is therefore not surprising that almost the entire sample had tried marijuana (97 percent) and ecstasy (92 percent). The lifetime prevalence for these drugs (the number of respondents who reported trying them at least once) equals, or nearly equals, that of alcohol. Around three-fourths of the sample were past-month users of beer and liquor, and just over 70 percent were past-month users of marijuana. Almost 80 percent had used ecstasy in the last year, and about one-third of the sample reported using it in the last month. Mushrooms was the only other drug that more than three-fourths of the sample had tried, although more than half of the sample had tried methamphetamine, cocaine, and LSD.

Regarding concurrent polydrug use, 77 percent of the participants admitted using two or more different substances, which included at least one illicit drug, concurrently during the last month, and 92 percent admitted using two or more substances concurrently over the past year. Although no comparable statistical data on simultaneous polydrug use were collected, we were able to gain some information on the extent to which different illicit and licit substances were used on the same occasion by analyzing the qualitative data. In the open-ended questions we asked, "Have you ever used drugs in combination with each other or with cigarettes and alcohol?" and in analyzing the answers discovered that 94 percent of the sample reported having combined two or more different substances and a further 30 percent reported having used three or more substances on any one occasion. The most commonly cited combinations, not surprisingly given the popularity of marijuana, ecstasy, and alcohol in our sample, were: marijuana and ecstasy (59 percent), and alcohol and marijuana (45 percent). Other combinations cited included ecstasy and alcohol (28 percent), ecstasy and acid (28 percent), and ecstasy and tobacco (28 percent). Similar to other researchers (Measham *et al.* 2001; H. Parker *et al.* 1998) we found that a substantial percentage of our respondents combine a range of different substances on the same occasion.

While these data provide a rough picture of the extent to which our respondents regularly combine different substances, we need to emphasize certain limitations concerning the precise accuracy of the qualitative data. First, a significant number of respondents seemed somewhat unsure how much combining they actually did at any one time. For instance, some described a laundry list of substances they consumed in the course of a night, but when asked specifically about what combinations of drugs they do, they reported that they "don't really combine drugs." The idea of drug-combining, for these respondents, has a narrower, more specific meaning than simply using multiple substances within a given evening. Second, participants seemed to assume that, when asked the question about combining drugs, the interviewer wanted to know if they had consumed two or more different drugs at the very same moment. In other words, if they took one drug at the beginning of a night out and then another at the end of the night to help them "to come down," they did not recognize this as a case of combining drugs. Finally, some of the club-drug users, when asked about combining drugs, admitted to polydrug use only if the effects of both drugs had been felt.

Given the difficulties that researchers themselves have had in defining precisely what qualifies as drug-combining or polydrug use, it is perhaps unsurprising that young drug users themselves display a similar ambivalence and lack of consensus as to what polydrug use might mean. While these caveats require that we interpret the precise numbers connected to their drug combinations with extreme caution, they should not be interpreted simply as weaknesses in the data. Instead they highlight the importance of examining the reasons that young users give for combining drugs, how they interpret their consumption of multiple substances, and how these subtleties could be missed by quantitative surveys that offer no room for these ambiguities. With this in mind, we now turn to consider in more detail the dominant themes that emerge from the participants' discussions of their drug consumption and drug combinations.

Combining illicit drugs to produce beneficial effects

The extent to which participants deliberately combine different substances in order to gain certain effects is a prominent theme within the data. In fact, these club-drug users provided lucid and detailed accounts of the reasons and motivations for their polydrug preferences – accounts which belie the notion of these young people as merely passive users swept up by forces and pressures external to them. While the interview data also highlight variations in individual preferences and perceptions of the pleasures to be gained and the risks to be encountered, overall, our respondents express the desire to achieve a particular desired effect. In fact, one of the primary reasons for combining different substances is simply that they enjoy the results: "I love candy flipping [acid and ecstasy]. ... That's a lotta fun. Love acid and nitrous. Love acid, pot, and nitrous. Love ecstasy and pot. ... Yeah, I definitely combine drugs" (Craig, 28). That they use and combine drugs for fun and pleasure may seem obvious, but it is a point that is generally overlooked in much of the epidemiology literature.

While these young people know that each individual substance taken has the potential to provide pleasure, they also know that consuming any substance involves risks. These potential effects, especially those that are negative, could then be modified if different substances are combined. Adding one substance is seen as ameliorating the effects of another. They actively seek information to aid them in choosing the right combinations. New club-drug users either sought information from peers, or went to Web sites to learn about which drugs to combine. They also, as Measham and colleagues have noted, "learn from their experimentation" (2001: 100). As users become more experienced they increasingly rely on their own experiences to guide them. "I'm a big fan of combinations. Once I ... was experienced enough with each one to know what they did, they're kinda like building blocks now" (David, 25). In fact, when describing how they came to combine specific drugs, participants note the extent to which their current drug-combining practices are based on previous experiments and that their current knowledge is based on a process of discovery. As Magnolia, 31, notes:

> Well, back then when I used it [GHB] frequently ... we were all about getting as high as we possibly could. ... We'd mix, like, speed with GHB. We did a lot of drugs mixing. We figured out which drugs were the best to use with which, which ones cancelled out ... you know, certain drugs' effects, and stuff like that. We found that doing speed and doing ecstasy was a great combo. Or doing GHB and doing speed was a great combo.

This language of experimentation, knowledge-building, and discovery is found throughout our interviews. These highlight the way that users mix planned drug combinations with more impulsive, experimental drug-combining. The particular results of these trial-and-error processes vary, however, and many of our participants express opposite views as to which drug combinations would result in the most pleasurable effects. However, club-drug users overall were consistent in identifying three major types of beneficial effects that encourage them to combine different substances: extension, enhancement, and reduction.

Extension

One motivation for drug combination is to use one substance to extend or prolong the effects of a different substance already consumed so that the drug high does not dissipate before participants want it to. In such cases, substances such as marijuana or GHB are used "to bring back up" (Kira, 31) the experience of being high. This effect is well described by Pat, 23, who discusses how taking GHB, while coming down from an ecstasy high, allowed him to continue its effects:

> I did [GHB] one time. And I was actually coming down off ecstasy, and it was a rave after party in Oakland. And I was totally coming down, like I ended up going to this party. It ended at two, and then I went to this after-party. And I was totally coming down off a hit of E, and I ended up doing one shot of G, and it totally just made me fully come back up, and I felt really ... I just totally felt like I came back up on the E.

In cases such as this, respondents use one drug to extend the effects of another. In other cases, combining drugs is done with the intention of enhancing or transforming the experience.

Enhancement

Certain drugs are used to intensify the effects of others, particularly ecstasy (see also Forsyth 1996; Hammersley *et al.* 1999; Solowij *et al.* 1992). Marijuana is frequently cited by the men and women we interviewed for its ability to enhance an existing drug experience. For example, according to Cary, 19, combining marijuana and mushrooms has the effect of making his experience more intense:

> When you're peaking, you smoke a bowl and you peak a little harder ... Definitely marijuana just intensifies any drug. Whatever it is, it all intensifies the situation. And ... you know, I would say with every drug I usually always put weed in with it.

Other drug combinations are believed not merely to intensify the ecstasy experience, but to transform the experience completely. Hallucinogens are believed to enhance the ecstasy high by adding "visuals" (Arthur, 23). Lydia, 19, describes the use of nitrous oxide while experiencing the effects of ecstasy as intensely pleasurable:

> Taking a hit of nitrous while you're rolling ... Nitrous is so intense anyway. ... It lasts for about a minute instead of thirty seconds. But it feels like ... That's the thing is, when you're taking nitrous, it feels like an eternity. And then all of a sudden you're back to your real life and it's only been, like, thirty seconds. You know, that's ... it's just really weird. And then ... so but it lasts longer, and it's more intense because you're already on another drug, and it's just ... all of the senses going at you the same time. It's just, like ... Whoa. That's the only way I can explain it, it's just an overall feeling of ... Whoa. Damn.

Lydia describes a sense of both increased intensity and increased duration, suggesting that the desire to enhance and extend the experiences of the drugs may often overlap.

Mushrooms are also viewed as working well with ecstasy. Aaron, 18, explains:

> 'Shrooms and ecstasy … it's almost like … going. … but for five minutes you could be rolling, and then five minutes you could be 'shrooming. You know, it's kind of an on and off, like … pulses of each one and stuff. So … it's pretty interesting. But for the most part, the general feeling there is neither rolling or 'shrooming. … it's almost like normalizing, where it's just like a euphoric state … 'cause they're high, they're under the influence, but it doesn't feel like they're being affected by anything.

The experience described by Aaron is particularly noteworthy because the result of combining these two substances produces an effect that is distinct from that of either mushrooms or ecstasy used independently. The pleasure experienced is over and beyond the possible effects of either drug alone and allows the user to reach a "euphoric" state, which is intriguingly described as being "normalized." In such cases, the transformation of the drug experience affected by combining is not simply quantitative (longer-lasting in duration, or a higher degree of a particular effect) but qualitative as well – it is a categorically different experience, in which the whole is greater than simply the sum of the parts.

Reduction

Combining different substances also has the potential of lessening or reducing the negative effects of certain drugs. For example, stimulants such as cocaine and amphetamines are described as reducing alcohol intoxication and are used by respondents to achieve a sense of sobriety. As Emma, 17, notes, taking cocaine while drunk makes her feel sober:

> You get drunk and it's nice and it's fun. … I come down off of alcohol, it's really weird, I get, like, so depressed after I drink. … Like, I feel terrible after I drink. Um, not so much a hangover … I just feel awful. … So, like, if coke was … near me, I'd probably beat someone down for some coke. And like … and then it really. … then it, like, makes you less, um, confused, I guess. And then you're, like, thinking straight. It sobers you up a little bit. You know, it makes you feel nice and you can have a nice conversation and go to sleep. You know, like, no worries, you know.

Another combination which has this effect is marijuana and ecstasy, which according to Pilar, 22, helps to "take the edge off" of the effects of ecstasy:

> What a lot of people hate about E is the speediness from it. Even if it's supposedly pure, or whatever, there's still something about it that just. … it's what makes your teeth grind and makes you all jittery, and uncomfortable, basically. And the weed definitely takes the edge off, like, so much, and it helps with the nausea and it helps with all the negatives effects, to

make it … the whole thing, like, pretty pleasurable, or as pleasurable as possible.

Using one drug to reduce the negative effects of another is also important to counteract the unpleasant effects of coming down from a "high." Aaron, 18, for example, describes the benefits of marijuana when coming down from speed:

Interviewer.   What about your comedown? What's that like?
Aaron.   Often … like a speed comedown. Like, depressing. Or … like … well, that's like just a plain comedown. But if there's weed around, then really the comedown's not that bad, it's like you're high. (*Laughs.*) You know, it's, like, a good transition.

The use of marijuana for this purpose has been noted by other researchers (Forsyth 1996; McDermott 1993; Riley *et al.* 2001); in fact, Sterk and colleagues discovered that more than 50 percent of their sample used marijuana "as their preferred drug … to come down from ecstasy" (Sterk *et al.* 2006: 213).

It is in the often elaborate plans of multiple drug consumption designed to ameliorate the negative effects of other drugs that we particularly see the active planning that goes into the structuring of the evening and the drug-taking more generally, issues we will examine in greater detail shortly.

Consuming non-illicit substances

In addition to combining different illicit substances to produce beneficial effects, participants also describe a series of non-illicit substances that they consume as precautionary steps. These include drinking water and orange juice, eating carbohydrates and taking herbal supplements and energy pills, such as 5-HTP, glucosamine, and "bumble bee/yellowjacket" pills to ensure that the risks associated with drug-taking are minimized. In fact, descriptions of polydrug use invariably contain a discussion of food and supplement use typically taken both prior to the event as well as during the coming-down or after-phase. For example, many men and women describe using food and food supplements as a type of "pre-loading" prior to ingesting drugs (see also B. C. Kelly 2007). The effects of these substances (e.g., having a full stomach) are believed to prepare the body for the physical hardship of drug use, thereby mitigating the possibility of adverse physical reactions, such as stomach upsets. Some participants involve themselves in highly developed, almost ritualistic consumption patterns. David, 25, elaborates:

So, the day before, start out with a high-protein diet and the 5-HTP … The protein helps the 5-HTP do its job, and vitamin B5 [B12] helps too. And the day of … what I've noticed in myself is … I have a really strong stomach, but if I'm gonna have stomach problems and be nauseous from E, it's gonna be because I ate wrong during the day … So on the day that I eat, I tend to eat low-volume high carbohydrates. Carbohydrates for energy. The day after, I go with the orange juice … Doughnuts are about the only thing I can make myself eat after rolling. Orange juice, obviously, for vitamin C and stuff. The doughnuts also have pretty good carbohydrates in them, and they'll help me have something in my stomach for when I take a crap load of vitamins and other antioxidants the next day. Then, once I've got an appetite back, high proteins again.

Again we see intensive active planning on the part of our respondents. They also speak at great length of the potentially negative effects of certain drugs, especially the consequences of ecstasy use on their brains. Participants evince great familiarity with research on the drugs they use. Many of our respondents refer to the reported effects of ecstasy on serotonin levels. To combat this they consume a series of supplements. Brian, 19, describes his method:

Brian.	I started taking 5-HTP …
Interviewer.	Do you think that helps?
Brian.	Yeah. Yeah, definitely. Because it makes it not such a fast … come-on? And not such a hard comedown.
Interviewer.	So you don't come up as fast, but you also don't come down as hard?
Brian.	Yeah. 'Cause of the … It balances out the serotonin.
Interviewer.	So when do you take that? You take it every day?
Brian.	Oh, no. I'll take it … like, when I'm doing E, I'll take it once before, once during … couple times after.
Interviewer.	A couple times … Like, within the same day? Or a day before?
Brian.	No, it's all within the same day. It's all within the same experience. Like just before I do it, just before I drop, I'll take 5-HTP and then maybe, if I remember, I'll take one, like, while I'm rolling, but probably won't. (*Laughs.*) And then towards the end I'll take, like, one, and then when I'm actually coming down I'll take another one. It helps. It mellows me out. It helps.

The meanings that using these licit substances have for the respondents – to reduce negative effects from their drug consumption – are not wholly different from the meaning that other illicit drug use has, such as in the case of marijuana, often used to aid in coming down. This shows the importance of considering illicit substances as part of a wide range of ingested substances consumed by young people in the context of polydrug use, rather than artificially separating these out in pre-determined, socially constructed, and narrow categories of what should count as polydrug use.

Combinations to be avoided

Just as the young men and women we interviewed have clear ideas about which substances to combine in order to obtain certain desired effects, their narratives also contain discussions about which combinations should be avoided. While not all participants agree on which combinations should be avoided, certain substances are mentioned more often. Of these, alcohol is the most commonly cited substance. Sixteen percent of respondents specifically noted that they would not combine alcohol with club drugs, and of these over 60 percent said they would never combine it with ecstasy. Two different types of narratives existed. The first dealt with potential *physical* dangers of combining alcohol and ecstasy, the second concerned issues of *social* proscription. Many of these respondents believe that combining alcohol with ecstasy is very dangerous: "Ecstasy and alcohol is bad. Very, very bad. It dehydrates you, and it's a sedative with an upper ... So it's not a good combination. It's actually really dangerous, too" (Anna, 23). This suggests that a relatively strong taboo exists that prevents some club-drug users from using alcohol with ecstasy. However, other respondents argue against this combination not because of the potential physical dangers but because they view it as socially inappropriate. Many explain that drinking alcohol and getting drunk are inappropriate behavior, especially at raves. (See Chapter 10 for further discussion of alcohol within the scene.)

As researchers on the dance scene have noted, a code of behavior exists in which alcohol is avoided and the events are generally free of "beer monsters" (see Hesmond-halgh 1998 and Measham *et al.*1998). In the same way, many of our respondents express the belief that alcohol is out of place at a rave.

> Liquor is not ... that important at the rave scene. People don't normally drink. I guess it's the way I feel about it and a lotta my friends feel about liquor. Some people don't know how to control it, and they're just very ... in an anger state. And the rave scene ... it's not a place where people get mad and angry. It's usually more of ... a happier place where you just feel ... you're there and you're enjoying yourself, no matter what the situation is. So it's more. ... E-related.
>
> (Amado, 22)

Nevertheless, in spite of these views about alcohol, it is clear that alcohol is not universally shunned. Factors influencing whether or not alcohol should be combined with ecstasy are often related more to the social context than to the substance. While ecstasy could be viewed as the quintessential substance of the rave, alcohol is more the defining substance in clubs: "Alcohol tends to play a big part ... You know at clubs they get a little more wild, they get a little more, whatever, they kind of, like, let go of themselves a little more" (Dwight, 29).

In addition to the potential of inappropriate disruptive behavior brought on by combining alcohol and drugs, respondents note three other reasons for not combining certain substances. First, some club drug users believe that combining particular substances does not merely have the potential of reducing the effects of individual drugs; they believe that certain combinations could negate the pleasurable effects completely. Such a possibility would defeat the purpose of taking the original drug, an eventuality well articulated by Cary, 19, who is clearly disappointed by the effects of combining ecstasy and methamphetamine:

> [L]ike ... the first time I did ecstasy it was the pure stuff. It was weird, because I ended up ... it was really stupid, I ended up doing a line of meth that night too.

Like, right after I'd done it. From what I hear, it cancels anything ... if you're having a bad trip or anything, you can bust a line of meth or coke and it'll sober you out. So ... I don't know, I was feeling it, but ... I wasn't sure if it was also like the meth too, 'cause it was a little bit of both mixed together, but ... the meth canceled a lot of the trip out. And I was disappointed.

Here, drug combining is not presented as dangerous or inappropriate, but rather as counterproductive.

Second, a few drug users describe themselves as purists in that they believe that combining different drugs took away from enjoying the pleasures afforded by a single drug. As Lydia, 19, notes:

I'm the type of person that likes to keep ... I like to keep my drugs separate. ... I just like pure experiences. ... I don't really like to mix anything, that's why I like to do nitrous ... while I'm sober, 'cause it's a pure experience of doing nitrous. ... I don't wanna hippie flip [ecstasy and mushrooms] or candy flip [ecstasy and acid] ... because ... I really don't wanna that much. ... So why would I wanna intensify my trip, you know? That's all.

While she enjoys many different drugs, it is important to her that she keeps their use separate. To combine drugs does not enhance the experience for her, but instead detracts from it.

Finally, some respondents express very pragmatic reasons for not combining different substances; specifically, that combining two substances would have no noticeable or obvious effect:

Iliana. I don't think you can get drunk [when using ecstasy]. I really don't. No matter how much you drink, you can't get drunk ... I did drink, like, once with it. But, like ... I drank, like, two beers and I was, like, "What am I doing? I'm on ecstasy. (*Laughs.*) I don't need to be drinking." And like it didn't do anything, really. And everyone that I've talked to that does says, like, they don't ... And, like, if ... on speed, like ... you can't.

Interviewer. Drink?

Iliana. You can drink, but you're not gonna get drunk.

Having learned about the various drugs from their friends, or from other sources of information, participants provide an often elaborate account of why they combine certain substances and why they refrain from mixing others. Their narratives also illustrate the extent to which the social context, whether it be a club or a rave, may also influence their use of certain combinations. This suggests that their decisions are based not solely on pharmacological effects. However, there exists another dimension which also plays a role in their decision-making and that is the dimension of time. In the final section we will show how time, whether in terms of the parameters of the night out or the timed effects of different substances, influences the reasons why they choose certain combinations and not others.

The importance of timing

A significant time dimension theme runs through the club-drug users' descriptions of combining different substances. In fact, much of their polydrug narratives is constructed around notions of time.[6] We find two different types of temporal organization in these drug-using narratives. The first is structured, planned, and organized by the external constraints of the dance event. The second is more flexible, unplanned, and organized by the user's extent of intoxication.

Structured time

In the first type we find a linear, chronological, and fixed notion of time which centers around using drugs to fit with the timing of the dance event itself and the night out. As a number of researchers have noted, dance events occur mainly at the weekend, which is viewed as a highly symbolic period where individuals can experience "a cathartic release from the working week" (Measham 2004a: 321. See also Hayward 2002). The weekend is a "time out from weekday pressures" (Measham 2004b: 210) in which the pursuit of hedonism takes place within a controlled manner. As Malbon (1999) has noted, dance activities typically revolve around set beginnings and endings as venues are increasingly governed by strict licensing restrictions that dictate the duration of the event. Given such time restrictions, using drugs to enhance the experience must take place within specified time boundaries. Although the men and women we interviewed consume substances both before and after dance events, the majority of their discussions on polydrug use revolve around dovetailing their drug use with the timing of the night out. This suggests an interesting paradox between the attempts to achieve a sense of timelessness or time out (MacAndrew and Edgerton 1969) through ingesting drugs and the necessity of accomplishing this experience within predetermined time constraints.

Thus, while the desired effects of polydrug use may vary, our respondents generally discuss their polydrug experiences within a linear notion of time fitted to the time restrictions of the night. David, 25, explains:

David.   I prefer to have two or three [drugs] throughout the night, depending on what period of the night I'm in. You know, for instance I always like to smoke a bowl [marijuana] at the end of the night. If I'm doing cocaine, I don't do it at the beginning of the night if I'm going to run out. Cocaine always leaves you wanting more, so I make sure that I have enough to last for whatever the last period of the night is ... I'd have some coke, for probably later in the evening. I wouldn't do it in the beginning, 'cause I wouldn't wanna run outta coke and have that kinda coke headache. You know, even though sometimes the E overpowers it. I love to have a little bit of

	GHB. That always spices things up. It would probably be just those three.
Interviewer.	How would you spread it out?
David.	Let's say we get there, like, eleven o'clock, take my tab of E, start feeling it around midnight. Around like one-thirty, two o'clock, I might do some GHB. If that came on, like, strong, if the mixture was strong ... 'cause I probably took another tab with that capful of GHB, I might do a little bit of cocaine just to, like ... it just kinda sharpens your senses up a little bit. I wouldn't do a lotta cocaine on those drugs, because ... the cocaine will kind of overpower 'em. ... But that would be later in the night, probably around three. And then I would definitely stop doing cocaine around ... probably around five, 'cause if I don't go to bed by ... seven o'clock, then I'm up for the day. It's like my clock resets. So seven's kinda my cutoff time, I gotta get in bed and be able to sleep. And if I've had cocaine within the last hour, hour-and-a-half, I won't be able to fall asleep.

Here we see a series of decisions made about which drugs to use in which combinations and sequences that are synchronized in order not only to gain a certain type of intoxication but also to ensure that the effects fit with the predetermined time parameters of the evening.

If an event is scheduled to last longer than usual, respondents make sure to consume drugs, such as methamphetamines, that enable them to keep active for the entire time. For example, Jason, 20, describes combining ecstasy with methamphetamine in order to meet the demands of an all-night rave:

E and crystal, mmm. When I decided I wanted to do E, and it was somewhat early in the night, and I was gonna be at a rave that's gonna last for a long time. And I knew that I wanted to roll, but I wanted to be not rolling the whole time; but I wanted to be alert. So I used a combination of the two.

In these narratives, polydrug use is carefully planned and timed to fit the external parameters of the event and the timing of drug combinations could be decided ahead of time.

Flexible time

The second notion of time apparent within the narratives is more flexible, influenced less by the time limits of the dance event, and governed instead by the effects of the participant's state of intoxication. In order to ensure the maximum effect of mixing two substances, the user has to time the ingestion of the second on the basis of the effects of the first. Participants believe that certain substances and certain combinations are inherently time-sensitive and that synchronizing the timing of when to consume specific drugs is an essential factor in maximizing the pleasure and managing any potential risks. As Devin, 19, comments: if you are experiencing an ecstasy high and if "you take it [marijuana] at the beginning when you first start rolling, it'll make you roll more"; [if, however,] "you take it, like … later, it'll make you go to sleep." Thus different outcomes could be attained by consuming the second substance at different stages of the initial drug trajectory.

In order to control the effects, participants apply a combination of timed-use techniques. As we have seen, many respondents consume additional substances in order to prolong or "maintain" the high. Similarly, respondents reported taking individual substances at different times in order to avoid negative interactions that might arise from combining different substances. The precise timing of the drug sequence could not be predetermined, as it depends on the evolving effects of the evening. For example, Craig, 28, describes how he spaced out his consumption of LSD, ecstasy, marijuana, and nitrous oxide:

> If I was going to combine, I'd start with acid. Then take ecstasy, then smoke pot, then do nitrous. … I'd usually wait till I felt like I was solidly at the peak of my acid before taking the ecstasy, so that I know where I'm gonna get to.'Cause you can never be sure how strong something is. And then wait for the comedown off the E to smoke. And then wait till you're high to do the nitrous. That's as combined as I would make an evening.

In his comment about the inability to fully predict the effects of a drug in advance, because of the varying intensity of effect, Craig highlights the degree to which the planning and timing must remain flexible to accommodate varying physical responses.

Spontaneity still operates: structured flexibility

The dominant narrative that emerges from our interviews is that of the rational and calculating user controlling his or her drug use by first preparing for the event by taking a series of ameliorating substances, such as carbohydrates and orange juice. While at the event, he or she consumes specific illicit and licit substances at different periods throughout the night out to attain an exciting and pleasurable evening. Finally, towards the end of the night, and as the intoxication diminishes, the respondent consumes other substances to ensure a pleasant transition back to everyday life. This is a picture of rational and controlled drug use where the individual drug user is an active agent engaged in a cost–benefit analysis in which he or she assesses the risks and measures them against the benefits (Coffield and Gofton 1994; Mayock 2005). However, as Measham has noted, it is important to "reintroduce emotionality to a conceptualisation of agency in contemporary consumption" (2004b: 209), a point evident in our own data, where, in addition to a picture of controlled drug use, there also exists a crosscutting and alternative narrative which describes more spontaneous and unplanned use. Such discussions of spontaneous drug use are more difficult to trace in the data, partly because respondents are typically much more specific about their planned use and this type of use tends to take on a much more central role in accounts of their experiences. Consequently, they seem more structured in time.

Nevertheless, peppered throughout their discussions of planned drug consumption are mentions of more spontaneous drug use. Spontaneous drug use in the narratives implies a notion of nonlinear-timed use, in that respondents disrupt their planned drug use by the sudden choice to consume another drug. Even those men and women who reported planning their polydrug use by researching information pertaining to drug effects on the Internet and plotting a planned course of action, when probed, admitted that they often use certain substances spontaneously, occasioned by meeting friends or finding themselves in a different situation.

The different degrees of spontaneity identified within the narratives can be plotted at different points along a continuum of planned versus spontaneous use. At one end, users describe a series of planned combinations consumed at different intervals and, at the other end, users describe impulsive consumption. In the middle there exist respondents who both describe planning their consumption and then being diverted from this plan. For example, Jacob, 26, discusses how he had taken ecstasy and then by chance met a friend and decided to take some cocaine:

> We had taken some E that was very chill and I was, like, at the club, I wanted to dance, I wanted to be social. And we ran into a girl that we knew from clubbing and partying and she had some [cocaine] and we bought some off her to, like ... as a boost kind of thing.

From this account we see that consuming cocaine had not been on the agenda for the evening, but the planned timing of events was impulsively amended to take advantage of this unforeseen opportunity of being able to use cocaine. In another example, Chace, 26, wandered into a different part of the venue and found nitrous available and decided to use it:

> About one o'clock I kinda took a break and started hanging out with a couple of friends ... in the chill room. ... Wound up going off into a separate area in the party and actually doing nitrous at the same time. And nitrous and E together is just ... really, really amazing. ... Wound up taking another half of a pill later on, and just, like ... chilling out.

This form of planned/spontaneous drug use can be described as *structured flexibility*. In such cases, participants begin the evening following a prearranged plan but, as the evening progresses, they find themselves either meeting new friends or being in a different setting and taking a drug which they had not initially planned for. However, they do not necessarily abandon their initial plans altogether.

We see another example of structured flexibility where Oliver, 19, describes how on his birthday he had attended a rave and was given ecstasy and methamphetamine by a friend who was also a dealer. The friend felt sorry for him because he was not having a great time:

> It was at a rave. ... I was hanging out with somebody, and he knew it was my eighteenth birthday, and he happened to be a drug dealer, and it was pretty

much, like, my eighteenth birthday present, you know. He gave me a pill of E and then he gave me meth – lines of meth. I was, like, "Hey, you know, eighteenth birthday, not going too well, sure, you know, why not?" ... I guess it was, like, "Hey, take something to try to feel better."

Interestingly enough, however, later on in the interview, Oliver tells the interviewer that he always prepares himself for the possibility of taking ecstasy by bringing with him his "rave pack":

[A] rave pack, is what I call it, that I take with me so that I ... before I take and after I take a drug. It's something called 5-HTP, and ... it's supposed to build artificial serotonin. And usually I take one a day before ... and then one a day afterwards, for a week. And I usually take five to ten thousand milligrams of vitamin C, three to four days before and after. ... I take [5-HTP] so that I don't get the kind of depressive ... you know, depletion effect. I also take zinc and iron, so that my jaw doesn't hurt afterward, to kinda cut down on the physical pain after you roll. Yeah, I do that as kind of a ritual. You know, you take that and always do it after and before.

While he admits to using drugs spontaneously, he nevertheless also plans for this possibility by always having his "rave pack" available.

In the above examples, while planning exists, spontaneous drug use also occurs. In the last two cases we highlight examples of spontaneous use with little or no planning. In the first case, the user attends a dance event equipped only with one drug, but, nevertheless, assumes that he can obtain other different substances by interacting with others. What substances these might be is unknown, as they will depend on who the user interacts with:

I'd usually get there [the club], like, around eleven. ... And I'd be there with a few friends. You know, we'd do, like, a little ... a couple lines before we'd go in, or we'd smoke ... maybe grab a drink ... and then you'd go to the dance floor and ... you'd meet someone ... then at this point I would take, like, another hit, and then I would just offer it to someone and, you know, they'd be, "Okay." ... Then they'd share what they would have ... and then you'd do a little bit of that, you know ... and ... you'd see someone you wanna talk to ... then sort of feel him out. ... It wasn't always, like, that they had drugs. ... And afterwards, like, you went home with them ... You party more ... use more drugs ... 'Cause everyone had a little bit with them, you know. Or if you didn't, you'd know someone. ... and you'd be able to get a little bit.

(Mohinder, 23)

Here we see the extent to which spontaneous drug use, while not planned, is determined by the social interaction that takes place and, in turn, the sharing of drugs operates to facilitate the social interaction. "I would just offer it to someone and ... they would share what they would have" is the reciprocal basis on which the interaction is facilitated and established. In this case, while the polydrug use is not planned, the user does expect that he will be able to involve himself in polydrug use.

In the last case, we see the user who is totally spontaneous in her polydrug use. Jasmine, 25, is intent on modifying an emotional state and is unconcerned with what substances she takes as long as her mood is altered:

> I didn't wanna be there [at a camp-out] and ... because of my emotional state, I really wasn't feeling like dancing, and I wasn't feeling the music, and I was like, "Okay, fuck it. So ... I'll have a couple drinks and I'll feel better." So I did that, didn't feel better. I was still, like ... depressed and I was, like, "Well, maybe if I do a bit o' coke I'll feel a little bit more excited, I'll feel better." Did some coke, still didn't work. I was, like ... more awake, but not any happier. So I was, like, "Well, fuck it, I'll eat some E." So I ate some E, that didn't do anything, and I was like, "Shit." So I smoked some pot, ate a mushroom cap ... And then ... the weird thing is that I did all that and then I went to bed at, like ... ten-thirty in the morning, and I slept, which seems ... impossible.

Given her depressed state of mind, she attempts to alter her mood by using whatever drugs are available. She has no idea of what she will ingest during the course of the evening and in fact on reflection is surprised that this concoction of different drugs had so little effect.

From all these cases, we see a range of different drug-using practices. We have users who have planned their entire evening of drug use. We have those who planned to take a specific substance but then decide to combine it with another substance given to them by a friend, or one that became available when they entered a new setting. We have those who appear not to have planned which specific drugs they intend to use but who nevertheless are prepared with ameliorating substances just in case they do take drugs. Finally, we have those who will consume whatever drugs are available to them in the course of the evening.

Conclusion

The data presented in this chapter validate the findings of much of the available research literature that highlights the extent to which polydrug use is a common characteristic of young people who attend electronic dance music events. As we have shown, our participants are involved in consuming a potpourri of substances both legal and illegal. However, although our data corroborate the results of contemporary epidemiology, they question both the dominant portrayal of the drug user as a passive consumer and the extent to which researchers in debating various definitional issues have neglected to consider the reasons and meaning ascribed to the mixing of drugs. While the literature has tended to focus on the patterns and types of drug consumed, we have concentrated on identifying the different reasons that users provide for their polydrug use. In so doing, we have seen the extent to which young users are active agents in deciding what to consume when enjoying the night out. By emphasizing the agency of our respondents we have described not only the combinations they both use and avoid, but also the meanings attached to these combinations.

Furthermore, we have highlighted the temporal organization of their drug use, a feature that has also been neglected in contemporary discussions of concurrent and simultaneous polydrug use. Given the extent to which our respondents tend to consume drugs exclusively at the weekend at public events or private parties, it is not surprising that issues of time would be important. As Measham (2004a, b) and others (Hayward 2002; Presdee 2000) have noted, unlike their counterparts in the late 1960s and 1970s, young drug users, at least as illustrated by our respondents, have not dropped out from society but instead are intent on enjoying themselves and their drugs within the societal confines of the acceptable time-out period at the end of the week. The weekend has become the time when a "controlled loss of control" (Measham 2004c: 338) takes place. Considering these restrictions, it is not unexpected that our respondents should plan their drug-using practices to fit their available leisure time. They seek a fun experience but are willing to attain this experience within societally acceptable parameters. However, while this sense of deliberation exists, it is also apparent from our respondents' narratives that on occasion their planning is interrupted and they consume other substances that they did not initially intend to use. In such cases, and in spite of their planning, the intoxicating effects of the drugs, coupled with the sensory pleasures of the event and interactions with their fellow partygoers may all result in their consuming a combination of substances not planned for, which may result in unanticipated consequences. What is significant, especially in the light of the extant literature, is not the fact that such events should occur, especially given the environments in which they operate, but the fact that both planned and spontaneous drug use are found to exist side-by-side in the single drug user. The occurrence of explicit planning and spontaneous drug-combining suggests that a simplistic dichotomy of use on the basis of planned versus spontaneous drug use may not accurately reflect the young drug user today.

In Part III we have examined the ways that the young club drug users we interviewed interpret and negotiate issues of risk and of pleasure in their consumption of drugs within the dance scenes. In the final part of the book we continue with these themes, but connect them with issues of identity and difference within the scene – particularly around issues of gender, sexuality, and race/ethnicity.

Part IV

Gender, social context, and ethnicity

Chapter 9

Drugs, gender, sexuality, and accountability in the world of raves

Introduction

In interviewing young men and women in the club and rave scenes, we found a stark difference in their descriptions of the culture and experiences of clubs and raves. They often described clubs as being alcohol-fueled meat markets, in which clothing styles and dancing styles are highly sexualized. Furthermore, gendered expectations are heavily enforced, and interactions with others often have a tinge of aggression (or sometimes outright fights and violence). Raves, on the other hand, are described as dominated by the drug ecstasy, by warmth and friendliness, and, while normative behavior encourages touching and feeling of friends and strangers, blatant sexual displays or expectations are frowned upon and more flexible gender dynamics are encouraged. These are the two stereotypical pictures of raves and clubs that most commonly emerge in our interviews. For many of the ravers, the specter of the club seems to operate as the "other" against which they define themselves, much like Thornton's (1996) clubbers' utilization of the opposition between underground and mainstream. However, the boundaries between the categories of rave and club, ecstasy and alcohol, sociability and sexuality are not necessarily nearly as neat as many of the descriptions initially seem to indicate. We find ecstasy and alcohol (among other substances) being consumed at or around both types of events, the opposition between ecstasy and sexuality that some young men and women described is far from universal in our sample, and while perhaps more open or flexible than clubs, many young men and women described continued enforcement of gendered norms at raves as well. In this chapter we will examine some of the dynamics of gender and sexuality as they operate in the rave scene, with particular emphasis on the connections between gender, sexuality, and ecstasy. In the next chapter we will examine the role of alcohol in these scenes, and key differences with the club (versus rave) scene, and the importance of context in shaping the experiences with substances, with gender, and with sexuality, in both scenes.

Gender and drugs

The stereotypical image of a drug user has, until recently, been that of a man – an image replicated within drug research literature. When women have appeared in the literature, it has traditionally been within a "pathology and powerlessness" perspective (Anderson 2008, see also Maher 1997), in which women drug users were portrayed as perpetual victims, their drug use treated as inherently pathological, and notions of women's agency or pleasures were missing. Although men comprised the norm in drug research, their gender typically remained unanalyzed or invisible (Broom 1995). Similarly, when sexuality was discussed within drug research, it was generally reduced to its problem status, analyzing the links between drug use and sexual disease transmission, for example. Rarely foregrounded were issues of the body, of gender or sexual identities, of pleasure and agency.

Feminist scholars achieved inroads in drug scholarship in the 1990s, highlighting women's agency and the centrality of gender dynamics in drug selling (Maher 1997; Taylor 1993) and drug consumption (Ettorre 1992), from inner-city drug use (Bourgois 1996; Hunt et al. 2002) to the dance/club scenes (Henderson 1996). Ettorre (2004) calls for "revisioning" women and drugs, contrasting the classical approach with her postmodern approach. The classical approach focuses on substance abuse and disease and on individualistic explanations; gender issues are often invisible, and, when acknowledged, simply naturalized (see also N. D. Campbell 2000). The postmodern approach, in contrast, emphasizes the consumption of drugs, the importance of pleasure, acknowledges the normalization of many drug cultures, and places difference (of gender, race, class, sexuality) at its center. Many of these issues have been important to studies of rave and club cultures, which emphasize the empowerment and freedoms experienced by women in these scenes. The work with this focus, though, remains more the exception than the norm.

Among these key exceptional works are Sheila Henderson's (1993a, 1996, 1999) analyses of women drug users in the dance scene, Maria Pini's study (1997, 2001) of women clubbers and ravers, and Fiona Hutton's (2006) book on gender, risk, and pleasure among women clubbers. Throughout Henderson's work she focuses not on women as drug victims, but rather on women using drugs as a part of their everyday leisure, actively seeking pleasure.[1] Pini examines the ways in which club drugs and the dance scene facilitate the challenging of normative heterosexuality among the women she interviewed, giving them a space to "lose it" within a dance context that privileges nonconformist gender displays. And Hutton points to the ways women in the club scene pleasurably engage with risk and aren't merely victims, arguing that certain club scenes (those associated with ecstasy or those in the underground) are empowering for women, examining the female producers, female drug sellers, as well as female clubgoers, who are often ignored in other analyses of these scenes.[2]

These key works focus on women in the British dance scenes and a comparable breadth of scholarship on the American context does not exist. And while all three mention issues of changing femininities and masculinities in these contexts, they focus primarily on women drug users, leaving explorations between the relationship between masculinities, club drugs, and the dance scenes less developed. In addition, while none of these ignores the issues of drugs entirely, it is the case that often the role, centrality, and effects of drugs within these scenes are downplayed or seen as secondary, leaving room for additional analysis that places drug issues more centrally at the core. This chapter, focusing on gender, sexuality, and ecstasy use in the San Francisco rave scene, attempts to address some of these lacunae through an analysis of the relationship between ecstasy and the accomplishment of gender in these social contexts, highlighting the freedoms and flexibility enabled but also the persistence of accountability within this youth cultural scene.

Gender and drug use in the sample

Of the 300 respondents interviewed, 276 (92 percent) had used ecstasy at some point in their lives. The qualitative analysis in this chapter draws from these 276 respondents. Among the ecstasy users, 47.5 percent were women and 52.5 percent were men. Seventy-five percent identified as heterosexual, 8 percent as homosexual, lesbian or gay, 14 percent as bisexual, and 3 percent as "other."

Generally, in the drug research field, although gender is increasingly examined, it is solely at the level of assessing different rates of drug use for men and women. Certainly this is a relevant area of inquiry and we did analyze these patterns among our respondents. We found that both the men and the women we interviewed were fairly widely drug-experienced (not surprising, as we specifically recruited club-drug users to interview). Men tended to have used or tried more substances in their lifetime (particularly the less used drugs), and men averaged a total of nine different drugs in their lifetime versus women's seven. Overall, though, these young men and women are quite similar in terms of drugs chosen. When we compared what drugs men and women in our sample had consumed in the prior year, for each of the twenty-five drugs that we looked at, a higher percentage of men had used each of these drugs than had women, although the only statistically significant differences were for ketamine, MDA, and "other" psychedelics (see Table 9.1). For the drugs most popular with the young men and women we interviewed (marijuana, ecstasy, and mushrooms), though, gender differences were nonsignificant. The only substances that we found a higher percentage of women consuming in the past year were cigarettes and hard liquor, although neither was a statistically significant difference. We found similar patterns in their past-month drug use. The only significant differences were that women were more likely to have used mushrooms. We found no significant differences between men and women in the age of initiation for any of the drugs. Data comparing particular dosing or amounts of drugs consumed proved to be unreliable, so we are unable to offer comparisons on those lines.

Certainly then, in our sample there is not the stark gender difference that earlier literatures on drug use might have given one to expect. These findings mirror those of Measham and colleagues (2001), who studied young men and women in the UK. They found men reportedly consuming drugs both more frequently and in somewhat greater quantities than women, along with wider repertoires of polydrug use, but with women apparently "catching up."

Doing gender and the performative pleasures of ecstasy

But what is left out by focusing on the quantitative differences in men and women's drug use? Although drug researchers now document gender differences in drug

Table 9.1 Gender and drug-use rates (%)

Drug	Lifetime prevalence		Past year prevalence		Past month prevalence	
	Men	Women	Men	Women	Men	Women
Tobacco, alcohol, marijuana						
Cigarettes	91	97	72	74	62	56
Beer	99	98	94*	84*	80	68
Hard liquor	98	99	89	91	75	80
Marijuana	96	88	88	87	73	68
Club drugs						
Ecstasy	90	94	81	79	34	34
LSD	66	51*	21	14	1	7
Mushrooms	81	73	55	54	13	22
Methamphetamine	59	51	34	32	12	15
Ketamine	41	32	27*	18*	2	3
GHB	31*	18*	13	11	3	2
Other illicit drugs						
Cocaine	62	59	44	37	16	14
Nitrous oxide	68*	55*	39	29	11	9
Poppers	16*	7*	8	2	3	1
MDA	19*	8*	10*	4*	1	0
Other psychedelics	37*	18*	14*	6*	3	11
DXM	14*	7*	6	1	1	0

*Statistically significant at or below the 0.05 level using chi-square.

consumption levels, much less often are the effects of drugs on the performance or accomplishment of gender examined sociologically. This is exactly what Fiona Measham calls for in her article "Doing gender, doing drugs," arguing that "[d]rug use is not just mediated by gender, but, far more significantly, drug use and the associated leisure, music, and style cultures within which drug use is located are themselves ways of accomplishing a gendered identity" (2002: 335). She draws on Messerschmidt's (1997) ideas of gender as structured action, which are rooted in the sociological analysis of the accomplishment of gender (West and Fenstermaker 1995; West and Zimmerman 1987), which argues that gender is not something we possess, or simply are, but rather something that we accomplish in social interactions. Measham argues that it's not just that gender influences doing drugs (e.g., men and women have different rates of drug use) but that "drug use itself can be seen as a way of doing gender" (2002: 335). Her call for more work examining the operation of drugs within the accomplishment of masculinity and femininity has gone unheeded for the most part, though, and most drug research neglects the questions she raises.

At first glance, there doesn't seem to be a huge difference in the way that women and men in our sample describe their experiences on ecstasy. Men and women both discuss feelings of empathy and openness. Both describe similar physical effects and the heightening of their senses. Many men and women stress that the drug is more sensory than sexual. This may lead to the belief that there is no real gendered element to the experience of ecstasy. However, considering the different gendered expectations for accomplishing a feminine versus a masculine identity in our society, the very same responses to ecstasy may have a very different meaning for a young man versus a young woman. There is a different meaning and implication to a young man expressing a greater ability to show physical affection and love to his same-sex friends than there is for a young woman, just as there's a different meaning for a young woman becoming increasingly sexually assertive while on ecstasy, compared to a young man with the same response. In the first example, the young man defies gender expectations, while the young woman does not; in the second the situation is reversed.

Cameron Duff (2008) provides tools that may be helpful for examining the connection between doing drugs and doing gender. In his article "The pleasure in context" he argues for the importance of attending to the "performative pleasures" of drugs. In so doing, he builds on the growing scholarly focus on the pleasures of drug consumption, but specifically highlights "The way that drug use was said to make possible certain types of performative behaviors, certain ways of 'being in the world' that are inaccessible, unthinkable, or just unlikely while sober" (Duff 2008: 386). In this article, Duff does not focus primarily on gender. Yet it seems ripe for a gendered analysis. To what degree are the pleasures of doing drugs connected to the pleasures of being a woman or a man in the world in ways that are inaccessible, unthinkable, or just unlikely while sober? Pini laid the groundwork for this in her analysis of women in the dance scene: "For such women, it is not simply attending a rave event which is pleasurable, but also the whole performance of an otherwise quite unlikely mode of femininity; a performance which rave culture is seen to make possible" (2001: 122), although in this aspect of her analysis she does not primarily focus on drugs *per se*, but more so on the social context of the dance scene, in which drugs may or may not play a part. These performative pleasures of drug use – specifically as they connect to performativity of gender and of sexual identities and practices – are a common theme in our interviews with young men and women in the San Francisco rave and club scenes as well.

A common theme in our respondents' narratives is enjoying the expressive qualities of ecstasy, the way that it allows them to be someone else, or to be who they "really" are, to express themselves and come out of their shell. For example, Cassie, 20 (heterosexual), says what's most enjoyable about using club drugs is that it allows an opportunity to "shake the cobwebs out," have fun, and express herself in a new way. Sometimes she wishes she could be more open and uninhibited, like she is on ecstasy, although she does wonder whether the drug turns her into a different person or whether it just unveils an existing part of her. (Among the ecstasy users we interviewed this is a matter of much debate – whether ecstasy reveals one's true, authentic self or whether it creates a fake persona and affect.) Similarly, Ling, 18 (heterosexual), says that ecstasy allows her to open up and to get over her fear of being at the center of things, of being a spectacle. These particular fears – of being too loud, of being too public, of being a spectacle[3] – were particularly expressed by young *women* we talked to, and particularly cited as advantages of ecstasy by them, perhaps reflecting the different gender expectations of social behavior for adolescent and young adult males versus females:

> I don't wanna say you get over your fears, but I think you do in a way sometimes. Like, your fear of being in public situations and not wanting to, like ... be kind of a ... a spectacle of yourself or ... you don't wanna be ... the odd person, you know. But then it's kinda like ... you don't care when you're on ecstasy ... and then, like, when you're sober, you still kinda have that feeling of, like, "I don't care what people think."
>
> (Ling)

This is not simply about the physiological effects of the drugs, however. The particular social nature and context of the setting of use, in this case raves, is essential to these performances and effects. Angelica, 20 (bisexual), describes the ways that the rave scene, both the social context and the drugs, frees one from typical inhibitions:

> The lines are blurred by all the drugs and by that feeling of, like, "we're never gonna see these people again and we're in this place." It's, like, a rave is so surreal ... because when I walk down the street in my big-ass pink pants and my like little shirt and my hair in pigtails and glitter and all, I would never walk around like that, you know, unless I was on my way to a party ... You're in such a different environment. ... you're gonna, like, act different and, like, take more risks, 'cause you don't really have anything to lose.

This social context is important to the pleasures of ecstasy for many of those we interviewed. For example, the collective experience of "dropping" ecstasy at a rave is very appealing to Ynez, 22 (heterosexual). She likes that everyone at the party feels the same thing at the same time, due to all being on ecstasy. In everyday life she feels like people cannot always communicate. However, on ecstasy all of those barriers are gone. Not only does she feel like she can say anything, she also feels like other people are interested in what she has to say. She feels like she can be herself. She can shed whatever roles she has to play in everyday life. No one judges anyone and there are no inhibitions. She attributes "99 percent" of the open, respectful behavior to the drug.

Natalie, 19 (heterosexual), explains that ecstasy made her accept who she is, to be okay with her body and her atypical sense of style. Overall, she thinks that using ecstasy at raves boosts her self-confidence. She describes people in her high school, who tended to belong to narrow, defined cliques, as "mean" and says she felt pressured to look thin, which she was not. While at raves she does not feel the pressure to look a particular way and feels comfortable about her body. She acknowledges that drug use probably plays a large role in the way in which people perceive and treat her there; however, Natalie says she likes experiencing what it feels like when everyone is "nice to you." She describes her immersion into rave culture, where she finally feels like she belongs:

> It was like the coolest thing … 'cause image was so important, especially where I lived. Like you were either a skater or a prep, or, you know, a Goth, or whatever. And, like, I didn't feel like I fit into any of those categories. And so then it was, like, "Oh, I'm a raver." Like, I finally figured out who I am.

Many of the ravers we interviewed contrast the freedom to be oneself at raves with what they experience at clubs, where they feel pressured to dress stylishly or provocatively and to put on a cool front. (See Chapter 10 for more analysis of these two contexts.) This is not simply a factor for young women we interviewed, but also for some young men who turn to raves to avoid the contexts in which narrow definitions of coolness and masculinity reign. As Paul, 21 (heterosexual), comments:

> I like the fact that you can go and dance and stuff like that [at clubs]. But, like … I also dislike the fact [that] … the whole atmosphere there is, like, so … "Mr. Cool Guy," and, like … Nobody's really themselves at clubs … it's just the whole front that you have to put on, to, like … I don't know, if you're looking for girls or whatever.

Or, as Brandon, 20 (heterosexual), puts it:

> You have to look really good [at clubs]. I don't think you have to look good to have fun. That's what turned me off, really, about clubs. You know, I don't think you have to be something that somebody else wants you to look like to have fun.

In the rave scene, on the other hand, they describe freedom to be who they are – a freedom often not enjoyed in day-to-day life. As Antonia, 20 (bisexual), argues, "The rave is still a place where you could be yourself and have fun. It made me learn. It made me realize, 'Don't be afraid to be yourself. Don't care what people are gonna say.'"

Ecstasy and sex

The idea that ecstasy enables a freedom from the kinds of sexualized sociability (Green and Halkitis 2006) expected in many nightlife scenes may seem quite surprising, given ecstasy's reputation among many people as being a "sexual" drug. Among the young club-drug users we interviewed, we found a wide range of opinions about the relationship between ecstasy and sex – from completely separating the two to seeing the two intimately fused, to seeing it as sexualized but not connected to sex *per se*. Some respondents go so far to say that it's "physically impossible" (Brian, 18, gay) to have sex while using ecstasy, and many, many respondents argue strongly that it is *not* a sexual drug. For these young ecstasy users, their priorities while on the drug are far from the sexual-hunt pastime that is assumed to dominate much of youth nightlife. Deana, 18 (heterosexual), says that it's a "misconception" that ecstasy is a sexual drug and that it makers her "very unsexual. Like, you love everybody, but you don't sexually love anybody." Similarly, Donna, 26 (heterosexual), adamantly argues that the appeal of ecstasy is unrelated to sexual pursuits of any kind:

> When I'm on ecstasy I wanna dance, and it's about being with my friends. It's not about … I could give a shit less about hooking up with guys, or meeting guys. It's about me and my friends having a good time, and … losing ourselves for a few hours.

This description seems to mirror that found in Henderson's (1993a) discussions of raves in the 1990s, with women dancing for their own pleasure, not as part of het-erosexual engagement or coupling, and Pini's interviews with British women in the dance scene: "For many women, rave represents an undoing of the traditional cultural association between dancing, drugged 'dressed up' women and sexual invitation, and as such opens up a new space for the exploration of new forms of identity and plea-sure" (1997: 154). In our own study we find this to be the case not only for many women, but also for a number of the young men we interviewed. Both men and women ravers emphasize as one of the positive aspects of raves the freedom from the pressures of sexualized display and interaction that are normative in other nightlife environments such as the club. Many men and women we interviewed also emphasize the empathetic and sociable over the sexual aspects of ecstasy. However, Donna's response is not a universal one and others do emphasize the effects ecstasy has on both their libido and on their emotionality.

The separation between ecstasy and sex in the rave scene has perhaps been pre-sented too categorically in some analyses of raves, sexuality, and gender. For other young men and women in the scene describe ecstasy as being used for sexual enhancement, that it "brings … love-making or sex to a different level" (Mike, 27, heterosexual). Some describe an enhanced libido while on the drug and say that it "brings out that sexual side" (Cassie, 27, heterosexual). However, Cassie, for exam-ple, stresses that though she's more sexual on ecstasy, it doesn't make her interested in sex (as in intercourse) itself. Instead, she and other respondents (men and women) emphasize the tactile enhancement of ecstasy and the physical and emotional intimacy with others that it enables.

These common effects of ecstasy on both men and women have some very inter-esting gender implications. For women, the increase in libido coupled with the loss of inhibitions creates an ability to express sexuality and sexual assertiveness in a way inconsistent with the gender expectation of conventional femininity. The gender implications for the effects of ecstasy on men may be even more extreme. The ability to feel sensitive and "lovey-dovey," to bond in an emotional way with other men, and to even express sexual feelings towards other men, are all distinct deviations from our culture's idea of acceptable and normative masculinity.

To understand the pleasures and appeals of ecstasy, then, it is necessary to attend to the way the drug enables certain performances and identities and the way it allows for different gendered selves. By examining the language our respondents use to talk about their own experiences as well as to describe how they perceive the experiences of others, it becomes clear both how ecstasy use contributes to normative gender deviation, and also how deviators are actively policed – in both word and action – by their friends and fellow partygoers. We examine issues of femininity and feminine sexuality before turning to issues of masculinity. In both cases we see both challenges to hegemonic gender expectations and the ongoing presence of gender accountability in this social setting.

Ecstasy, sexuality, and femininities

One common gender assumption is that men are inherently more sexual, and more sexually aggressive, than women. Many women who use ecstasy seem to turn this idea on its head because not only do some describe the ecstasy experience as a sexual one and aggressively act on those urges, but many men and women we interviewed seem to invest in the idea that it is actually a *more* sexual experience for women. They describe ecstasy as enabling women to be not just sexual objects, but sexual subjects in their own right.

In general, respondents described women on ecstasy as "more, like, this touchy-feely," "flirtatious," and "more sexual" than they would be otherwise. Women are also described as becoming more sexually assertive. As Becky, 21 (heterosexual), noted of her ecstasy experience:

Interviewer. Did you socialize much or dance?
Becky. I didn't really talk. I just remember trying to kiss every guy I seen.

This sexual assertiveness from women runs counter to the ideas that women are not interested in sex and will not initiate sexual encounters. Whether ecstasy allows them to express feelings they already harbored, or creates new sensations, the fact remains that it is considered a deviation from conventional femininity for a young woman to express her sexuality in such a manner.

Of course, this is not unambiguously "progress." We want to guard against an optimistic a reading of women's expanded roles in nightlife and raves and expanded substance consumption. As Chatterton and Hollands comment:

> Despite evidence that some young women have pushed the boundaries of gendered nightscapes, many are increasingly taking on behaviors characteristic of young men in this sphere … rather than challenging male domination of mainstream nightlife spaces by creating alternative female cultures, young women appear to be simply competing on men's terms through a crude "equality" paradigm [i.e., proving they can be as "bad" as young men].
>
> (Chatterton and Hollands 2003: 155)

Still, a number of women we interviewed do describe their experiences using ecstasy and at raves as rather liberating or empowering.

In addition, ecstasy use also seems to facilitate non-normative behavior in that it allows some heterosexual women to explore same-sex contact. Dana, 22 (heterosexual), explains:

> It's just, like, girls being really fucked up on ecstasy and, like, making out with each other ... It just feels so good to be touched. It feels like ... I don't know. It's really, like, sexual, actually. It's real ... so good to, like, touch.

Young women we interviewed connect this both to the increased pleasure of touching that ecstasy enables as well as a lowering of inhibitions. In addition, women using ecstasy expressed not only a change in their sexual behavior and inhibitions, but there also seems to be a sense that, in the context of ecstasy use, different and non-normative behaviors are more permissible. As one woman explains, "if you haven't ever made out with ... girls, and, like, make out with them, you know ... it would be fine" (Claire, 24, heterosexual). Antonia, a bisexual young woman, 18, argues that using ecstasy, along with the overall openness of the rave scene, has helped her to become more comfortable with her sexuality, more comfortable with being attracted to women.

In many of these narratives, ecstasy is invoked by young men and women to explain or excuse non-normative gender practices. Peralta analyzed the role that alcohol can play in providing a face-saving excuse for gender-non-normative behavior, examining "how alcohol-related excuses counteract the deviance associated with gender norm violation and ease the shame associated with inappropriate gender displays" (2008: 373). Our findings parallel his, where he emphasizes the license alcohol, or in our case ecstasy, gives young women to take risks, and be bolder in pursuit of romantic partners, protecting against the shame or stigma that might otherwise accompany these behaviors. However, Peralta suggests that the risks of gender assessment, or what we will discuss as "accountability," are suspended while the user is under the influence of alcohol (or, presumably, ecstasy). We found, however, that even in this setting, even on ecstasy, accountability does not disappear entirely.

Policing ecstasy-using women: risk and accountability

Despite individual ecstasy-using women who feel these displays of sexuality are acceptable and accepted, at least while on ecstasy or in the context of the rave scene, this non-normatively feminine behavior does not go unnoticed by other ecstasy users and people in the dance scene. As with many transgressions of gender norms, others move quickly to try and stop the transgression from occurring or to reframe it in a more gender-normative context.

Gender and sexuality should not be conflated – they are distinct aspects of identity and social organization. Yet they're deeply intertwined. A large part of what comprises normative gendered behavior in our society is tied up with the performance and accomplishment of (hetero)sexual identities and practices. Part of accomplishing femininity is complying with norms of heteronormativity, just as assumptions about appropriate heterosexual behaviors involve conventional femininities or masculinities. It is not that these are strictly or uniformly followed. Indeed, that is far from the case, and challenges to these standards are an important part of social interactions and daily life. But these are the standards to which people in a culture are all constantly potentially accountable. People's actions and interactions are conducted in the context of being held potentially accountable for living up to gendered expectations of what it means to be or act like a man or a woman (Fenstermaker *et al.* 1991; West and Zimmerman 1987). However, the salience of gender, and the level of accountability, may vary in different social contexts. Accountability (Heritage 1984) has been a fundamental concept from the earliest versions of "doing gender," or "doing difference" (West and Fenstermaker 1995; West and Zimmerman 1987). But accountability is too often overlooked in some adoptions of the doing-gender model, especially as the doing of gender often slides into notions of volitional performance.[4] Our analysis of young men's and women's gender accomplishment in the rave scene and with ecstasy use, though, highlights the continuing presence of this gender accountability, even in this social context that would initially appear to be freer of strict gender expectations.

Often, women using ecstasy are physically stopped from expressing some of the less gender-normative effects of ecstasy such as an increase in sexual behavior. A number of the men we interviewed discussed needing to "protect" female ecstasy users from doing "something they'll regret." These women are assumed to be unable to make decisions for themselves or to be inherently at risk (despite the reputation of raves as a "safe space"). Jamie, 19 (heterosexual), explains that he likes being with girls at raves, but this introduces onerous responsibilities:

Jamie.   I learned that, like, having girls around, you know, you got to take care of 'em.

Interviewer.   Oh, really? What do you mean?

Jamie.   'Cause sometimes they just get too fucked up … Give 'em water. Escort 'em to the bathroom, 'cause you don't know if some other ecstasy fiend is gonna hop on your girl. When I used to have, like, a girlfriend, we used to go ravin' and droppin'. I wouldn't trust her, basically.

Interviewer.   Oh. You didn't trust her or you didn't trust the people?

Jamie.   I didn't trust the people out there, either, 'cause that's what ravers are like. You know, I walked in on hella people that were having sex at raves. And, like, I knew she was, like, one of those girls that was, like, "Oh, I was fucked up." I was, like, "That's no fuckin' excuse."

He implies that women use ecstasy as a feeble excuse to explain inappropriate behavior – and that their behavior needs excusing.

These protective or dismissive behaviors are often justified by saying things like: women "don't know what they're doing, but guys takes advantage of them" (Amado, 22, heterosexual). Although the language of "men taking advantage of women" is frequently used in these narratives, these young men rarely discuss "policing" those men who take advantage, and instead focus on policing the women's behavior that is seen as enabling this. And it is not merely the "preying" behaviors of men that they worry about, but a woman's own aggressive sexual behavior is seen as something from which she needs protection. Of course, under the influence of drugs or alcohol, people sometimes *do* engage in activity they might not otherwise and which they may later regret. However, respondents seem much less concerned about men engaging in sex they may regret or being "taken advantage of" due to the effects of ecstasy:

> So I would always say, maybe if it was a guy, I would say, you know, "Just go with some friends, enjoy yourself." If it was a woman, I would say, "Just be careful. Make sure you're looked after during your night out. Don't go alone, don't do it ... " I would never recommend doing it alone.
>
> (Keith, 32, heterosexual)

But it was not only men regulating or policing the sexual behaviors of women on ecstasy. Throughout the interviews we heard descriptions of women policing one another.[5] The young women we interviewed, as with the men, are most worried about other women engaging in sexual behaviors they would regret; men's sexual practices, even if enabled by the disinhibitory effects of ecstasy and other club drugs, were normalized and seen as not a problem, not something that they need to be protected against:

Kim.	Basically it's, like, my group of friends, we all look out for each other, and if we see someone with some random guy, like, we'll pull them away and, like, "Do you know who's behind you?" Just like, "You know this guy is, like ... ?" Basically make sure they know what they're doing.
Interviewer.	Now what about guys? Do any of the guy friends you go with, if they were making out with a random girl, would you do the same thing?
Kim.	Actually I don't think I would. It's just like, Oh, there's that guy over there making out with someone. Like, roll your eyes and ... whatever.

(19, heterosexual)

So, as many ravers attempt to curb the non-normative sexuality of their female friends and peers while using ecstasy, they in no way attempt to curb the very same behaviors, which comprise normative sexuality, of their male friends. Luis, 20 (heterosexual), describes the systems of self-policing and policing among female friends he sees at raves.

> People try to get all ... you know ... Dudes try to pick up on girls while they're tweaking. But a lotta the times, you know, the girls come with their friends. That's, like, the best thing. The girls come with their friends, so that the friends will watch 'em: "No, you're not going in there." Really. It's like ... I know a couple girls that do that ... they always bring the friend that's sober. That one sober one regulates them all ... to watch out, and make sure the girls ain't doing nothing that they'll regret tomorrow ... Good friends do that.

As the above sections show, ecstasy challenges gender assumptions by creating a situation in which women are able to express their sexuality more easily – including being assertive and experiencing same-sex contact. But despite this ability of ecstasy to blur the edges of gender expectations, it is not strong enough to counter the constant gender policing that keeps it in check. Even in this seemingly more open environment, this does not mean that the accomplishment of gender is free from being held accountable for doing appropriate gender norms by others.

Ecstasy, sexuality, and masculinities

Among those works that focus on gender, clubs, and drugs, the emphasis of analysis has primarily been on the role of women and femininities, but masculinity is very important to this story as well. Although men have traditionally been at the center of drugs research, their maleness or their masculinity has generally not been a topic of analysis until recently (Broom 1995). In the club/dance-scene literatures, analysts have highlighted (though often not focused on) the changing roles for men and the changing expectations regarding masculinity found in these scenes and spaces. Commentators note the increased acceptability of displays of emotion, of friendliness, of non-traditional masculine displays and attire, and less acceptance of aggression and sexually predatory behavior in these scenes (see Avery 2005; Henderson 1997, 1999; McRobbie 1995; Measham et al. 2001; Pini 1997). We clearly see these challenges to traditional masculinity in the discussions of rave and ecstasy cultures among the young men and women we interviewed. However, these interview narratives also make clear that gender deviations are not accomplished without being potentially held accountable to more conventional standards of masculinity, even within these scenes.

Although ecstasy allows women to push gender boundaries by expressing their sexuality more openly as subjects, overall the ecstasy experience is one that can better be categorized as a more conventionally "feminine" one. Participants often use conventionally feminine signifiers such as "lovey-dovey" and "emotional" to describe their ecstasy experiences. Some explicitly assign a gender to ecstasy: as one respondent says, he previously thought it was "a drug for the woman" (Mike, 27, heterosexual). One way in which ecstasy allows men to transgress traditional gender boundaries is by making it unnecessary to be traditionally "aggressive" and masculine. As Amy, 22 (bisexual), explains:

> Guys definitely have a different frame of mind. I mean, it's so funny, becaus, like, when you go to like a rave … like, I've seen, like, one of these guys drop a pill [take ecstasy] and, like, it's really weird, because they're, like, "I love you!" And you're like, "Whoa, dude. You're like a hella hard-core gangster." I mean, they turn nice … and they're like all of a sudden all lovey and stuff, and you're just like, "Whoa!" I mean, like it's really weird.

She describes men on ecstasy as transformed from "hella hardcore gangsters" to "nice" and "lovey," a dramatic (albeit, to her, "weird") difference. This description of change is echoed by many other men and women we interviewed. They describe men as being less aggressive, and a key factor here is the absence of alcohol at raves, and the prevalence of ecstasy instead:

> Maybe it's 'cause everyone's on E, and you don't wanna be an asshole when you're on E ... Like, for guys, like they'll be a lot more aggressive when they're drunk than when they're on E. Like a guy'll come up to you and give you a hug on E, but he'll ask you, like, your name at least first. [Laughs.] You know what I mean?
>
> (Angelina, 20, bisexual)

In their relationships with women, men describe a change in perception while using ecstasy. Some of this transformation is connected to having a lesser emphasis on casual sex and "hooking up." Paulo, 27 (heterosexual), compares the behavior of men (including himself and his friends) when they are on ecstasy to how they may act at other times, when their "whole goal" is to "hook up with a girl." Instead, he says:

> Once they do take the pills that sometimes it ... that they end up seeing this other side of it too, that it's more to it than just wanting to go hook up with somebody, that there's more to this person, you know, than just sex.

These descriptions of men being more emotional, open, able to connect with same-sex friends more easily, and being able to appreciate the opposite sex for less sexual reasons are all considered conventionally *feminine* characteristics. But, for these young men, the ecstasy experience allows them to escape their gender expectations and have a different sort of experience. "Male bonding," in particular, seems to be enabled by the use of ecstasy. More than any other explicit gender reference, the men and women we interviewed make note of the fact that men could have the kind of close, loving, same-sex friendships (perhaps more typical of young women) while on – and because of – ecstasy and the norms of ecstasy in the rave settings.

> Especially for ... for young men, like, you know, twenty years old. You just don't go around like telling all your guy friends, like, how awesome they are. So it was awesome, you know, that one time.
>
> (Bob, 25, heterosexual)

Similarly, Luis, 20 (heterosexual), explains that ecstasy at raves opens up wholly different communicative abilities for young men to express themselves to other young men:

> Like, a lotta stuff that you would normally not say, just 'cause you're guys and ... guys are less ... 'Cause guys, you know, we're not sentimental beings here towards each other, you know. We'll just be, like, "Oh, that's gay. I'm not gonna tell him that. He might think I'm gay or something." [Laughs.]

Here we see that ecstasy allows him to communicate in a more affectionate and appreciative way than typically allowed – and that some of the reasons for the usual reserve are due to concerns about seeming "gay." (These concerns, we will see in the next section, are not completely escapable, even at raves.) One thing elided over by this young man, and by many of those we interviewed, is whether it's purely the drug that they think enables this behavior, or the specific social context of the raves. The two are so seemingly inseparable in many of these descriptions, even though some also use ecstasy in very different settings.

While for some, like Luis, it appears that their different behavior is confined to the social context of raves, or to when they are using ecstasy, others argue that this new openness and ability to express affections between men spills out into their everyday world as well. Tom, 20 (heterosexual), describes his interactions with his male friends as being transformed even while sober and in other contexts, a change he attributes to prior ecstasy use:

> Like ... usually, like, when I see my friends ... I'm, like, "Hey, man." Give 'em a hug ... I mean, normally if I didn't do ecstasy, I probably would just, like, you know, handshake ... But ... it's just ... a lot easier now, because it's happened before and it's just like ... I really love my friends a lot, so ... I'm not like afraid to express it.

Some of the young men argue that ecstasy allows them to be more physically affectionate with other men, something they don't always feel free to experience in everyday life. Paulo, 27 (heterosexual), explains that what makes his behavior different when on ecstasy is that he's always "giving more hugs to people, to even, like, my guy friends." And Charles, 23 (heterosexual), describes even more intimate affection between himself and his male friends:

> Like, it's, like, your boys, you're all, like, leaning on each other. It's like, yeah, you hold each other. Not necessarily massaging or kissing or nothing. But, you know, it's like very, like just like family. Everyone just talks together, just chilling, right?

Peralta (2008), in his study of the effects of alcohol on the accomplishment of gender among college students, notes two major divisions in how alcohol and gender-deviant behaviors for men are accomplished. On the one hand, he discusses those men who intentionally practice gender-nonconformist behaviors while drinking, using alcohol to counter the negative labels associated with such behavior. On the other hand, there are those for whom alcohol leads to "gender blunders" – accidental gender-norm violations, for which alcohol provides a *post facto* excuse, for those who fear marginalization. This can be seen particularly in the instances of those heterosexual-identified men who engage in same-sex intimacies while on ecstasy or at raves. Although for many of the men ecstasy opens up homo*social* bonding, for others ecstasy helps enable homo*sexual* practices (although in most of the described cases this is limited to kissing, touching, and "making out"). Some straight men we interviewed describe sexual experiences with same-sex partners while on ecstasy, while some of the bisexual and gay men cite ecstasy use as a factor in some of their first same-sex experiences.

Donnie, 20 (bisexual), explains that the use of ecstasy opened him up to different people and eventually opened him up to his own bisexual identity:

> I didn't like gay people at all. I think they're totally weird and whacked and I didn't understand 'em, and I took ecstasy and I totally saw the beauty, and I was just all, like … it opened me up … It's not that they're weird. I'm just as weird as they are, because … they're enjoying each other, they're loving each other for human beings, not because they're this certain way or anything. Which I also found out about myself, that I can do the same …

Not all of the men with these experiences later identify as bisexual or gay. Curt, 20, identifies as heterosexual, but has "made out" with other men on ecstasy, something he doesn't regret (nor does he see it as a threat to his heterosexuality).

> You just lose all possible inhibitions … you're in this setting of a rave, where it's almost, like, anything goes … I've ended up, like, making out with random people, like, guys even, 'cause I just didn't care, I was, like, so high.

In this example, as in others, we can see the fluidity of sexual roles and norms, challenging the idea of sexuality or sexual identity as static or fixed.

In dealing with this topic, we also found a second group – who understand their same-sex actions to be blunders, and who use ecstasy as an excuse:

Interviewer.   Did you ever do anything you regretted the next day while you were on ecstasy? …

Carlos.   Like when I made out with some guy … the next day I was, like, "Oh, my gosh." 'Cause, like … I guess I gave him my number, and he called me. I was, like, "Dude, don't call me. Obviously I had to have been on drugs hardcore. I'm not like that, so let's not even go there."

(Carlos, 18, heterosexual)

He says that "obviously" he had to have been on drugs – what else would explain this behavior on his part? He "obviously" wouldn't do it otherwise. And these behaviors, while on ecstasy, are something he wants to put behind him, later, when sober and out of that rave. In fact, this same issue – of heterosexual men kissing men at raves and disavowing it the next day – poses a problem for some of our gay and bisexual respondents, such as Dave, 21 (bisexual), who describes straight men he's made out with at raves who later disavowed the behavior by excusing it due to substance use:

Dave.   I've made out with straight guys.

Interviewer.   And how do you feel about that?

Dave.	I thought they were so gay. I totally thought they were gay.
Interviewer.	And then what happened? When did you find out they were straight?
Dave.	Afterwards. They'd be like, "We were really fucked up, huh?" And I'd be like, "Yeah."

As with the case of ecstasy, sexuality, and femininity, there are more and more flexible gender options and norms in the social context of raves, which are perceived to be influenced by the consumption of ecstasy. As with the case of the women, however, there are limits to this openness, and gender remains policed and the system of gender accountability still shapes interactions and experiences in this context.

Policing, accountability, and ecstasy-using men

Ecstasy use does not excuse men from conventional expectations to accomplish heterosexual masculinity entirely. As with the policing of female sexuality described above, so too are men's gender performances policed by their peers within the rave scene, despite the setting's reputation for total openness and acceptance. Users themselves, along with the larger community, are quick to outline unacceptable behavior through the language they use, and in some cases physically prevent unacceptable behavior from occurring. While some ravers find these breaks from conventional gender expectations to be freeing, others find them disturbing or problematic.

The fact that raves' gendered interactions are a break from their everyday expectations for appropriate conventions of masculinity is evinced by the reactions of some of the ravers – while many of these respondents approve of these differences, they also describe them as "weird" or as something that made them laugh, at least upon initial encounters.

> You know, everybody was … and I remember I wanted to laugh, because there was, like, these guys or whatever, and they're always hard, and they were like, "man, I really love you." And the other guy was like, "Yeah, I love you, too." Right. And I wanted to laugh.
>
> (Socorro, 19, heterosexual)

Ecstasy's effects on transforming masculine affect and behavior are described as positive for most of the respondents, although some express uneasiness that having these sorts of interactions somehow undercuts their masculinity and makes them seem "gay." And the accusation of the "gayness" of certain behaviors is the primary way in which young men are held accountable for their gendered behaviors at raves.

Some of the young men we interviewed attempt to distance themselves from the more "feminine" aspects of ecstasy in a number of ways. Some consciously try to avoid or stop feminine behaviors while using:

> When, you know, you're on E, you're just very emotional and stuff like that. I have this very, like, strong emotional … blockade, I guess. I don't really like to show it in front of people that I don't really know. So I think, like – I was acting

a certain way and then I stopped, and I was thinking, like, "How am I acting?" And I was, like, "Okay, I don't wanna act that way."

(Chad, 22, heterosexual)

Others police the border of gender appropriateness by labeling any who transgress it with negatives – such as in this case by discussing men on ecstasy who are "E-tarded" and therefore "gay." Tracee, 18 (heterosexual), says that men act "gay" while under the influence of ecstasy:

Just how they talk, like nice ... I think guys just look gay on it, all of 'em. It just brings out their gay side, I guess. It's really funny. Like ... some guys that act tough, you know. But then when they're on E, it's like they're nice and like ... their body language is just totally different. Like they don't wanna hurt you or hurt your feelings or anything.

Although when she expands upon this point it's clear that she doesn't actually mean anything regarding their sexuality or sexual behaviors, rather she's (perhaps derogatorily) discussing different gender practices, less typically masculine affect and display. In this case "being gay" means being nice, not tough, having a different body language, and not wanting to hurt people.

This sentiment, that ecstasy makes you "gay" or is perceived as doing so, is one shared by many of young ravers and clubbers we talked to, and some actively avoided ecstasy because they were worried about it:

I hated X [ecstasy]. At the time. I'd never tried it, but I always ... the guys that I met were too fruity when they were on [it] and we were always convinced, we were, like, "Ecstasy is just gonna turn me into half a fag." You know. And I don't wanna be like that. I mean, I was so anti-X.

(Pat, 23, heterosexual)

Importantly, though, even though some men and women use "gay" to describe ecstasy users, they use it only to describe male ecstasy users. So, it is not simply using "gay" as a synonym for "lame" or "uncool," as is often the case in youth slang. These accusations are often disconnected from any actually sexual behavior or interactions on the men's part. That is because, in this case, "gay" hardly refers to a sexuality, but instead to what the respondents see as an *inappropriate masculinity* – or men who are inappropriately feminine.

Some of these young men physically distance themselves from situations in which they may behave in ways deemed inappropriate. These young men go out of their way to make sure that same-sex contact never happens, or avoid using ecstasy in settings that are predominantly male:

I don't like to take a bunch of E with a bunch of males. But that's just me. I mean lots – some males do. But, I mean, it's just usually at someone's house, intimate setting, you're just kicking back on E. Kind of paired off or ...

(Bryan, 24, heterosexual)

So men, like women, must police themselves both by using language to distance themselves from non-normative behavior and also by not placing themselves in situations that may lead to undesirable gender or sexual behavior. These men are held accountable to others and hold themselves accountable to normative masculine heterosexuality. In fact, due to the more feminine effects of ecstasy, men have to be even more careful than women to police themselves. As one young woman notes:

> And then there's a lotta people that, like, talk a lotta mess about, like, people who wear candy [the bright, plastic jewelry favored by many ravers]. Especially if they're guys. The guys get a lotta heat, like … I don't know, from people.
>
> (Alicia, 17, heterosexual)

Conclusion

This chapter offers an analysis of gender and sexuality explorations and gender accountability in the context of young people's ecstasy use in the rave scene in San Francisco. We focused not primarily on whether gender differences shape drug use patterns or prevalence, but rather on how ecstasy use, and practices surrounding it, help to shape the accomplishment of gender in a particular youth cultural scene. This is a very specific community or subculture and certainly their experiences are not generalizable to all young adults, nor even to all young adult drug users. Yet they serve as a reminder of the ongoing significance of the concept of accountability within analyses of the doing or accomplishment of gender, a concept that too often disappears when "doing gender" is mistakenly reduced to some kind of optional or volitional performance. Early analyses of the rave scene, particularly by UK researchers, tended to emphasize the ways in which the rave scenes and ecstasy use provided an arena for the renegotiation of gender relations or alternative spaces for men and women to involve themselves in gender bending. However, although this was true to some extent in our study, our research highlights the extent to which raves and ecstasy did not necessarily mean the complete overthrow of more traditional forms of femininity and masculinity.

Because men and women both operate against the backdrop of two very different sets of gender expectations, we cannot examine their experiences with exactly the same lens. Just as it is outside gender expectations for women to be sexually aggressive, it is perfectly within the realm of gender conventionality for young men. Conversely, the sensitivity and emotional nature that is usually positively attributed to women may be attacked and belittled when it appears in men. Many members of the ecstasy-using community embrace the gender flexibility that ecstasy allows. However, this does not preclude many of these behaviors from being seen and treated as deviations even in this context. Gender accountability is not so easily escaped, it seems.

This chapter has focused primarily on gender and sexuality with respect to the drug ecstasy and the social setting of the rave. In the next chapter, we broaden our focus to contrast the experiences our respondents describe with alcohol and to the additional social context of the dance club, in which norms of sexuality and gender may differ greatly. In doing so, we further theorize about the meaning and significance of *context* in understanding gender, sexuality, drug use, and youth-cultural scenes.

Chapter 10

Alcohol, gender, and social context

Introduction

As we have seen in the previous chapter, the development of raves in the late 1980s and 1990s contributed to significant changes in the gendered behavior of young men and women, at least within the dance scene. In an attempt to explain these changes, sociologists and cultural studies theorists argued that the replacement of alcohol by ecstasy as the preferred drug of choice by young clubbers was a critical factor. Whereas ecstasy intoxication led to integrative behavior, alcohol intoxication among clubbers led to violent and disruptive behavior. Although such explanations, which exclusively focused on the substances themselves, could be accused of pharmacological determinism (Measham *et al.* 2001), and while not wishing to fall into such a trap ourselves, it is, nevertheless, the case that the young men and women we interviewed presented far different narratives about the behaviors associated with alcohol intoxication compared to that of ecstasy or other club drugs.

While the young club drug users that we interviewed portray ecstasy as leading to positive outcomes, their descriptions of the effects of alcohol intoxication are much more negative. In fact, some of the men and women save their most negative descriptions in the entire interview for drunken behavior. Drunks in the dance scene are viewed as a nuisance and described as "pushy," "volatile," "belligerent and nasty." As one participant notes, people on alcohol are "idiots." Consequently, an initial reading of these narratives suggest that not only are the effects of ecstasy and those of alcohol viewed in very different ways, ecstasy is seen as generally leading to positive developments, whereas drinking alcohol is much more likely to result in problematic behavior. However, a deeper examination of the alcohol consumption discourse reveals the extent to which the characterization of alcohol-related behavior is not simply a discussion about the effects of becoming drunk, but is also a discussion about gendered behavior around drinking and appropriate and inappropriate drinking contexts. Discussions about drunkenness are primarily about male drinking behavior and are largely described as taking place within the context of the club. It became apparent that drinking alcohol within the rave context is perceived as inappropriate. Moreover, as we will show, in addition to negative descriptions of drunken male behavior, a strong anti-alcohol ideology pervades these descriptions. However, in spite of this anti-alcohol narrative, these very same respondents themselves drink alcohol, and, for most of them, alcohol represents an important mind-altering substance. In fact, not surprisingly, the vast majority had experienced their first intoxication moment by consuming alcohol. Consequently, in examining the discourse of alcohol among our young participants, we need to situate these narratives not only within a gendered context, but also within an analysis of the role of social context if we are to understand why alcohol consumption is described in such negative ways.

Alcohol and gender

As many researchers have noted, gender is a strong predictor of drinking behavior (Wilsnack *et al.* 1994). Gender differences "in drinking behavior are so ubiquitous that men's drinking predominates for virtually all ages, ethnic groups, religions, education levels, incomes and categories of marital status" (Lemle and Mishkind 1989: 213). In general, men are more likely to drink, are more likely to drink heavily, and are more likely to experience problems with their drinking. These overall gender characteristics are also true cross-culturally. In almost every culture men drink more than women (Heath 2000; Holmila and Raitasalo 2005). For example, Fillmore's (1984) analysis of thirty-nine longitudinal studies from fifteen countries highlights the extent to which men "in every country and every age group ... drank larger quantities, drink more frequently and report more drinking problems than women" (cited in Wilsnack *et al.* 1994). Although these differences existed across all age groups, age does influence the extent to which male and female drinking differs. According to the National Survey on Drug Use and Health, in the US alcohol consumption, notably binge and heavy drinking, tends to increase rapidly among youth until the age of 21 and decreases slowly after that point (Substance Abuse and Mental Health Services Administration 2007), with individuals between the ages of 21 and 25 reporting the highest rates of alcohol use of any age group. As Foxcroft and Lowe have noted, "in a period of approximately ten years young people go from individuals who have never had an alcoholic drink to individuals who as an age group comprise the heaviest drinking section of the population" (1997: 215). During this period male adolescents in general drink more heavily than their female counterparts, although the extent of the differences varies by age.

Not only do men tend to consume larger amounts of alcohol than women, but the significance and meaning of drinking alcohol may be different. For example, initiation into drinking for boys is often viewed as a "rite of passage" into manhood. "Along with his first sexual experience, [drinking] ... is one of the fundamental activities by which a boy is initiated as a man" (Lemle and Mishkind 1989: 214). To drink is to be masculine and to drink heavily is to be even more masculine, "heavy drinking symbolizes masculinity more than lighter drinking, and the more a man tolerates his alcohol, the more manly he is deemed" (Lemle and Mishkind 1989: 214). Male drinking, especially in young male groups, is often prescribed male behavior (Gutmann 1996) and is associated with risk-taking activities, excitement, and aggression. Consequently, drinkers are viewed as manly not solely because they drink, but because their drinking is linked with other behaviors which are also connected with the image of being masculine (Lemle and Mishkind 1989). For example, notions of honor are frequently intertwined with drinking, and when the drinker's honor is impugned violence may then be the result (Burns 1980; R. N. Parker 1995). Given this strong association between drinking and becoming a man, what are the characteristics of our respondents' alcohol consumption? Is this dominance of male drinking obvious?

Young men's and women's drinking patterns

In our sample, both men and women drink. All but two of the 300 respondents had consumed alcohol at some point in their lifetimes (and the two abstainers were both only 17 years old), and the vast majority (96 percent) had used at least one form of alcohol (beer, wine, spirits/hard liquor) in the year prior to the interview. However, in spite of this overall prevalence, the frequency with which our respondents consumed alcohol did vary. While nearly one-quarter (24 percent) drank beer less than once per month in the previous year, more than one-third (36 percent) drank beer more than once a week. The results for hard liquor were similar, with 27 percent consuming liquor less than once a month and 28 percent drinking liquor more than once a week. Wine was consumed much less frequently than either beer or hard liquor, and 49 percent consumed it less than once a month. These data show that overall individuals within our sample possess a wide range of experiences with alcohol. We do, however, see some gender differences in alcohol consumption rates.

As expected, men tend to consume beer and hard liquor more frequently than women, although men and women reported drinking wine with similar frequencies. One-third (33.3 percent) of all hard-liquor-using men reported using hard liquor, on average, more than once per week, versus only 21 percent of hard-liquor-using women. Similar trends emerged for past year use of beer: 41 percent of male beer-drinkers used beer, on average, at least once per week in the previous year, versus only 30 percent of female beer users.

Age is an additional characteristic that is significantly related to frequency of respondents' alcohol use. Despite the fact that all but two of the young men and women we interviewed had tried alcohol at some point in their lives, people who were under the legal drinking age tended, unsurprisingly, to use alcohol less frequently than individuals who were over the age of 21 (the legal drinking age in the US) (see Table 10.1). For example, whereas more than half (51 percent) of all beer-using respondents over the age of 21 reported consuming it, on average, once per week or more in the year prior to the interview, only 22 percent of participants under the age of 21 did so. Similar trends emerged for wine and hard liquor, which were used, on average, once per week or more by 20 percent and 36 percent (respectively) of men and women over the age of 21 and only 1 percent and 20 percent (respectively) of young men and women under the age of 21. In other words, while the legality of alcohol consumption appears to have little bearing on young people's decisions to try alcohol for the first time – as evidenced by the fact that all but two of our 158 respondents under the legal drinking age had tried alcohol at some point in their lives – there are significant differences with respect to the frequency with which those respondents use alcohol. These differences may be the result of

Table 10.1 Age and frequency of alcohol use in the past year

Type of alcohol	0 days		Less than once per week		Once per week or more		Total	
	%	n	%	n	%	n	%	n
Beer (*n* = 296)								
Gender:								
Male	6	(9)	53	(85)	41	(66)	100	(160)
Female	14	(19)	56	(76)	30	(41)	100	(136)
Age group:								
Under 21	13	(20)	65	(100)	22	(34)	100	(154)
21 and older	6	(8)	43	(61)	51	(73)	100	(142)
Wine (*n* = 284)								
Gender:								
Male	12	(19)	77	(117)	11	(17)	100	(153)
Female	13	(17)	78	(102)	9	(12)	100	(131)
Age group:								
Under 21	15	(22)	84	(122)	1	(2)	100	(146)
21 and older	10	(14)	70	(97)	20	(27)	100	(18)
Hard liquor (*n* = 292)								
Gender:								
Male	9	(14)	58	(90)	33	(52)	100	(156)
Female	7	(10)	71	(97)	21	(29)	100	(136)
Age group:								
Under 21	8	(12)	72	(110)	20	(31)	100	(153)
21 and older	9	(12)	55	(77)	36	(50)	100	(139)

such factors as the lack of availability of alcohol to individuals who are under 21, the absence of available settings in which to consume it, and maybe even less of a desire to consume alcohol. Simply noting the frequency of alcohol consumption, though, does not illuminate the meaning of subjective experience of drinking for these young men and women, for which we must turn to their narratives of their alcohol experiences.

Initiation to intoxication

The young men and women we interviewed tend to start using alcohol at an earlier age than any other drug besides marijuana. The median age of initiation to beer, wine and hard liquor use was 15 years for participants in our sample, with few significant differences between men and women. (The exception is with regard to use of beer: women started using beer, on average, at 14, versus 15 for men.) Respondents tended to start using beer regularly before other types of alcohol (16 years versus 18 years for wine and 17 years for hard liquor) but at the same age as marijuana. As these data demonstrate, many young men and women start using alcohol well in advance of the age at which they are able to do so legally, and in many cases have experiences using alcohol prior to trying any other licit or illicit drug. In fact, when looking at qualitative descriptions of their first alcohol-using experiences, it becomes clear that most participants experienced intoxication for the first time with alcohol. In many cases, they express the sentiment that they "had no idea" what to expect from their alcohol-using experiences prior to using alcohol for the first time and, in many cases, describe encountering problems with regard to dosage. For example, some describe using a very small amount of alcohol in the company of friends, and remembered believing that they were intoxicated despite the fact that they probably had not consumed enough alcohol to actually be intoxicated. Other young men and women describe seriously overestimating the amount of alcohol that would be required to become intoxicated, which in some cases produced dangerous, or at least unpleasant, results. However, the majority of our participants describe their experience as generally positive and are able to laugh at their naivety surrounding their earliest experiences with alcohol and, in many cases, with intoxication. It is only later that the negative discourses around alcohol use seem to develop, particularly as they relate to using alcohol in an inappropriate manner or inappropriate context.

Some participants discuss alcohol-initiation experiences during which they were surprised by the effects of the drug, and have difficulty describing their precise reaction, but found the experience to be a generally positive one. Thomas, 21, says of his first experience getting "buzzed" on alcohol: "I didn't know it was a buzz at that time, but I decided to do some. Talk a lot more. Just felt happy." And Jacob, 26, describes using alcohol for the first time as "kind of funny … Totally kind of new … a new feeling." When recalling her first experience using alcohol, Maria, 15, says:

> We drank. But, um, it was weird. I was, like, "Oh, I feel weird." But then I liked the feeling because we laughed a lot and stuff like that. But, like, nothing bad or anything like that happened to us. We just came home and went to sleep.

As she describes, alcohol made Maria feel "weird," but simultaneously contributed positively to her experience with her friends. It is also interesting to note the manner in which she emphasizes that "nothing bad happened" as a result of her experience, almost as though she expected something to go wrong.

Along similar lines, many of the people we interviewed describe their first experience using alcohol as not only a surprising one, but as a fortuitously positive one, which enhanced their personality and interaction with others. Ray, 22, for example, describes his first alcohol-using experience in the following way:

> It gave me this feeling like I'd never actually felt. Like, where you were just, like … the whole state of being drunk, um, not being, like, yourself. That was a fun aspect, especially when you're around people that are just, like, jokers and fun characters, just enhances it even more.

In Ray's narrative we see that the experience of being drunk was novel, and unlike anything he'd ever experienced. It is interesting to note the extent to which Ray believes that being drunk means "not being like yourself" and the extent to which that is viewed as a positive, if not the defining, aspect of the experience. As with ecstasy, there is disagreement among our respondents over whether intoxicating drugs allow one to be "oneself," to uncover hidden parts of themselves, or whether it allows them to be someone else entirely. According to Ray, this experience is further enhanced by the presence of other men, whom he refers to as his "skater buddies" as well as "jokers" and "fun characters." The tone of Ray's discussion suggests that, despite the fact that he had never used alcohol prior to the occasion he mentions, he is examining his experience from a position of authority, which may be the result of the retrospective nature of the interview, but may also be indicative of a desire to project a particular image of himself as a skilled drinker, starting with his earliest drinking experiences. What is central to his narrative, however, is the discussion of his alcohol use as a positive experience, particularly as it relates to his ability to interact with others.

We see similarly positive discussions of drinking behaviors in the narratives of other young men. When discussing the aspects of his first alcohol-using experience that he enjoyed, Jason, 20, lists "just being drunk and chatting. Playing cards." In this statement we see the extent to which the state of being drunk defines the experience, as well as the centrality of chatting and playing cards, both of which suggest a relaxed atmosphere and socialization. A number of other young men remember that they felt, "hella happy," "comfortable with everybody," and "able to carry on conversations with people [they] didn't know" during their first alcohol-using experiences. These descriptions lack the naivety or loss of control presented in many accounts of early drinking experiences, and instead provide a portrait of an alcohol user who is not only in control of his use but enhanced by it, particularly as it concerns his ability to relate to other men.

Many of the young women we spoke with also talked about their first alcohol-using experiences as positive. For example, Ynez, 22, comments on the first time she used alcohol:

> I got a buzz, I felt dizzy, I felt, like, happy. Everything was funny. Everybody else, like, was feeling the same way, so it was like … if you can imagine, everybody's funny, everybody thinks you're funny, it was just, like, a good time, you know. And you feel, like, less inhibited, you know, so you feel more brave or whatever. It was nice, it was a good feeling.

Much like the young men that we discussed above, Ynez discusses her first experience using alcohol as a positive one, and notes that the drug contributed to feelings of disinhibition and facilitated interactions with other individuals who were also using alcohol. However, rather than describe herself as "drunk," she notes that alcohol made her feel "dizzy" and "happy" and contributed to a positive experience with friends. We see similarly positive descriptions of experiences from other young women we interviewed. Take, for example, Maria, 15, who says of the physical experience of using alcohol for the first time: "I felt like I was floating. Like I was light on my feet," and Lucy, 19, who describes the feeling as "hyper, excited, enthusiastic, happy – like positively emotional."

While neither Maria nor Lucy explicitly states that she got *drunk* during her first experience using alcohol, a few women we interviewed did reference getting drunk during their first experiences with the substance. However, unlike many of the men we interviewed, drunkenness was not necessarily the primary goal of drinking. Sarah, 28, for example, remembers the first time that she got drunk:

> It was just sort of a typical high-school party ... and I got really, really drunk ... I was, like, "Woo-hoo. I'm seventeen. I'm at a party." And it was my first kinda, like, "party" party, you know what I mean? And, like, people were going crazy and drinking and having a good time. And there were some older kids there and stuff, so. Just hung out, drank.

Much like the young men that we discussed above, Sarah discusses her first experience using alcohol as a positive one, and notes that the drug made her feel *less inhibited* and *more brave* in a social context. However, unlike some of the men we interviewed, who describe *being drunk* as the best part of their first experience using alcohol, Sarah frames her experience within the context of the party, and expresses the sentiment that she used alcohol for the first time as a means of *having a good time* and *going crazy* at the party. While it may be true that alcohol use and intoxication defined one's inclusion or membership within the context of this particular party, Sarah did not name getting drunk as the primary reason for her alcohol use, as did many of the young men we interviewed. Rather, she views her alcohol use as a means of taking full advantage of her youth, and her first party. In other words, she describes her alcohol use as the product of the context in which she finds herself and the people that she's with.

From these narratives we see the extent to which the young men and women we interviewed view their first experiences with alcohol as positive, and recognize the potential that alcohol has to shape a their perceptions of their environment and enhance sociability. However, one significant difference is the emphasis that young men place on being *drunk*, whereas young women describe more specific physiological and emotional effects of the drug. That is not to say that *no* women describe getting drunk during their first experience using alcohol, as some certainly did, rather it suggests that even when young women are discussing instances during which they were drunk, they are more likely than men to use language to describe far more than their state of intoxication. While this may be seen as a reflection of the richness of the narratives of the young women we spoke with relative to that of many of the young men, as women may be more descriptive in their language to begin with, it may also be interpreted as a reflection of what many other researchers have described as a generalized feeling of unacceptability of women's intoxication, particularly in public drinking contexts (Fillmore 1984; Herd 1997; Leigh 1995; Morgan 1983; Room 1996; Warner *et al.* 1999). The young women we spoke with, while they may very well have been drunk during their first alcohol-using experiences, may not describe themselves as such, or list *drunkenness* as the defining aspect of their experience, because it is less socially acceptable for them to be drunk, or, presumably, even to discuss occasions during which they were drunk. Researchers have demonstrated that even in settings in which women's drinking is accepted, it is less acceptable for women than men to lose control when under the influence of alcohol (McDonald 1994; Warner *et al.* 1999), with women who display alcohol intoxication being judged more harshly than their male counterparts (Fillmore 1984; Finch and Munro 2007; Leigh 1995). Alcohol use among women is often viewed as being in conflict with traditional notions of femininity (Herd 1997; Ricciardelli *et al.* 2001; Warner *et al.* 1999) and even leads people to perceive alcohol-using women as more sexually available than non-alcohol-using women (Bogren 2008; Finch and Munro 2007; George *et al.* 1995; Leigh 1995; A. M. Young *et al.* 2007). As we saw in our participants' discussions of their first alcohol-using experiences, men and women perceive their alcohol-using experiences differently, and are subject to different norms of alcohol use.[1]

With this connection between alcohol use and gender/sexuality in mind, we pass from our discussion of our participants' initial, early experiences with alcohol use and intoxication to their patterns of use in their current lives. The remainder of this chapter focuses on the practices and ideas about alcohol consumption in two key arenas of leisure activity and consumption for the young people we interviewed: dance clubs and rave events. In particular, we will examine alcohol and the contexts in which it is used as it intersects with issues of gender and sexuality.

Drinking and meaning: the importance of social context

Anthropologists have long examined the way that context not only determines whether or not drinking is viewed as appropriate or inappropriate, but also the way in which context may influence the drinking behaviors and the meanings and values associated with those behaviors. As Heath has noted "drinking is an act that has very different meanings and connotations depending on where it takes place. The ways people feel about drinking or about other people's drinking, and about the changes in behavior that sometimes result from drinking, are all colored by the setting and evaluations of it" (2000: 44). Researchers have identified a number of key factors that need to be considered when examining the influence that social context has on drinking.[2] These include the physical setting or structure of the context, the type of event, the characteristics of the social groupings present within the social context, including social class, gender, age, and ethnicity, as well as the values of the group and its ability to modify behaviors through sanctions (Zinberg 1984).

There are a number of different ways that one could contrast raves from clubs: clubs are licensed, permanent venues, whereas raves are one-off events sometimes in unlicensed or illegal venues and often do not serve alcohol; clubs in the US are restricted to those over 21, or in some cases to those over 18, whereas raves, particularly unlicensed or underground raves, are all-ages events; and clubs tend to play more mainstream, Top 40 or hip-hop music, while raves more frequently feature a DJ who performs independently produced electronic dance music. While many of the same people go to both clubs and raves, and our respondents sometimes discuss them interchangeably, most of the people we interviewed mark clear distinctions between the two nightlife arenas, in terms of the norms, ethos, traditions, and general experience. First, they distinguish the two on the basis of the favored intoxicating substance in each setting: the dominant substances ingested at raves are illicit drugs, especially ecstasy, whereas at clubs the dominant substance is alcohol. Although other drugs may be present at clubs, they are much less central. Second, clubs are primarily perceived as "meat markets" or sexual arenas, whereas raves are described as far less sexually oriented, particularly in the sense of "pick ups" or "hook ups." Within our respondents' narratives, these two issues – the dominance of alcohol versus ecstasy, and the degree of sexualization in the nightlife setting – are not separate matters, but appear again and again as deeply intertwined.

One way in which the sexual meat-market aspect of clubs versus raves can be seen is in the different norms and expectations connected to clothing and attire. The distinction that Gloria, 19, makes between raves and clubs is echoed in many of our interviews with young ravers:

> At a rave … you can go as yourself. You can go in your pajamas, for all you care. Try pulling that at a club. … [At clubs] a guy's gonna try to front. You know, "Oh, I have this, this, and that" … Girls … they always … I don't know, they're gonna jump up on, you know, the little cages and … shake their booty … At a rave, you don't really have to do that to get attention … At a rave, you can pretty much go up and talk to anybody.

She argues that the rave scene provides the people in attendance an opportunity to be themselves, whereas the club scene is an environment in which attendees are expected to dress in a particular way – which for women nearly universally includes scanty, provocative clothing – and overt displays of sexuality are the norm. Many of the men and women we interviewed cite stringent dress codes and entry policies, which give preferred treatment to groups of beautiful women while denying it to men, as a way of selling not only sex appeal, but also alcohol. In other words, they believe that if the club environment weren't so centered on sex, then the men and women in attendance wouldn't need to depend on alcohol to facilitate flirtation and overtly sexual behaviors. In contrast, raves are relaxed and comfortable, which many people attribute to the fact that alcohol use is discouraged or, in some cases, entirely absent. In the discussion that follows, we will explore the relationship between alcohol and the contexts in which it is used, particularly as it relates to the behavior of attendees within each scene.

First, we turn to the place of alcohol at raves, where alcohol isn't necessarily entirely absent but is "officially" frowned upon by dominant subcultural values. Then we contrast these experiences with those of nightclubs, where alcohol is seemingly ever-present.

Drinking and raves

Age and the choice between raves and clubs

There is a clear relationship between age – and specifically being over or under the legal drinking age – and primarily attending clubs versus raves. Relatively few

(13 percent) of the young people under the age of 21 we interviewed describe themselves as attending primarily or exclusively clubs. However, more than half (53 percent) of those over the age of 21 cite dance clubs as their primary nightlife destinations. While many minors describe attending clubs that cater specifically to individuals under the age of 21, or state that they use fake IDs or other means of gaining entry into "21 and over" clubs before they are legally of age to do so, there are significant differences in the types of events young people choose to attend. Correspondingly, the vast majority (78 percent) of respondents under the age of 21 attend primarily or exclusively raves, versus only 37 percent of respondents age 21 or older. In many of the qualitative interviews our participants describe (and sometimes complain about) the very youthful culture of the rave scene, which many credit to the fact that many raves are underground and can therefore be attended by individuals under the age of 21 (or even under 18) who cannot attend mainstream club events legally.

Take, for example, Thomas, 21, who believes that there is a direct relationship between an individual's rave attendance and his or her age:

> I think younger kids start off with raves, because clubs they can't get into. I think more people move from raves to clubs than clubs to raves. Maybe because people who start off with clubs, they usually like clubs because they like being clean, they like to dress up nice, they like to wear nice clothes, and like have alcohol and meet people. Raves are just too crazy and wild for them. And a lot of time clubbers are older and they don't really want to go with high-school kids to a rave.

Thomas believes that individuals choose to attend raves because they are not yet able to attend club events legally, which he explains is the reason why most people transition from raves to clubs rather than vice versa. While Thomas does discuss alcohol as a motivating factor for club attendance, which reinforces the link between legal age of alcohol consumption and alcohol use, he also discusses a number of other positive aspects of club attendance that are not related to age, which could be seen as motivating factors for attendance, including cleanliness and the manner of dress of individuals in attendance at clubs. He contrasts this environment in which patrons "have alcohol and meet people" to the rave environment, which he describes as "crazy and wild."

Others, however, question the idea that there is a rave-to-club progression or that attending clubs is a sign of more maturity. When asked whether she believes there is a progression from raves to clubs, Cassie, 27, responds:

> I would say that like, when you are just coming of age to drink and everything, you're gonna be more likely to go to a club, you know. And then you're burnt out on that and, like, do more of the things with people you already have met, and things like that. Really, if you're single you're more likely to go to clubs, you know. But progression? It's hard to say.

Cassie herself is a raver, and at 27 on the older side of the rave age spectrum; clearly this plays a role in her disagreement with the notion that one inevitably moves from raves to clubs. However, we see in Cassie's narrative that she agrees that club attendance, age, and alcohol use are closely related. At this point in her life Cassie prefers to attend raves rather than clubs because she has established herself and found a community of friends in a network of older ravers. She also alludes to periods during which she felt that she had become burnt out on the club scene. However, she, like many of our older participants, also acknowledges the fact that, for most people, turning 21 and "coming of age to drink" goes hand in hand with club attendance. This point of initiation to legal alcohol use was central to many of our participants' discussions of their club attendance and, for many, played a role in their decision to stop attending raves and start attending clubs exclusively.

Opposition to alcohol at raves

While some of the young people we interviewed attribute an absence of alcohol at raves to the age of attendees or the fact that raves are typically held in non-permitted venues (as we discussed in Chapter 2 in our description of the differences between raves and clubs), many others describe a culture particular to raves that is conducive to and permissive of ecstasy use, but renders alcohol use not only inappropriate, but in many cases offensive. For example, James, 26, recalls being surprised and disappointed that alcohol was served at the first rave he attended:

> It was really crowded. There were just people all over the place, laying on the ground. And I was … I was not liking it. You know, you couldn't walk anywhere. It was steaming hot. They even had an alcohol bar. And I thought that was kind of weird, even though that was, like, my first party. I knew I didn't like alcohol and I knew alcohol kind of made people, you know, really not as friend [sic]. And I didn't get good vibes from it.

He attributes this to the negative effects that alcohol has on the individuals who use it, namely that they are less friendly than individuals who are not using alcohol. James is not alone, among those we interviewed, in believing that alcohol is out of place at raves. His sentiments are echoed by many other respondents, including those who use alcohol on a regular basis, and approve of alcohol use in other contexts, but nevertheless disapprove of alcohol at raves. Take, for example, Serena, 16, who attends raves only occasionally, who says of individuals' behavior at raves, "When they're on E at raves and stuff they're more calm, friendlier, and stuff. Other than having a whole bunch o' drunks at a rave, where they're all fighting and violent and stuff. Yeah, that's different."

It is interesting to note that while Serena was only asked to describe people's behavior at raves, she chooses to describe those behaviors as they relate to the substances that they choose to use (or to abstain from) within the context of the rave scene. This statement reflects the sentiments expressed by many of our participants about the centrality of substance use, particularly ecstasy, to their experience in the rave scene. However, this contrast between ecstasy and alcohol also reflects the sentiments of many of our participants about the negative effects of alcohol, and the extent to which it is perceived as inappropriate within the rave scene. Descriptions of individuals who choose to use alcohol at raves are frequently reduced to, as Serena describes it, "a whole bunch o' drunks" who are violent and aggressive. Chad, 22, makes a similar comparison between the behavior of patrons at clubs and raves:

> I think at clubs you're ... definitely if you go with a big group of people, you can be more inclined to get into a fight. Raves, on the other hand – because usually people are on ecstasy and they're all happy and stuff – they don't ... you know, they're just happy. Whereas clubs, you can get pretty belligerent. And a lotta stuff happens. You know, guy looks at a girl, and the girl ... And then you drink too much, and then that's how, you know, you get in big arguments with people just wanting to start shit.

Like Serena, Chad makes a comparison between clubs and raves on the basis of the substances people choose to use in each context, and the effects of the substances on the general tone of the event. However, unlike Serena, Chad is a regular club attendee, and describes himself as a heavy alcohol user, yet he still describes his negative impressions of what happens when people, notably men, drink too much. As we see in Chad and Serena's narratives, alcohol users' actions are not granted the nuanced understanding or interpretation that is typically granted to the actions of ecstasy users, who are described as not only "calm and friendlier," but are also described as social, talkative, compassionate, and loving. In fact, in many cases, the same young men and women who, when discussing their first alcohol-using experiences, describe the positive effects of alcohol on their personalities and interactions reference only the potentially negative effects of alcohol within the context of the rave scene. Despite having positive experiences with alcohol in the past, and in some cases using alcohol on a regular basis, the young men and women we spoke with have a nearly universal ideological opposition to alcohol, particularly within the rave scene. These individuals construct alcohol users as unfriendly, aggressive, violent, which is, in many ways, the exact opposite of the manner in which they discuss ecstasy use and ecstasy users. This dichotomous relationship between alcohol use and ecstasy use closely parallels our participants' descriptions of the differences between the club and rave scenes. As we will demonstrate in the section that follows, alcohol use is central to many of our participants' involvement in the club scene; however, even in this context, in which alcohol use is not only accepted, but often assumed, it carries with it significant negative associations, particularly as it concerns the behaviors of men, and the construction of the club environment as a location for sexual advances.

Drinking and clubs: context and gender

As noted in the previous section, most of the young people we spoke with believe that alcohol has no place within the rave scene on the grounds that it makes people aggressive and unfriendly, which contradicts what many believe is supposed to be the idea of PLUR (Peace, Love, Unity and Respect) that many people view as central to the rave scene. Most of our participants say that they choose to attend raves to hear particular DJs, dance, meet new people, and in many cases, use drugs. It is interesting to note that many of those same individuals cite nearly identical reasons for attending club events, and are not always able to pin down just what the difference is between a rave and a club. However, their qualitative descriptions of clubs, and the people who attend them, are fraught with negative feelings about unwanted sexual advances, violence, aggression, and other generally unpleasant behaviors, all of which are blamed on alcohol and an entire group of alcohol users who are unable to control their behavior. This perception of the negative effects of alcohol use would not be surprising at all if our participants were not themselves current alcohol users. But this is simply not the case, since almost all of the people we interviewed were current users of alcohol. What is it about the club scene that leads individuals to hold such negative views of alcohol and alcohol use, and how do they reconcile their own alcohol use, with their impressions of other people's alcohol use as negative?

What does club attendees' alcohol use look like?

Given our available data, it is impossible to know the precise location and context of our respondents' drug and alcohol use; however, there are significant patterns with respect to their type of event attendance and rates of consumption of alcohol. For example, men and women who attend primarily or exclusively clubs are far more likely than respondents who attend primarily or exclusively raves to use beer or hard liquor, on average, once per week or more (55 percent versus 23 percent for beer; 43 percent versus 16 percent, for liquor). These trends hold true when controlling for gender: while men involved in all types of dance scenes tend to consume alcohol more frequently than women, both men and women who attend primarily or exclusively club events use beer and hard liquor more frequently than men or women who primarily or exclusively attend rave events.

Additionally, while age may be seen as a potentially confounding factor when comparing alcohol use among ravegoing and clubgoing populations (due to the fact that the majority of our respondents who attend primarily or exclusively clubs are over the age of 21 and, therefore, are able to consume alcohol legally), we found that young men and women under the age of 21 who attend primarily or exclusively clubs used beer and hard liquor more frequently than respondents under the age of 21 who attend primarily or exclusively raves. While it is impossible to know the extent to which this alcohol use took place within the club itself, these data suggest that there is a significant relationship between club attendance and frequency of alcohol use among young people involved in the San Francisco Bay Area dance scene, even among individuals who cannot consume alcohol legally within the scene.

While our quantitative data *suggest* that alcohol is closely related to involvement in the club scene, the young men and women who attend clubs and raves that we spoke with unequivocally state that the club environment is shaped by the alcohol use within it. This connection is most apparent in young men's and women's descriptions of the manner in which alcohol use transforms club environment into a meat market, where overt displays of sexuality are rampant, alcohol-induced aggression is common, and women are seen as being mistreated by the drunk men in attendance. Take, for example Ling, 18, who says of the club scene:

> You know, just what I see, like … all the guys are there to … get a girl's number, to go hook up with a girl. And like for girls, like … well, from my experience, like … we just wanna dance. So you know, you see all the guys on the wall not dancing, and all the girls are, like, dancing and, like … It's kinda like … the vibe there is negative. Everyone for themselves, like … you know, like, it's all about, "Who's got the best car? … Oh, look at her. Those are fake." … And then plus you gotta lotta drunk people too. I think that adds to it, you know. And when you're drunk, you just wanna pick a fight, I noticed. Or guys do. So it's just like more fights at clubs … I think it's a negative vibe.

In Ling's description of the club scene, we see, first and foremost, a description of the extent to which male clubgoers treat the scene as an opportunity to meet and "hook up" with women, and transform the environment into a meat market. According to Ling's description, as well as the descriptions of many other men and women we interviewed, her primary motivation for attending clubs is to dance; however, she feels her ability to enjoy the experience is hampered by the men in attendance. While Ling does not name alcohol as the sole cause of such overt displays of sexuality and the "negative vibe" in clubs, she does name drunkenness as the source of male fighting and aggression. It should be noted that Ling uses hard liquor, on average, twice per week, yet she still expresses highly critical views of the men and their alcohol use in the club scene.

Tanya, 19, echoes Ling's sentiments about men making sexual advances at clubs. When speaking about people's behavior at a club, she says:

> You can tell who was drunk and who wasn't. And who was buzzed. And the music was different, the environment … And … like … the guys were more, like … the guys would come up to dance with us, they were more … they would sort of grab you or, like … if they did touch you, you would get offended, or … you would not be as open to like dance with them and be okay with them as you would at a rave.

Like Ling, Tanya speaks very generally about "guys" at clubs who "grab you" and "touch you," which she finds offensive; however, she notes that this would not necessarily be the case at a rave. Tanya, like many of the other young people we interviewed, implies that raves are environments in which behaviors such as dancing with and touching people you don't know are acceptable, while those behaviors are viewed as unacceptable, and even threatening at clubs. In other words, what is viewed as a relatively innocent and friendly interaction at a rave, where there is a preexisting culture of openness and respect for others is viewed as an offensive and disrespectful act in the already sexually charged environment of the club. This relationship between substance choice (i.e., alcohol versus ecstasy) and the type of dancing at a club or a rave is a common theme in many of our interviews. Like Tanya, many of them discuss feeling comfortable dancing on their own at raves, or dancing with groups of people they don't know; however, in a club, this behavior becomes aggressive and offensive.

Ling and Tanya's discussions of men and male behaviors in the club scene are representative of many of the young men and women we spoke with. When speaking generally about obnoxious behavior in the club scene, the perpetrators of that behavior are nearly uniformly men; however, contrary to what one might expect, far more men than women complain about men's behavior. For example, Arturo, 23, speaks with disdain about the men at clubs, whom he describes as the "jocks ... the guys that are out there in the fraternities and they're going to pick up chicks, and they wear muscle shirts ... and, like they ... you know, go there, get drunk." In this statement, Arturo clearly differentiates himself from the "jocks" and reduces them to nothing more than men in "muscle shirts" who want to "pick up chicks" and "get drunk." Arturo not only implies that these men lack emotional complexity, at least as it pertains to their behavior within the club, but he also suggests that his behavior is different. This type of "othering" is typical of many of the young men that we interviewed; these men recognize the bad behavior of others, and in so doing, are implicitly asserting that they are not guilty of these same offenses.

We see similar complaints about men's behavior in clubs from Paxton, 23, who frames his discussion of those behaviors in a comparison between acceptable behaviors within the club and rave scenes. First, he asserts that "Guys don't go to raves to pick up chicks." He implicitly contrasts this with clubs by asserting that he "wouldn't take E at a club, because I wouldn't wanna have to deal with some guy ... totally drunk on alcohol picking up on my girlfriend." Here we see the manner in which alcohol-using, clubgoing men are portrayed in many of our participants' narratives: they take advantage of women who are under the influence of alcohol and other substances because they are in an environment where it is perceived as being acceptable to do so. Very few men and women we interviewed talked about this male alcohol-using behavior in clubs without making a comparison to the rave scene, where there is not a culture of a meat market, and, as Paxton states, "guys don't go ... to pick up chicks." It is also interesting to note that most men complain about other men's drunken behavior because of offenses committed not toward them, but to the women in attendance. Some focus on the particular threat to "their" women – their girlfriends or friends – while others resent that in that environment their own actions get perceived as a pick-up, even if not intended in that way. Thomas, 21, avoids clubs, especially hip-hop clubs, where, he says, his actions are misinterpreted: "If I just try to talk to someone, they think I'm either hitting on them or trying to start something."

Not all discussion of alcohol use at clubs was negative, however. We did interview a few young people – primarily women – who discuss their own alcohol use and their sexual behaviors in clubs in a positive manner. Take, for instance, Donna, 26, who in describing her behavior at clubs says:

> I mean ... you know, you drink a lot, act stupid ... You know, they do a lot of shots and ... beer – and ... Oh, we used to hook up with lotsa guys. I mean, not ... When I say hook up, it's, like ... we'd kiss couple different guys in a night or whatever. And then, "Hee, hee, hee." Then we'd go home, and it was

all hunky-dory. There was no one coming home with us. It was nothing like …
a big deal, you know. It was fun, that was it.

This is a rare instance in which we see one of the people we interviewed speaking frankly about their own intoxication and behavior while using alcohol. Donna acknowledges that her behavior while drunk may be considered "stupid" by some, and attempts to downplay the extent to which her "hooking up" while drunk could be interpreted as reckless and irresponsible, but emphasizes that in the end, everything "was all hunky-dory." We see a similar response to a question about appropriate behavior at clubs and raves from Laura, 19.

Like, at raves, I never make out with anybody. Like, I'd kiss somebody on the lips. But I remember, like, I'd make out at a club, 'cause I was really drunk. See, that's the big difference too. Like, you know. I've drunk at a club, I'm, like, more … like affectionate. I'm affectionate on E too, but it's a different kind of affectionate. Whereas when you're drunk you wanna kiss everybody, right? So. (Laughs.) You've been in college, you know. So. I think that's … yeah, that's different.

Much like Donna, Laura discusses her overtly sexual behavior while at clubs, but acknowledges that she would not have made out with people if she hadn't been drunk. She also addresses the interviewer directly to emphasize that her experience is not unusual – that, in fact, it is common to "wanna kiss everybody" while using alcohol, at least within the context of a club or in college settings. As noted above, narratives like Donna's and Laura's were unusual in our sample. Most of the people we interviewed spoke very generally about their alcohol use, particularly within the context of the rave and club scene, and tend to dissociate themselves from individuals who use alcohol and cause trouble. Those individuals who are cited as being drunk, out of control, aggressive, and who, in many ways, are responsible for transforming the club into a meat market, are male, almost without exception. However, it should be noted that men do not discuss the negative effects of their own drunkenness, but rather more frequently discuss the drunkenness of others. In other words, it is not their drinking that is the problem – although most of the men who complain about the alcohol use of others are regular alcohol users themselves – rather, the problem is the inability of other men to control themselves while using alcohol. Women, on the other hand, are either protected by their male friends and boyfriends (as seen in our male respondents' descriptions) or, in rarer instances, discuss taking advantage of the freedom alcohol affords them to let loose and release their inhibitions in a manner normally deemed inappropriate for young women (McDonald 1994; Warner et al. 1999).

Conclusion

Perhaps the most striking feature of our examination of alcohol use within our sample is the ambivalence with which many of the young men and women we interviewed discuss their alcohol use and the fact that the extent to which they discuss their alcohol use differs from the way they discuss their use of other drugs. While many of the young people we interviewed spoke at length about the specific emotional and physiological effects of the club drugs they use, they make an effort to distance themselves from their own alcohol use. Nearly all of the young people we interviewed have used alcohol at some point in their lives, and most are current alcohol users, yet their descriptions of their own alcohol use are relatively limited. What emerges in place of young people's descriptions of their own alcohol use are descriptions of the alcohol use of others, namely men, and the power that alcohol has to shape a particular social context. Women are nearly universally absent from discussions of drunken behavior, and drunk men are reduced to a monolithic category characterized by aggressive, abusive, belligerent, out-of-control behavior. They are defined solely by their alcohol use and the behaviors that take place while they are under the influence of alcohol. To a large extent their agency as alcohol users is ignored, and their behaviors are described as being shaped by the product of alcohol use, which is seen as enhancing a version of masculinity. As it concerns gender performances, this loss of agency appears to be linked to a reversion to stereotypically gendered behaviors and social norms. These traditional conservative performances of gender roles stand in marked contrast to some of the descriptions of the relationship between the performance and negotiation of gender within the rave scene and the use of ecstasy that we discussed in Chapter 9. While those discussions at times reinforce gender stereotypes and roles, at times they also challenge them. They afford ecstasy use and users a degree of complexity that is not granted to alcohol use and alcohol users.

In fact, in many ways the young men and women we interviewed were eager to discuss their disdain for alcohol, and frequently acknowledged the capacity of ecstasy and other illicit drugs to enhance their personalities and interactions with others, while speaking of alcohol in almost entirely negative terms. Drawing upon Thornton's (1996) concept of "subcultural capital," which confers status upon individuals on the basis of a self-definition as an "authentic" member of a particular subculture, we can examine the rejection of alcohol use, at least at an ideological level, as a marker of authenticity and, consequently, possession of subcultural capital within the rave scene. In their "othering" of alcohol users, and their descriptions of the male-chauvinist behaviors of alcohol-using men, our participants assert an authentic position within the rave scene, which, for many reasons, is viewed as incompatible with alcohol use. They reject what they describe as the overtly sexual mainstream, consumption-oriented culture of alcohol use and the club scene in favor of the rave scene and ecstasy use, which are for the most part underground and illicit.

Within the context of the rave scene, a rejection of mainstream, alcohol-using culture serves as a means of defining membership. However, in greater society, drug use carries with it a stigma not found within the drug-normalized environment of the rave, and is characterized as irrational, dangerous, risk-taking behavior. In our participants' narratives, the position of importance and legitimacy granted to illicit drug use relative to alcohol use may be interpreted as a means of justifying behaviors that are likely to be perceived as harmful or dangerous by others. In other words, by constructing a distinctly anti-alcohol narrative, particularly on the basis of the drug's status as an instrument in the production of gender inequality and sexual harassment, young people are able to frame ecstasy as a viable alternative to alcohol use despite its illegality. However, it is impossible to determine the extent to which this factor influenced our participants' perceptions of alcohol use and its relationship to social context. Future research needs to focus not only on the meanings of drug use, but on the meanings of illicit drug use relative to alcohol and other legal drugs and the role of those meanings in the shaping of drug-using social contexts.

Chapter 11

Asian American youth

Consumption, identity, and drugs
in the dance scene

Introduction

Raves and electronic dance music (EDM) clubs are often described, both in the popular press and in scholarly accounts, as a primarily white, middle-class phenomenon (Measham *et al.* 2001; Yacoubian and Urbach 2004). However, as soon as we started observing and interviewing participants in raves and dance clubs in the San Francisco Bay Area we were immediately struck by the prevalence of Asian Americans in these scenes. While the early rave scene in San Francisco may have been predominantly white, today white and Asian American participants describe the increasing prominence of Asian Americans as a significant turning point in the rave and dance-club scenes. This belies two popular misconceptions. First, that the rave and electronic dance music scenes in the US are completely white-dominated affairs; Asian Americans have generally been ignored or invisible in media and scholarly analyses of these scenes. (See Maira 2002 for an important exception and Zhou and J. Lee 2004 for more on Asian American youth studies more generally.) Second, that Asian Americans cannot be drug users. Stereotypes about Asian Americans as a "model minority" tend to preclude an understanding of drug use among Asian American youth and the drug literature has tended to replicate this pattern. The available research data on Asian American drug use is relatively limited in comparison with the availability of research on other major ethnic groups; the available data on Asian American *club-drug* use is even scantier.

Asian Americans represent one of the fastest-growing ethnic groups in the US. While in 1960 they represented less than 1 percent of the total US population, today they account for 10.2 million (or 3.6 percent) of the total population (Barnes and Bennett 2002). The San Francisco Bay Area is one of the largest centers of Asian American presence in the US. In the Bay Area there are over 1.4 million residents of Asian descent, comprising just over 20 percent of the overall population (US Census Bureau 2000). Not only has contemporary immigration altered the size of the Asian population in the US, it has also increased its diversity. Today the panethnic term "Asian American" includes a much greater ethnonational diversity than was imagined by those who organized the Asian American movement in the 1960s (Barringer *et al.* 1993; Espiritu 1992; Hollinger 1995). In the San Francisco area dozens of distinct nationalities are represented, and prominent Asian American subgroups include: Chinese/Taiwanese (36 percent of the area's Asian American population), Filipino (27 percent), South Asians (12 percent), Southeast Asians (14 percent), Japanese (7 percent), and Korean (4 percent).[1]

However, in spite of the growing significance of Asian Americans within the US, and in spite of the concern about young people's drug use, the available research data on young Asian American drug use are relatively limited in comparison with the availability of research on other major ethnic groups. Epidemiological studies of Asian American drug use have often lacked "sufficient numbers of cases to examine patterns of drug use among young people who were not members of the three largest racial and ethnic groups (whites, African Americans, and Hispanic Americans)" (Wallace *et al.* 2002: S74). Most national studies either omit mention of Asian Americans entirely, or lump Asian Americans into a broader (and generally unstudied) category of "other" (Ja and Aoki 1993: 61; Ono 2005). The two major national studies of drug use – Monitoring the Future (MTF) and the National Household Survey on Drug Abuse (NHSDA) – still do not provide complete information about Asian American drug use due to small sample sizes.

Beyond the question of sample sizes, one of the primary reasons for the neglect of Asian Americans in drug scholarship has been the belief that drug use among Asian Americans is not a problem. This belief has stemmed in part from the results of a few national surveys that found for Asian Americans "much lower overall use prevalence rates than most other ethnic/racial groups" (Austin 1999: 208). This portrayal seems to confirm the stereotype of Asian American youth as a model minority. Increasingly, however, this assumption is viewed as erroneous. More recent publications, especially those drawing from locally based studies, highlight the extent to which substance use is significant and increasing within Asian American communities (Harachi *et al.* 2001; Ja and Aoki 1993; Jang 1996; Nemoto *et al.* 1999; O'Hare and Tran 1998; So and Wong 2006; Zane and Huh Kim 1994). The available data on Asian American *club-drug* use is even less developed, but indicators point to this as an area to be watched (Yang and Solis 2002). According to MTF, between 1996 and 2000 Asian American twelfth-graders consistently had one of the lowest rates of drug use. However, for certain substances, including hallucinogens, LSD, and some stimulants, Asian Americans reported annual use at a rate higher than African Americans (Johnston *et al.* 2002) and another study found comparatively higher rates of lifetime ecstasy use among Asian American youth than other groups (Substance Abuse and Mental Health Services Administration 2003; Yacoubian and Urbach 2004). Other studies have suggested key differences among ethnonational subgroups of Asian Americans in initiation and degree of substance use (Harachi *et al.* 2001; M. Y. Lee *et al.* 2002). The NHSDA also indicates that although Asian Americans generally have one of the lowest rates of drug use, like other ethnic groups, Asian American *youth* and young adults have tried and are using drugs at higher rates than older Asian Americans, indicating that this is a group to be watched in the future.

Many young Asian Americans are increasingly involved in the club and rave scenes, and within these scenes they are experimenting with and using club drugs. While embarking upon our study of the social context of club-drug use in the San Francisco Bay Area, we quickly became aware of the presence and prevalence of

Asian American youth in these scenes. Some local reports suggested that approximately 30 percent of attendees at electronic dance music events were Asian American (Mills 1998; Nishioka 2000) and our own fieldwork at local raves showed some events in which Asian Americans were in the majority, a scenario described in many of our interviews as well. In addition, there is a growing and thriving Asian American dance-club scene in the Bay Area. The prominence of Asian Americans in San Francisco's nightlife is reflected in the large number of Asian American DJs, promoters, and Asian American specific nightclubs. In our mapping of the San Francisco club scene (see Chapter 5 for more details), we identified 126 electronic dance music (EDM) venues, fourteen of which hosted Asian clubs or Asian nights, some of which occur on a weekly or monthly basis. A total of 475 clubs (individual events which take place in venues) were also identified, of which sixty-one clubs catered specifically to Asian American communities.

The Asian dance scene is itself quite diverse – encompassing a variety of music styles and genres, events both underground and commercial, and overall styles of scenes that vary considerably. While there are a few nationally specific clubs (such as "K clubs" frequented by Korean Americans), most of the Asian clubs tend to draw a diverse, pan-Asian clientele. Asian Americans in our sample choose the different clubs they attend based on a number of characteristics, including the ages of attendees, the type of music they prefer (hip-hop versus trance versus house), the style of the club (casual versus dressy), the type of people who attend the clubs (e.g. a college crowd, an "elite" crowd, or a more general population), and the organization promoting the event.

It is against this backcloth that we examine the drug-using experiences of a group of young Asian Americans in the dance/club/rave scenes in the Bay Area. In considering their experiences, which for many of the participants are primarily positive, we attempt both to situate their drug use within the wider social context of their lives and to connect their use and their involvement in the dance scene with their different social groupings. While some researchers (Austin 1999; Harachi *et al.* 2001; Ja and Aoki 1993; Jang 1996) have criticized the existing work for its unitary image of Asian Americans, we discovered that important additional subgroup variations exist which cross-cut ethnonational differences. These divisions are based not solely on ethnicity but on social, generational, cultural, and stylistic features. In examining the importance of these subgroup variations we hope to provide a more nuanced and contextualized investigation of drug use among Asian American young people not typically found in epidemiological studies.

Unlike many of the epidemiological studies on Asian American youth, whether national or local, we have adopted a primarily qualitative approach to the study of the social context of drug use. Within this analysis, we have sought to examine the different types of involvement of young Asian Americans in the electronic dance music scene. We consider the different social groups of which they are a part and within which they attend dance events and consume drugs. In addition to examining the role of drugs within their lives and their social groups, we highlight the ways in which they actively construct and negotiate their identities around these different social groupings. We demonstrate how different Asian American youth groups negotiate their identity by socially and culturally constructing peer-group boundaries in order to distinguish themselves and their own social group from other perceived groups within the scene. Throughout our analysis, we were struck by the nuanced explanations of drug consumption and Asian American cultures provided by our respondents. We found that while the conventional theoretical perspectives of immigration and substance use – which focus on issues of assimilation and acculturation – provide some leverage for understanding these experiences, they are not sufficient for understanding all of the stories told by these young, Asian American drug users.

Sample

Of the 300 young adults we interviewed for this book, fifty-six self-identified as Asian or Asian American. These fifty-six young Asian Americans were split evenly by gender, and had a median age of 20. The respondents were of seven different ethnic groups/national origins: Chinese (28.6 percent), Filipino (26.8 percent), Vietnamese (12.5 percent), Korean (10.7 percent), Indian (8.9 percent), Japanese (5.4 percent), and Taiwanese (3.6 percent). An additional two respondents claimed the general category of "Asian" as their ethnicity. Thirteen of the respondents reported that they were of mixed heritage, although they listed their Asian ethnic group as their primary ethnic identity. Sixty-eight percent were born in the US (59 percent in California), and all but one of the foreign-born respondents were born in Asia or the Philippines. The reported mean length of time living in the US for these foreign-born respondents was fifteen and a half years. Seventy-five percent reported having parents who were born in Asia, 12.5 percent claimed one parent was born in Asia and one in the US, and an additional two respondents said a parent was born in a non-Asian country.

Drug use in the sample

As with the overall sample of club-drug users and individuals in the rave/club scenes that we interviewed, we found widespread use of marijuana and ecstasy, drug experimentation with a variety of other substances (with some people being regular/frequent users and others only very occasional), and primarily weekend or leisure-time use of these drugs (see Table 11.1). For the two most popular drugs – marijuana and ecstasy – we see almost identical rates of lifetime use and comparable rates of past-year and past-month use, comparing Asian American versus non-Asian American participants: within both groups, 97 percent reported lifetime marijuana use, 94 percent of Asian Americans reported ecstasy use versus 91 percent of non-Asian Americans. The Asian Americans in the sample were generally less likely to report lifetime and past-year use of most of the other drugs we studied (except for poppers). However, for many of the drugs the past-month use was more equal between the two groups. Still, however, the Asian Americans in our sample reported drug use much higher than that of the general population (Asian American specifically, or overall) and displayed a wide range of experimentation. Sixty-six percent have tried mushrooms, 46 percent have tried methamphetamine, 41 percent cocaine, and 33 percent have tried LSD.

Table 11.1 Asian American ethnicity and drug-use rates (%)

Drug	Lifetime prevalence		Past-year prevalence		Past-month prevalence	
	Asian Americans	Non-Asian Americans	Asian Americans	Non-Asian Americans	Asian Americans	Non-Asian Americans
Marijuana	97	97	81	90	61	74
Ecstasy	94	91	80	80	29	35
LSD	33	67	4	21	0	5
Mushrooms	61	87	37	60	9	20
Methamphetamine	46	58	26	36	11	14
Ketamine	33	38	19	24	4	2
GHB	20	27	9	16	4	2
Cocaine	41	66	27	45	11	17
Nitrous oxide	43	68	29	36	7	11
Poppers	13	11	7	4	3	1
Opium	14	36	3	15	0	4
Pill opiates	44	59	31	43	7	16
Amphetamines	17	35	10	14	6	5

While the majority of the Asian American sample (75 percent of men and 50 percent of women) have tried at least five or more drugs, including marijuana and the recreational use of prescription drugs, the extent of their use of some of these drugs varies. While approximately 62 percent of those who have tried marijuana estimate that they have used it more than fifty times in their lives, 35 percent said the same about methamphetamine and 28 percent about ecstasy. However, the majority of respondents who have ever tried LSD (55 percent), mushrooms (56 percent), GHB (91 percent), and ketamine (75 percent) said that they used them on only five or fewer occasions. Slightly less than half of the respondents who have ever tried methamphetamine (46 percent) or cocaine (44 percent) said they used them only one to five times.

This data, although limited in terms of sample size, suggest a picture of primarily recreational or "weekend," rather than daily or very frequent, use. If their use of these drugs is often recreational and associated with leisure activities, then it is likely that much of their use of these drugs takes place within their social groups. To further our understanding of drug use in this sample, it is therefore important for us to examine their social groups and the role of these drugs within that framework.

During our interviews with young men and women involved with club-drug use and the rave and club scenes, the importance of, and diversity among, Asian Americans in these scenes became more and more apparent. This led us to begin, in 2005, a second study, an offshoot of the first one, which focused specifically on Asian Americans in this scene. In this second study (CDA), in which we interviewed 250 young Asian American club-drug users in the club scenes, we screened and recruited participants using the same methods and criteria as in the original club-drugs (CD) study that is the focus of much of this book. The interview schedules in both research studies included many of the same questions about participation in the scene as well as the same drug-use matrix to measure patterns of drug consumption by the participants. However, in the newer Asian American (CDA) study, we included additional sets of questions focusing on their family background, their experiences with immigration or migration, experiences with Asian cultural traditions, and involvement in Asian American club scenes. Because the Asian American sample was larger in this second study, we were able to recruit participants from a more diverse range of Asian American subgroups and levels and types of experiences in the club/rave scenes and we draw from narratives from both samples in our qualitative analysis in this chapter. The general levels of participation and of drug use in the two groups are fairly comparable.

While in the first study (CD) the sample of Asian Americans ($n = 56$) was too small to find meaningful intra-group differences in drug-use patterns, we did attempt to probe this issue in the second (CDA) study with its larger sample size ($n = 250$).[2] We looked for differences in drug consumption between foreign- and American-born respondents but found few significant differences. The issues of immigration status and acculturation loom large in the Asian American drug-use literature as factors to account for drug-use rates (Amodeo *et al.* 1997; Bhattacharya 2002, 2004; O'Hare and Tran 1998; Zane and Huh Kim 1994). However, our data produced no statistically significant relationships between lifetime drug-use rates and immigration status or age at immigration and there were relatively few significant differences between American- and foreign-born respondents' use of drugs in the previous year (see Table 11.2).

We did find some significant variation in the types of drugs used across ethnic groups (see Table 11.2). Japanese American respondents, for example, reported the highest rates of lifetime use of LSD, mushrooms, prescription amphetamines, and tranquilizers (a finding that has occurred in other studies as well; see Price *et al.* 2002; Substance Abuse and Mental Health Services Administration 2006, although see also Wong *et al.* 2004). Filipino respondents reported the highest rate of lifetime methamphetamine use out of any Asian ethnic group (66 percent), whereas South Asian and Southeast Asian respondents reported the lowest rates of lifetime methamphetamine use (27 percent and 33 percent, respectively). Southeast Asians were the least likely of all Asian ethnic groups to have used wine, LSD, mushrooms, prescription tranquilizers, and salvia in the previous year. South Asian respondents reported the highest rates of lifetime cocaine use (70 percent), almost double the rate of use among Southeast Asians (35 percent). These findings indicate that there are significant differences among various Asian American subgroups with respect to drug use and reflect the diversity rather than homogeneity of the broad category captured within "Asian American."

While the data suggest some interesting differences in drug consumption among different ethnonational subgroups, and certainly this is an area perennially in need of further investigation and large-scale studies, in examining our respondents' qualitative interviews we were often struck more by the commonalities among these groups in *narratives* about their drug consumption and their ethnic identities. This is not to suggest that the Asian American youth we interviewed are homogeneous or unitary. Far from it; this is an eclectic and diverse group of young people and we will discuss

Table 11.2 Asian American subgroups and lifetime drug-use rates (%)

Drug	Nativity		National subgroup					
	American-born	Foreign-born	Chinese/Taiwanese	Filipino	Southeast Asian	South Asian	Japanese	Korean
Marijuana	97	99	97	100	100	96	100	100
Ecstasy	94	96	99	93	96	92	100	91
LSD	38	37	36*	51*	23*	35*	60*	43*
Mushrooms	65	63	67*	71*	49*	73*	93*	71*
Methamphetamine	40	47	35*	66*	32*	27*	47*	43*
Ketamine	17	12	18	25	9	15	13	5
GHB	14	22	21	23	11	12	7	10
Cocaine	49	50	44*	61*	35*	69*	53*	62*
Nitrous	32	33	41	39	18	27	40	43
Prescription opiates	58	50	55	59	51	62	53	57
Amphetamines	24	21	23*	18*	11*	35*	40*	38*
Tranquilizers	21	21	26*	32*	2*	12*	40*	29*
Salvia	19	9	26*	7*	2*	15*	47*	19*

*Statistically significant at or below the 0.05 level using chi-square.

a variety of different narratives offered by them. But the key differences between and among them are often much more salient around issues of lifestyle, taste, and consumption, and not always the more typically looked for dimensions of immigration generation or national background.

Simply looking at the drug-use histories and prevalence rates of our respondents can only get us so far, though. For these numbers alone tell us very little about the meaning or context of drug consumption in the lives of these young Asian Americans. To get a sense of the meaning and significance of drug consumption within their lives, we turn to their own words, their own narratives of explanation.

Asian American groupings, ethnicity, and the dance scene

Social composition and salient characteristics

In order to understand fully the role of drugs within these Asian American youth groupings we need first to examine their social composition and their salient characteristics. In spite of the fact that the issue of ethnicity was not a central focus of our initial research, it is nevertheless a central feature of our respondents' social groups. Ethnicity-related issues emerge in many of the interview narratives, and it is clear that ethnicity plays an important role in the formation of their friendship groups and in their patterns of interaction while participating in the dance/club scenes. As we will show, while for some respondents issues of pan-Asianism are important, for others negative and stereotypical views about other Asians, intermixed with stylistic features of dress and musical choice, are pivotal in establishing and maintaining their friendship groups.

The Asian American men and women we interviewed were split between those who socialize in primarily or exclusively Asian American social groups (sometimes of their specific ethnicity, e.g. Chinese, Filipino, etc., but many times of more pan-Asian, multiethnic configurations), and those who socialize primarily in mixed-ethnicity social groups (sometimes predominantly white, sometimes with members of many different racial/ethnic groups).[3] These patterns are also apparent in the types of clubs and dance events that the young men and women attend – with some gravitating primarily to Asian clubs and dance events in which Asian Americans are in the majority, while others prefer mixed-ethnicity clubs, predominantly white clubs, or predominantly African American clubs (depending in large part on the community the respondent grew up in as well as their musical tastes and preferences).

Many of those active in the Asian club scene report they prefer it because it is comfortable and familiar. As Charles, 23, noted, "Those are the people I've been used to hanging with. So, those are the people I party with." Some also mention that they prefer Asian clubs because they are free to dance and enjoy themselves without judgment. These individuals explain that at ethnically diverse clubs they feel socially repressed and intimidated by African Americans and whites, whom they perceive as judgmental. Nhean, 21, for example, comments that at Asian clubs it's easier for him to "let go." He is more cautious of his actions around people of other ethnic backgrounds and sometimes feels like he is being scrutinized by others for "acting wild."

On the other hand, many of the young Asian Americans who have an aversion to the Asian club scene say that they don't participate because they feel that the scene is materialistic and cliquey. Max, 31, spoke extensively about his disdain for Asian clubs, stating that he does not fit in because he doesn't associate with the "dress to impress mentality," which he feels is characteristic of the Asian scene. Others argue that the Asian scene is too status-oriented or too insular.

Some Asian Americans who predominantly attend mixed-ethnicity events discuss their preferences in terms of the norms of the rave/dance scene. Diversity in the scene and finding commonalities with people from different backgrounds is an important aspect of their raving experience:

> Going to raves ... helped me to realize, like, to be openminded ... it also made me see, like, there are a lotta interesting people, and you do not have to just, like ... be contained to like one specific group ... Like don't be afraid to talk to other people, just because, like, they may not be your same ethnicity, or they may not dress the same as you.

> (Ling, 18)

This diversity in people of different ethnicities reflects, according to some of the young men and women we interviewed, the ethic of PLUR (peace, love, unity, and respect) that attracted many of them to the scene.

Disidentification and creating the Asian "other"

Regardless of whether our respondents are in Asian-dominated or mixed ethnic groups, a significant and striking number of them make a point of distinguishing themselves and their groups from *other* Asians and other Asian groups. Within their narratives, they describe themselves in opposition to "others" in the scene. This process of group separation and boundary maintenance (Hunt and Satterlee 1986) has been examined by a number of researchers looking at ethnicity (Kibria 1998, 2000; Nagel 1994; Song 2003). These researchers have emphasized the ways in which ethnic social groups use identity boundaries both to "disrupt the often stereotypical assumptions people make about one another" (Song 2003: 21) and to distance themselves from other ethnically defined groups. For example, Kibria (2002), in her research on second-generation Asian Americans, uses Goffman's (1963) work on disidentification to examine young Asian Americans' resentment of the idea of intra-Asian affinity. She describes "disidentification" as "the distancing of members of one Asian ethnic group from another" (Kibria 2002: 78). By establishing and constructing the "other," our respondents strengthen their own group identity and cohesion (Barth 1969; Wallman 1978). To do this, many of our respondents draw "on popular stereotypes of Asians" (Kibria 2002: 89). For example, they use stereotypical terms, such as "Asian gangsters," "FOB," and "rice rockets," and characterize other Asian groups on the basis of these "types."

To the respondents, length of time spent in the US is a critically important distinguishing characteristic, and those who are newly arrived are often referred to as FOBs: "Like, fresh off the boat, someone who comes directly from Taiwan or China and still holds traditional values ... Someone who is less. ... whitewashed, I guess you could say" (Henry, 23).

In addition to using stereotypes of other Asians as FOBs, or gangsters, our respondents often associate these particular characteristics with specific dance scene locations and venues, thereby emphasizing the extent to which "spatial divisions and socially segmented consumption patterns" exist within the dance scene (Hollands 2002; see also Skelton and Valentine 1998). For instance, a young Filipina (Lillian, 22) contrasts those Asians like herself who attend hip-hop or reggae clubs with those other "mainstream" Asians who go to clubs specializing in trance or house music:

Lillian.   If you go to a trance or a house club there's a lot of Caucasians there.
                There's Asians and stuff like that, but the Asians there are mainstream,
                like, they're racers.
Interviewer.   What's a racer?
Lillian.   Racers, like, they have Hondas or Accuras that's very "souped up,"
                I guess you'd say, and they'd race. They're called rice rockets. You
                know, Asians like rice and their cars are like the rockets that go off
                or whatever ... You wouldn't really find those people at a hip-hop
                and reggae club like I go to. But you can see them at mainstream
                clubs, like ... places where they play commercial music ... I like
                going to clubs that are multicultural ... It was mostly urban people,
                but the mainstream Asians try to come and ... so I mean, not that I'm
                discriminatory to the people who are mainstream, but it's just a whole
                different vibe.

Many of the young Asian Americans' attitudes toward other Asians are not only based on individual behaviors or styles but are also coupled with the general accusation that the involvement of Asians has caused the dance scene to deteriorate. The decline of the scene in their eyes is the result of both the number and the type of young Asians that can now be found attending dance events. This point is emphasized by a number of our respondents who describe, somewhat wistfully, the scene as it was when they first attended a dance event. At that time, according to them, fewer Asians were visible at events, whereas today Asians have now "flooded" the scene. For example, Doug, 19, explains how much better the scene had been when frequented primarily by whites. Once certain types of Asians had begun to attend, the scene was "ruined." More specifically, the scene had declined because these new attendees did not know about nor embrace its central philosophy of PLUR. Today, according to this young man, attendees do not respect each other.

When rave started, it started with white people ... Then Asian people started to go ... [and] ... it kind of ruined the scene because Asians just go there and drop

E. And they tend to go in groups, and then the groups, like, if you don't ... if you're not with the group, then you're being hated on. Kind of, like, "Oh, you're not in the same clique," you know ... And that just ruins the whole purpose of the rave, the peace, love, unity and respect. There's no respect, you know ... some Asians are cool, you know. They're like me, just there to dance; it's all about the music. But some Asians just ruined the whole purpose of a rave.

The theme of Asians undermining the purpose and the spirit of the rave and the dance scene in general is elaborated on by Henry, who notes how, when he first went to a rave, he considered everyone a friend, but with commercialization and the influx of Asians the scene has become "hostile."

So far, we have seen the extent to which some of these Asian American respondents, whether in predominantly Asian groups or groups of mixed ethnicity, maintain the cohesion of the group by distinguishing themselves and their friends from other "types" of Asians. This disidentification, as Kibria (2002: 89) has noted, is achieved by "establishing one's difference from the other." In the case of these young men and women, they do it by demarcating themselves from others within the dance scene whom they portray as less "cool," exhibiting inappropriate behavior, or even as having tarnished the scene and its initial ideology. The respondents avoid these "other" Asians by attending "underground" as opposed to "mainstream" events, where few if any "unacceptable" Asians attend. Whereas the behaviors and motives of others are illegitimate, the respondents believe that their own motives for attending and their own behaviors are legitimate and "cool." This is precisely the same process of distinction identified by Malbon (1999) and Thornton (1996) (drawing on Bourdieu 1984), except that for these respondents the process is based on ethnic characteristics. By distinguishing themselves in this manner they further confirm their differences from the Asian other.

We have discussed above the social groups in which our respondents exist and the divisions and boundaries that mark out these different Asian groupings. The characteristics on which these groups are based include being Asian and nonwhite in a white society, wanting to associate only with other Asians, wanting to socialize with others from different ethnic groups and, finally, wanting to avoid and distance oneself from the uncool Asians in the scene. Given these different social groupings, what role do ecstasy and other drugs play within them? How do these young men and women understand their drug use *vis-à-vis* their ethnic identities?

Assimilation, acculturation, ethnicity, and substance use

To the degree that Asian American youth have been studied in the drug and alcohol literatures, issues of ethnicity and identity have tended to be subsumed under a focus on immigration[4] and assimilation. In this research tradition, researchers have examined the effects of assimilation on the drug and alcohol-using behaviors of immigrant youth. In so doing they have utilized the concept of acculturation – a minority group's adoption of the "cultural patterns" of the host society.

Growing initially out of the seminal work of Milton Gordon (1964), assimilation theory generally posited that acculturation was a large one-way process from less to more acculturated.[5]

In adopting this concept, drug and alcohol researchers have tended to focus on two themes. First, they have examined the extent to which immigrant youth alter their substance-using behaviors and "converge with those of the host culture as they become integrated into their new social environment" (Johnson et al. 2002: 944). While immigrant children may possess little prior knowledge or experience of alcohol or illicit drug use, as they become assimilated into the host society they may begin to adopt a different set of norms and values, which increases their likelihood of using alcohol and drugs. In adopting the culture of the host society they forgo the protective nature of their parents' culture and are therefore more at risk of drug and alcohol use and problems. In other words, acculturation will lead to changes in substance use (Rodriguez et al. 1993; see also Caetano 1987; Caetano and Mora 1988; Price et al. 2002).

"Acculturative stress" is the second research focus in the study of substance use and immigrant youth. Within this perspective, instead of examining the impact of the host culture on normative drug and alcohol use, researchers have investigated the extent to which the very process of acculturation and its related stress may increase substance use among immigrant youth. Caught between two competing and often conflicting cultures – their own or their parents' "traditional" culture and their newly adopted culture – young immigrants may turn to drugs and alcohol as "coping mechanisms" to reconcile potentially conflicting pressures (see, for example, Berry et al. 1987; Bhattacharya 2002; Bhattacharya and Schoppelrey 2004). In the former research focus, the emphasis is on the potential risk for increased drug and alcohol use because of adopting the norms of the host culture; in the latter focus, the emphasis is placed squarely on the effects of acculturation itself.

In recent years, the underlying perspective that provides the foundation for either side of this debate – assimilation theory – has come under great scrutiny among sociologists and cultural theorists. Indeed, by 1993 Nathan Glazer had published an essay titled "Is assimilation dead?" and Alba and Nee argued that the theory of assimilation had "fallen into disrepute ... In recent decades assimilation has come to be viewed by social scientists as a worn-out theory which imposes ethnocentric and patronizing demands on minority peoples struggling to retain their cultural and ethnic integrity" (1997: 827). Critics charge acculturation research with oversimplifying cultural complexities and with conceptualizing immigrants as passive actors. Researchers adopting acculturation theory have also been criticized for assuming that "identification with the country of origin uniformly decreases with time spent in the US and that it rarely intensifies" (Gutmann 1999: 173) and that changes in the behavior of young immigrants can be attributed solely to changes in place as opposed to temporal changes. Contemporary sociological research on youth cultures, ethnicity, and immigration have significantly questioned the static and essentialist notions of ethnic identity underlying assimilation and acculturation and in so doing have provided us with new conceptual tools for analyzing the relationship between ethnic identity and substance use.

In the case of Asian American identity, researchers have demonstrated how different Asian ethnic groups negotiate identity through interaction both within and outside their communities. Asian Americans can choose from "an array of pan-ethnic and nationality-based identities" (Nagel 1994: 155; see also Espiritu 1992; Kibria 2000; Maira 2002), though these choices are constrained by continuing structural inequalities. The notions of "core" and unchanging Asian values, of cultural continuity, and of the gradual linear change in the ethnic group's adaptation to their new home (Thai 1999; Wu 2003; Zia 2000) that underlie much discussion of Asian American acculturation have been increasingly challenged. Instead, social constructionists argue that "ethnicity is emergent" and situational – neither constant nor guaranteed – and can fluctuate over time (Song 2003). While this social constructionist model may be ascendant in contemporary sociological research on racial and ethnic formations, it is not yet fully integrated into the drug and alcohol literatures' inquiries into immigration, which retain a focus on assimilation via their use of the concept of acculturation, nor into the drug field's treatment of ethnicity, which can sometimes be somewhat static and monolithic.

Thus we argue for bringing together these social constructionist models with the drug and alcohol scholarship on immigration and ethnicity. First, this would mean treating Asian American youth not as passive actors but instead as active players in shaping their (ethnic) identities and (drug) consumption choices. Second, it requires questioning the static and essentialist notions of ethnic identity contained in much of the literature on immigrant youth. Instead we emphasize "the fluid, situational, volitional, and dynamic character of ethnic identification, organization, and action – a model that emphasizes the socially 'constructed' aspects of ethnicity, i.e. the ways in which ethnic boundaries, identities, and cultures are negotiated, defined, and produced through social interaction inside and outside ethnic communities" (Nagel 1994: 152). Such developments, we will argue, are more useful in helping to understand the ways in which young Asian Americans discuss their ethnic identities, their sense of who they are, and their drug use. Finally, we wish to move our discussion of Asian American drug use beyond the traditional debates of acculturation and assimilation and additionally situate it more within the recent research on youth cultures, identities, and the consumption of commodities.

While the acculturation perspectives are not without utility – especially if they are deployed in a manner that does not assume that youth passively succumb to either acculturation or substance use, but actively manage and negotiate both – the acculturation paradigm cannot tell the whole story. Recent youth cultural research has emphasized the importance of examining the role of consumption – of music, cars, clothes, or drugs – in constructing an identity and a lifestyle, particularly within youth cultures (Miles 2000); drug consumption needs to be situated within this broader context of consumption (Hunt and Barker 2001). Though such work has tended to focus on white, and to a lesser extent African American, youth (see Maira 2000 for an important exception), we argue for the utilization of these concepts to examine and understand the construction of identity for our young Asian American respondents.

In this chapter, we examine the narratives of these young Asian Americans to see how they explain and how they make sense of their own drug consumption and their own ethnic identities. We find three distinct narratives utilized by respondents in the interviews. While two of these are resonant with the issues of acculturation or acculturative stress, the third narrative indicates a different phenomenon: a normalization of club drug use within some Asian American youth cultures.

Clashing cultures? acculturative stress and Asian culture as explanations for drug use

Some of the descriptions and explanations of drug use provided by our respondents sound almost perfectly like they could come from a drug researcher within the acculturative stress paradigm. These young men and women describe their drug consumption as growing directly out of their experiences of being Asian American, and, in particular, out of the experiences of feeling "in between" or torn between Asian and American cultures.

In some narratives, such explanations are salient only for their supposition about why *other* Asian Americans may use drugs. Marisa, 31, for example, speculates that "if they're newly immigrant, their parents are working all the time, they don't have enough time to, you know, understand their kids, and they're not doing well in school ... they turn to drugs." She does not think, though, that experiences with immigration or with Chinese identity have anything to do with her own drug consumption. Other young Asian Americans, though, speak in great detail about how they think their own drug-use histories have grown out of their experiences with immigration, with culture clash, or with difficulties feeling at home in American and/or Asian cultures. Amanda, 33, for example, specifically describes her illicit drug use as a form of "self-medication" and as a response to feelings of loneliness, anxiety, and depression that she connects to her ethnic identity and to feelings of disconnect with Filipino culture (in part due to being a lesbian, and in part due to the physical and metaphorical distance that she says all American-born Filipinos experience): "Oh, let's just smoke weed, or let's just take acid, let's just snort some coke. You know, it's like everything was to sort of disguise the fact that I had real emotions about stuff that I couldn't understand." She speculates that she wouldn't have turned to drugs if she had been able to find "support or a community ... that I can relate to or relates to me."

Other respondents specifically attribute their drug use to a response to the "culture clash" that they experience as Asian Americans – as both Asian and American. A young Indian woman, who immigrated to the US as a teenager, describes herself as an "in-betweener" – fitting in fully neither with other Indian-born immigrants nor with American-born Indians. At times she felt intense pressure to choose between these two groups and two cultures, though more recently she realized "we don't have to choose. We are happy being a bit of everything ... stuck in between, and we don't have to pick sides" (Reena, 22). Her first club-drug experiences were with another "in-betweener" in the same position that she was in, and, while her drug-using networks have greatly expanded since then, she still finds a particular resonance with that identity.

An even more common version of "culture clash" described by our respondents occurs with second-generation immigrants in conflict with their first-generation parents. Kini, 23, for example, discusses parental pressure to excel academically and the desire to appear as an honorable daughter – a theme that emerged in many of our interviews. She specifically invokes the term "culture clash," echoing a recurrent trope in our interviews. These expectations, which grew out of her parents' experiences of being raised in China, she argues, may be difficult to meet for young *Americans* like herself. She describes Chinese culture as "repressed," as shut down emotionally, as precluding free expression of thoughts and problems. Within her narrative, all of these combine to explain her drug use:

> If I was raised in a different atmosphere, I probably wouldn't have been so exposed ... if I wasn't so repressed maybe ... if I was able to talk to my parents or have conversations with them about concerns I was having ... I wouldn't have to turn to other people ... And I think it did contribute to, you know, drug usage.

Finally, Eean, 28, describes his own drug use as a response to depression: "drugs are just mechanisms to deal with, you know, whatever pain ... you go through." He further elaborates that this may be particularly true within Asian American communities due to stigmas associated with mental health problems and treatment "mental health is a private matter ... no one must find out ... in the Asian community. You know, we don't really talk about too many things like that."

These self-explanations for drug consumption echo some discourses within treatment and etiology literatures regarding drug use as a coping mechanism for other underlying problems. These young men and women go beyond merely psychological explanations in connecting these states to their negotiation of ethnic identity, the conflicting expectations of Asian and US culture. Yet, to do justice to their explanations, it should be pointed out that, contrary to many of the drug literatures, this is not always seen as a negative or problematic response to these issues. Amanda, 33, for example, specifically denies any regret for her extensive drug use, even though she has successfully gone through drug treatment: "I don't regret having had my experiences with all those drugs and heroin. I really don't, because it really forced me to go inside myself to understand ... I would not have had those experiences to ... grow on or ruminate."

Maira and Soep have criticized overreliance on what they call the "simplistic trope of the 'culture clash'" (2004: 259) in studies of Asian (and other immigrant) youth cultures. Such work, they charge, "has tended to neglect the engagement of youth with popular culture and their more nuanced understandings of race, especially, and also of gender and sexuality" (ibid.). They call for moving beyond the limited narratives of acculturation and culture clashes, which have overwhelmingly dominated studies of Asian American youth. As we will argue below, we agree with them about the importance of engagements with popular culture and that acculturation explanations are far from sufficient – much cannot be reduced to issues of culture clash. However, our respondents' narratives indicate that it would not be prudent to drop these models altogether. For, despite any skepticism about the concept that we may have brought into our analysis initially, the trope of "culture clash" continues to have a great deal of salience and resonance for many (but not all) of the young Asian Americans we interviewed; they independently raise these explanations on their own as they attempt to make sense of and interpret their own experiences with drug consumption.

Yet also key are the ways our respondents describe actively managing, shaping, creating, or negotiating their drug-using experiences and their identities as Asian Americans. If the acculturative-stress model is to truly help explain the meaning of drug use among young Asian Americans, it must be deployed in such a manner that understands the *meaning* of drug consumption for them and takes seriously their role as agents, rather than presenting them as pawns, torn between two cultures or passively turning to or "succumbing" to drugs.

While the first group of respondents explain the relationship between their ethnic identity and their substance use in terms familiar from the acculturative stress research, others offer explanations of their own drug use in terms of increasing acculturation and/or Americanization (compared to less acculturated Asians). It is to this second group that we now turn.

Model minorities? acculturation leading to substance use

One of the most dominant stereotypes of Asian Americans today is that they comprise a "model minority"; in contrast to other racial/ethnic minorities, Asian Americans are depicted as hard-working, successful, less likely to be impoverished or involved in crime or substance use. Critiques of this perspective abound within Asian American studies. Kibria (1998: 951–55), for example, provides a helpful summary of the problems engendered by the model-minority myth. She notes that while this image of Asian Americans contrasts with earlier images of Asians as being unassimilable, inscrutable, tricky, or immoral heathens and that it seems to situate Asians in a privileged position in the US racial hierarchy, the "model minority" construction raises difficulties of its own. Within media discourses of Asians as a model minority, for example, the idea of a threatening "yellow peril" remains and can help sustain the racial marginality of Asian Americans in US society. This is because it is often used to pit Asians against other minorities. In addition, empirical evidence utilized to demonstrate Asian American success tends to be based on pooled Asian American statistics, obscuring socioeconomic diversity (and even polarization) among subpopulations of Asian Americans.

Interestingly, one set of our Asian American participants often themselves invoke images of Asian Americans as a model minority. They describe Asian Americans, as a group, as unlikely to use drugs or to participate in the dance/rave/club scenes and their discussions of why this is so often dovetail with the dominant model-minority discourse. Or, more precisely, they describe *most* Asian Americans in this way. They, themselves, are exempt from this categorization. They describe themselves as unique, atypical, unlike most Asian Americans – and they argue that a major factor separating them from other Asians is their attendance at clubs/raves and their substance use.

These men and women argue that Asian American drug use is relatively unusual. A young Chinese American woman, for example, speculates that "there would be a lower amount of drug use among Asian Americans ... I think it's not in our culture" (Stacy, 24). In contrast to others in our sample, many of these young Asian Americans tend to be in social networks that are of mixed ethnicities or are not predominantly Asian American. Or, in other cases, they maintain multiple, distinct social networks, including Asian American peer groups (who do not use drugs) and non-Asian drug-using groups, keeping the two separate.

These young Asian Americans need to reconcile their belief in the infrequency of drug use among Asian Americans with their own, often rather extensive, drug use. For some, this distinction is a source of pride, proving that they are different or breaking the mold. Bradley, 24, for example, asserts that he may be "unique" among other South Asians because he's used more drugs and alcohol than them. He argues that most Indians aren't using drugs, "and even if they are … because Indian people are generally conservative, they wouldn't talk about it, they wouldn't expose the fact that they were on a certain drug." He feels "somewhat isolated" from other young South Asians, arguing that he has more in common with "just normal American kids." Similarly, Jin, 25, who is heavily involved in the rave scene, explicitly distinguishes himself from other Chinese Americans due to (among other things) his drug consumption.

I can't just call myself Chinese, 'cause when I think of just a Chinese kid, I don't think of a person like me [who] … does, like, psychedelic drugs [laughs], or does, like, drug education volunteering that's not, like, anti-drug … These things that … I don't know, that I associate with, like … I don't know … white kids or white people.

In both of these examples, the respondents associate white culture or American culture (and the two are often used interchangeably) with drug consumption, and Asian, Indian, or Chinese cultures are seen as in opposition to this.

While these two young men wear their "uniqueness" like badges of pride, others who experience drug consumption as a feature that distinguishes them from other Asian Americans express feelings of anxiety, shame, or worries that they're losing or "selling out" their (Asian) culture and their family's traditions. Tara, 26, for example, avoided the Filipino community on her college campus due to her drug use, which she feared would stigmatize her.

And I remember thinking, "God, I wonder if they're using, too." … "I wonder if this is something that's acceptable … Do other Filipino kids do this?" I remember thinking that, like, "Am I being less Filipino because I'm hanging out with some white people and Vietnamese people and doing drugs with them or … ?" I kinda had a hard time with that. [I] didn't know if I was being true to my people.

She equated using drugs with losing her culture or undermining her authenticity as a Filipina, which threw her into what she calls an "identity crisis." While she eventually discovered other drug-using Filipino and Asian Americans at clubs and raves (a "mind-boggling" experience for her), she still carefully manages her drug use *vis-à-vis* Asian identity, being careful not to inappropriately use (or exhibit signs of) drugs within what she deems unsuitable cultural contexts: "Asians, when we do drugs, it's at a very specific place, like raves, and a very specific context, like the privacy of your own home."

In the narratives of these respondents, acculturation and Americanization (though not precisely in those terms) are very much tied up with substance use and assumed to be causal – the more American one is, the more likely to use drugs; the more Asian one is, the less likely, according to these respondents' explanations. These respondents appear to experience Asian and American identities as bifurcated and feel pressure to choose one or the other – unlike some of our other respondents, they do not experience their "in-betweenness" as a strength to be cherished.

In some ways they are the opposite of the first group. Whereas the first group view their drug use as a natural outgrowth of their experiences as Asian Americans (and the culture clashes that can result from this), this second group experience drug consumption as something oppositional to Asian American identity. One thing that both narratives hold in common, though, is the sense that drug-using identities and ethnic identities are carefully and actively managed and negotiated by each of these young people; their narratives very much belie the notion of ethnic identity (or drug-using identity) as a category one passively occupies, or something that can simply be used as an independent variable in our analyses. While in many ways their explanations of their own drug use are reminiscent of the sorts of etiologies dominant in much of the drug literatures' explanations of immigration and ethnicity, our respondents remind us of the important role of agency in these processes, an agency that is too often missing within drug scholarship.

Yet not everyone finds their identities as Asian Americans, as both Asian and American, as a source of culture clash or alienation. Not everyone finds anything unusual about Asian Americans as drug consumers. For a third group, their experiences of drug consumption, and the relationships they posit between substance use and ethnic identity, are not particularly resonant with the issues raised within acculturation perspectives in the drug and alcohol scholarship. For these young Asian Americans, in our final group, issues of style, consumption, taste, and differences within Asian American communities have much greater salience in how they understand the context of their drug use. Moreover, the narratives of drug use presented by these young Asian Americans indicate a *normalization* of Asian American drug use in these youth cultures.

Normalized Asian American drug consumption?

The drug-normalization thesis argues that illicit drug consumption, which has traditionally been seen as extraordinary, unusual, or deviant, is becoming normative, accepted, and part of the everyday in many youth cultures. H. Parker and colleagues (1998) found that in the UK drug use was no longer confined to the subcultural margins, but has become an undeniable aspect of mainstream youth cultures (see also H. Parker 2005). Indicators of this normalization include the degree to which drug use is widespread and drugs are made easily accessible, the approaches to "sensible" drug use and cost–benefit analyses constructed by young drug users, a growing social and cultural accommodation to drug use (particularly marijuana use), and the prominence of drugs and drug symbols in popular and consumer culture. This perspective has been less developed in the US than in the UK (for exceptions see Lankenau and Sanders 2007; MacKenzie *et al.* 2005). However, with drug-use rates in the two countries being comparable (Shiner and Newburn 1999), and with drugs having a similarly prominent place in much of youth culture, this is an area in need of further development in understanding drug consumption – and youth culture much more generally – in the US.[6] However, in a country as diverse and heterogeneous as the US, one might expect uneven levels of drug normalization within various youth cultures (for youth cultures in the US are far too variegated to speak of "youth culture" in the singular). With the stereotypes of Asian Americans as a model minority unlikely to use drugs, one might expect a lesser degree of drug normalization within Asian American youth cultures. While our study is not a comparative one, and we cannot assess relative degrees of normalization in different ethnic youth cultures, our research certainly indicates the presence of at least some Asian American youth cultures in which club-drug use is expected, everyday, mundane; in a word: normalized.

This third group of narratives actually represent the majority of Asian Americans we interviewed. These respondents spoke to us for hours about their ethnic identity, their culture and family traditions, and about their long histories of drug use and their involvement in the dance scenes. Yet, after hours of these interviews, they often made no explicit connections between their ethnic identities and their substance use. They tended not to remark at all on this. Within these narratives, Asian American drug use was seen as *unremarkable*; it was completely taken for granted.

Some of these young Asian Americans describe certain dance scenes (Asian dance clubs, but also the rave scene more generally) as increasingly dominated by Asians and by the drug ecstasy. For these respondents, the two (Asians and ecstasy) go hand in hand. One Chinese American woman describes her first impressions of a rave in a way we saw repeated in numerous interviews: "There were a lot of Asians ... Everywhere, on the dance floor ... it felt like everybody was on E. I know of a couple people that were sober, but ... pretty much everyone was on E" (Denise, 24). Many describe ecstasy as being on par with alcohol, in terms of prevalence and acceptability:

> E is the biggest thing they do, we do ... At the Asian clubs that's the most prevalent, more than any other drug. More than marijuana ... I would say it's equal to alcohol ... E, it almost seems ... accepted ... like smoking or drinking alcohol, it's ... "Oh, it's not that bad."
>
> (Derek, 27)

When pondering why the club scene is increasingly popular and the reasons for the growth of the Asian club scene, one Chinese American simply speculates, "perhaps it's the drugs, perhaps it's the alcohol" (Travis, 26). An affinity between Asian Americans and substance use, or rather, use of particular substances, including ecstasy and alcohol, is simply taken as a given.

Indeed, this has become so normalized that Derek describes a popular Asian dance event "almost like a social networking place, where it's not really a rave. It's people getting to know each other ... professionals going to talk to each other ... you build contacts and stuff." He compares it to dinner parties or cocktail parties of the past, although, rather than wine and cocktails, the substances of choice may be club drugs, particularly ecstasy. However, in this description the drugs are an almost incidental, mundane part of the broader social context.

This group is not easily categorized in terms of experiences with acculturation. It includes highly acculturated third-generation Asian Americans and recent immigrants who socialize in predominantly Asian/Asian American social networks. Some of these respondents prefer Asian clubs, while others frequent mixed clubs (though often in ethnically homogeneous and/or pan-Asian social groups). Their drug use is not necessarily tied up with being more or less acculturated or Americanized (and some discuss drug-using experiences in Asia), nor do they tend to describe experiences that indicate "acculturative stress." Any "culture clashes" that they may describe are between finely distinguished subcultures, between different "types" and styles of Asian Americans, often distinguished through music preferences and clothing styles (as in the examples of disidentification in the earlier section). Neither Asian American identity, nor that of being a drug consumer, is problematic for these youth; they are accepted, normalized aspects of their existence. The sorts of differentiations they make are not so much about whether or not they would try drugs (that is taken as a given by these young Asian Americans), nor to what degree this is influenced by being Asian/Asian American. Instead, they focus on much finer distinctions – distinctions based on different ways of being Asian within club-drug settings and communities: how to display and perform one's subcultural affiliations; how to dress like a gangster, or a "Hong Kong girl," or a hipster; how to avoid being perceived as an FOB or a "square" Asian. Within these narratives, drug consumption can be understood only if placed in the context of a whole other range of consumption choices – of clothes, cars, drinks, and music. This is not a universal, across-the-board phenomenon for young Asian Americans. Certainly for the young Asian Americans discussed in the previous section (who represent a significant, but minority, group, within our sample) Asian American drug use is far from perceived as the norm. And there do appear to be significant ethnonational differences with respect to drug normalization. Drug use is described as normalized particularly within Chinese American and other East Asian youth cultures (both by insiders and outsiders to these cultures). To a lesser degree this appears to be true for many Southeast Asian and Filipino respondents (although drug-use patterns here are a bit different, with ecstasy playing a less central role). However, there is near unanimity among our South Asian respondents that drug use continues to be stigmatized in South Asian American communities, including in youth cultures. "Typically Indian people get wrapped up in drinking but not in drugs" (Gauri, 28).[7] "Within the South Asian scene ... the only drugs I ever saw being done was ... booze. And some weed ... Never heard of anything else" (Deepak, 24). Though many South Asian youth may use drugs (including, of course, all of our South Asian respondents in this study), this is something that tends to be done discreetly, hidden from view. Further exploration of cultural differences between and among Asian American subgroups will be important in the future to discern the reasons for the differential acceptability of drug consumption in various youth cultures in the US and beyond.

Conclusion: Asian American youth and drug consumption in the context of globalization

In our diverse group of young Asian American club drug users we found different patterns of social network participation in their involvement in the dance scenes. Their choice of dance events, music, style of dress and drugs represent features of their own or their social group's identity. Far from being passive consumers, they actively decide on and choose the commodities they consume, and they develop their identities partly around this consumption. This process of consumption is inherently social (Appadurai 1986a) and consuming these commodities, whether it be drugs, dance events or drinks, operates as a "medium of exchange" (Strathern 1987) in interpersonal relations, mediating and consolidating relationships between individuals and social groups.

By examining the social lives of these young Asian Americans, their involvement in the dance scene, and their use of drugs, we have also attempted to illustrate the possible importance of intra-ethnic divisions within the scene. So far, the available literature, with only a few exceptions (Huq 2003; Measham *et al.* 2001; Sharma *et al.* 1996), has tended to downplay ethnic divisions within the scene. In our respondents' narratives they not only describe their activities, their social worlds, and the role of drugs, they also discuss the ways in which their activities and consumption practices differ from others in the scene. Significantly enough, given their structural position as ethnic minorities, the groups or individuals whom some respondents characterize as cool are whites, whereas the people and groups they seek to distinguish themselves from are other Asians, and specifically stereotypical Asians, referred to as Asian gangsters and FOBs. They portray these stereotypical Asians in disparaging ways and argue that, while their own motives and activities are cool, the motives and behaviors of these others are "uncool." Their critique of other Asian Americans is not only that they are uncool, but that they are partly responsible for bringing about the overall decline in the scene, undermining its original PLUR philosophy, and encouraging its contemporary commercialization. While sociocultural distinctions based on notions of cultural capital within the dance scene have been identified by some researchers (see Thornton 1996), as yet few writers have examined the possible ways in which young adults in the scene may construct an ethnic dimension to those distinctions. In this chapter we have attempted to show how Asian American youth in the dance scene create social divisions within their own ethnic groupings. Paradoxically, while embracing and wanting to be part of a scene that upholds the ideology of PLUR, some respondents note, and in some cases help to create, social and cultural divisions that undermine the "unity." However, other respondents are less concerned about, or are not aware of, this ideology, and instead focus their experiences of the dance scene solely around their own social groups, thus furthering the perceived boundary markers and separation between participants.

When examining the meaning of young Asian American drug consumption in the scene, we found three distinct types of narratives invoked to explain their own drug use. One group notes difficulties arising from their Asian American identities, the experience of culture clash, and stresses associated with acculturation and Americanization, and they view their own substance use as an outgrowth of this. A second group view their drug consumption as unusual among Asian Americans and see their drug use as indicative of the degree to which they've grown apart from Asian culture and toward white/American culture. A third group see neither their identities as Asian Americans, as drug users, nor as Asian American drug users as problematic. Drug use is a normal, accepted, mundane part of their leisure time, not something they view as problematic, shameful, or unusual.

In discussing these narratives, one can sometimes fall into the trap of making sharp contrasts between Asian and American cultures, between host culture and immigrant culture. Our respondents themselves often paint these distinctions as either – or. Yet in this increasingly globalized world such distinctions are increasingly problematic to make.

Given increased globalization and the import and export of cultural products and cultural notions, we can no longer assume that even a new immigrant youth does not have some preconceptions of the culture or cultures he or she is coming into, particularly those notions that are transmitted through the media and popular culture. Furthermore, drug and alcohol use and abuse are not limited to any particular country, although accessibility may vary, and it is a mistake to assume that immigrant youth have had no previous exposure to such behaviors. Nor are Asian American immigrants, even second and third-generation immigrants, cut off from Asian culture after migrating to the US – communication and travel back and forth between Asia and the US are increasingly common, and participants in Asian American club-drug scenes sometimes also participate in such scenes within Asia.

In choosing and creating their lifestyle and, consequently, their identity, immigrant youth today, like other youth groups, are consumers within both a local and global market and are able to connect with developments in youth cultures far beyond the communities in which they live. Through the use of Internet Web sites and chat rooms they can remain informed of new developments in youth cultures whether that be in the field of music, of dance, of dress, or of drugs. As Osgerby has noted:

> Groups of young people far removed from one another in terms of time and space became audiences for the same sets of messages and images and, in many respects, come to share the same cultural vocabulary. By the early nineties, therefore, it was possible for the first time to speak of a "global" dimension to many youth styles and cultures.
>
> (Osgerby 1998: 199)

Young people utilize and adapt features of these global cultures and fuse them with elements from their own more localized cultures in order to create a distinct identity. Their ability to create an identity and an associated lifestyle based on a more global perspective raises important questions for assimilation theorists, who have focused solely on the impact of American culture on more traditional immigrant cultures. While assimilation theorists have focused on immigrants adopting the host culture in favor of their own or their parents' culture, they have failed to consider the extent to which immigrant youth today are able to draw upon many different cultures and create a more distinctive, a more idiosyncratic and hybrid identity. In so doing they no longer follow a linear progression of assimilating, but as Modood (1997) has noted, they are assimilating *on their own terms*. The fact that most of the respondents in our sample negotiate those varying and sometimes conflictual identities points to the complexity and pressures of those often competing cultural attractions and strains. Even when attempting to understand the role of the party scene and club drugs in the lives of Asian Americans, the variations and diversity of experiences that cannot be fully rationalized or explained by ethnic groupings point to the complexity inherent in an analysis of Asian American identity.

Conclusion

The research outlined in *Youth, Drugs, and Nightlife* began in 2001 when we commenced fieldwork in San Francisco and began to interview young people who used club drugs and attended either raves or clubs. As with much sociological research, by the time the results are published the social situation has changed. Since 2001 much has occurred both in the dance scene in San Francisco and in the drug-using habits of the young people whom we interviewed. However, although we began the work nearly eight years ago, our research on San Francisco's nightlife has continued through the present and we have been able to witness changes along the way. Some changes are centered around the inevitable evolution and transformation of musical styles, genres, and preferences. Most significantly for this book, while the club scene, including the electronic dance music (EDM) scene, continues to be strong in San Francisco, raves surely play a far less central role in nightlife now. Other changes, though, are centered in the social and political context surrounding nightlife. For example, as we noted in Chapter 5, issues of nightlife regulation and control have been contentious and in flux over this time period. One key change in this arena in the first decade of the century has been a shift from an emphasis on curbing or controlling drug use to curbing or controlling violence in and around nightlife venues. Undoubtedly, by the time this book arrives on the shelves, further developments in the nighttime economy will have occurred. But the purpose of this book is not solely to chart developments around drug use and this particular dance scene. Many of the themes at the core of this book are ones we feel are important for any sort of research on the drug-using practices of young people and the social contexts and scenes in which this use is embedded. These themes continue to be of importance regardless of the historical nature of some of the research.

As we noted in our introduction, one of the reasons for writing this book, besides documenting the lives and experiences of the young people we interviewed, is to emphasize the necessity of enriching drug epidemiological research with the insights from sociological and cultural studies work on youth cultures. Epidemiological data are essential if we are to understand the wider picture of young people's drug use and also important if we are to chart the emergence and transformation of different drug trends in the US, Europe, and other parts of the globe. But a too heavy reliance on survey methodology nevertheless has some very serious limitations, in spite of its aura of scientific credibility. Too much survey research is conducted in a way that ensures that the research process is divorced from "the human particulars of both researchers and those they studied" (Ferrell *et al.* 2008: 162). In the very process of separating the research process from people, survey research fails to capture the essential nature of human experiences and the meanings associated with doing drugs. With this in mind, we have argued that contemporary epidemiological research omits three critically important features of young peoples' drug use: *context, pleasure,* and *agency* – three features which are inextricably intertwined. These themes are important not only for understanding young people's drug use, but also for policy practitioners committed to encouraging a safer environment within which young people use both legal and illegal substances.

An understanding of the social context in which young people consume their drugs is an essential component if we are to examine the meaning of youthful drug use. In this research the central social context were raves and dance parties, the attendance of which was a central feature of our respondents' leisure activities. As a number of researchers have noted, the nighttime economy has expanded significantly since 1990 (Chatterton and Hollands 2003; Hadfield 2006; Talbot 2007) and this has provided an important focus for youthful leisure practices which has also provided a "greater space of illicit drug use" (Shiner 2009: 236). Therefore, in an attempt to understand the role of drugs within the lives of young people, we must also consider how drugs operate within this environment and comprehend the intrinsically social aspect of their consumption. Our attempt to situate drug use within this social contextual framework did not focus only on the local context, for we also sought to provide an even wider framework within which to understand their drug use. Consequently, we examined the national context and specifically the development of increasing legislative controls not only on ecstasy and other club drugs but also on raves and clubs. Finally, given the extent to which the electronic dance music scene has developed into a global phenomenon, we situated the activities and experiences of our respondents against the backcloth of these global developments. An analysis of the wider perspective illustrates the extent to which the local is influenced by the global as well as the ways in which the global scene relies on borrowing and modifying local cultural practices.

The importance of pleasure in our respondents' drug use was obvious when we came to examine their narratives on the attraction of mind-altering substances. While many researchers in the drug field have played down this element, others (Siegel 1989; Walton 2001) have argued for a long time that the desire to become intoxicated is an age-old pursuit. Although researchers, heavily invested in the problem paradigm, may not wish to acknowledge this central human desire, the importance of getting high and having fun was paramount in the interviews with our respondents. From this we have argued that any analysis of youthful drug use which omits to acknowledge the importance of pleasure fundamentally fails to understand a basic feature of young people's drug consumption. But our discussion of our respondents' desire to have fun did not occur in a social vacuum, for we also emphasized the necessity of situating their desire to consume drugs primarily within the nighttime dance scene. As O'Malley and Mugford (1993) have noted, having fun at night allows them to overcome the mundane, or, as J. Young (1971) argued, it allows them to express their "subterranean values." In fact, drugs and raves can be viewed as a replaying and a reworking of "subcultural experiences of previous generations, signifying a gesture of avoidance and a shirking of adult responsibility in favor of a universe of pleasure and play" (Shiner 2009: 237).

However, while emphasizing the feature of pleasure, we also sought to understand and examine how our respondents viewed the risks associated with drug use. Given the extent to which our sample is a well-educated, middle-class population, it is not that surprising that they were quite aware of possible drawbacks attached to their drug use. These young club-drug users took active steps to understand and mitigate the potential risks that club drugs, in various combinations, pose. But, in addition, we find that the risks associated with drug use, whether that be the illegality of the substance or the negative pharmacological side effects, were sometimes elements that enhanced the attraction and the potential pleasure of the drugs. Risk and pleasure are not completely opposed, as involving oneself in risky activities may itself be pleasurable (Lyng 1990). The more the media and prevention officials emphasized the inherent dangers of drugs, the more some young people wished to experiment. Having tried them and found them to be pleasurable and rarely encountering the dangers they had been warned of, they continued to use. And they carried on using until other factors began to lessen their enjoyment, whether because they no longer frequented the environments where drug use was common, or because continuing to use interfered with other important aspects of their lives, including work, school, or relationships.

In negotiating the arenas within which to use, and deciding on how to balance risk and pleasure, notions of agency were particularly apparent. Unlike media representations of young people, our respondents were not gullible, easily led, or just plain misguided; instead, they were active actors intent on negotiating their lives within certain structural constraints. These constraints operated in different ways for different people, depending on their gender or their ethnicity, among other factors. While young people are often characterized as a homogeneous group, our respondents were not. These differences played an important role in how they experienced drugs. For example, although our analysis revealed similar drug-use rates for women and men, notions of acceptable ways of being intoxicated differed considerably. Furthermore, ethnic differences were also critically important in understanding young people's relationships to drug use. Many of the Asian American respondents exhibited complex relationships with their drug use, which were related to their attempts to construct a stable identity and balance the often conflicting pressures of being more Asian or more American. In both cases, gender and ethnicity operated not just as individual sociodemographic characteristics or markers, but, more important, as socially constructed group determinants.

While noting the general thematic elements that our research revealed, we would not wish to underestimate the specificity of conducting research in the San Francisco Bay area. This book examines the drug use and experiences of a group of young people who attend nighttime events in San Francisco. As we noted in Chapter 5, San Francisco has had a long and varied nightlife history. This history has had an impact on the ways that nightlife has come to be organized. This history is also apparent in how our respondents describe their drug-using experiences. For many of our participants, pleasure in using drugs resided solely in having a good time, but, for others, drug pleasures were more long-term and life-changing. These latter respondents described how the longer-term positive effects produced changes both in how they saw themselves and how they wished to interact with others. Like many others, they wished to transcend the mundane, but they also sought more. For those who sought long-term changes emanating from their drug use, their narratives contained notions of alternative lifestyles or ways of interacting with others that reflected notions of communality and spirituality that have existed in the culture of San Francisco's dance scene for decades – an alternative lifestyle first expressed by the Beatniks of the 1950s and 1960s and then by the Hippies of the 1960s and 1970s and today can be seen in the writings of Burning Man aficionados (J. Beck and Rosenbaum 1994; St. John 2004).

The importance of noting the specificity of the San Francisco dance scene and drug-related practices can be found not solely in how our respondents viewed the significance and meaning of their drug use, it is even apparent in the specific sociodemographic characteristics of our sample. As we saw in Chapter 2, the majority of our sample was white or Asian American and middle class. Missing from the rave and electronic dance music club scene in San Francisco were young, predominantly low-income, Latinos and African Americans. Having an enjoyable time at an organized rave or upscale dance club could be very expensive, especially when one calculated the costs of the entry fees, refreshments, special outfits, and the preferred drug of choice. Such costs were prohibitive for young minority, working-class youth. But issues of cost were not the only factors prohibiting a greater involvement of low-income ethnic-minority youth; cultural issues also played a role. The absence of African American and Latino youth also reflected the lack of appeal of the rave scene for these young people and the alternative attraction of hip-hop. Hip-hop events were more likely to take place in affordable local neighborhood venues and less prevalent at some of the mega-clubs and particularly absent at the raves. However, we do not wish to paint these youth scenes as different or separate from one another.[1] While the "club drugs" discussed throughout this book – and especially ecstasy – have been traditionally associated with the rave and EDM scenes, we do now increasingly see evidence of the popularity of ecstasy in some hip-hop scenes as well. This is particularly the case in San Francisco's hyphy hip-hop scene, in which raps about "thizzing" (using ecstasy) have been popular in recent years. And certainly hip-hop music is not foreign to many of the young men and women we interviewed, regardless of race or class. Indeed, many of the young clubbers in particular were sometimes highly engaged with the hip-hop scene. An important area for future research will be to further explore the linkages, similarities, and differences in the cultures and meanings of drug use in these varying youth cultures and dance/music scenes. Further comparative work on different youth dance and drug scenes in the US is sorely needed.

But the need for comparative qualitative research on drugs and youth cultures does not end at the boundaries of the US. In considering the global nature of dance cultures, we soon realized the importance of studying drugs and youth cultures within a crossnational comparative perspective. Part of the scene's initial impact and its continuing success as a global phenomenon has been its association with a range of illicit substances. In fact, marketing the scene also meant marketing illegal drugs, especially ecstasy, and the belief that a "chemical generation" had developed. However, as noted in Chapter 3, while sociologists, anthropologists, and cultural studies researchers have examined in much detail the development of globalization and "contemporary youth cultural practice" (Pilkington and Johnson 2003), researchers in the drug field have spent much less time examining the global nature of drugs and the dance scene. Nor have they sought to understand the way in which local forces influence global features. Moreover, while some drug research has certainly identified regional variations, much of the work has neglected to examine the extent to which the meaning of drug use within these youthful events contains both similarities and dissimilarities. From our initial attempts to compare the drug-using practices of young people in San Francisco, Hong Kong, and Rotterdam it has become increasingly clear that respondents in these locales share similar motives of pleasure-seeking in consuming ecstasy and topping it up with other drugs in the dance scene. Beyond this, however, we observed that young people in San Francisco, Hong Kong, and Rotterdam attach very different meaning to their drug use. In commencing to chart potential cultural differences in youthful drug use in different parts of the world, we would hope to emphasize the importance of conducting crossnational qualitative research in the future.

Notes

Introduction

1 See for example Orlov (2009). Even in Britain it is certainly not the case that the club scene has waned entirely. Moreover, Measham and Moore (2009) found higher levels of ecstasy and cocaine use in Manchester dance-club surveys than ten years earlier; thus club drug use continues to be strong, at least among those still in the scene.
2 Tammy Anderson has also completed a book on raves and clubs in Philadelphia: *Rave Culture: the alteration and decline of a music scene* (2009). See also Perrone (2009), which is on "club kids" in New York City.
3 Exceptions include Hutton (2006), Jackson (2004), and Measham *et al.* (2001).
4 As we will discuss in Chapter 2 there has been much discussion as to whether raves and related dance scenes represent a distinct subculture (with some theorists proposing instead the concepts of "tribes," "lifestyles," or "scenes," the latter term gaining increasing acceptance in the UK.
5 For a few exceptions of American work engaging with the normalization thesis see Bahora *et al.* (2009) on the normalization of ecstasy in Atlanta, Lankenau and Clatts (2002) on normalization and ketamine in New York, and MacKenzie *et al.* (2005) on normalization of marijuana use among San Francisco gang members.
6 See Michael Shiner's book *Drug Use and Social Change* (2009) for an interesting discussion of the differences in illicit drug use between the US and the UK.

1 Epidemiology meets cultural studies

1 The National Institute on Drug Abuse's (NIDA) classification includes under the heading "club drugs" the following individual substances: ecstasy, LSD, methamphetamine, GHB, ketamine, Rohypnol. This, however, does not necessarily completely match the experiences of drug-using clubgoers. Our own research, for example, has found that other substances, including cocaine, poppers, and magic mushrooms, are popular within the club scene.
2 Although not all epidemiologists work within the social problems emphasis, for the purposes of this chapter we focus on those within the epidemiological tradition that appear most central in the club-drug literature. We must note, though, that some epidemiologists would argue that the frequency of equating drug use with drug abuse is not an inherent tendency of epidemiology, but rather a misuse of it (Duncan 1997; Terris 1987, 1990, 1992).
3 The one city that is an exception to this was Athens, where the rave scene was heavily dominated by men (80 percent).
4 In noting the emphasis in epidemiology on the problematic nature of drug use, we do not wish to give the impression that issues of pleasure have been completely absent in epidemiological research on drugs. See for example Terris (1975).
5 Baudrillard dismissed "the discotheque as the lowest form of contemporary entertainment" (Thornton 1996: 1).

6 For a further discussion of these forms of control see Hunt *et al.* (2000, 2002).
7 This point is also made by Alexander (2000) in her discussion of Asian gang members in the UK.
8 See for example Hutton (2006) and Jackson (2004).

2 Clubbers, candy kids, and jaded ravers

1 Ecstasy is the street name for the drug methylenedioxymethamphetamine (MDMA) (although "ecstasy" is commonly adulterated with other substances as well and is rarely pure MDMA). LSD, commonly called "acid," is the abbreviation for lysergic acid diethylamide. GHB is the abbreviation for gamma-hydroxybutyric acid and Rohypnol is the trade name for the drug flunitrazepam. In addition to these drugs, cocaine and "magic" mushrooms (psylocibin), as well as the most prevalent drug, marijuana, are commonly used drugs in the club setting in our study, despite not being labeled as "club drugs" in official government publications.
2 We use the term "mainstream" here advisedly in the sense that there is no one mainstream or no one alternative. As Thornton (1996) makes clear, the term "mainstream" is a socially constructed category against which, or in opposition to, dance-club attendees construct their own identities. "The mainstream is the entity against which the majority of clubbers define themselves" (Thornton 1996: 5). Consequently given its constructed nature, the precise characteristics of the "mainstream" may be frequently contested.
3 For a similar discussion of the difference between attending raves and being a raver see K. Moore's (2004) discussion of the distinction between going clubbing and being a clubber.
4 All names used to identify participants in this study are pseudonyms, to protect their anonymity.
5 See Hollands (2002) and Northcote (2006) for the importance of bringing together analyses of youth development and transitions (on a more structural/economic level) with youth cultures and nightlife.
6 We additionally collected data on our respondents' use of a variety of other drugs: crack cocaine, heroin, PCP, other pharmaceuticals, and "research" chemicals, although most of these had much, much lower prevalence rates and did not appear to play a major role in the scenes being studied.
7 Here in our definition of "drugs" we are including marijuana and the recreational use of prescription drugs, but not alcohol.
8 Of course we must caution here that the data on lifetime prevalence should be interpreted carefully, as the validity of these data is somewhat unknown. It is difficult for most respondents to accurately recall the number of times they have used a substance over the course of many years, especially when they have used it numerous times. We must also acknowledge the potential difference that might exist between men and women in their estimation of lifetime prevalence, such that some respondents might be more likely to over- or underreport (whether purposefully or unintentionally), and this tendency could be connected to gender, among other factors.

3 Clubbing, drugs, and the dance scene in a global perspective

1 The following discussion is not meant as a definitive history of the development of electronic dance music. Other writers have provided much more comprehensive accounts. See Collin (1997), Reynolds (1999), Shapiro (1999), and Silcott (1999).
2 While noting these origins of the rave scene we should nevertheless remember the cautionary comments made by Connell and Gibson (2003), who argue that there is a tendency for musical histories to identify "authentic origins" in tracing the development of new music scenes. In the case of the rave scene, linking its origins to New York, Chicago, and Detroit implies a more serious musical heritage.

3 There appear to be competing versions as to the origins of house music. For example, Rietveld offers two possibilities. First, "house" referred to the meaning that a special restructuring of songs could be heard only at the Warehouse club. A second meaning is that "house" referred to "a group of partying people" (1998: 17).

4 As it happened Oakenfold, with another friend, had attempted unsuccessfully to introduce house music to London in 1985, as a result of having gone to the Paradise Garage in New York. Later Oakenfold argued that the missing element in 1985 had been ecstasy.

5 The names of the clubs have been altered to ensure their anonymity.

4 Youth, US drug policy, and social control of the dance scene

1 The Illicit Drug Anti-Proliferation Act was signed into law through the PROTECT (Prosecutorial Remedies and other Tools to End the Exploitation of Children Today) Act of 2003 (S. 151, 108th).

2 D. Moore and Valverde call the term club drugs "an unstable array of substances" (2000: 527). NIDA defines "club drugs" as MDMA, GHB, Rohypnol, LSD, ketamine and methamphetamine.

3 Today these numbers appear to be on the rise again (Johnston et al. 2007).

4 Hereinafter we will refer to the Hillory J. Farias and Samantha Reid Date-Rape Drug Prohibition Act of 2000 as the Date-Rape Drug Prohibition Act.

5 The Fariases' family attorney claimed an additional test conducted by a DEA agent contradicted the initial ruling that her death was the result of a GHB overdose. The spokesperson for the family said they had been informed that "according to a DEA report, the amount of GHB in the teen's body was not sufficient to have caused her death" (Rendon 1997: A34).

6 The ecstasy-related death of 18-year-old Leah Betts in 1995 led to a period of intense news media commentary and political debate in the UK.

7 Senator Graham introduced the Ecstasy Anti-Proliferation Act of 2000, which was co-sponsored by both Grassley and Biden.

8 Senator Biden later introduced the 2002 RAVE Act and the subsequent Illicit Drug Anti-Proliferation Act of 2003.

9 Specifically they mounted a class action suit against a plea bargain, resulting from a federal prosecution against two managers and a promoter of the State Palace Theater in New Orleans, charged under the Federal Crack House Statute. The ACLU argued that the banning of these legal objects violated the First Amendment. Ultimately an appeals court agreed with the ACLU and found that the government had violated the First Amendment and had failed to provide conclusive evidence that a ban on such items "would reduce the use of club drugs" (Kardan 2003: 112). Other cases in which the federal government had prosecuted club owners under the Crack House legislation were also defeated.

10 Interestingly enough, because prescription drugs are viewed as beneficial, the consumption of these drugs is not targeted.

5 Uncovering the local

1 In addition to our 2001–03 interviews with those in the dance scene, many interviews in this chapter are taken from our study of changing modes of regulation for San Francisco's nightlife. We interviewed fifteen key informants who represented a variety of stakeholders in the city – police officers, city officials, nightclub owners, DJs, promoters, and managers – in 2007 and 2008. See Moloney et al. (2009).

2 Though the numbers of clubs are taken from our initial mapping of the scene, we have continued studying and collecting data on the nightlife of the city, up through 2008, when our focus was on the changing modes of nightlife regulation. Many of the interviews with nightclub owners, operators, or promoters quoted in this chapter come from this more recent phase of our research.

3 And the "live–work" spaces that have been one of the district's fastest-growing segments are exempt from the city's requirements that developers set aside a percentage of units for affordable housing, thus further contributing to the low- and middle-income housing squeeze in San Francisco (Alejandrino 2000: 9).

4 Of course, this region wasn't empty before the bars, nightclubs, restaurants, etc., started moving in in the 1980s, and it wasn't always dominated by industry. In the first half of the twentieth century working-class families and industry both dominated the region, though by the 1950s the families had largely been pushed out by "urban development" and revitalization strategies, such as the building of the convention center. (See Godfrey 1997 for more on this history.)

5 However, the degree of dominance of branded pubs in the UK is sometimes overstated, and certainly independent pubs continue to exist and open. See Hadfield and Measham (2009) for an overview of the British nighttime economy.

6 For an examination of the uneven history of growth and anti-growth activism in San Francisco see Godfrey (1997).

7 However, the adult entertainment venues/strip clubs in the city (which we're not focusing on in this chapter) tend to be owned by one company located out of state, according to one of our police interviewees.

8 We would not want to imply that low-income residents have not been displaced by gentrification in the SoMa district as well; however, much of this displacement occurred decades ago, prior to more recent expansions in the district (Graham and Guy 2002).

9 The original grand jury report advocating the creation of an Entertainment Commission did address some drug issues, and "harm reduction" is explicitly within the EC's mandate. However there was consensus among the professionals we interviewed (police, city officials, and owners/operators) that drugs just "aren't that big of a problem" in nightclubs in the present moment, and especially not if compared to the problem of violence. Some do compare the present day to the 1990s, when the rise of club drugs did lead to some prominent drug overdoses at clubs. One thing that is not entirely clear, however, is if they're saying (a) drugs are used less, or (b) drugs are still widely used in clubs but it's not really a problem these days (more discreet/fewer health problems), or (c) drugs are a problem but it's dwarfed by the problem of violence.

10 Later, one EC representative complained in an interview, though, that while the EC is receiving a lot of heat recently, the nightclubs that have been the sites of violence were actually ones that were licensed in the police, pre-EC regime. He asks, "So if the police had the ability to proactively, through a magic wand or a piece of paper, make it safer, then how come the violence that we have seen has primarily occurred at venues that the police department gave and conditioned those permits?" (interview).

11 He also presents a middle group – those who aren't starting fights or being blatantly inappropriate, but whose noise (such as loud cellphone conversations outside) infuriate neighbors and bring unwanted regulatory attention (interview).

12 Oakland and Richmond are suburbs across the bay, known for their sizable African American populations and notorious in recent years for gang-related violence.

13 One police officer, who is rather disdainful of the EC in general for being too permissive, laughs at the idea that the EC wouldn't give permits to a hip-hop club, because he thinks they'd give permits to anyone: "If you said you were gonna have baby-throwing contests on the weekends, they'd give you the license" (interview).

6 The "great unmentionable"

1 Whereas Partridge (1978), for example, suggests a more sociocultural explanation, arguing that there exists a long-held European–North American consensus view that illicit drugs are inherently bad because of an intense dislike and mistrust of altered states of consciousness, Tiger (1992) has suggested that industrialized societies have devalued notions of pleasure.

2 One exception to this would be the work of Thornton (1996), who focused less on the internal happenings of the clubs themselves and more on the extent to which rave culture could be characterized as a subculture in the traditional sense.

3 One exception to this would be the work of Jackson (2004), who examines the pleasurable elements of the "clubbing" experience. His focus is on the body and the sensuous and pleasurable experiences of clubbing.

4 However, it is also important to note that some researchers have suggested that taking ecstasy and attending dance events may gradually become routinized themselves and hence predictable and mundane. See for example Reith (2005) and Shewan et al. (2000).

5 This idea has also been examined by Maffesoli (1996) who developed the notion of neotribes.

6 This division based on short-term versus long-term effects has been noted by other researchers. For example, J. Beck and Rosenbaum (1994) examined the extent to which different types of ecstasy users (therapeutically or recreationally oriented) would emphasize short-term versus longer-term effects.

7 Feeling that one now understands the meaning of life is not unusual for drug users. For example, Coleridge, De Quincy, and Huxley all described similar effects for mind-altering drugs (Boon 2002; De Quincy 1971; Huxley 1954).

8 Some researchers have referred to this process of self-improvement as ego-work. See Reith (2005).

9 For a fuller discussion see N. Campbell (2004) and Ortner (1998).

7 Drug use and the meaning of risk

1 For example, see Lyng's (1990) research on edgework.

2 Exceptions include Duff (2003); France (2000); W. Mitchell et al. (2004); and M. Plant and M. L. Plant (1992).

3 While Douglas adopts what can be described as a weak social constructionist model, she does not subscribe to the argument that there are no real dangers – "the reality of the dangers is not at issue" (Douglas 1992: 29).

4 For example, see National Institute on Drug Abuse (2008).

5 For a further discussion see Henderson (1993b) and Hunt et al. (2002).

6 The term comes from Hunter S. Thompson (Lupton 1999a: 151).

7 The transgressive nature of the music can be seen in the UK government's Criminal Justice and Public Order Act (1994), which defined rave music as "music that includes sounds wholly or predominantly characterised by the emission of a succession of repetitive beats" (Presdee 2000: 117).

8 See also Hutton (2006) for an analysis of the gendered aspects of this, in which she examines the pleasures women clubbers take in their risky behaviors.

8 Combining different substances in the dance scene

1 Many researchers in the US suggest that the term "polydrug" became common parlance as a result of the federal government's increasing concern about multiple drug use in the early 1970s. See Bourne (1974).

2 Johnston (1975) notes this as a component of the cultural debate surrounding the legalization of marijuana.

3 One possible reason for this may be separation between research on alcohol and illicit drugs. See Hunt and Barker (2001).

4 The other definitions of polydrug use include effects (Sidney Cohen 1981) and specific combinations (Leri et al. 2003).

5 Exceptions to this include Boeri et al. (2008), B. C. Kelly (2007), and Schensul et al. (2005b).

6 For a further discussion of notions of time see Munn (1992).

9 Drugs, gender, sexuality, and accountability in the world of raves

1 However, some (e.g. Measham *et al.* 2001) worry that this work that focuses on women's pleasures could fall prey to fueling the ideas of women drug users as selfish hedonists. Still others, though, ask, "What's wrong with women selfishly seeking pleasure through the use of drugs ... What's wrong with the pursuit of pleasure?" (Hutton 2006: 23).
2 Moore (2007), however, points out that Hutton problematically dichotomizes mainstream and underground clubs and, while Hutton (2006) emphasizes the agency of women in the underground scenes, she may be ignoring the agency of "mainstream" women.
3 For more on young women, sexuality, and being a "spectacle" see Skeggs (2003).
4 This same problem is found in appropriations of the concept of "gender performativity," despite the fact that gender performativity as initially theorized by J. Butler (1990, 1995) is explicitly distinguished from optional performance. For more on the connections between the accomplishment or doing of gender and gender performativity see Moloney and Fenstermaker (2002).
5 For a different example of young women policing each other's sexual behaviors, with parallels but in a different social context (that of female gangs), see Joe-Laidler and Hunt (2001).

10 Alcohol, gender, and social context

1 Studies of alcohol use in the UK have demonstrated that patterns of men's and women's behavior may be converging (see, e.g., M. L. Plant and M. Plant 2001; Williamson *et al.* 2003). Other European researchers have posited that this convergence in drinking patterns may be the result of a convergence of male and female gender roles, and a broadening of the types of arenas to which women have access (Bloomfield *et al.* 2001); however, their results indicated that, of the four countries they studied, only one, Finland, demonstrated patterns of gender convergence of alcohol use. Future research needs to focus on the effect of changing gender roles and norms on patterns of alcohol use, as the topic is the subject of considerable dispute in the field of alcohol research (see, e.g., Holmila and Raitasalo 2005; M. L. Plant 2008).
2 However, in spite of the importance of social context or social setting on the resulting behaviors, a number of researchers have remarked on the extent to which the elements of social context have lacked conceptual clarity. For example, Fagan noted that the social processes within social contexts that influence alcohol-related violence "have been only vaguely specified" (1993: 163). Duff has argued that "the precise nature of social contexts remains uncertain, typically reduced to some vague notion of background, culture or setting ... the provenance and ontology of contexts remains unclear" (2007: 504).

11 Asian American youth

1 The South Asian category includes those of Indian, Pakistani, Bangladeshi, and Sri Lankan descent. The Southeast Asian category includes those of Hmong, Indonesian, Laotian, Malaysian, Thai, Vietnamese, and Cambodian descent.
2 For more on the quantitative analysis of our CDA data see Fazio *et al.* (in press), which focuses additionally on significant differences within Asian American drug use along the lines of gender and sexual orientation.
3 In our initial sample of fifty-six Asian Americans – close to half (twenty-four) are in primarily Asian groups, fourteen are in mixed-ethnicity groups, and the remainder did not specify.
4 As of the 2000 U.S. census, 49.2% of Asian Americans are foreign born (first generation), and 23.7% are the children of immigrants (second generation) (Logan 2001 Cited in Min 2006).

5 For analysis and critique of acculturation perspectives see Alba and Nee (2003) and Kivisto (2005). Assimilation theorists have developed more sophisticated models over the years, for example Portes and Zhou's (1993) segmented assimilation approach. Yet even these more sophisticated models do not escape all of the problems identified by assimilation theory's critics, discussed in the next section.

6 Shiner and Newburn (1999) use this data to argue *against* the normalization thesis, demonstrating that in neither the US nor in Great Britain has illicit drug use become a majority activity. We agree with them about the dangers of exaggerating these claims. However, they do point out that drug use is on the rise among youth in both countries and additionally point to the importance of focusing not just on prevalence statistics but also on the attitudes of the youth themselves. It is to the latter type of analysis that we are confining our comments about normalization. Our sampling frame explicitly excluded non-drug users, so we are making no claims about overall trends in drug use among Asian Americans. Instead, we will examine attitudes about and perceptions of normalization among this sample of drug-experienced Asian Americans (most of whom do not think they differ much from Asian American youth at large).

7 This idea of alcohol being particularly dominant in the Indian community was commonly mentioned in the interviews, and in our quantitative analysis of the second, larger sample we found that 100 percent of our South Asian respondents were current users of hard alcohol (whereas for all other ethnic groups the range was from 70 percent to 79 percent).

Conclusion

1 See also the work of Sterk *et al.* (2006, 2007) on the significant involvement of African American youth in the dance scene in Atlanta, as well as Maira's (1998) work in New York, highlighting the importance of hip-hop in the dance culture of young South Asians.

Bibliography

Abbott-Chapman, J., and Denholm, C. (2001) "Adolescents' risk activities, risk hierarchies and the influence of religiosity," *Journal of Youth Studies*, 4: 279–97.

Adlaf, E., and Smart, R. G. (1997) "Party subculture or dens of doom? An epidemiological study of rave attendance and drug use patterns among adolescent students," *Journal of Psychoactive Drugs*, 29: 193–98.

Agar, M., and Reisinger, H. S. (2003) "Going for the global: the case of ecstasy," *Human Organization*, 62: 1–11.

Aitchison, C. (2004) "From policy to place: theoretical explorations of gender–leisure relations in everyday life," in W. Mitchell, R. Bunton, and E. Green (eds) *Young People, Risk and Leisure: constructing identities in everyday life*, Basingstoke: Palgrave Macmillan.

Akram, G., and Galt, M. (1999) "A profile of harm-reduction practices and co-use of illicit and licit drugs amongst users of dance drugs," *Drugs: Education, Prevention and Policy*, 6: 215–25.

Alba, R., and Nee, V. (1997) "Rethinking assimilation theory for a new era of immigration," *International Migration Review*, 31: 826–74.

Alba, R., and Nee, V. (2003) *Remaking the American Mainstream: assimilation and contemporary immigration*, Cambridge, MA: Harvard University Press.

Alejandrino, S. V. (2000) *Gentrification in San Francisco's Mission District: indicators and policy recommendations*, San Francisco, CA: Mission Economic Development Association (MEDA).

Alexander, C. E. (2000) *The Asian Gang: ethnicity, identity, masculinity*, Oxford: Berg.

Algemeen Dagblad (1992) "Gabbers komen er niet in" (Gabbers not allowed), *Algemeen Dagblad*, March 31, p. 15.

Allott, K., and Redman, J. (2006) "Patterns of use and harm reduction practices of ecstasy users in Australia," *Drug and Alcohol Dependence*, 82: 168–76.

Amodeo, M., Robb, N., Peou, S., and Tran, H. (1997) "Alcohol and other drug problems among Southeast Asians: patterns of use and approaches to assessment and intervention," *Alcoholism Treatment Quarterly*, 15: 63–77.

Anderson, T. (2008) "Introduction," in T. Anderson (ed.) *Neither Villain nor Victim: empowerment and agency among women substance abusers*, New Brunswick, NJ: Rutgers University Press.

Anderson, T. (2009) *Rave Culture: the alteration and decline of a music scene*, Philadelphia, PA: Temple University Press.

Appadurai, A. (ed.) (1986a) *The Social Life of Things: commodities in cultural perspective*, Cambridge: Cambridge University Press.

Appadurai, A. (1986b) "Introduction: commodities and the politics of value," in A. Appadurai (ed.) *The Social Life of Things: commodities in cultural perspective*, Cambridge: Cambridge University Press.

Armstrong, D. (1995) "The rise of surveillance medicine," *Sociology of Health and Illness*, 17: 393–404.

Armstrong, S. (2004) *The White Island: two thousand years of pleasure in Ibiza*, London: Bantam Press.

Asghar, K., and DeSouza, E. (eds) (1989) *Pharmacology and Toxicology of Amphetamine and Related Designer Drugs*, NIDA Research Monograph No. 94, Rockville, MD: National Institute on Drug Abuse.

Associated Press (1984) "Fourteen San Francisco sex clubs told to close to curb AIDS," *New York Times*, October 10. Online. Available HTTP: <http://query.nytimes.com/gst/fullpage.html?sec=health&res=9B04EED6133BF933A25753C1A962948260&n=Top/News/Health/Diseases,%20Conditions,%20and%20Health%20Topics/AIDS> (accessed December 17, 2008).

Austin, G. A. (1999) "Current evidence on substance abuse among Asian-American youth," in B. W. K. Yee, N. Mokua, and S. Kim (eds) *Developing Cultural Competence in Asian-American and Pacific Islander Communities: opportunities in primary health care and substance abuse prevention*, Washington, DC: Center for Substance Abuse Prevention.

Avery, A. P. (2005) "'I feel that I'm freer to show my feminine side': folklore and alternative masculinities in a rave scene," in S. J. Bronner (ed.) *Manly Traditions: the folk roots of American masculinities*, Bloomington, IN: Indiana University Press.

Avni, S. (2001) "Pulse of the city," *San Francisco Magazine*, 48: 81–91.

Back, L. (1996) *New Ethnicities and Urban Culture: racisms and multiculture in young lives*, New York, NY: St. Martin's Press.

Bahora, M., Sterk, C. E., and Elifson, K. W. (2009) "Understanding recreational ecstasy use in the United States: a qualitative inquiry," *International Journal of Drug Policy*, 20: 62–69.

Barker, J. C., Hunt, G., Evans, K., Harris, S., and Earnest, G. (n.d.) "The GHB experience: convergent results from two qualitative studies," unpublished paper.

Barnes, J. S., and Bennett, C. E. (2002) "The Asian population, 2000," US Census. Online. Available HTTP: <http://www.census.gov/prod/2002pubs/c2kbr01–16.pdf> (accessed December 17, 2008).

Barrett, S. P., Gross, S. R., Garand, I., and Pihl, R. O. (2005) "Patterns of simultaneous polysubstance use in Canadian rave attendees," *Substance Use and Misuse*, 40: 1525–37.

Barringer, H. R., Gardner, R. W., and Levin, M. J. (eds) (1993) *Asian and Pacific Islanders in the United States*, New York, NY: Russell Sage Foundation.

Barth, F. (ed.) (1969) *Ethnic Groups and Boundaries*, Boston, MA: Little Brown.

Bauman, Z. (1998) *Globalization: the human consequences*, Cambridge: Polity Press.

Beck, J., and Rosenbaum, M. (1994) *Pursuit of Ecstasy: the MDMA experience*, Albany, NY: State University of New York Press.

Beck, U. (1992) *Risk Society: towards a new modernity*, London: Sage Publications.

Beck, U. (1994) "The reinvention of politics: towards a theory of reflexive modernization," in U. Beck, A. Giddens, and S. Lash (eds) *Reflexive Modernization: politics, tradition and aesthetics in the modern social order*, Cambridge: Polity Press.

Beck, U. (1995) *Ecological Politics in the Age of Risk*, Cambridge: Polity Press.

Beck, U. (1996) "Risk society and the provident state," in S. Lash, B. Szerszynski, and B. Wynne (eds) *Risk, Environment and Modernity: towards a new ecology*, London: Sage Publications.

Bennett, A. (1999a) "Hip hop am Main: the localization of rap music and hip-hop culture," *Media, Culture and Society*, 21: 77–91.

Bennett, A. (1999b) "Subcultures or neo-tribes? Rethinking the relationship between youth, style and musical taste," *Sociology*, 33: 599–617.

Bennett, A. (2000) *Popular Music and Youth Culture: music, identity and place*, New York, NY: St. Martin's Press.

Berridge, V. (1988) "The origins of the English drug 'scene', 1880–1930," *Medical History*, 32: 51–64.

Berry, J. W., Kim, U., Minde, T., and Mok, D. (1987) "Comparative studies of acculturative stress," *International Migration Review*, 21: 491–511.

Bhattacharya, G. (2002) "Drug abuse risks for acculturating immigrant adolescents: case study of Asian Indians in the United States," *Health and Social Work*, 27: 175–83.

Bhattacharya, G. (2004) "Health care seeking for HIV/AIDS among south Asians in the United States," *Health and Social Work*, 29: 106–15.

Bhattacharya, G., and Schoppelrey, S. L. (2004) "Preimmigration beliefs of life success, post-immigration experiences, and acculturative stress: South Asian immigrants in the United States," *Journal of Immigrant Health*, 6: 83–92.

Biden, J. (2002) "Biden Bill targets rave promoters who seek to profit by putting teens at risk," press release, June 18. Online. Available HTTP: <http://biden.senate.gov/press/press_releases/release/?id=938608fa-5095-47fd-8d15-97a4e5b5791b> (accessed 16 December 2008).

Blackman, S. (2004) *Chilling out: the cultural politics of substance consumption, youth and drug policy*, New York, NY: Open University Press.

Bloomfield, K., Gmel, G., Neve, R., and Mustonen, H. (2001) "Investigating gender convergence in alcohol consumption in Finland, Germany, the Netherlands, and Switzerland: a repeated survey analysis," *Substance Abuse*, 22: 39–53.

Boeri, M. W., Sterk, C. E., Bahora, M., and Elifson, K. W. (2008) "Poly-drug use among ecstasy users: separate, synergistic, and indiscriminate patterns," *Journal of Drug Issues*, 38: 517–42.

Bogren, A. (2008) "Women's intoxication as 'dual licentiousness': an exploration of gendered images of drinking and intoxication in Sweden," *Addiction Research and Theory*, 16: 95–106.

Boon, M. (2002) *The Road of Excess: a history of writers on drugs*, Cambridge, MA: Harvard University Press.

Bourdieu, P. (1984) *Distinction: a social critique of the judgement of taste*, London: Routledge.

Bourgois, P. (1996) *In Search of Respect: selling crack in el barrio*, New York, NY: Cambridge University Press.

Bourne, P. G. (1974) "Polydrug abuse: considerations in a national strategy," *American Journal of Drug and Alcohol Abuse*, 1: 147–58.

Boys, A., Lenton, S., and Norcross, K. (1997) "Polydrug use at raves by a Western Australian sample," *Drug and Alcohol Review*, 16: 227–34.

Bradbury, J. A. (1989) "The policy implications of differing concepts of risk," *Science, Technology and Human Values*, 14: 380–99.

Brewster, B., and Boughton, F. (1999) *Last night a DJ saved my life*, New York, NY: Grove Press.

Broom, D. H. (1995) "Rethinking gender and drugs," *Drug and Alcohol Review*, 14: 411–15.

Brown, J. (2003) "Your glowstick could land you in jail: the latest incarnation of the Rave Act punishes drug users and bystanders alike – and tramples civil liberties," Salon.com, April 16.

Online. Available HTTP: <http://dir.salon.com/story/mwt/feature/2003/04/16/rave/index. html> (accessed December 16, 2008).

Bucholtz, M. (2002) "Youth and cultural practice," *Annual Review of Anthropology*, 31: 525–52.

Bukoski, W. J. (1991) "A framework for drug abuse prevention research," in C. G. Leukefeld and W. J. Bukoski (eds) *Drug Abuse Prevention Intervention Research: methodological issues*, NIDA Research Monograph No. 107, Rockville, MD: National Institute on Drug Abuse.

Bulwa, D. (2008) "New violence draws safety warning to SF clubs," *San Francisco Chronicle*, January 18. Online. Available HTTP: <http://www.sfgate.com/cgi-bin/article/article?f=/c/a/2008/01/18/BALMUHAP4.DTL> (accessed December 16 2008).

Bunton, R., and Burrows, R. (1995) "Consumption and health in the 'epidemiological' clinic of late modern medicine," in R. Bunton, S. Nettleton, and R. Burrows (eds) *The Sociology of Health Promotion: critical analyses of consumption, lifestyle and risk*, New York, NY: Routledge.

Bunton, R., Crawshaw, P., and Green, E. (2004a) "Risk, gender and youthful bodies," in W. Mitchell, R. Bunton, and E. Green (eds) *Young People, Risk and Leisure: constructing identities in everyday life*, Basingstoke: Palgrave Macmillan.

Bunton, R., Green, E., and Mitchell, W. (2004b) "Introduction. Young people, risk and leisure: an overview," in W. Mitchell, R. Bunton, and E. Green (eds) *Young People, Risk and Leisure: constructing identities in everyday life*, Basingstoke: Palgrave Macmillan.

Burns, T. F. (1980) "Getting rowdy with the boys," *Journal of Drug Issues*, 10: 273–86.

Butler, J. (1990) *Gender Trouble: feminism and the subversion of identity*, New York, NY: Routledge.

Butler, J. (1995) *Bodies that Matter*, New York, NY: Routledge.

Butler, M. J. (2006) *Unlocking the Groove: rhythm, meter, and musical design in electronic dance music*, Bloomington, IN: Indiana University Press.

Byqvist, S. (1999) "Polydrug misuse in Sweden: gender differences," *Substance Use and Misuse*, 34: 195–216.

Caetano, R. (1987) "Acculturation and drinking patterns among US Hispanics," *British Journal of Addiction*, 82: 789–99.

Caetano, R., and Mora, M. E. (1988) "Acculturation and drinking among people of Mexican descent in Mexico and the United States," *Journal of Studies on Alcohol*, 49: 462–71.

Calafat, A., Fernández, C., Juan, M., Bellis, M. A., Bohrn, K., Hakkarainen, P., Kilfoyle-Carrington, M., Kokkevi, A., Maalsté, N., Mendes, F., Siamou, I., Simon, J., Stocco, P., and Zavatti, P. (2001) *Risk and Control in the Recreational Drug Culture: SONAR project*, Palma de Mallorca: IREFREA.

Campbell, C. (1989) *The Romantic Ethic and the Spirit of Modern Consumerism*, Oxford: Blackwell.

Campbell, N. (ed.) (2004) *American Youth Cultures*, New York, NY: Routledge.

Campbell, N. D. (2000) *Using Women: gender, drug policy, and social injustice*, New York, NY: Routledge.

Carrington, B., and Wilson, B. (2002) "Global clubcultures: cultural flows and late modern dance music culture," in M. Cieslik and G. Pollock (eds) *Young People in Risk Society: the restructuring of youth identities and transitions in late modernity*, Burlington, VT: Ashgate Publishing.

Carrington, B., and Wilson, B. (2004) "Dance nations: rethinking youth subcultural theory," in A. Bennett and K. Kahn-Harris (eds) *After Subculture: critical studies in contemporary youth culture*, Basingstoke: Palgrave Macmillan.

Cavan, S. (1972) *Hippies of the Haight*, St. Louis, MI: New Critics Press.

Celentano, D., Valleroy, L., Sifakis, F., Mackellar, D., Hylton, J., Thiede, H., McFarland, W., Shehan, D., Stoyanoff, S., Lalota, M., Koblin, B., Katz, M., and Torian, L. (2005) "Associations between substance use and sexual risk among very young men who have sex with men," *Sexually Transmitted Diseases*, 33: 1–7.

Chagnon, N. A. (1977; 3rd edn 1983) *Yanomamö: the fierce people*, New York, NY: Holt Rinehart & Winston.

Chatterton, P., and Hollands, R. (2002) "Theorising urban playscapes: producing, regulating and consuming youthful nightlife city spaces," *Urban Studies*, 39: 95–116.

Chatterton, P., and Hollands, R. (2003) *Urban Nightscapes: youth cultures, pleasure spaces and corporate power*, London: Routledge.

Chonin, N. (2002) "The beat goes on: SF's dance scene survived the blows," *San Francisco Chronicle*, March 10. Online. Available HTTP: <http://www.sfgate.com/cgi-bin/article.cgi?f=/c/a/2002/03/10/PK183434.DTL> (accessed December 18, 2008).

Cieslik, M., and Pollock, G. (eds) (2002) *Young People in Risk Society: the restructuring of youth identities and transitions in late modernity*, Burlington, VT: Ashgate Publishing.

Coffield, F., and Gofton, L. (1994) *Drugs and Young People*, London: Institute for Public Policy Research.

Cohen, Sidney (1981) *The Substance Abuse Problems*, New York, NY: Haworth Press.

Cohen, Stanley, and Taylor, L. (1976; 2nd edn 1992) *Escape Attempts: the theory and practice of resistance to everyday life*, New York, NY: Routledge.

Colfax, G., Coates, T. J., Husnik, M. J., Huang, Y., Buchbinder, S., Koblin, B., Chesney, M., Vittinghoff, E., and EXPLORE Study Team (2005) "The role of poly-substance use in high-risk sex: longitudinal patterns of methamphetamine, popper (amyl nitrite), and cocaine use and high-risk sexual behavior among a cohort of San Francisco men who have sex with men," *Journal of Urban Health: Bulletin of the New York Academy of Medicine*, 82: i62–i70.

Collin, M. (1997; 2nd edn 1998) *Altered State: the story of ecstasy culture and Acid House*, London: Serpent's Tail.

Collins, P. (1998) "Negotiating selves: reflections on 'unstructured' interviewing," *Sociological Research Online*, 3: 1–21.

Collins, R. L., Ellickson, P. L., and Bell, R. M. (1999) "Simultaneous polydrug use among teens: prevalence and predictors," *Journal of Substance Abuse*, 10: 233–53.

Collison, M. (1996) "In search of the high life: drugs, crime, masculinities and consumption," *British Journal of Criminology*, 36: 428–44.

Community Epidemiology Work Group (1995) *Epidemiological Trends in Drug Abuse: advance report*, Rockville, MD: National Institute on Drug Abuse.

Community Epidemiology Work Group (2001) *Epidemiologic Trends in Drug Abuse*, Vol. I, *Highlights and Executive Summary*, Rockville, MD: National Institute on Drug Abuse.

Connell, J., and Gibson, C. (2003) *Sound Tracks: popular music, identity and place*, London: Routledge.

Crane, D. (2002) "Culture and globalization: theoretical models and emerging trends," in D. Crane, N. Kawashima, and K. Kawasaki (eds) *Global Culture: media, arts, policy, and globalization*, New York, NY: Routledge.

Critcher, C. (2000) "'Still raving': social reaction to ecstasy," *Leisure Studies*, 19: 145–62.

Critcher, C. (2003) *Moral Panics and the Media*, Buckingham: Open University Press.

D'Andrea, A. (2007) *Global Nomads: techno and new age as transnational countercultures in Ibiza and Goa*, New York, NY: Routledge.

De Quincey, T. (1971) *Confessions of an English Opium Eater*, New York, NY: Penguin Classics.

Deehan, A., and Saville, E. (2003) "Calculating the risk: recreational drug use among clubbers in the south-east of England," Home Office Online Report 43/03. Online. Available HTTP: <http://rds.homeoffice.gov.uk/rds/pdfs2/rdsolr4303.pdf> (accessed January 20, 2009).

Degenhardt, L. (2005) "Drug use and risk behaviour among regular ecstasy users: does sexuality make a difference?" *Culture, Health and Sexuality: An International Journal for Research, Intervention and Care*, 7: 599–614.

Degenhardt, L., Barker, B., and Topp, L. (2004) "Patterns of ecstasy use in Australia: findings from a national household survey," *Society for the Study of Addiction*, 99: 187–95.

Dibbets, H. (1988) "De terreur van the summer of love," *Haagse Post*, August 20.

Diebold, D. (1988) *Tribal Rites: San Francisco's dance music phenomenon, 1978–1988*, Northridge, CA: Time Warp.

Dobkin de Rios, M. (1990) *Hallucinogens: cross-cultural perspectives*, Prospect Heights, IL: Waveland Press.

Dore, M. H. (2002) "Targeting ecstasy use at raves," *Virginia Law Review*, 88: 1583–623.

Douglas, M. (1966) *Purity and Danger: an analysis of the concepts of pollution and taboo*, London: Routledge.

Douglas, M. (1985) *Risk: acceptability according to the social sciences*, London: Routledge.

Douglas, M. (1992) *Risk and Blame: essays in cultural theory*, London: Routledge.

Douglass, F. M., and Khavari, K. A. (1978) "The drug use index: a measure of the extent of polydrug usage," *International Journal of the Addictions*, 13: 987–93.

Dowling, G. P. (1990) "Human deaths and toxic reactions attributed to MDMA and MDEA," in S. J. Peroutka (ed.) *Ecstasy: the clinical, pharmacological and neurotoxicological effects of the drug MDMA*, Boston, MA: Kluwer.

Drug Abuse Warning Network (2004) "Club drugs, 2002 update," *The DAWN Report*, July. Substance Abuse and Mental Health Services Administration, Office of Applied Studies. Online. Available HTTP: <http://www.oas.samhsa.gov/2k4/clubDrugs/clubDrugs.pdf> (accessed January 21, 2009).

Drug Enforcement Administration (2000) "Drug statistics: DEA meth lab seizures, national totals," US Department of Justice and Drug Enforcement Administration. Online. Available HTTP: <http://web.archive.org/web/20010405143136/http://www.usdoj.gov/dea/stats/drugstats.htm> (accessed April 16, 2008).

Drug Policy Alliance Network (2003) "Legislative history of the Rave Act." Online. Available HTTP: <http://www.drugpolicy.org/communities/raveact/legislative/> (accessed December 16, 2008).

Duff, C. (2003) "The importance of culture and context: rethinking risk and risk management in young drug using populations," *Health, Risk and Society*, 5: 285–99.

Duff, C. (2005) "Party drugs and party people: examining the 'normalization' of recreational drug use in Melbourne, Australia," *International Journal of Drug Policy*, 16: 161–70.

Duff, C. (2007) "Towards a theory of drug use contexts: space, embodiment and practice," *Addiction Research and Theory*, 15: 503–19.

Duff, C. (2008) "The pleasure in context," *International Journal of Drug Policy*, 19: 384–92.

Duncan, D. F. (1997) "Uses and misuses of epidemiology in assessing drug policy," *Journal of Primary Prevention*, 17: 375–82.

Dyson, M. E. (2007) *Know what I mean? Reflections on hip-hop*, New York, NY: Basic Civitas Books.

Earleywine, M., and Newcomb, M. D. (1997) "Concurrent versus simultaneous polydrug use: prevalence, correlates, discriminant validity and prospective effects on health outcomes," *Experimental and Clinical Psychopharmacology*, 5: 353–64.

Eliade, M. (1964) *Shamanism: archaic techniques of ecstasy*, Princeton, NJ: Princeton University Press.

Eliscu, J. (2001) "The war on raves," *Rolling Stone Magazine*, 869: 21, May 24.

English, Camper (2004) "Bad reputation, or, How to shut down nightlife and why we shouldn't," *San Francisco Bay Guardian*, June 16–22, 38/38. Online. Available HTTP: <http://www.sfbg.com/38/38/cover_nightlife.html>.

Epstein, J. S. (ed.) (1994) *Adolescents and their Music: if it's too loud, you're too old*, New York: Garland Publishing.

Espiritu, Y. L. (1992) *Asian American Panethnicity: bridging institutions and identities*, Philadelphia, PA: Temple University Press.

Ettorre, E. (1992) *Women and Substance Use*, New Brunswick, NJ: Rutgers University Press.

Ettorre, E., and Miles, S. (2002) "Young people, drug use and the consumption of health," in S. Hendersen and A. Petersen (eds), *Consuming Health: The Commodification of Health Care*, London: Routledge.

European Monitoring Centre for Drugs and Drug Addiction (1997) *New Trends in Synthetic Drugs in the EU: epidemiology and demand-reduction responses*, Insights series 1, Lisbon: EMCDDA.

European Monitoring Centre for Drugs and Drug Addiction (2002) *Report on the Risk Assessment of Ketamine in the Framework of the Joint Action on New Synthetic Drugs*, Risk Assessments series 3, Luxembourg: Office for Official Publications of the European Communities. Online. Available HTTP: <http://www.emcdda.europa.eu/html.cfm/index33341EN.html> (accessed December 2, 2008).

European Monitoring Centre for Drugs and Drug Addiction (2007) "Annual report, 2006. The state of the drugs problem in Europe," EMCDDA. Online. Available HTTP: <http://ar2006.emcdda.europa.eu/en/home-en.html> (accessed August 20, 2007).

experiencefestival.com

Fagan, J. (1993) "Set and setting revisited: influences of alcohol and illicit drugs on the social context of violent events," in S. E. Martin (ed.) *Alcohol and Interpersonal Violence: fostering multidisciplinary perspectives*, Rockville, MD: US Department of Health and Human Services.

Fazio, A., Joe-Laidler, K., Moloney, M., and Hunt, G. (in press) "Gender, sexuality, and ethnicity as factors of club drug use among Asian Americans," *Journal of Drug Issues*.

Fenstermaker, S., West, C., and Zimmerman, D. H. (1991) "Gender inequality: new conceptual terrain," in R. L. Blumberg (ed.) *Gender, Family and Economy: the triple overlap*, Newbury Park, CA: Sage Publications.

Ferrell, J., Hayward, K., and Young, J. (2008) *Cultural Criminology: an invitation*, Los Angeles, CA: Sage Publications.

Fikentscher, K. (2000) *"You better work!" Underground dance music in New York City*, Hanover, CT: Wesleyan University Press.

Fillmore, K. M. (1984) "'When angels fall': women's drinking as a cultural preoccupation and as reality," in S. C. Wilsnack and L. J. Beckman (eds) *Alcohol Problems in Women: antecedents, consequences, and intervention*, New York, NY: Guilford Press.

Finch, E., and Munro, V. E. (2007) "The demon drink and the demonized woman: socio-sexual stereotypes and responsibility attribution in rape trials involving intoxicants," *Social Legal Studies*, 16: 591–614.

Foderaro, L. W. (1988) "Psychedelic drug called ecstasy gains popularity in Manhattan nightclubs," *New York Times*, December 11, p. 26.

Forsyth, A. J. M. (1996) "Places and patterns of drug use in the Scottish dance scene," *Addiction*, 91: 511–21.

Foxcroft, D. R., and Lowe, G. (1997) "Adolescents' alcohol use and misuse: the socializing influence of perceived family life," *Drugs: Education, Prevention and Policy*, 4: 215–29.

France, A. (1998) "'Why should we care?' Young people, citizenship and questions of social responsibility," *Journal of Youth Studies*, 1: 97–111.

France, A. (2000) "Towards a sociological understanding of youth and their risk-taking," *Journal of Youth Studies*, 3: 317–31.

Fritz, J. (2000) *Rave Culture: an insider's overview*, Victoria, BC: SmallFry.

Furlong, A., and Cartmel, F. (1997) *Young People and Social Change: individualization and risk in late modernity*, Buckingham: Open University Press.

Furst, P. T. (1976) *Hallucinogens and Culture*, Novato, CA: Chandler & Sharp.

Galanter, M. (1974) "Why the 'haves' come out ahead: speculations on the limits of legal change," *Law and Society Review*, 9: 95–160.

Garofoli, J. (2002) "A push for the right to party loudly in SF," *San Francisco Chronicle*, July 1. Online. Available HTTP: <http://www.sfgate.com/cgi-bin/article.cgi?f=/c/a/2002/07/01/BA235663.DTL> (accessed December 10, 2008).

Garratt, S. (1998) *Adventures in Wonderland: a decade of club culture*, London: Headline.

Gautier, F. (2004) "Rapturous ruptures: the 'instituant' religious experience of rave," in G. St. John (ed.) *Rave Culture and Religion*, London: Routledge.

George, W. H., Cue, K. L., Lopez, P. A., Crowe, L. C., and Norris, J. (1995) "Self-reported alcohol expectancies and postdrinking sexual inferences about women," *Journal of Applied Social Psychology*, 25: 164–86.

Gibson, C. (1999) "Subversive sites: rave culture, spatial politics and the Internet in Sydney, Australia," *Area*, 31: 19–33.

Giddens, A. (1990) *The Consequences of Modernity*, Stanford, CA: Stanford University Press.

Giddens, A. (1991) *Modernity and Self-identity: self and society in the late modern age*, Stanford, CA: Stanford University Press.

Giddens, A. (1994) "Living in a post-traditional society," in U. Beck, A. Giddens, and S. Lash (eds) *Reflexive Modernization: politics, tradition and aesthetics in the modern social order*, Cambridge: Polity Press.

Giddens, A. (1998) "Risk society: the context of British politics," in J. Franklin (ed.) *The Politics of Risk Society*, Cambridge: Polity Press.

Gilbert, J., and Pearson, E. (1999) *Discographies: dance music, culture and the politics of sound*, New York, NY: Routledge.

Gilroy, P. (1987) *There ain't no black in the union jack: the cultural politics of race and nation*, London: Unwin Hyman.

Gilroy, P. (1993) *The Back Atlantic: modernity and double consciousness*, Cambridge, MA: Harvard University Press.

Giroux, H. A. (2000) "Disposable youth/disposable futures: the crisis of politics and public life," in N. Campbell (ed.) *American Youth Cultures*, New York, NY: Routledge.

Giulianotti, R. (1997) "Drugs and the media in the era of postmodernity: an archaeological analysis," *Media, Culture and Society*, 19: 413–39.

Glassner, B., and Loughlin, J. (1987) *Drugs in Adolescent Worlds: burnout to straights*, New York, NY: Palgrave Macmillan.

Glazer, N. (1993) "Is assimilation dead?" *Annals of the American Academy of Political and Social Science*, 530: 122–36.

Godfrey, B. J. (1997) "Urban development and redevelopment in San Francisco," *Geographical Review*, 87: 309–33.

Goffman, E. (1963) *Stigma: notes on the management of spoiled identity*, Englewood Cliffs, NJ: Prentice-Hall.

Gordon, M. M. (1964) *Assimilation in American Life*, New York, NY: Oxford University Press.

Goss, J. (2001) "Designer drugs: assess and manage patients intoxicated with ecstasy, GHB, or rohypnol – the three most commonly abused designer drugs," *Journal of Emergency Medicine*, 26: 84–93.

Graham, S., and Guy, S. (2002) "Digital space meets urban place: sociotechnologies of urban restructuring in downtown San Francisco," *City: Analysis of Urban Trends, Culture, Theory, Policy, Action*, 6: 369–82.

Green, A. I. (2007) "On the horns of a dilemma: institutional dimensions of the sexual career in a sample of middle-class, urban, black, gay men," *Journal of Black Studies*, 37: 753–74.

Green, A. I., and Halkitis, P. N. (2006) "Crystal methamphetamine and sexual sociality in an urban gay subculture: an elective affinity," *Culture, Health and Sexuality: an international journal for research, intervention and care*, 8 (4): 317–33.

Griffin, C. (1993) *Representations of Youth: the study of youth and adolescence in Britain and America*, Cambridge: Polity Press.

Griffin, C. (1997) "Troubled teens: managing disorders of transition and consumption," *Feminist Review*, 55: 4–21.

Gross, S. R., Barrett, S. P., Shestowsky, J. S., and Pihl, R. O. (2002) "Ecstasy and drug consumption patterns: a Canadian rave population study," *Canadian Journal of Psychiatry*, 47: 546–51.

Gutmann, M. C. (1996) *The Meanings of Macho: being a man in Mexico City*, Berkeley, CA: University of California Press.

Gutmann, M. C. (1999) "Ethnicity, alcohol, and acculturation," *Social Science and Medicine*, 48: 173–84.

Haas, C. (2005) "Owner and promoter liability in 'club drug' initiatives," *Ohio State Law Journal*, 66: 511–68.

Hadfield, P. (2006) *Bar Wars: contesting the night in contemporary British cities*, Oxford: Oxford University Press.

Hadfield, P., and Measham, F. (2009) "England and Wales," in P. Hadfield (ed.) *Nightlife and Crime: social order and governance in international perspective*. Oxford: Oxford University Press.

Halkitis, P. N., and Parsons, J. T. (2002) "Recreational drug use and HIV risk sexual behavior among men frequenting gay social venues," *Journal of Gay and Lesbian Social Services*, 14: 19–38.

Hall, S. (1992) "New ethnicities," in J. Donald and A. Rattansi (eds) *'Race', Culture and Difference*, London: Sage Publications.

Hall, S., and Jefferson, T. (eds) (1976) *Resistance Through Rituals: youth subcultures in post-war Britain*, London: Hutchinson.

Hammersley, R. (2005) "Theorizing normal drug use," *Addiction Research and Theory*, 13: 201–3.

Hammersley, R., Ditton, J., Smith, I., and Short, E. (1999) "Patterns of ecstasy use by drug users," *British Journal of Criminology*, 39: 625–47.

Hammersley, R., Khan, F., and Ditton, J. (2002) *Ecstasy and the Rise of the Chemical Generation*, New York, NY: Routledge.

Harachi, T. W., Catalano, R. F., Kim, S., and Choi, Y. (2001) "Etiology and prevention of substance use among Asian American youth," *Prevention Science*, 2: 57–65.

Harnden, A. (2006) "San Francisco Entertainment Commission: how this city manages entertainment and events," Responsible Hospitality Institute. Online. Available HTTP: <http://

rhiclearinghouse.net/RHICH_ShowColumns.aspx?RecID=448> (accessed December 10, 2008).

Harrison, M. (ed.) (1998) *High Society: the real voices of club culture*, London: Piatkus.

Hayward, K. (2002) "The vilification and pleasures of youthful transgression," in J. Muncie, G. Hughes, and E. McLaughlin (eds) *Youth Justice: critical readings*, London: Sage Publications.

Heath, D. B. (2000) *Drinking Occasions: comparative perspectives on alcohol and culture*, Philadelphia, PA: Brunner/Mazel.

Heaven, P. C. L. (1996) *Adolescent Health: the role of individual differences*, London: Routledge.

Hebdige, D. (1979) *Subculture: the meaning of style*, London: Methuen.

Henderson, S. (1993a) "Fun, fashion and *frisson*," *International Journal of Drug Policy*, 4: 122–29.

Henderson, S. (1993b) "Luvdup and de-elited: responses to drug use in the second decade," in P. Aggleton, P. Davies, and G. Hart (eds) *AIDS: facing the second decade*, New York, NY: Falmer Press.

Henderson, S. (1996). ""E" types and dance divas': gender research and community prevention," in T. Rhodes and R. Hartnoll (eds), *AIDS, Drugs and Prevention*, London: Routledge.

Henderson, S. (1997) *Ecstasy: case unsolved*, London: Pandora.

Henderson, S. (1999) "Drugs and culture: the question of gender," in N. South (ed.) *Drugs: cultures, controls and everyday life*, Thousand Oaks, CA: Sage Publications.

Herd, D. (1997) "Racial differences in women's drinking norms and drinking patterns: a national study," *Journal of Substance Abuse*, 9: 137–49.

Heritage, J. (1984) *Garfinkel and Ethnomethodology*, Cambridge: Polity Press.

Hesmondhalgh, D. (1998) "The British dance music industry: a case study of independent cultural production," *British Journal of Sociology*, 49: 234–51.

Hier, S. P. (2002) "Raves, risks and the ecstasy panic: a case study in the subversive nature of moral regulation," *Canadian Journal of Sociology*, 27: 33–57.

Hill, D. (1999) "Mobile anarchy: the house movement, shamanism and community," in T. Lyttle (ed.) *Psychedelics Reimagined*, New York, NY: Autonomedia.

Hodkinson, P. (2002) *Goth: identity, style and subculture*, Oxford: Berg.

Hodkinson, P. (2007) "Youth cultures: a critical outline of key debates," in P. Hodkinson and W. Deicke (eds) *Youth Cultures: scenes, subcultures and tribes*, New York, NY: Routledge.

Holiday, B. (1956) *The Lady sings the Blues*, New York, NY: Doubleday.

Hollands, R. (2002) "Divisions in the dark: youth cultures, transitions and segmented consumption spaces in the night-time economy," *Journal of Youth Studies*, 5: 155–71.

Hollinger, D. (1995) *Post-ethnic America: beyond multiculturalism*, New York, NY: Basic Books.

Holmila, M., and Raitasalo, K. (2005) "Gender differences in drinking: why do they still exist?" *Addiction*, 100: 1763–69.

Howes, D. (ed.) (1996) *Cross-cultural Consumption: global markets, local realities*, London: Routledge.

Hunt, G., and Satterlee, S. (1986) "Cohesion and division: drinking in an English village," *Man*, new series, 21: 521–37.

Hunt, G., MacKenzie, K., and Joe-Laidler, K. (2000) "'I'm calling my mom': the meaning of family and kinship among homegirls," *Justice Quarterly*, 17: 1–31.

Hunt, G., and Barker, J. C. (2001) "Socio-cultural anthropology and alcohol and drug research: towards a unified theory," *Social Science and Medicine*, 53: 165–88.

Hunt, G., Joe-Laidler, K., and Evans, K. (2002) "The meaning and gendered culture of getting high: gang girls and drug use issues," *Contemporary Drug Problems*, 29: 375–415.

Hunt, G., and Evans, K. (2003) "Dancing and drugs: a cross-national exploration," *Journal of Contemporary Drug Problems*, 30: 779–814.

Huq, R. (1996) "Asian kool? Bhangra and beyond," in S. Sharma, J. Hutnyk, and A. Sharma (eds) *Dis-orienting Rhythms: the politics of the new Asian dance music*, Atlantic Highlands, NJ: Zed Books.

Huq, R. (2003) "From the margins to mainstream? Representations of British Asian youth musical cultural expression from Bhangra to Asian underground music," *Young: Nordic Journal of Youth Research*, 11: 29–48.

Huq, R. (2006) *Beyond Subculture: pop, youth and identity in a postcolonial world*, New York, NY: Routledge.

Hutton, F. (2006) *Risky Pleasures? Club cultures and feminine identities*, Burlington, VT: Ashgate Publishing.

Huxley, A. (1954) *The Doors of Perception and Heaven and Hell*, New York, NY: Harper.

Ingham, J., Purvis, M., and Clarke, D. B. (1999) "Hearing places, making spaces: sonorous geographies, ephemeral rhythms, and the Blackburn warehouse parties," *Environment and Planning D: Society and Space*, 17: 283–305.

Ives, R., and Ghelani, P. (2006) "Polydrug use (the use of drugs in combination): a brief review," *Drugs: Education, Prevention and Policy*, 13: 225–32.

Ja, D. Y., and Aoki, B. (1993) "Substance abuse treatment: cultural barriers in the Asian-American community," *Journal of Psychoactive Drugs*, 25: 61–71.

Jackson, P. (2004) *Inside Clubbing: sensual experiments in the art of being human*, Oxford: Berg.

Jang, M. (1996) "HIV/AIDS education and prevention in the Asian American and Pacific Islander communities," in M. K. Moore and M. L. Forst (eds) *AIDS Education: reaching diverse populations*, Westport, CT: Praeger.

Jansen, K. L. R. (1999) "Ecstasy (MDMA) dependence," *Drug and Alcohol Dependence*, 53: 121–24.

Jenkins, P. (1999) *Synthetic Panics: the symbolic politics of designer drugs*, New York, NY: New York University Press.

Joe-Laidler, K. (2004) "Globalization and the illicit drugs trade in Hong Kong," in C. Sumner (ed.) *The Blackwell Companion to Criminology*, Malden, MA: Blackwell.

Joe-Laidler, K. (2005) "The rise of club drugs in a heroin society: the case of Hong Kong," *Substance Use and Misuse*, 40: 1257–78.

Joe-Laidler, K., and Hunt, G. (2001) "Accomplishing femininity among girls in the gang," *British Journal of Criminology*, 41: 656–78.

Joe-Laidler, K., and Hunt, G. (2008) "'Sit down to float': the cultural meaning of ketamine use in Hong Kong," *Addiction Research and Theory*, 16: 259–71.

Joe-Laidler, K., Hodson, D., and Traver, H. (2000) "The Hong Kong drug market," final report to the UNICRI on the UNDCP global study in illicit drug markets, Hong Kong: Centre for Criminology, University of Hong Kong.

Johnson, T. P., Vangeest, J. B., and Cho, Y. I. (2002) "Migration and substance use: evidence from the US National Health interview survey," *Substance Use and Misuse*, 37: 941–72.

Johnston, L. (1975) "Defining the term 'polydrug use'," in J. Elinson and D. Nurco (eds) *Operational Definitions in Socio-behavioral Drug Use Research*, NIDA Research Monograph No. 2, Rockville, MD: National Institute on Drug Abuse.

Johnston, L. D., O'Malley, P. M., and Bachman, J. G. (2002) *Monitoring the Future National Survey Results on Drug Use, 1975–2001*, Vol. I, *Secondary School Students*, NIH Publication No. 02-5106), Bethesda, MD: National Institute on Drug Abuse.

Johnston, L. D., O'Malley, P. M., Bachman, J. G., and Schulenberg, J. E. (2003) *Monitoring the Future National Survey Results on Drug Use, 1975–2003*, Vol. I, *Secondary School Students*, NIH Publication No. 04-5507, Bethesda, MD: National Institute on Drug Abuse.

Johnston, L. D., O'Malley, P. M., Bachman, J. G., and Schulenberg, J. E. (2007) *Monitoring the Future National Survey Results on Drug Use, 1975–2006*, Vol. II, *College Students and Adults ages 19–45*, NIH Publication No. 07-6206, Bethesda, MD: National Institute on Drug Abuse.

Jones, S. T. (2005) "Burner season: local promoters, partyers, and DJs have transformed burning man – and in the process redefined SF's club and underground dance scenes," *San Francisco Bay Guardian*, 39 (37), June 15–21. Online. Available HTTP: <http://www.sfbg.com/39/37/cover_barsclubs_burningman.html> (accessed September 1, 2008).

Jordan, T. (1995) "Collective bodies: raving and the politics of Gilles Deluze and Felix Guattari," *Body and Society*, 1: 125–44.

Joyson, V. (1984) *The Acid Trip: a complete guide to psychedelic music*, Todmorden: Babylon Books.

Kardan, S. (2003) "The government's new war on drugs: threatening the right to dance!" *New England Journal on Criminal and Civil Confinement*, 29: 99–128.

Katz, J. (1988) *Seductions of Crime: moral and sensual attractions in doing evil*, New York, NY: Basic Books.

Kelly, B. C. (2007) "Club drug use and risk management among 'bridge and tunnel' youth," *Journal of Drug Issues*, 37: 425–43.

Kelly, P. (2000) "Youth as an artefact of expertise: problematizing the practice of youth studies in an age of uncertainty," *Journal of Youth Studies*, 3: 301–15.

Kempster, C. (1996) *History of House*, London: Sanctuary Publishing.

Kibria, N. (1998) "The contested meanings of 'Asian American': racial dilemmas in the contemporary US," *Ethnic and Racial Studies*, 21: 939–58.

Kibria, N. (2000) "Race, ethnic options, and ethnic binds: identity negotiations of second-generation Chinese and Korean Americans," *Sociological Perspectives*, 43: 77–95.

Kibria, N. (2002) *Becoming Asian American: second-generation Chinese and Korean American identities*, Baltimore, MD: Johns Hopkins University Press.

Kitwana, B. (2002) *The Hip Hop Generation: young blacks and the crisis in African-American culture*, New York, NY: Basic Civitas Books.

Kivisto, P. (2005) "The revival of assimilation in historical perspective," in P. Kivisto (ed.) *Incorporating Diversity: rethinking assimilation in a multicultural age*, London: Paradigm Publishers.

Klingemann, H., and Hunt, G. (eds) (1998) *Drug Treatment Systems in an International Perspective: drugs, demons and delinquents*, Thousand Oaks, CA: Sage Publications.

Klingemann, H., and Sobell, L. C. (ed.) (2007) *Promoting Self-change from Addictive Behaviors: practical implications for policy, prevention, and treatment*, New York, NY: Springer.

Kohn, M. (1992) *Dope Girls: the birth of the British drug underground*, London: Granta Books.

Lagos, M. (2008) "Club violence still rampant in North Beach," *San Francisco Chronicle*, September 29. Online. Available HTTP: <http://www.sfgate.com/cgi-bin/article.cgi?f=/c/a/2008/09/29/MNQK130KAN.DTL> (accessed September 29, 2008).

Lalander, P. (1997) "Beyond everyday order: breaking away with alcohol," *Nordic Studies on Alcohol and Drugs*, 14: 33–42.

Lankenau, S. E., and Clatts, M. C. (2002) "Ketamine injection among high-risk youth: preliminary findings from New York City," *Journal of Drug Issues*, 32: 893–905.

Lankenau, S. E., and Sanders, B. (2007) "Patterns of ketamine use among young injection drug users," *Journal of Psychoactive Drugs*, 39: 21–29.

Laughey, D. (2006) *Music and Youth Culture*, Edinburgh: Edinburgh University Press.

Lee, M. Y., Law, F. M., Eo, E., and Oliver, E. (2002) "Perception of substance use problems in Asian American communities by Chinese, Indian, and Vietnamese American youth," *Journal of Ethnic and Cultural Diversity in Social Work*, 11: 159–89.

Leigh, B. C. (1995) "'A thing so fallen, and so vile': images of drinking and sexuality in women," *Contemporary Drug Problems*, 22: 415–34.

Lemle, R., and Mishkind, M.E. (1989) "Alcohol and masculinity," *Journal of Substance Abuse Treatment*, 6: 213–22.

Lenton, S., Boys, A., and Norcross, K. (1997) "Raves, drugs and experience: drug use by a sample of people who attend raves in Western Australia," *Addiction*, 92: 1327–37.

Leri, F., Bruneau, J., and Stewart, J. (2003) "Understanding polydrug use: review of heroin and cocaine co-use," *Addiction*, 98: 7–22.

Leshner, A. I. (2000) "Club drugs aren't 'fun drugs'," National Institute on Drug Abuse. Online. Available HTTP: <http://www.nida.nih.gov/Published_Articles/fundrugs.html> (accessed September 16, 2008).

Levine, H. G. (2003) "Global drug prohibition: its uses and crises," *International Journal of Drug Policy*, 14: 145–53.

Levy, B. A. (2004) "When cute acronyms happen to bad legislation: the reducing America's vulnerability to ecstasy 'RAVE' Act," *Northwestern University Law Review*, 98: 1251–89.

Lewis, L. A., and Ross, M. W. (1995) *A Select Body: the gay dance party subculture and the HIV/AIDS pandemic*, New York, NY: Cassell.

Lipsitz, G. (1994) *Dangerous Crossroads: popular music, postmodernism and the poetics of place*, London: Verso.

Lloyd, R., and Clark, T. N. (2000) "The City as an Entertainment Machine," Research Report No. 454, Annual Meeting of the American Sociological Association, San Francisco, CA.

Lovatt, A. (1996) "The ecstasy of urban regeneration: regulation of the night-time economy in the transition to a post-Fordist city," in J. O'Connor and D. Wynne (eds) *From the Margins to the Centre: cultural production and consumption in the post-industrial city*, Aldershot: Arena.

Lull, J. (1995) *Media, Communication, Culture: a global approach*, Cambridge: Polity Press.

Lupton, D. (1999a) *Risk*, London: Routledge.

Lupton, D. (ed.) (1999b) *Risk and Sociocultural Theory: new directions and perspectives*, Cambridge: Cambridge University Press.

Lupton, D., and Tulloch, J. (1998) "The adolescent 'unfinished body', reflexivity and HIV/AIDS risk," *Body and Society*, 4: 19–34.

Lyng, S. (1990) "Edgework: a social psychological analysis of voluntary risk taking," *American Journal of Sociology*, 95: 851–86.

Lyng, S. (ed.) (2005a) *Edgework: the sociology of risk-taking*, New York, NY: Routledge.

Lyng, S. (2005b) "Sociology at the edge: social theory and voluntary risk-taking," in S. Lyng (ed.) *Edgework: the sociology of risk-taking*, New York, NY: Routledge.

MacAndrew, C., and Edgerton, R. B. (1969) *Drunken Comportment: a social explanation*, Chicago, IL: Aldine.

McCambridge, J., Winstock, A., Hunt, N., and Mitcheson, L. (2007) "Five-year trends in use of hallucinogens and other adjunct drugs among UK dance drug users," *European Addiction Research*, 13: 57–64.

McCann, U. D., Szabo, Z., Scheffel, U., Dannals, R. F., and Ricaurte, G. A. (1998) "Positron emission tomographic evidence of toxic effect of MDMA ('ecstasy') on brain serotonin neurons in human beings," *Lancet*, 352: 1433–37.

McDermott, P. (1993) "MDMA use in the north-west of England," *International Journal of Drug Policy*, 4: 210–21.

McDonald, M. (ed.) (1994) *Gender, Drink and Drugs*, Providence, RI: Berg.

MacKenzie, K., Hunt, G., and Joe-Laidler, K. (2005) "Youth gangs and drugs: the case of marijuana," *Journal of Ethnicity in Substance Abuse*, 4: 99–134.

McKirnan, D. J., and Peterson, P. L. (1989) "Psychosocial and cultural factors in alcohol and drug abuse: an analysis of a homosexual community," *Addicted Behaviors*, 14: 555–63.

McMillan, D. (2005) "HRC rules gay bar owner violates civil rights," *San Francisco Bay Times*, April 28. Online. Available HTTP: <http://www.sfbaytimes.com/index.php?article_id=3625&sec=article> (accessed December 16, 2008).

McRobbie, A. (1993) "'Shut up and dance': youth culture and changing modes of femininity," *Cultural Studies*, 7: 406–26.

McRobbie, A. (1994) *Postmodernism and Popular Culture*, New York, NY: Routledge.

McRobbie, A. (1995) "Recent rhythms of sex and race in popular music," *Media, Culture and Society*, 17: 323–31.

McRobbie, A. (ed.) (1997) *Back to Reality? Social experience and cultural studies*, Manchester: Manchester University Press.

Maffesoli, M. (1996) *The Time of the Tribes: the decline of individualism in mass society*, Thousand Oaks, CA: Sage Publications.

Maher, L. (1997) *Sexed Work: gender, race, and resistance in a Brooklyn drug market*, Oxford: Clarendon Press.

Maira, S. (1998) "Desis reprazent: Bhangra remix and hip-hop in New York City," *Postcolonial Studies*, 1: 357–70.

Maira, S. (2000) "Henna and hip-hop: the politics of cultural production and the work of cultural studies," *Journal of Asian American Studies*, 3: 329–69.

Maira, S. (2002) *Desis in the House: Indian American youth culture in New York City*, Philadelphia, PA: Temple University Press.

Maira, S. (2003) "TranceGlobalNation: Orientalism, cosmopolitanism, and citizenship in youth culture," *Journal of Popular Music Studies*, 15: 3–33.

Maira, S. (2004) "Imperial feelings: youth culture, citizenship, and globalization," in M. M. Suárez-Orozco and D. B. Qin-Hilliard (eds) *Globalization: culture and education in the new millennium*, Berkeley, CA: University of California Press.

Maira, S., and Soep, E. (2004) "United states of adolescence? Reconsidering US youth culture studies," *Young*, 12: 245–69.

Maira, S., and Soep, E. (eds) (2005) *Youthscapes: the popular, the national, the global*, Philadelphia, PA: University of Pennsylvania Press.

Malbon, B. (1999) *Clubbing: dancing, ecstasy and vitality*, New York, NY: Routledge.

Males, M. A. (1999) *Framing Youth: ten myths about the next generation*, Monroe, ME: Common Courage Press.

Manning, P. (2006) "There's no glamour in glue: news and the symbolic framing of substance misuse," *Crime, Media, Culture*, 2: 49–66.

Manning, P. (ed.) (2007) *Drugs and Popular Culture: drugs, media, and identity in contemporary society*, Portland, OR: Willan Publishing.

Marshall, J. (1993) "Harder than hardcore," *The Europe Issue*, 116: 85–86.

Martin, A. (2007) "Forum: close clubs at 4 a.m., offer owners training," *San Francisco Examiner*, April 14. Online. Available HTTP: <http://www.examiner.com/a-673772~Forum–Close_clubs_at_4_a_m–offer_owners_training.html> (accessed December 18, 2008).

Martin, D. (1999) "Power play and party politics: the significance of raving," *Journal of Popular Culture*, 32: 77–99.

Mattison, A. M., Ross, M. W., Wolfson, T., Franklin, D., and HNRC Group (2001) "Circuit party attendance, club drug use, and unsafe sex in gay men," *Journal of Substance Abuse*, 13: 119–26.

Maxwell, J. C. (2005) "Party drugs: properties, prevalence, patterns, and problems," *Substance Use and Misuse*, 40: 1203–40.

May, R. A. B. and Chaplin, K. S. (2008) "Cracking the code: race, class, and access to nightclubs in urban America," *Qualitative Sociology*, 31: 57–72.

Mayock, P. (2005) "'Scripting' risk: young people and the construction of drug journeys," *Drugs: Education, Prevention and Policy*, 12: 349–68.

Measham, F. (2002) "'Doing gender' – 'doing drugs': conceptualizing the gendering of drugs cultures," *Contemporary Drug Problems*, 29: 335–73.

Measham, F. (2004a) "The decline of ecstasy, the rise of 'binge' drinking and the persistence of pleasure," *Probation Journal: The Journal of Community and Criminal Justice*, 51: 309–26.

Measham, F. (2004b) "Drug and alcohol research: the case for cultural criminology," in J. Ferrell, K. J. Hayward, W. Morrison, and M. Presdee (eds) *Cultural Criminology Unleashed*, London: GlassHouse Press.

Measham, F. (2004c) "Play space: historical and socio-cultural reflections on drugs, licensed leisure locations, commercialisation and control," *International Journal of Drug Policy*, 15: 337–45.

Measham, F., and Moore, K. (2009) "Exploring patterns of weekend polydrug use within local leisure scenes across the English night time economy," *Criminology and Criminal Justice*, 9 (4).

Measham, F., Newcombe, R. and Parker, H. (1994) "The normalization of recreational drug use amongst young people in north-west England," *British Journal of Sociology*, 45: 287–312.

Measham, F., Parker, H., and Aldridge, J. (1998) "The teenage transition: from adolescent recreational drug use to the young adult dance culture in Britain in the mid-1990s," *Journal of Drug Issues*, 28: 9–32.

Measham, F., Aldridge, J., and Parker, H. (2001) *Dancing on Drugs: risk, health and hedonism in the British club scene*, New York, NY: Free Association Books.

Melechi, A. (1993) "The ecstasy of disappearance," in S. Redhead (ed.) *Rave off: politics and deviance in contemporary youth culture*, Brookfield, VT: Avebury.

Merchant, J., and MacDonald, R. (1994) "Youth and the rave culture, ecstasy and health," *Youth and Policy*, 45: 16–39.

Messerschmidt, J. W. (1997) *Crime as Structured Action: gender, race, class, and crime in the making*, Thousand Oaks, CA: Sage Publications.

Miles, S. (2000) *Youth Lifestyles in a Changing World*, Philadelphia, PA: Open University Press.

Miller, C. (2002) "Show's over: why the hell do the cops get to decide what kind of music plays in SF?" *San Francisco Bay Guardian*, October 23. Online. Available HTTP: <http://

www.sfbg.com/37/04/cover_show_over.html> (accessed December 18, 2008).

Mills, A. C. (1998) "I like the nightlife, Bebe," *Metroactive*. Online. Available HTTP: <www.metroactive.com/papers/metro/04.23.98/cover/asian-nites1–9816.html> (accessed December 18, 2008).

Milroy, C. M. (1999) "Ten years of 'ecstasy'," *Journal of the Royal Society of Medicine*, 92: 68–72.

Mitchell, T. (1996) *Popular Music and Local Identity: rock, pop and rap in Europe and Oceania*, New York, NY: Leicester University Press.

Mitchell, W., Bunton, R., and Green, E. (eds) (2004) *Young People, Risk and Leisure: constructing identities in everyday life*, Basingstoke: Palgrave Macmillan.

Modood, T. (1997) "Difference, cultural racism and anti-racism," in P. Werbner and T. Modood (eds) *Debating Cultural Identity*, London: Zed Books.

Moloney, M., and Fenstermaker, S. (2002) "Performance and accomplishment: reconciling feminist conceptions of gender," in S. Fenstermaker and C. West (eds) *Doing Gender, Doing Difference*, New York, NY: Routledge.

Moloney, M., Hunt, G., Bailey, N., and Erez, G. (2009) "Changes in the nighttime economy: the case of San Francisco," in P. Hadfield (ed.) *Nightlife and Crime: social order and governance in international perspective*, Oxford: Oxford University Press.

Moore, D. (2004) "Beyond 'subculture' in the ethnography of illicit drug use," *Contemporary Drug Problems*, 31: 181–212.

Moore, D. (2008) "Erasing pleasure from public discourse on illicit drugs: on the creation and reproduction of an absence," *International Journal of Drug Policy*, 19: 353–58.

Moore, D., and Valverde, M. (2000) "Maidens at risk: 'date rape drugs' and the formation of hybrid risk knowledges," *Economy and Society*, 29: 514–31.

Moore, K. (2004) "A commitment to clubbing," *Peace Review*, 16: 459–65.

Moore, K. (2007) Book review, "*Risky Pleasures: club cultures and feminine identities*," *Crime, Media, Culture*, 3: 402–5.

Moore, K., and Miles, S. (2004) "Young people, dance and the subcultural consumption of drugs," *Addiction Research and Theory*, 12: 507–23.

Morgan, P. (1983) "Alcohol, disinhibition, and domination: a conceptual analysis," in R. Room and G. Collins (eds) *Alcohol and Disinhibition: nature and meaning of the link*, NIAAA Research Monograph No. 12, Washington, DC: US Government Printing Office.

Muggleton, D. (2000) *Inside Subculture: the postmodern meaning of style*, New York, NY: Berg.

Munn, N. D. (1992) "The cultural anthropology of time: a critical essay," *Annual Review of Anthropology*, 21: 93–123.

Nagel, J. (1994) "Constructing ethnicity: creating and recreating ethnic identity and culture," *Social Problems*, 41: 152–76.

National Drug Intelligence Center (2001) "Raves," *Information Bulletin*, Product No. 2001-L0424-004. Johnstown, PA: US Department of Justice. Online. Available HTTP: <http://www.usdoj.gov/ndic/pubs/656/656p.pdf> (accessed December 18, 2008).

National Institute on Drug Abuse (1999) "Facts about MDMA (ecstasy)," *NIDA Notes*, 14: tearoff. Online. Available HTTP: <http://www.nida.nih.gov/NIDA_Notes/NNVol14N4/tearoff.html> (accessed December 17, 2008).

National Institute on Drug Abuse (2008) "Info facts: MDMA (ecstasy)," National Institute on Drug Abuse. Online. Available HTTP: <http://www.drugabuse.gov/PDF/Infofacts/MDMA08.pdf> (accessed December 16, 2008).

Nemoto, T., Aoki, B., Huang, K., Morris, A., Nguyen, H., and Wong, W. (1999) "Drug use behaviors among Asian drug users in San Francisco," *Addictive Behaviors*, 24: 823–38.

Newcombe, R. (1992) "A researcher reports from the rave," *Druglink*, 7: 14–15.

Nishioka, J. (2000) "Ravelicious: Asian American kids on the rave and ecstasy train," *Asian Week*, April 12.

Northcote, J. (2006) "Nightclubbing and the search for identity: making the transition from childhood to adulthood in an urban milieu," *Journal of Youth Studies*, 9: 1–16.

Nutt, D., and Williams, T. (2004) "Ketamine: an update, 2000–2004," Ketamine Report Appendix, Report for Advisory Council on the Misuse of Drugs. Online. Available HTTP: <http://drugs.homeoffice.gov.uk/publication-search/acmd/ketamine-report-annexes.pdf?view=Binary> (accessed December 10, 2008).

O'Brien, K. (2004) Book review, "*Inside Clubbing: sensual experiments in the art of being human,*" *British Journal of Sociology*, 55: 596–97.

O'Connor, B. (1994) "Hazards associated with the recreational drug 'ecstasy'," *British Journal of Hospital Medicine*, 52: 507–14.

O'Hare, T., and Tran, T. V. (1998) "Substance abuse among Southeast Asians in the US: implications for practice and research," *Social Work in Health Care*, 26: 69–80.

Olaveson, T. (2004) "'Connectedness' and the rave experience: rave as new religious movement?" in G. St. John (ed.) *Rave Culture and Religion*, London: Routledge.

O'Malley, P., and Mugford, S. (1991) "The demand for intoxicating commodities: implications for the 'war on drugs'," *Social Justice*, 18: 49–75.

O'Malley, P., and Mugford, S. (1993) "Crime, excitement, and modernity," in G. Barak (ed.) *Varieties of Criminology: readings from a dynamic discipline*, Westport, CT: Praeger.

O'Malley, P., and Valverde, M. (2004) "Pleasure, freedom and drugs: the uses of 'pleasure' in liberal governance of drug and alcohol consumption," *Sociology*, 38: 25–42.

Ono, K. (2005) *Asian American Studies after Critical Mass*, Malden, MA: Blackwell.

Operario, D., Choi, K.-H., Chu, P. L., McFarland, W., Secura, G. M., Behel, S., MacKellar, D., and Valleroy, L. (2006) "Prevalence and correlates of substance use among young Asian Pacific Islander men who have sex with men," *Prevention Science*, 7: 19–29.

Orlov, P. (2009) "School-age DJ's: old-school style," *New York Times*, January 4, Music Section, pp. 12–13.

Ortner, S. B. (1998) "Generation X: anthropology in a media-saturated world," *Cultural Anthropology*, 13: 414–40.

Osborne, B. (1999) *The A–Z of Club Culture: twenty years of losing it*, London: Sceptre.

Osgerby, B. (1998) *Youth in Britain since 1945*, Oxford: Blackwell.

Owen, F. (2003) *Clubland: the fabulous rise and murderous fall of club culture*, New York, NY: St. Martin's Press.

Paglia, A., and Room, R. (1999) "Preventing substance use problems among youth: a literature review and recommendations," *Journal of Primary Prevention*, 20: 3–50.

Parker, H. (2005) "Normalization as a barometer: recreational drug use and the consumption of leisure by younger Britons," *Addiction Research and Theory*, 13: 205–15.

Parker, H., Aldridge, J., and Measham, F. (1998) *Illegal Leisure: the normalization of adolescent recreational drug use*, London: Routledge.

Parker, H., Williams, L., and Aldridge, J. (2002) "The normalization of 'sensible' recreational drug use: further evidence from the North West England Longitudinal Study," *Sociology*, 36: 941–64.

Parker, R. N. (1995) "Bringing 'booze' back in: the relationship between alcohol and homicide," *Journal of Research in Crime and Delinquency*, 32: 3–38.

Partridge, W. L. (1978) "Uses and nonuses of anthropological data on drug abuse," in E. M. Eddy and W. L. Partridge (eds) *Applied Anthropology in America*, New York, NY: Columbia University Press.

Pearson, G., Ditton, J., Newcombe, R., and Gilman, M. (1991) "Everything starts with an 'E'," *Druglink*, 6: 10–11.

Peralta, R. R. (2008) "'Alcohol allows you to not be yourself': toward a structured understanding of alcohol use and gender difference among gay, lesbian, and heterosexual youth," *Journal of Drug Issues*, 38: 373–99.

Perrone, D. (2009) *The High Life: club kids, harm, and drug policy*, Monsey, NY: Criminal Justice Press.

Peroutka, S. J. (ed.) (1990) *Ecstasy: the clinical, pharmacological and neurotoxicological effects of the drug MDMA*, Boston, MA: Kluwer.

Perry, I. (2004) *Prophets of the Hood: politics and poetics in hip-hop*, London: Duke University Press.

Petersen, A., and Lupton, D. (1996) *The New Public Health: health and self in the Age of Risk*, Thousand Oaks, CA: Sage Publications.

Pilkington, H., and Bliudina, U. (2002) "Introduction," in H. Pilkington, E. Omel'chenko, M. Flynn, U. Bliudina, and E. Starkova (eds) *Looking West? Cultural globalization and Russian youth cultures*, University Park, PA: Pennsylvania State University Press.

Pilkington, H., and Johnson, R. (2003) "Peripheral youth: relations of identity and power in global/local context," *European Journal of Cultural Studies*, 6: 259–83.

Pini, M. (1997) "Women and the early British rave scene," in A. McRobbie (ed.) *Back to Reality? Social experience and cultural studies*, Manchester: Manchester University Press.

Pini, M. (2001) *Club Cultures and Female Subjectivity: the move from home to house*, Basingstoke: Palgrave Macmillan.

Plant, M., and Plant, M. L. (1992) *Risk-takers: alcohol, drugs, sex and youth*, London: Tavistock/Routledge.

Plant, M. L. (2008) "The role of alcohol in women's lives: a review of issues and responses," *Journal of Substance Use*, 13: 155–91.

Plant, M. L., and Plant, M. (2001) "Heavy drinking by young British women gives cause for concern," *British Medical Journal*, 323: 1183–89.

Portes, A., and Zhou, M. (1993) "The new second generation: segmented assimilation and its variants," *Annals of the American Academy of Political and Social Science*, 530: 74–96.

Presdee, M. (2000) *Cultural Criminology and the Carnival of Crime*, London: Routledge.

Price, R. K., Risk, N. K., Wong, M. M., and Klingle, R. S. (2002) "Substance use and abuse by Asian Americans and Pacific Islanders: preliminary results from four national epidemiologic studies," *Public Health Reports*, 117: 39–50.

Redhead, S. (1990) *The End-of-the-century Party: youth and pop towards 2000*, New York, NY: St. Martin's Press.

Redhead, S. (ed.) (1993) *Rave off: politics and deviance in contemporary youth culture*, Brookfield, VT: Avebury.

Redhead, S. (1997) *Subcultures to Clubcultures: an introduction to popular cultural studies*, Malden, MA: Blackwell.

Reilly, R. (2001) "GHB prohibition: codification of moral mass hysteria," *disinfo.com*. Online. Available HTTP: <http://www.disinfo.com/archive/pages/article/id1430/pg3/index.html> (accessed March 5, 2008).

Reinarman, C. (1997) "The social construction of drug scares," in P. A. Adler and P. Adler (eds) *Constructions of Deviance: social power, context, and interaction*, Belmont, CA: Wadsworth.

Reinarman, C. (2003) "Response: geo-political and cultural constraints on international drug control treaties," *International Journal of Drug Policy*, 14: 205–8.

Reith, G. (2005) "On the edge: drugs and the consumption of risk in late modernity," in S. Lyng (ed.) *Edgework: the sociology of risk-taking*, New York, NY: Routledge.

Release (1997) *Release Drugs and Dance Survey*, London: Release.

Rendon, R. (1997) "DEA disputes family's claim about drug test," *Houston Chronicle*, February 8, p. A34.

Reynolds, S. (1998a) *Energy Flash*, London: Picador.

Reynolds, S. (1998b) "Rave culture: living dream or living death?" in S. Redhead (ed.) *The Clubcultures Reader*, Malden, MA: Blackwell.

Reynolds, S. (1999) *Generation Ecstasy: into the world of techno and rave culture*, New York, NY: Routledge.

Rhodes, T. (1995) "Theorizing and researching 'risk': notes on the social relations of risk in heroin users' lifestyles," in P. Aggleton, P. Davies, and G. Hart (eds) *AIDS: safety, sexuality and risk*, Bristol, PA: Taylor & Francis.

Ribbens, J., and Edwards, R. (1998) "Living on the edges: public knowledge, private lives, personal experience," in J. Ribbens and R. Edwards (eds) *Feminist Dilemmas in Qualitative Research: public knowledges and private lives*, London: Sage Publications.

Ricciardelli, L. A., Connor, J. P., Williams, R. J., and Young, R. M. (2001) "Gender stereotypes and drinking cognitions as indicators of moderate and high risk drinking among young women and men," *Drug and Alcohol Dependence*, 61: 129–36.

Rietveld, H. C. (1998) *This is our House: house music, cultural spaces and technologies*, Brookfield, VT: Ashgate.

Riley, S., and Hayward, E. (2004) "Patterns, trends, and meanings of drug use by dance-drug users in Edinburgh, Scotland," *Drugs: Education, Prevention and Policy*, 11: 243–62.

Riley, S., James, C., Gregory, D., Dingle, H. and Cadger, M. (2001) "Patterns of recreational drug use at dance events in Edinburgh, Scotland," *Addiction*, 96: 1035–47.

Rivera, R. Z. (2003) *New York Ricans from the Hip-hop Zone*, New York, NY: Palgrave Macmillan.

Rodriguez, O., Adrados, J.-L. R., and De La Rosa, M. R. (1993) "Integrating mainstream and subcultural explanations of drug use among Puerto Rican youth," in M. R. De La Rosa and J.-L. R. Adrados (eds) *Drug Abuse among Minority Youth: advances in research and methodology*, NIDA Research Monograph No. 130, Rockville, MD: National Institute on Drug Abuse.

Room, R. (1996) Review article "Gender roles and interactions in drinking and drug use," *Journal of Substance Abuse*, 8: 227–39.

Room, R., and Paglia, A. (1999) "The international drug control system in the post-Cold War era: managing markets or fighting a war?" *Drug and Alcohol Review*, 18: 305–15.

Rose, T. (1994) *Black Noise: rap music and black culture in contemporary America*, Middletown, CT: Wesleyan University Press.

Rosenbaum, M. (2002) "Ecstasy: America's new 'reefer madness'," *Journal of Psychoactive Drugs*, 34: 137–42.

Sachdev, M. V. (2004) "The party's over: why the Illicit Drug Anti-proliferation Act abridges economic liberties," *Columbia Journal of Law and Social Problems*, 37: 585–625.

Salasuo, M., and Seppälä, P. (2005) "The party scene of Helsinki," *Nordic Studies on Alcohol and Drugs*, 22: 142–45.

Saldanha, A. (2002) "Music, space, identity: geographies of youth culture in Bangalore," *Cultural Studies*, 16: 337–50.

Sample, C. J. (1977) "Concept of polydrug use," in L. G. Richards and L. B. Blevens (eds) *The Epidemiology of Drug Abuse: current issues*, NIDA Research Monograph No. 10, Rockville, MD: National Institute on Drug Abuse.

Samuels, S. (2000) "Dance: they also dance who party the night away," *New York Times*, August 20. Online. Available HTTP: <http://query.nytimes.com/gst/fullpage.html?res= 9D07EFDB1E3FF933A1575BC0A9669C8B63&sec=&spon=&pagewanted=all> (accessed December 16, 2008).

San Francisco civil grand jury (2000) "Club permits," 1999–2000, San Francisco Civil Grand Jury Report. Online. Available HTTP: <http://www.sfgov.org/site/courts_page.asp?id= 3731> (accessed December 18, 2008).

San Francisco civil grand jury (2007) "The Entertainment Commission: a work in progress," 2006–07, San Francisco Civil Grand Jury Report. Online. Available HTTP: <http://www.sfgov.org/site/uploadedfiles/courts/entertainment_commission_report. pdf> (accessed December 18, 2008).

San Francisco Mayor's Office (2007) "Sustaining our prosperity: the San Francisco economic strategy," Mayor's Office of Economic and Workforce Development and ICF International Economic and Planning Systems. Online. Available HTTP: <http://www.sfgov.org/site/ uploadedfiles/yw1/SFES090607final.pdf> (accessed December 18, 2008).

Sanders, A. (2005) "Late night wakes up in the city," *San Francisco Business Times*, 8 April. Online. Available HTTP: <http://www.bizjournals.com/sanfrancisco/stories/2005/ 04/11/story3.html> (accessed December 18, 2008).

Sanders, J. (2002) "Nightclub supporters get glimmer of hope: commission to oversee permit process," *San Francisco Chronicle*, September 12. Online. Available HTTP: <http://www. sfgate.com/cgi-bin/article.cgi?f=/c/a/2002/09/12/DD174649.DTL> (accessed December 18, 2008).

Schensul, J. J., Convey, M., and Burkholder, G. (2005a) "Challenges in measuring concurrency, agency and intentionality in polydrug research," *Addictive Behaviors*, 30: 571–74.

Schensul, J. J., Diamond, S., Disch, W., Bermudez, R., and Eiserman, J. (2005b) "The diffusion of ecstasy through urban youth networks," *Journal of Ethnicity in Substance Abuse*, 4: 39–71.

Sellars, A. (1998) "The influence of dance music on the UK youth tourism market," *Tourism Management*, 19: 611–15.

Shapiro, H. (1999) *Waiting for the Man: the story of drugs and popular music*, London: Helter Skelter Publishing.

Sharma, S., Hutnyk, J., and Sharma, A. (eds) (1996) *Dis-Orienting Rhythms: the politics of the new Asian dance music*, Atlantic Highlands, NJ: Zed Books.

Shewan, D., Dargano, P., and Reith, G. (2000) "Perceived risk and risk reduction among ecstasy users: the role of drug, set, and setting," *International Journal of Drug Policy*, 10: 431–53.

Shiling, C. (1993) *The Body and Social Theory*, London: Sage Publications.

Shiner, M. (2009) *Drug Use and Social Change*, Basingstoke: Palgrave Macmillan.

Shiner, M., and Newburn, T. (1999) "Taking tea with Noel: the place and meaning of drug use in everyday life," in N. South (ed.) *Drugs: cultures, controls and everyday life*, London: Sage Publications.

Siegel, R. K. (1989) *Intoxication: life in pursuit of artificial paradise*, New York, NY: Dutton.

Silcott, M. (1999) *Rave America: new school dancescapes*, Toronto: ECW Press.

Simpson, D. D., and Sells, S. B. (1974) "Patterns of multiple drug abuse, 1969–1971," *International Journal of the Addictions*, 9: 301–14.

Single, E., Kandel, D., and Faust, R. (1974) "Patterns of multiple drug use in high school," *Journal of Health and Social Behavior*, 15: 344–57.

Sjö, F. (2005) "Drugs in Swedish club culture: creating identity and distance to mainstream society," in P. Lalander and M. Salasuo (eds) *Drugs and Youth Cultures: global and local expressions*, NAD publication No. 46, Helsinki: Nordic Council for Alcohol and Drug Research (NAD).

Skeggs, B. "Becoming repellent: the limits to propriety," paper presented at the British Sociological Association annual conference, 2003, "A Sociological History of the BSA Social Futures: Desire, Excess and Waste," University of York, April 2003.

Skelton, T., and Valentine, G. (eds) (1998) *Cool Places: geographies of youth cultures*, New York, NY: Routledge.

Smith, K. M., Larive, L. L., and Romanelli, F. (2002) "Club drugs: methylene dioxymethamphetaine, flunitrazepam, ketamine hydrochloride, and ë-hydroxybutyrate," *American Journal of Health-System Pharmacy*, 59: 1067–76.

Smith, P. H. (ed.) (1992) *Drug Policy in the Americas*, Boulder, CO: Westview Press.

So, D. W., and Wong, F. Y. (2006) "Alcohol, drugs, and substance use among Asian-American college students," *Journal of Psychoactive Drugs*, 38: 35–42.

Soellner, R. (2005) "Club drug use in Germany," *Substance Use and Misuse*, 40: 1279–93.

Solowij, N., Hall, W., and Lee, N. (1992) "Recreational MDMA use in Sydney: a profile of 'ecstasy' users and their experiences with the drug," *British Journal of Addiction*, 87: 1161–72.

Song, M. (2003) *Choosing Ethnic Identity*, Cambridge: Polity Press.

South of Market Health Center (2007) "SoMA's story: the evolution of a community," SOMA History. Online. Available HTTP: <http://www.smhcsf.org/soma.html> (accessed December 18, 2008).

Spencer, P. (1985) *Society and the Dance: the social anthropology of process and performance*, Cambridge: Cambridge University Press.

St. John, G. (ed.) (2004) *Rave Culture and Religion*, London: Routledge.

Sterk, C. E., Theall, K. P., and Elifson, K. W. (2006) "Young adult ecstasy use patterns: quantities and combinations," *Journal of Drug Issues*, 36: 201–28.

Sterk, C. E., Theall, K. P., and Elifson, K. W. (2007) "Getting into ecstasy: comparing moderate and heavy young adult users," *Journal of Psychoactive Drugs*, 39: 103–13.

Stevens, J. (1987) *LSD: the storming of the heavens*, New York, NY: Atlantic Monthly Press.

Strathern, M. (1987) "Relations without substance," in L. Lindstrom (ed.) *Drugs in Western Pacific Societies: relations of substance*, Lanham, MD: University Press of America.

Straw, W. (1997) "Communities and scenes in popular music," in K. Gelder and S. Thornton (eds) *The Subcultures Reader*, London: Routledge.

Substance Abuse and Mental Health Services Administration (2003) "Racial and ethnic differences in youth hallucinogen use," The NHSDA Report, August 15, Rockville, MD: Office of Applied Studies, Substance Abuse and Mental Health Administration. Online. Available HTTP: <http://www.drugabusestatistics.samhsa.gov/2k3/youthHallucinogens/youthHallucinogens.pdf> (accessed December 18, 2008).

Substance Abuse and Mental Health Services Administration (2006) "Table 1.67a, Nonmedical use of pain relievers in lifetime, past year, and past month among persons aged 18 or older, by demographic characteristics: numbers in thousands, 2004 and 2005," Office of Applied Studies, Substance Abuse and Mental Health Administration. Online. Available HTTP: <http://oas.samhsa.gov/NSDUH/2k5NSDUH/tabs/Sect1peTabs67to132.htm> (accessed December 17, 2008).

Substance Abuse and Mental Health Services Administration (2007) "Table 2.16b, Alcohol use, binge alcohol use, and heavy alcohol use in the past month, by detailed age category: percentages, 2006 and 2007," Office of Applied Studies, Substance Abuse and Mental Health

Administration. Online. Available HTTP: <http://drugabusestatistics.samhsa.gov/NSDUH/2k7NSDUH/tabs/Sect2peTabs1to42.htm#Tab2.16B> (accessed December 17, 2008).

Talbot, D. (2006) "The Licensing Act 2003 and the problematization of the night-time economy: planning, licensing and subcultural closure in the UK," *International Journal of Urban and Regional Research*, 30: 159–71.

Talbot, D. (2007) *Regulating the Night: race, culture and exclusion in the making of the night-time economy*, Aldershot: Ashgate.

Taylor, A. (1993) *Women Drug Users: an ethnography of a female injecting community*, Oxford: Clarendon Press.

Taylor-Gooby, P., and Zinn, J. (2005) "Current directions in risk research: reinvigorating the social?" Social Contexts and Responses to Risk Network (SCARR) Working Paper, ESRC (Economic and Social Research Council). Online. Available HTTP: <http://www.kent.ac.uk/scarr/papers/taylor-goby&Zinn%20Wk%20Paper8.05.pdf> (accessed December 10, 2008).

Temple, J. (2008) "Shifting demographics hint at SoMA's future," *San Francisco Chronicle*, March 9. Online. Available HTTP: <http://www.sfgate.com/cgi-bin/article.cgi?f=/c/a/2008/03/09/MN9RVCUV9.DTL> (accessed December 18, 2008).

Ter Bogt, T., and Engels, R. C. M. E. (2005) "'Partying' hard: party style, motives for and effects of MDMA use at rave parties," *Substance Use and Misuse*, 40: 1479–1502.

Ter Bogt, T., Engels, R., Hibbel, B., Wel, F. V., and Verhagen, S. (2002) "'Dancestasy': dance and MDMA use in Dutch youth culture," *Contemporary Drug Problems*, 29: 157–81.

Terris, M. (1975) "Approaches to an epidemiology of health," *American Journal of Public Health*, 65: 1037–45.

Terris, M. (1987) "Epidemiology and the public health movement," *Journal of Public Health Policy*, 8: 315–29.

Terris, M. (1990) "Public health policy for the 1990s," *Journal of Public Health Policy*, 11: 281–95.

Terris, M. (1992) "Healthy lifestyles: the perspective of epidemiology," *Journal of Public Health Policy*, 13: 186–94.

Thai, H. C. (1999) "'Splitting things in half is so white!' Conceptions of family life and friendship and the formation of ethnic identity among second generation Vietnamese Americans," *Amerasia Journal*, 25: 53–88.

Thomas, H. (ed.) (1997) *Dance in the City*, New York, NY: St. Martin's Press.

Thornton, S. (1996) *Club Cultures: music, media and subcultural capital*, Hanover, NH: Wesleyan University Press.

Thrasher, F. (1927) *The Gang*, Chicago, IL: University of Chicago Press.

Tiger, L. (1992) *The Pursuit of Pleasure*, Boston, MA: Little Brown.

Tossmann, P., Boldt, S., and Tensil, M.-D. (2001) "The use of drugs within the techno party scene in European metropolitan cities," *European Addiction Research*, 7: 2–23.

Tramacchi, D. (2004) "Entheogenic dance ecstasis: cross-cultural contexts," in G. St. John (ed.) *Rave Culture and Religion*, London: Routledge.

Turner, V. W. (1969; Cornell Paperbacks edn 1977) *The Ritual Process: structure and anti-structure*, Ithaca, NY: Cornell University Press.

US Census Bureau (2000) "Pct43. Sex by place of birth by citizenship status [31] – universe: total population. Racial or ethnic grouping: Asian alone or in combination with one or more other races," Detailed Tables, American FactFinder. Online. Available HTTP: <http://tinyurl.com/c2ow3f> (accessed January 23, 2009).

US Congress Senate Caucus on International Narcotics Control (2001a) *Ecstasy: Underestimating the Threat: hearing before the Senate Caucus on International Narcotics Control, One Hundred Sixth Congress, second session, July 25, 2000* , Washington, DC: US Government Printing Office.

US Congress Senate Caucus on International Narcotics Control (2001b) *America at Risk: the ecstasy threat: hearing before the senate caucus on international narcotics control, United States Senate, One Hundred Seventh Congress, first session, March 21, 2001*, Washington, DC: US Government Printing Office.

Van de Wijngaart, G. F., Braam, R., de Bruin, D., and Fris, M. (1999) "Ecstasy use at large-scale dance events in the Netherlands," *Journal of Drug Issues*, 29: 679–702.

Verhagen, S., Wel, F. V., Bogt, T. T., and Hibbel, B. (2000) "Fast on 200 beats per minute: the youth culture of Gabbers in the Netherlands," *Youth and Society*, 32: 147–64.

Wagner, D. (1997) *The New Temperance: the American obsession with sin and vice*, Boulder, CO: Westview Press.

Wallace, J. M., Bachman, J. G., O'Malley, P. M., Johnston, L. D., Schulenberg, J. E., and Cooper, S. M. (2002) "Tobacco, alcohol, and illicit drug use: racial and ethnic differences among US high school seniors, 1976–2000," *Public Health Reports*, 117: S67–S75.

Wallman, S. (1978) "Boundaries of 'race': processes of ethnicity in England," *Man*, 13: 200–17.

Walsh, D. (1993) "'Saturday night fever': an ethnography of disco dancing," in H. Thomas (ed.) *Dance, Gender and Culture*, New York, NY: St. Martin's Press.

Walton, S. (2001) *Out of it: a cultural history of intoxication*, London: Hamish Hamilton.

Ward, J., and Fitch, C. (1998) "Dance culture and drug use," in G. V. Stimson, C. Fitch, and A. Judd (eds) *Drug Use in London*, London: Leighton.

Warner, J., Weber, T. R., and Albanes, R. (1999) "'Girls are retarded when they're stoned': marijuana and the construction of gender roles among adolescent females," *Sex Roles*, 40: 25–43.

Weber, T. R. (1999) "Raving in Toronto: peace, love, unity and respect in transition," *Journal of Youth Studies*, 2: 317–36.

Weil, A. T. (1972) *The Natural Mind*, Boston, MA: Houghton Mifflin.

West, C., and Fenstermaker, S. (1995) "Doing difference," *Gender and Society*, 9: 8–37.

West, C., and Zimmerman, D. H. (1987) "Doing gender," *Gender and Society*, 1: 125–51.

Williams, L., and Parker, H. (2001) "Alcohol, cannabis, ecstasy and cocaine: drugs of reasoned choice amongst young adult recreational drug users in England," *International Journal of Drug Policy*, 12: 397–413.

Williamson, R. J., Sham, P., and Ball, D. (2003) "Binge drinking trends in a UK community-based sample," *Journal of Substance Use*, 8: 234–37.

Willis, P. (1977) *Learning to Labor: how working class kids get working class jobs*, New York, NY: Columbia University Press.

Willis, P. (1978) *Profane Culture*, London: Routledge & Kegan Paul.

Wilsnack, S. C., Wilsnack, R. W., and Hiller-Sturmhofel, S. (1994) "How women drink: epidemiology of women's drinking and problem drinking," *Alcohol Health and Research World*, 18: 173–81.

Wilson, B. (2006) *Fight Flight or Chill: subcultures, youth, and rave into the twenty-first century*, Montreal: McGill-Queen's University Press.

Winick, C. (1960) "The use of drugs by jazz musicians," *Social Problems*, 7: 240–53.

Winstock, A. R., Griffiths, P., and Stewart, D. (2001) "Drugs and the dance music scene: a survey of current drug use patterns among a sample of dance music enthusiasts in the UK," *Drug and Alcohol Dependence*, 64: 9–17.

Wolcott, H. F. (1974) *African Beer Gardens of Bulawayo: integrated drinking in a segregated society*, Rutgers Center of Alcohol Studies Monograph No. 10, New Brunswick, NJ: Rutgers Center of Alcohol Studies.

Wong, M. M., Klingle, R. S., and Price, R. K. (2004) "Alcohol, tobacco, and other drug use among Asian American and Pacific Islander adolescents in California and Hawaii," *Addictive Behaviors*, 29: 127–41.

Wright, M. A. W. (1999) "The symbolic challenge of a new cultural movement: ecstasy use and the British dance scene, 1988–1998," unpublished thesis, City University, London.

Wu, F. H. (2003) "The arrival of Asian Americans: an agenda for legal scholarship," *Asian Law Journal*, 10: 1–12.

Yacoubian, G. S., and Urbach, B. J. (2004) "Exploring the temporal relationship between race and the use of ecstasy: findings from the National Household Survey on Drug Abuse," *Journal of Ethnicity in Substance Abuse*, 3: 67–77.

Yang, P. Q., and Solis, P. (2002) "Illegal drug use among Asian American youths in Dallas," *Journal of Ethnicity in Substance Abuse*, 1: 17–38.

Young, A. M., McCabe, S. E., and Boyd, C. J. (2007) "Adolescents' sexual inferences about girls who consume alcohol," *Psychology of Women Quarterly*, 31: 229–40.

Young, J. (1971) *The Drugtakers: the social meaning of drug use*, London: Paladin.

Young, J. (2007) *The Vertigo of late Modernity*, London: Sage Publications.

Zane, N., and Huh Kim, J. (1994) "Substance use and abuse," in N. W. S. Zane, D. T. Takeuchi, and K. N. J. Young (eds) *Confronting Critical Health Issues of Asian and Pacific Islander Americans,* Thousand Oaks, CA: Sage Publications.

Zhou, M. (1997) "Segmented assimilation: issues, controversies, and recent research on the new second generation," *International Migration Review*, 31: 975–1008.

Zhou, M., and Lee, J. (2004) "Introduction. The making of culture, identity, and ethnicity among Asian American youth," in J. Lee and M. Zhou (eds) *Asian American Youth: culture, identity, and ethnicity*, New York, NY: Routledge.

Zia, H. (2000) *Asian American Dreams: the emergence of an American people*, New York, NY: Farrar Straus & Giroux.

Zinberg, N. E. (1984) *Drugs, Set, and Setting: the social bases of controlled drug use*, New Haven, CT: Yale University Press.

Zinko, C. (2005) "Club scene grows up: the party isn't over in SF – it has just moved on to smaller, mellower places. Nights of excess in huge venues give way to calmer gatherings in more intimate settings," *San Francisco Chronicle*, December 2, pp. A1, A20.

Index